CW01424955

ALLIED
DUNBAR

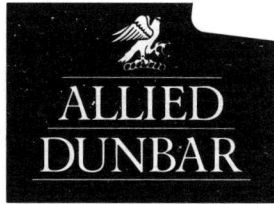

INVESTMENT
AND
SAVINGS HANDBOOK
1995–96

ALLIED DUNBAR

INVESTMENT

AND

SAVINGS HANDBOOK

1995–96

General Editor

Harry Littlefair
Investment Consultant

© Allied Dunbar Assurance plc 1995

ISBN 0 75200 0756

Published by

Pearson Professional Limited
Maple House, 149 Tottenham Court Road, London W1P 9LL

Associated Offices
Australia, Belgium, Canada, Hong Kong, India, Japan, Luxembourg,
Singapore, Spain, USA

All rights reserved. No part of this publication may be reproduced,
stored in a retrieval system, or transmitted, in any form or by any
means, electronic, mechanical, photocopying, recording, or otherwise,
without either the prior written permission of the copyright holder for
which application should be addressed in the first instance to the
publishers, or a licence permitting restricted copying issued by the
Copyright Licensing Agency Ltd,
90 Tottenham Court Road, London W1P 9HE.

No responsibility for loss occasioned to any person acting or refraining
from action as a result of the material in this publication can be
accepted by the authors or publishers.

The views and opinions of Allied Dunbar may not necessarily coincide
with some of the views and opinions expressed in this book which are
solely those of the authors and no endorsement of them by Allied
Dunbar should be inferred.

A CIP catalogue record for this book is available from the
British Library.

Printed and bound in Great Britain by
Mackays of Chatham

Preface

The Allied Dunbar Investment and Savings Handbook is now in its six-teenth year of publication. This year's edition covers, as usual, all the major areas and aspects of investment. Of the 21 chapters in the Handbook, 19 are devoted to specific investment areas and the remain-ing two, the first and the last, are the Introduction and a chapter on Investor Protection. A new chapter (Chapter 6) has been added which covers the increasingly important area of derivatives. All the chapters have been fully revised and updated.

Where investment decisions lead the reader into other specialised areas, eg inheritance tax, the making of wills etc, reference should be made to other products in the Allied Dunbar Library.

It is important to note that Scottish law varies from English law on many subjects, but in most aspects of tax, trusts and domicile, the two systems coincide.

The Law is stated as at 31 December 1994 but the 1995 Finance Act has been included.

My wholehearted thanks go out to all the authors both old and new for their hard work and punctuality.

Harry Littlefair
May 1995

Some favourite investment maxims from our authors

'Buy low, sell high.'   (Anon)

'If it's obvious, it's obviously wrong.'   (Joe Granville)

'Market dogmatists frequently bark up the wrong trees.'
(David Fuller)

'Beware of company chairmen who either:
   a) wear more gold than is in the balance sheet
   b) have an all-year-round sun tan.'   (David Ballance)

'Don't be afraid to leave something for the next investor, no one ever, in reality, buys at the bottom and sells at the top.'   (idem)

'Beware of fashion, especially amongst product launches. If everyone is offering the same thing it's probably not a good idea, eg the rash of Convertible Unit Trusts launched after the 1987 crash.'   (idem)

'Finally, there is no such thing as a free lunch, if the reward is that high or the risk that low there is probably a catch somewhere.'
(idem)

'Investment decisions should not be driven by tax considerations alone.'   (Harry Littlefair)

'Gilt-edged stocks are the riskiest investment of all for the long-term investor.'   (idem)

'Endeavour to chain-link decisions. Before dealing in a stock look back at what has happened (if anything) since your previous transaction in that stock, and relate this to the change in the share price.'
(idem)

'Test the extremes. Suppose you are tempted to buy for a 20 per cent gain, but fear a 20 per cent fall. Ask yourself a different question — which is more likely, a doubling or a halving of the share price?'   (idem)

'If it sounds too good to be true — it is.'   (Jeremy Burnett Rae)

'All markets are cyclical and short-term performance is more about timing of investment and sale decisions than anything else.' (Geoff Abbott)

'When all advisers and commentators are in agreement be warned — the market is approaching the top or the bottom of its current cycle.' (idem)

'When property values fall below the cost of the bricks and mortar on site — start buying.'   (idem)

'In depressed markets lenders will always try to support you through into the recovery phase — so as to be sure of getting all their money back.' (idem)

'When you observe a strong consensus, take the opposite view.' (David Fuller)

'Trust in a sufficiency of wealth as the by-product of a good life.' (John Train)

'Soar not too high to fall; but stoop to rise.'
(Philip Massinger 1583–1640, from *The Duke of Milan*)

'When choosing an investment for tax reasons follow the "Yellow Box Principle''. Do not enter the box unless your exit is clear.' (Stuart Reynolds)

'Learning from your own mistakes is all very well, but learning from the mistakes of others is cheaper.'

'Experience is the name everyone gives to his mistakes.' (Oscar Wilde)

'An economist is an expert who will know tomorrow why the things he predicted yesterday didn't happen today.' (Prof L J Peter)

'The riskiest place to leave your long-term investments is in a deposit account.'   (DW Adams)

'The best time to invest is when you have the cash.'

'The closest you can come to safety in investing is to buy shares in many countries and many industries.'

Contributors

Geoffrey Abbott, Dip FBA (Lon) FRICS, is Agricultural Investment Partner and Head of Purchases & Sales Department in Smiths Gore (Chartered Surveyors) based in their London Office. He was assisted by a number of his partners in their sixteen offices throughout England & Scotland.

Douglas W Adams, MA, MBA, is Marketing Director at Templeton Investment Management Ltd, the UK subsidiary of the worldwide Franklin Templeton Group. Templeton manage over £6.7bn in emerging markets portfolios. Mr Adams is an economist by profession.

William Adams is the Base Metal Research Analyst at Rudolf Wolff & Co Ltd; the company was one of the founding members of the London Metal Exchange in 1876. He is involved in fundamental and technical analysis of the markets and in the operation of technical trading systems.

Malcolm Baker, BCom, MSI(DIP), is Director of the European Investment department at Threadneedle Investment Managers Ltd. In addition, he has substantial experience in global investment.

David Ballance, MA (Oxon), is with Threadneedle Investment Managers Ltd working as an Investment Manager specialising in European equities.

Michael Box, BSc, PhD, is a Director of Threadneedle Investment Managers Ltd with responsibility for the use of derivative instruments and investment techniques having a mathematical content.

Andrew Bull, ARICS, is a Partner at Jones Lang Wootton, the world's largest independent property consultants with specific responsibilities for the investment strategy and implementation of two UK pension funds.

Jeremy Burnett Rae, MA (Oxon), Barrister, is Investment Secretary of Threadneedle Investment Managers Ltd which manages over £30bn in international investments on behalf of Allied Dunbar and Eagle Star.

Peter Howe, LLB, Barrister, is Company Secretary and a Divisional Director in the legal department of Allied Dunbar Assurance plc. The legal department provides a complete legal and technical service to companies in the Allied Dunbar Group. Financial Services legislation is his principal area of specialisation.

Vince Jerrard, LLB, ACII, Solicitor, is the Legal Director of Allied Dunbar Assurance plc. Mr Jerrard has contributed chapters to other Allied Dunbar publications, including the *Tax Handbook*, *Capital Taxes Guide* and the *Business Law and Tax Guide*.

Harry Littlefair was, up to his retirement in 1988, Vice Chairman of Allied Dunbar Unit Trusts plc and Allied Dunbar Asset Management plc having previously been Managing Director of both. Today he is an adviser to four pension funds and a Director of Persimmon plc, Geared Income Investment Trust plc, River Plate and General Investment Trust plc, and Metrotect Industries plc.

Paul Manduca, BA (Oxon), is the founding Chief Executive of Threadneedle Asset Management Ltd.

John Myers, Lessia Djakowska and Susan Farrell are from Solon Consultants, a specialised research firm that focuses on property and alternative investments. John Myers is also a visiting professor at Strathclyde Business School and has been a contributor to the *Allied Dunbar Investment and Savings Handbook* since it was first published in 1980.

Stuart Reynolds, LLB, is a Divisional Director in the Legal Department of Allied Dunbar Assurance plc where his primary responsibility is in relation to the development of new life assurance and pension products for the Company.

John Smithard, LLB, formerly a Member of The Stock Exchange and now a Member of the Securities Institute, is with the investment management division of stockbrokers James Capel & Co.

Mike Wilkes is a Senior Tax Manager with Pannell Kerr Forster, an international firm of chartered accountants. He specialises in the taxation of Lloyd's underwriters and foreign domiciled individuals, but also deals with the general taxation affairs of a number of other personal clients.

Contents

1 Introduction

Paul Manduca — Threadneedle Asset Management Ltd

This book, which was first published in 1980, is aimed primarily at the investment adviser and is designed to give an annual update on the various types of investment. Most chapters include a section designed to cover highlights of the previous year, a preview of the coming year and a view on the next year or two based on current thinking.

This chapter covers the following topics:

- the investment adviser;
- types of investor;
- ways of arranging and holding investments;
- the nature of an investment;
- investment policy;
- trustees; and
- overseas investors.

1.1 Introduction

The basic principles of investment do not change. It is only the influences on investment policy that are likely to alter over the years. These influences are primarily of a political and economic nature, that is to say, the world economic climate and, for the UK investor, the economic and taxation policies of the government of the day.

The task of the investment adviser is always to ensure that the client's asset portfolio is well balanced and robust in the face of changing investment conditions. When interest rates are exceptionally high, as they have been during much of the last two decades, the appeal of short-term deposits can be hard to resist. However, as we have seen, interest rates can fall sharply, leaving clients with the twin problems of declining real value and declining income. The adviser must always be prepared if necessary to lean against the winds of investment fashion in order to ensure that his clients achieve the right balance of risk and reward to suit their personal circumstances through a portfolio which can deliver a satisfactory result regardless of fashion.

1.2 The investment adviser

Today's investment adviser has the unenviable burden of coping with more and more information about an increasing choice of investments. Nowadays, more investment media exist than ever before, described in an ever growing mass of literature, commented on by experts of varying experience and qualifications in an environment of proliferating legislation.

Against that background, the investment adviser — solicitor, accountant, stockbroker, insurance broker, bank manager or anyone else — has five main responsibilities:

(1) He needs to know which investment media are available and to establish which are suitable for his individual clients (particularly so following the passing of the Financial Services Act 1986).

(2) He needs to know which questions to ask about which investment medium and where to find the answers.

(3) He needs to be able to support his decision and, if necessary, show that his advice is not influenced by the method of remuneration.

(4) He must be able to make arrangements for a particular investment (or disinvestment) to be made on behalf of his clients.

(5) He will need to be kept up to date on a fast-changing regulatory framework which applies to all those in the business of providing investment advice.

Most important of all, he has to recognise his own limitations and to look for advice himself. That is the purpose of this book, which identifies the main investment media, identifies the investor for whom they are suitable or unsuitable (posing the main questions which should be asked about each medium) and provides signposts to the specialist consultants or dealers and to the legal, fiscal and other technicalities.

1.3 Types of investor

This book is concerned with people advising individual investors (including trustees and family investment companies). It is essential that the adviser identifies the particular category of investor to which his client belongs. It would be impossible to devise a precise categorisation which is exhaustive and so it follows that the adviser must take into account a number of personal factors in appraising both the investor and also the investment and disinvestment situations with which he is concerned. These factors will include the investor's age and health, his intention with regard to his place of residence and/or domicile, his willingness to accept risk, his willingness to participate in the choice of investments and his capacity to delegate.

1.4 Ways of arranging and holding investments

All the foregoing assumes considerable sophistication on the part of the investment adviser and also a willingness to give his time, for which he will obviously expect to be remunerated. The fact that investors of moderate means are usually unwilling to pay for this level of individual attention has meant that collective investment media have developed hand-in-hand with the relative decline of individually tailored investment portfolios. A corollary of this development is that an ever-growing body of legislation and regulation (see Chapter 21) has had to be developed to protect the small saver against fraud or against unscrupulous salesmanship.

In respect of many of the specific investments, comment is made on methods of arranging and holding those investments, although a number of such methods are common to many investment media. It is beyond the scope of this book to give detailed explanations or advice on either the mechanics of establishing and conducting the particular 'vehicle' or its taxation implications. The investment adviser will be aware that the principal ways in which investments can be arranged and held are:

(1)   by personal direct investment by the individual;
(2)   through a trust or settlement (including a will trust);
(3)   in partnership with others;
(4)   through a family investment company.

1.5 The nature of an investment

1.5.1 Capital and income

The two basic elements of investment are capital and income. At one end of the scale, the capital remains constant while the income produced may vary (eg bank and building society deposits); at the other end, there are non-income-producing assets (such as commodities and works of art), where no income is produced but the capital value fluctuates.

Between the two extremes, there are many variations. Gilt-edged securities can produce a constant level of income and a known repayment value at maturity. Short dated securities will have more certainty over the rise (or fall) in capital values to maturity whereas values of long-dated gilts will vary considerably as interest rates rise and fall. Investments in property or equities will produce variations in both capital value and income. Life assurances, such as single premium bonds, in theory produce no income while they are held as an investment, but in practice this disadvantage can be overcome by the various withdrawal plans which are available (see Chapter 14).

1.5.2   Inflation

An essential third element in evaluating investments is inflation. The need for a hedge against inflation has had a strong influence on investment policy since the 1960s. As inflation rates fluctuate, opinions will vary widely on what represents an effective hedge; inflation has different consequences for different people. Commodities, works of art or tangible assets may turn out to be a good hedge against inflation, but the same hope of finding a good hedge often underlies investment in land, buildings and shares in companies, both domestic and overseas. The list is endless; and the investor must take his pick, according to his own philosophy or judgement.

This is also an area where fashion can play a part. The current view is that inflation provides only a modest threat to markets which, on analysis would seem to mean that it has been below 3 per cent for just over three years. People with not particularly long memories will recall inflation at seven times that level and everybody has to take account of the fact that the reduction in inflation has brought other ills in its wake such as unemployment. A future administration might feel that unemployment is not a 'price worth paying' and the long-term investor has to be ready for this.

1.5.3   Time

A fourth investment dimension is the time factor. In most, if not all, of the following chapters, references are made to fluctuations, trends and fashions affecting the various markets. Within a long-term trend, there are likely to be many short-term fluctuations, caused by a myriad of factors. When to buy and when to sell are therefore difficult decisions for the investor. He can be guided by professional advisers who have knowledge of the technical factors affecting a particular market but who can only express an opinion on political factors and the general state of the economy and who can therefore make only intelligent general forecasts not amounting to precise predictions. For those who invest overseas, fluctuations in exchange rates form a further element in the evaluation of investments.

1.6 Investment policy — general principles and special factors

1.6.1 Diversification

The first maxim for practically every investor should be diversification (indeed, for trustees the Trustee Investments Act 1961 prescribes diversification, although its provisions can be excluded when a trust is created). Diversification can be achieved by investing in varying kinds of investments but can also be achieved within a particular class of investment.

There will always, of course, be the investor who has to commit, or to leave committed, a substantial part of his capital in one particular way (eg the man who has built up a substantial business). It might also be thought that the small investor with little money to invest would have little scope for diversification but unit trusts (see Chapter 8) or bonds (see Chapter 3) indirectly provide diversification.

1.6.2 Balance

The investor should as far as possible have a balanced portfolio. A part of his capital should be earmarked for security and invested in, for example, building society or bank deposits. However, every investor should also look for a measure of capital appreciation as a hedge against inflation, so a part of his capital should be invested in equity-type investments. The precise balance will depend on the individual circumstances and inclinations of the particular investor.

1.6.3 Advice of specialists

The investor should be guided by the advice of the various specialists in the markets discussed in this book. They all provide a service which, if well performed, is a valuable one, for which they quite properly charge fees. However, they all wish to sell their wares and another reason for diversification is to avoid total dependence on the judgement and integrity of any one particular specialist.

Any investor investing overseas should pay particularly close regard to the advice of specialists familiar with the markets in the countries concerned. The additional advice required will cover such things as marketability, banking arrangements and (particularly in the case of purchase of property) legal advice to ensure that the investor obtains a good title.

1.6.4   Taxation

The general rule is that, whilst full account should be taken of likely tax implications, investment policy should not be dictated by tax. It is often the case, for example, that decisions tend to be unduly influenced by capital gains tax considerations. The investor has to balance the right time to sell an investment which is showing a profit against a loss of use of the money required to pay the tax. In general terms, investors should not be deterred from realising investments simply by capital gains tax considerations alone.

Investments with favourable tax treatment include national savings certificates (see Chapter 2) and life assurances (see Chapter 14) which continue to have capitals gains tax benefits and, in the case of certain trust policies, inheritance tax benefits as well. Other tax-efficient investments include TESSAs and PEPs (see Chapter 20).

These tax benefits are a good reason for investing in this way. However, there is no guarantee that, over a given period, they will necessarily produce a better return than investments which have no tax benefits at all. Not only may these other investments have compensating benefits (eg better capital appreciation), future tax legislation could alter or even nullify tax benefits that are now available; yet another reason for a policy of diversification.

1.6.5   Commission and expenses of buying and selling

At one end of the scale, there is no explicit cost at all in investing money in a building society or bank deposit. Commission on the purchase of gilt-edged securities is small, while for equities it is reasonable, although *ad valorem* stamp duty on purchases will also be payable (see Chapter 3). Commissions on equities vary from broker to broker following the abolition of fixed commissions in 1986.

At the top end of the scale comes the art market where the total commission can be as high as 20 per cent+VAT (see Chapter 18). The investor hoping to make an eventual gain must realise that, immediately after purchase, the item may be worth only around 80 per cent of the amount paid (or even less, where VAT is taken into account).

1.6.6   Buying and selling prices

On The Stock Exchange, separate buying and selling prices are quoted, the difference between these prices being the market-maker's turn or potential profit. The same principle can apply to other markets and, with certain assets (eg jewellery), the fact that the asset has only second-hand value the moment it has been purchased must be taken into account.

1.6.7 Other benefits

Investments should not be considered only by reference to pure investment criteria. Property may be purchased as a home or, eg if it is a farm, to provide a livelihood. Life assurance brings with it the element of family protection. Works of art (unless stored away in a safe deposit) bring pleasure to the owner and collector.

1.6.8 Methods of investment

The normal method of investment is for the investor, either personally or through an agent, to buy and sell individual investments (and he could give his agent discretionary power to buy and sell on his behalf). The investor can either buy the investment outright or acquire options to buy at some time in the future. Alternatively, he may be able to buy a future, which effectively gives full exposure to fluctuations in the value of the underlying asset, but at a much lower cost.

The same type of investment can sometimes be acquired through different means. For example, investment in property can be by direct purchase of property (see Chapters 9–12), shares in a property company (see Chapter 3) or property bonds (see Chapter 3). Overseas investment can be through investment trusts or unit trusts (either based in the UK or offshore) holding overseas investments, or in UK companies with substantial overseas activities.

1.6.9 Gearing

For the smaller investor, borrowing can only be a sensible strategy if tax relief is available on the loan interest. Under the present law, tax relief for loan interest is available for loans for the purchase of a house as a principal residence (the ceiling being £30,000) but this relief is reducing in value as the rate of tax relief is being reduced (to 20 per cent in the 1994/95 tax year and 15 per cent for the 1995/96 tax year).

Such borrowing, however, will only appeal to an investor with free assets who thinks he can invest these assets so as to produce greater capital appreciation. It would be pointless, for example, for the cautious investor to borrow from a building society and then reinvest the amount borrowed in a building society (or other equally safe investment) because the interest paid would exceed the interest received and the only beneficiary would be the building society itself.

For the wealthy investor, borrowing is less a question of tax relief than of altering the shape of the asset portfolio. For example, consider an investor with £250,000 who buys a house for £150,000. If he buys the property without a mortgage, he will have a £150,000 stake in the property market and £100,000 invested elsewhere. If he takes a £100,000 mortgage, he will have an unchanged stake in the property market but £200,000 invested elsewhere.

1.7   Trustees

Trustees are usually appointed by a settlement or a will. They can, however, be bare trustees, nominees or attorneys for others (under a power of attorney) who might well be infants or persons under some disability. They also include anyone who owes a fiduciary duty of care to others.

For investment purposes their 'bible' is the Trustee Investments Act 1961, although its provisions are often expressly varied by the trust instrument itself. The principles that the Act lays down are discussed below.

1.7.1   Suitability of investments for the trust

Normally the question of what investments are suitable for a particular trust involves considering the interests of the beneficiaries under that trust. If there is a life tenant and remaindermen, then the trustees must ensure that the income produced for the life tenant is reasonable, but at the same time they must consider security of capital and possible capital appreciation for the remaindermen. Where there are infant beneficiaries, a special duty of care is required.

1.7.2   Diversification

In a normal trust, the trustees could be in breach of trust if they do not diversify the trust investments. In a small trust, diversification can be achieved through the medium of, for example, unit trusts or investment trusts. However, diversification can be a problem in the fairly common case where a settlor has built up a business through a company and settled shares in that company upon trust for his children. In this case the trust instrument should include the appropriate authority for the trustees to continue to hold that investment even though that approach does not lead to diversification.

1.7.3   Expert advice

Trustees must obtain and consider proper advice from a specialist in the relevant field of investment. This principle is seldom expressly excluded.

Unless there is a specific provision in the trust instrument to the contrary, trustees must make investment decisions personally (and cannot delegate this to the expert adviser).

1.7.4 Authorised investments

The Act specifies the kinds of investment in which trustees are authorised to invest and states that at least half the trust fund should be invested in the 'narrower range' and that the balance can be invested in the 'wider range'. Investments in the 'narrower range' include deposits with approved banks and building societies, gilt-edged securities, mortgages on property and debentures of companies that, first, have an issued and paid up share capital of at least £1m and, secondly, have paid dividends (however small) on the whole of their ordinary share capital in each of the previous five years. The 'wider range' includes unit trusts and ordinary shares in companies satisfying the conditions stated above for debentures in the narrower range.

It is fairly general practice nowadays for trust instruments to confer express powers of investment, overriding the provisions of the Trustee Investments Act 1961 in this respect, and it is quite usual for the trustees to be given very wide powers in the interests of flexibility. The investment clause will always require close examination because, either by design or as a consequence of bad drafting, the powers actually given may not be so wide as appears at first sight. An investment in its narrow legal sense is an income-producing instrument. Consequently, if trustees are to be given powers to buy houses as residences for beneficiaries or to use capital for improving or repairing them, specific powers must be included. Again, if trustees are to be permitted to invest in assets such as capital shares with no participation in the profits of the company or chattels or commodities or currency, specific powers must be given. Specific powers must also be given in respect of insurances and assurances.

1.7.5 Caution

In their own interests trustees should tend to be cautious and adopt a conservative policy. They must act within the principles laid down in the trust or settlement deed and the Trustee Investments Act 1961. Their first duty is to familiarise themselves with the powers of investment that they have been given and whether these are restricted as specified in the Act or whether, as is often the case, they are given the powers of an absolute owner, but even then they must ensure that they are given *all* the powers of an absolute owner.

If a known liability arises (and this commonly occurs on the death of a testator, where a liability to inheritance tax may arise), the trustees or the personal representatives should set about covering that liability, if necessary by realising investments and placing the money on deposit with a bank or with building societies or even by investing in short-dated gilts. A prudent trustee who does this cannot be criticised if the market in those realised investments then goes up, but, conversely, a trustee who does not do this is open to criticism if the market goes down.

1.8   Overseas investors

1.8.1   Exchange control

A UK investor can invest in any country in the world without restriction, although he will be subject to whatever restrictions the country in which he plans to invest may impose. Conversely, an overseas investor can freely invest in the UK but he may be subject to exchange control provisions imposed by his country of residence.

1.8.2   Taxation

Detailed advice on taxation is outside the scope of this book and so the comments made below are necessarily only in very general terms. Overseas investors (and also immigrants and emigrants) have to be particularly aware of taxation considerations, which for them depend on domicile and residence.

For tax purposes, a person is regarded as resident in the UK if he is physically present in this country for 183 days or more in any tax year, or, if over a period of four such years, he is present in this country for an average of three months or more in each tax year.

He will be regarded as 'ordinarily resident' if he is habitually resident in the UK year after year and will continue to be regarded as ordinarily resident if he usually lives in this country but is in fact physically absent (eg on a long holiday) for even the whole of any tax year.

Inheritance tax

Liability to UK inheritance tax depends basically on domicile. The investor domiciled in the UK will be subject to inheritance tax on his worldwide assets, whereas an investor not domiciled in the UK will be subject to inheritance tax on his UK property or investments only.

Domicile is a concept of general law and is determined by a range of factors. Broadly speaking, domicile is where the individual has his permanent home. It is distinct from nationality or residence and an individual can have only one domicile at a time.

An individual would normally acquire a domicile of origin from his father when he was born, though this may change if the person on whom the individual was dependent at the time, changed his domicile before the individual was aged 16.

Married women who married before 1974 automatically acquired their husband's domicile, though they may now change it to a domicile of their choice.

Anyone over the age of 16 has the legal power to apply for a new domicile of choice. However, it is not at all easy to do and will usually require proof that the individual has severed all connections with his existing country and intends to settle permanently in a new country.

Capital gains tax

Liability to capital gains tax depends on UK residence or 'ordinary residence' for tax purposes. The general rule is that the investor ordinarily resident in the UK is subject to capital gains tax and the investor not ordinarily resident in the UK is exempt from it. Investors immigrating to or emigrating from the UK should take advice on the timing of the sale of assets so as to avoid any liability to capital gains tax.

Income tax

Liability to income tax depends on residence, but there are certain concessions for people not domiciled in the UK. Many factors, including the provisions of double taxation agreements, are relevant and the investor must take professional advice.

1.8.3   Other restrictions

Normally, an overseas investor can invest in any form of UK investment without problems. However, difficulties might arise where the investor ultimately wanted to export the investment (particularly where it is a work of art) or where the investment involves a liability in the UK (which could arise with, say, an investment in leasehold property as the landlord might require a UK resident guarantor).

1.9   Conclusion

If there is any conclusion to be drawn for the investor and the investment adviser from the foregoing analysis, it is that nothing is constant and that continual review and permanent vigilance are essential. The investment strategies appropriate to one investor may not be right for another and those suitable for one particular generation of investor, may be wholly inappropriate for the next generation, when the investment climate and the law may have changed. Even a strategy appropriate now may be inappropriate in the future by which time the investor will have aged and his needs and his family circumstances will have changed.

1.10   Income tax rates, allowances, and National Insurance rates from 6 April 1995

Table 1.1   Income tax rates 1995/96

Bands of taxable income £	Rate %	Tax on band £
0–3,200	20	640
3,201–24,300	25	5,275
Over 24,300	40	—

Table 1.2   Personal allowances

(1)   Personal and married couple's allowances
The rates which will apply for 1995/96 (equivalent figures for 1994/95 in italics) are:

Age	Personal allowance £		Married couple's allowance £	
Under 65	3,525	*3,445*	1,720	*1,720*
65 to 74	4,630	*4,200*	2,995	*2,665*
75 and over	4,800	*4,370*	3,035	*2,705*

Note: The income limit for persons aged 65 and over is £14,600. Where the taxpayer's total income exceeds this limit, the age-related allowances are reduced by £1 for every £2 of income over the limit. The allowances are not reduced below the level of the basic personal or married couple's allowances.

(2)   Additional allowance and widow's bereavement allowance — unchanged at £1,720.
(3)   Blind person's allowance — unchanged at £1,200.

National Insurance contributions 1995/96

Table 1.3 Contracted-in

Employer contributions			Employee contributions		
Earnings £pw	% of all earnings		Earnings £pw	% on first £58	% on remainder
0–57.99	0		0–57.99	0	0
58–104.99	3.0		58–440	2	10
105–149.99	5.0		Over 440	2	10% up to £440
150–204.99	7.0				
205–440.00	10.2				
Over 440	10.2				

Table 1.4 Contracted-out

Employer contributions			Employee contributions		
Earnings £pw	% on first £58	% on remainder	Earnings £pw	% on first £58	% on remainder
0–57.99	0	0	0–57.99	0	0
58–104.99	3.0	0.0	58–440	2	8.2
105–149.99	5.0	2.0	Over 440	2	8.2% up to £440
150–204.99	7.0	4.0			
205–440.00	10.2	7.2			
Over 440	10.2	7.2/10.2*			

*7.2% of earnings between £58 per week and £440 per week 10.2% on excess.

Self-employed contributions

Class 2 Contributions: where profits are over £3,260, flat weekly rate increased from £5.65 per week to £5.75 per week.

Class 4 Contributions: 7.3 per cent on profits between £6,640 and £22,880 per annum.

These rates take effect from 6 April 1995.

1.11   Capital gains tax

Capital gains tax is charged on real capital gains. A person who makes a gain is allowed to deduct not only his actual acquisition value (in addition to the costs of acquisition and disposal) but also a proportion of the acquisition value which represents the increase in the RPI between the month of acquisition and the month of disposal.

Up until the November 1993 Budget, it was permissible to use indexation relief to create or increase a capital loss. From 30 November 1993, indexation relief may only be used in this way in relation to transactions prior to 30 November 1993.

The intention of the new rules was that, in all future transactions, indexation relief should only be used to reduce or extinguish a gain, not create or increase a loss. The rule was relaxed as the Finance Bill made its way through the committee stages; indexation may continue to be used in this way but only for the 1993/94 and 1994/95 tax years and only up to an overall limit of £10,000.

2 Unlisted investments

John Smithard, of James Capel & Co

2.1 Types of unlisted security

This chapter deals with the most commonly available forms of investment which do not have an official quotation or market price. It includes investments issued by the government through National Savings, by local authorities, by building societies and by other financial institutions wishing to raise money, and in general can only be redeemed by the borrower.

With some exceptions, these securities provide the investor with interest until they mature, whereupon he receives the return of his original capital. Although the rates of return on some of these investments might not always compare favourably with returns on other forms of investment, some have taxation advantages up to a specific amount, particularly for the higher rate taxpayer. Other investments covered in this chapter may produce no income in the course of their lives, but give a guaranteed improvement in capital value on maturity. Premium bonds give no guarantee of income or capital appreciation but offer the holder a chance in draws for tax-free prizes. A comparison of rates of return, the limitations on amounts invested, and conditions of withdrawal are set out in Table 2.1 on pp 16 and 17.

2.2 Review of 1994

With the government still running a huge public sector borrowing requirement in 1994, National Savings had to play its role fully, and in calendar 1994 contributed a net £4.6bn towards government funding. Very much a tale of two halves, the net contribution in the first six months of the year was £3.2bn. The first quarter was by far the best for some time, but funding from this source tended to peter out as the year went on, and especially as base rates turned up in the autumn. By the end of December 1994, there was a total of £51bn invested in National Savings products, up from around £46.5bn a year earlier.

Table 2.1   Current rates of return and conditions (April 1995)

Investment	Return (% pa)		Amount invested		Withdrawal notice (days)	Notes
	Gross*	Net*	Min	Max		
1 National Savings Bank: Ordinary accounts Investment accounts	$2.0-3.3^0$ $5.3-6.0$	$1.5-2.4^0$ $3.9-4.5$	£10 £20	£10,000 £100,000	£100 on demand 30	[0]Depending on balance, first £70 free of tax
2 National savings certificates (42nd issue)	5.85^1 (tax free)		£100	£10,000	8	[1]Equivalent to 7.7% to basic-rate taxpayers: further £10,000 if from re-investment of expired NSC
3 National savings index-linked certificates (8th issue)	Increase in RPI^2 (tax free)		£100	£10,000	8	[2]Paid on withdrawal if after one year, with tax-free interest. Further £10,000 if from matured NSC
4 National savings children's bonus bonds	7.9 (tax free)		£25	£1,000	8	If held for 5 years
5 National savings income bonds	$6.5-6.8$	$4.9-5.1$	£2,000	£250,000	3 months	
6 National savings capital bonds	7.8	5.8	£100	£250,000	8	
7 National savings FIRST option bonds	6.4	4.8	£1,000	£250,000	8	
8 National savings pensioner's guaranteed income bonds	7.5	5.6				

		(tax free)				Other terms
						...month's interest at 5.2% on each bond eligible for draw
10 Local authority mortgage bonds: 1 year	7.4	5.5				Other terms available
11 Commercial banks: Deposit accounts (7 day)	1	0.8	25p	None	7[5]	[5]But may be withdrawn on demand subject to deduction of 7 days' interest from balance
High Interest cheque	5.5–6.9	4.1–5.1	£1,000	None	None	
Certificates of deposit	6.0[6]	4.5	£50,000	None	Marketable security	[6]3-month term and 6-month term
12 Building societies: Share accounts	1.5–5.5	1.1–4.1	£1		On demand[7]	[7]Up to £300 in cash or £5,000 by cheque; above £5,000 branch refers to head office
Premium accounts	6.0–7.8[8]	4.5–5.8[8]	£500	None	0–12 months	[8]Rates vary according to size
13 Certificates of tax deposit	2.5–6.3[9] / 1.3[10]	1.9–4.7[9] / 0.9[10]	£2,000	None	0–12 months	[9]If withdrawn for payment of tax [10]If withdrawn in cash
14 Treasury bills	6.0	4.5	£5,000	None	Marketable security	

*Based on tax at the basic rate of 25%

Perhaps the most popular product during the year was premium bonds. The arrival of the National Lottery seems to have stimulated a good deal of interest in random draws, and while the top prizes may never be able to match those on offer each Saturday from the Lottery, premium bonds are gaining in popularity helped by the fact that one's stake can be returned by having the bonds repaid. Following close behind in terms of new money raised were the new Pensioner's Bonds, with fixed-interest and index-linked certificates also attracting some interest, but nowhere near as much as in 1993.

Some products were withdrawn. The Save As You Earn scheme was dropped so that National Savings could concentrate 'on its core activities'; the building societies provide adequate SAYE schemes. The Yearly Plan was also to be withdrawn in February 1995, probably due to lack of interest in what seemed a rather cumbersome product, although investors at least were allowed to complete the year's payments to achieve the next plan certificate.

2.3   Types of unlisted investment

2.3.1   National Savings Bank accounts

The National Savings Bank is guaranteed by the government and is operated by the Post Office as agent. Two types of account — ordinary accounts and investment accounts — are available.

Anyone aged seven years or over can open an account in his or her own name, and an account can be opened on behalf of a younger child by his parent or legal guardian although withdrawals and encashments are not allowed until the child is seven. Friendly societies and other classes of investor can also open accounts.

Interest on both types of account is credited annually on 31 December. In the case of ordinary accounts, this is for each complete calendar month. For investment accounts, interest is calculated from the day funds are deposited until the day prior to withdrawal. There is a maximum amount which can be withdrawn daily from an ordinary account, and all withdrawals from an investment account require one month's notice.

Interest is paid gross (ie without deduction of tax at source). In the case of ordinary accounts an individual is given exemption from basic and higher rate income tax for the first £70 interest. If a husband and wife each have an account, they can each claim exemption up to this level, although if they hold a joint account the exemption is £140. However, there is no such exemption for the higher gross interest earned on investment accounts.

Although the limit on income tax exemption for ordinary accounts is relatively low, a holding up to this level may be attractive for higher rate taxpayers.

Accounts can be opened by completing a simple form available from almost any branch of the Post Office. The account holder receives a pass book in which all deposits and withdrawals are entered. The minimum for each deposit is £10 (ordinary account) and £20 (investment account) and the maximum holding is £100,000 (investment account).

The pass book no longer needs to be sent in once a year for the adding of interest, as this will be done on the next occasion that it is received by the National Savings Bank.

2.3.2 National savings certificates

National savings certificates are guaranteed by the government. They cannot be sold to third parties. A number of different issues of certificates have been made over the years.

A maximum individual holding is specified for each issue of national savings certificates. Trustees and registered friendly societies and charities approved by the director of savings can also buy certificates.

No interest is paid, but after a stated period of time the certificates can be redeemed at a higher value than the original purchase price. The total rate at which the value appreciates during this period is indicated on the certificate and in the prospectus. However, the value builds up by the addition of increments at the end of the first year and each subsequent period of three months. The full table, showing how the value rises more steeply towards the end of the period and levels off after the end of the period, is available from the details issued by the Department of National Savings. Certificates from the seventh issue earn interest at the general extension rate after maturity. The general extension rate is a variable rate of interest for matured certificates when they have completed their fixed period terms and is currently only 3.51 per cent gross.

The capital appreciation is free from both income tax and capital gains tax. The minimum holding is £100 and the maximum £10,000 in the current issue, but holders may have a further £20,000 worth of certificates if these arise from reinvestment of a holding in an earlier issue.

The certificates can be a suitable form of savings for children, although parents and children should also consider children's bonus bonds (see **2.3.7**). For the pure investor they are not suitable for non-taxpayers or for short-term savings; but for the investor paying tax at the higher rate, the certificates may be attractive. Application forms are available from most branches of the Post Office and banks.

Holdings should be reviewed from time to time, particularly since new issues may carry more attractive rates of capital appreciation than those already held. A review of holdings should certainly be made at the end of the specified period as the general extension rate is usually unattractive.

Any number of certificates can be cashed at one time, on at least eight working days' notice, and repayment forms are available at most branches of the Post Office and banks.

2.3.3   National savings index-linked certificates

As with national savings certificates, these certificates are guaranteed by the government. They cannot be sold to third parties.

There is no lower age limit for holding these certificates, although encashment is not allowed until a child reaches the age of seven, except in special circumstances. No more than 400 certificates of £25, ie £10,000 at initial purchase price can be held in the current issue unless they came from a reinvestment of mature certificates in which case the limit is increased by £20,000. The minimum holding is four certificates, costing £100.

If a certificate is encashed within the first year, the purchase price only is repaid, unless it is a reinvestment certificate. If the certificates are held for more than a year, the redemption value is equal to the original purchase price, increased in proportion to the rise in the RPI between the month of purchase and the month of redemption. In the event of a fall in the RPI, the certificates can be encashed for the original purchase price in the first year, and not less than their value at the previous anniversary otherwise. After the death of a holder, indexation can continue for a maximum of 12 months.

The latest issue guarantees a return above the rate of inflation for a five-year term by offering extra tax-free interest as well as indexation. The amount of extra interest credited to the holding rises in each year of the life of the certificate after its second anniversary and is itself inflation-proofed. Details of these calculations are shown in the prospectus available at post offices.

After the fifth anniversary, certificates continue to earn interest and index-linking, but on such terms as the Treasury may decide. As with national savings certificates, capital appreciation is exempt from income tax and capital gains tax.

Certificates are suitable for individuals who do not need immediate income but are seeking protection in real terms for the amount invested. Higher rate taxpayers in this category will find the certificates particularly attractive. Application forms are obtainable from most branches of the Post Office.

2.3.4 National savings income bonds

As with national savings certificates, these bonds are guaranteed by the government. Anyone aged seven years or over can buy income bonds and they may be bought for children under seven, but there are two special conditions:

(1) interest is normally credited to a national savings bank account in the child's name;
(2) the bond is not normally repayable until the child reaches seven.

Friendly societies and other classes of investor can also buy these bonds.

Gross interest is paid on a monthly basis but the interest is subject to tax. Investors may cash in part of their holding in multiples of £1,000, but they must keep a minimum balance of £2,000. Investors should be aware of the following terms of repayment:

(1) for repayments in the first year, interest is credited at half the rate from the date of purchase to the date of repayment on the amount repaid;
(2) for repayments after the first year, interest is paid in full.

Three months' notice of repayment is required. The maximum holding is £250,000. If the investor dies, the money can be withdrawn without any formal period of notice and with interest paid in full up to the date of repayment.

A slightly higher interest rate is given for amounts exceeding £25,000. Rates of interest are variable.

The bonds are particularly suitable for investors who require high regular income, who can afford to tie up at least £2,000 for a minimum period of 12 months and are not subject to tax. Income is paid monthly, on the fifth of each month. The first payment is made on the next interest date after the bonds have been held for six weeks. Application forms are obtainable from branches of the Post Office. Investors aged 65 or over should also compare the rates with those available on pensioner's guaranteed income bonds.

2.3.5   National savings capital bonds

The bonds are guaranteed by the government. They may be held by individuals, by children and by trustees of a sole individual.

Bonds are bought with a £100 minimum and a £250,000 maximum and give a rate of return fixed at the date of purchase. Although called capital bonds, they accrue interest which is capitalised on each anniversary of the purchase date, and this accrued interest must be notified to the Inland Revenue on the individual's tax return (and income tax paid, if necessary, before actual receipt of the capitalised interest at the date of maturity). An annual statement of value, showing the capitalised interest, is sent to the bondholder shortly after the end of each tax year.

The capitalised interest accrues at an increasing rate during the life of the bond and the full advertised compound rate will be received only if held to maturity. This occurs on the fifth anniversary of the purchase date, before which the bondholder will have been reminded by the bond office of the imminence of maturity.

Repayment can be requested at any time for a minimum amount of £100, provided this leaves at least the minimum holding. No capitalised interest accrues before the first anniversary.

Depending on the level of interest rates available elsewhere, capital bonds may prove an excellent investment for an individual who pays little or no income tax and who can tie up his funds for five years, assuming that interest rates will move downwards in the intervening period.

2.3.6   FIRST option bonds

FIRST option bonds are a means of lump sum saving in a government security, the returns on which are guaranteed for one year at a time. The interest rate for the first year is set at the time of purchase and the interest, net of basic rate tax, is capitalised within the bond on the first anniversary. At the same time, holders are notified of the next year's interest rate and this accrues, again net of basic rate income tax, on the value of the bond, being added to the capital at subsequent anniversaries.

The amount held in the FIRST option bond must not be reduced by subsequent withdrawals to below the minimum holding of £1,000, but up to £250,000 may be held in total in one, or any number of bonds.

FIRST is an acronym for Fixed Interest Rate Savings, Tax-paid. Interest accrues daily but is added only on the anniversary; an improved rate is given on a bond exceeding £20,000, although an amalgamation of a number of bonds to make £20,000 or over would not qualify. Bonds may be purchased and held by anyone aged 16 or over, and by trustees.

Withdrawals should be made only on anniversary dates for, if not, only half the stated interest rate accrues since the last anniversary on the capitalised interest at that date. No interest is given on a withdrawal in the first year.

FIRST option bonds have been designed for basic rate taxpayers looking for a competitive return who can make lump sum payments which they intend to hold for at least one year. Non-taxpayers, who would need to reclaim tax deducted at source, might find other national savings instruments paying gross interest more convenient. Higher rate taxpayers, who will need to find a further tax payment, might consider tax-free investments.

Applications for bonds are made to National Savings on prospectus forms available from branches of the Post Office.

2.3.7 Children's bonus bonds

These bonds are guaranteed by the government and are designed to encourage children to save. They can be bought to a maximum of £1,000 by or for children under 16, although they can be held to the age of 21. The minimum holding is £25 and the bonds are available in multiples of £25. After five years, holders will receive a bonus payment and the bonds will then attract interest at extension terms yet to be announced.

All interest, and the bonus, will be exempt from income tax and need not be declared to the Inland Revenue. The proposed return should be in excess of that available on normal five-year fixed rate certificates. Repayment will normally be made to a parent or guardian only if the holder is then still below the age of 16.

They may prove attractive to parents wishing to give capital to children, for there will be no liability to income tax on the interest which in most other circumstances is deemed still to belong to the parent if it exceeds a token level of £100.

2.3.8 Pensioners' guaranteed income bonds

This national savings product has been designed to produce a competitive income return for older investors who wish to fix a monthly return for a period of five years despite any change in the level of interest rates during that period.

Interest is paid without deduction of income tax, although it is subject to income tax. This will be of certain benefit to non-taxpayers, who need not make a reclaim of tax already deducted at source. Interest is paid monthly on the 19th of each month, but only to a bank or building society account.

The bonds can only be bought by individuals of 65 years of age or older, or held in trust for a beneficiary who has reached that age. The minimum limit for each purchase is £500, but any amount above this level can be bought, up to a maximum of £20,000 for each individual. Application forms are available at Post Offices, with applications being made to National Savings.

Interest is earned on each day that the bonds are held. Repayment is subject to 60 days' notice, although no interest will be paid for the notice period. However, there is no loss of interest on the repayment of the bonds on their fifth anniversary, or on the death of a holder. The amount of each repayment must be at least £500, and there must be at least a £500 minimum holding retained after any withdrawal. Applications for repayment are also made direct to National Savings.

At the time of the fifth anniversary of the bond, holders should receive a reminder notifying them of the rate of interest for the next five-year period. Holders will then need to make a decision as to whether to leave the bonds in place or to have them redeemed and reinvest in an alternative investment. This will depend on the bond-holders' needs at that time and the prevailing level of interest rates, although it is the intention to offer pensioners a competitive return for their savings.

2.3.9 Premium bonds

Premium bonds are guaranteed by the government. They cannot be sold to third parties.

Any person aged 16 or over can buy the bonds, and a parent, grandparent or legal guardian may buy bonds on behalf of a child under 16. A bond cannot be held in the name of more than one person or in the name of a corporate body, society, club or other association of persons. Prizes won by bonds registered in the name of a child under the age of 16 are paid on behalf of the child to the parent or legal guardian.

Bonds are sold in units of £1 and purchases must then be in multiples of £10 subject to a minimum purchase at any time of £100 up to a maximum of £20,000 per person.

No interest is paid, but a bond which has been held for one full calendar month is eligible for inclusion in the regular draw for prizes of various amounts. The size of the monthly prize fund is determined by applying one month's interest at a predetermined rate to the total value of the eligible bonds at that time. This rate is reviewed from time to time. Bonds can be encashed at any time. All prizes are free of income tax and capital gains tax.

Every month over 290,000 prizes are paid, ranging from £50 to £1m.

Premium bonds are suitable for higher rate taxpayers who do not wish to receive income and can set aside some savings with no guaranteed return but with the chance of receiving a tax-free prize. They are also a 'fun' investment for any investor who wishes to take the chance of a prize, knowing he can always have the return of his cash investment. The odds against winning any prize are 15,000 to 1 for each unit.

Application forms are available at branches of the Post Office and from banks. Winning bondholders are notified in writing at their last recorded address and lists of winning numbers are advertised in newspapers. Repayment forms are available at branches of the Post Office and from banks.

2.3.10   Government stock

Gilts, gilt-edged, or government stock represent a loan to the Bank of England, repayable on a fixed future date and, with the exception of index-linked gilts, on which a fixed rate of annual interest is payable to the holder. By far the largest active market for gilts is through The Stock Exchange, but they can also be bought and sold across Post Office counters through the National Savings movement. There are certain benefits to individuals in doing so, although transactions take slightly longer to process.

The full range of gilt-edged stock is now available through National Savings. Potential investors must decide whether to buy stock which has a high income return with perhaps restricted capital growth prospects, or even a guaranteed fall in value if held to redemption; a low income return and a guaranteed rise in value until maturity; or a balance between the two. In the majority of cases, investment in index-linked stock will protect the capital against inflation until redemption, while providing a low, but inflation-proofed, income.

Gilts can also be bought when offered by the Bank of England through application forms published in the national newspapers.

Interest on gilts bought on the National Savings register is paid without deduction of income tax and so gilts can certainly be considered by non-taxpayers and, depending on their return, by others who normally pay tax. Basic rate and higher rate taxpayers will have to account for the tax due on the interest at their marginal rate. There is no liability to capital gains tax on profits made on the redemption or sale of gilts.

The main characteristics of gilts are described in **3.5.1**.

Application forms are available from the Post Office. Investors can buy either a fixed nominal amount of stock, or they can invest a certain amount of cash. The maximum that can be invested on any one day is £25,000, but there is no maximum holding in one or any stock. When buying or selling through National Savings, the delay between sending the application and the purchase or sale of the stock means that no guarantee can be given to the price paid or received as the market value of gilts fluctuates throughout the day. Sales are made by sending in the appropriate completed application form and the stock certificate. Commission charges are often considerably lower than those charged by stockbrokers.

2.3.11   Local authority mortgage bonds

These borrowings are secured on the revenues of local authorities, which have the power to levy the council tax. It is generally assumed that the government would stand behind such borrowings, although it has no legal commitment to do so.

A minimum investment is usually specified: this varies between authorities but is smaller than for local authority negotiable bonds (ie less than £1,000).

Local authority mortgage bonds are issued for a fixed term, usually between two and seven years and, unlike local authority negotiable bonds, in which there is a market on The Stock Exchange, they cannot normally be sold to third parties.

Interest is subject to income tax and is paid after deduction of basic rate tax. Non-taxpayers will therefore have to claim a rebate of tax, while higher rate taxpayers will be assessed for the balance of tax due.

Deposits are suitable for the investor who is seeking a competitive rate of interest and is prepared to tie up his capital for a fixed term. An investor who may require to realise his investment more quickly should explore the possibility of negotiable bonds.

Authorities seeking deposits advertise in the national press, stating the period, rate of interest paid and details of where applications should be made. Deposits are acknowledged by the issue to the holder of mortgage bonds.

2.3.12 Commercial banks — current accounts, deposit accounts, savings accounts and certificates of deposit

Deposits with banks carry no government guarantee and their security therefore lies in the reputation and viability of the bank concerned. Certificates of deposit (CDs) are bearer documents and can be sold to third parties, whereas deposit and savings accounts represent a non-assignable debt from the bank to the holder.

There are normally no pre-conditions to opening a deposit or savings account with a commercial bank. However, the minimum sum for an investment in CDs is usually fairly high.

Interest, which is paid at regular intervals on accounts, can be varied by the bank as the general level of interest rates and the bank's own base rate change. Seven days' notice of withdrawal is required for deposit accounts. The interest on CDs is fixed for the duration of the certificates — normally between three months and five years.

Interest on deposit and savings accounts is paid net of basic rate tax which may be reclaimed if tax deducted at source exceeds the total tax due. Higher rate taxpayers will be given credit for the tax at basic rate.

Deposit and savings accounts are useful means of investing funds which may be needed at short notice. CDs are suitable for large deposits and consequently earn a higher return than deposit or savings accounts. Since 1 January 1991, banks have been able to offer tax exempt special savings accounts (TESSAs), see **2.3.15** and also Chapter 20.

Deposit and savings accounts may be opened, and CDs purchased, by instruction and transfer of cash to the bank concerned.

Bank account statements should be kept for reference. Since CDs are bearer documents, they should be held in safe custody.

2.3.13 National Girobank deposit accounts

National Girobank is a specialist banking subsidiary of the Post Office. It operates both current and deposit accounts and high interest accounts.

To open a deposit account the investor must first have opened an ordinary (ie current) account, for which the minimum age is 15.

Interest is credited to the deposit account or may be transferred to the current account at the depositor's option. Interest is paid net of basic rate tax which can be reclaimed.

Like the deposit and savings accounts of commercial banks, National Girobank deposit accounts are suitable for investors who may require to withdraw money at short notice. The return on the account should be compared with that available on commercial bank deposit accounts.

Current accounts and deposit accounts may be opened by completing application forms available at most branches of the Post Office. Withdrawals can be made by cashing cheques at up to two nominated Post Office branches.

2.3.14   Building society accounts

Building societies offer share accounts, various higher interest accounts, term bonds and save-as-you-earn contracts. None of these investments can be sold to third parties. Security lies in the reputation and viability of the building society concerned. Since 1 January 1991 building societies have been able to offer tax exempt special savings accounts (TESSAs), see **2.3.15** and Chapter 20.

The minimum age for entering into an SAYE contract is 16, but any of the other forms of savings may be undertaken by children aged seven or over. For younger children an account may be opened in the name of trustees (normally the child's parents). SAYE contracts are open only to individuals and cannot be undertaken on joint accounts.

Building societies compete for deposits not only with banks but also with each other (their offices are often open to the public for longer hours than the banks during the week and are also open on Saturday mornings). On lump sum investments, interest is usually paid every six months, although in some cases monthly. On SAYE contracts the bonus is fixed at the outset and paid at the end of the fifth and the seventh years, but other savings plans bear interest rates which, although specified at the time of investment, vary from time to time with the general level of interest rates. A period of notice is specified for withdrawals from share accounts but is in practice seldom required except for large sums. There may be penalties for early withdrawal from term bonds.

Since April 1991 basic rate tax is deducted from gross interest, but this can be reclaimed if tax deducted at source exceeds the total tax due. Higher rate taxpayers are liable for the balance of tax at those rates on the gross amount.

Since February 1989 building societies have been able to pay interest gross to depositors in certain instances.

The simplicity of building society deposit and share accounts and the ease with which small withdrawals can be made on demand, coupled with the sound record of building societies, make them attractive for basic or higher rate taxpayers. Application forms are available from local branches of the building societies. Passbooks are issued for most types of investment, although certificates are in some cases issued in respect of fixed term contracts.

2.3.15   Tax exempt special savings accounts (TESSAs)

TESSAs were announced in the 1990 Budget and were introduced on 1 January 1991. They provide a means of longer-term saving, tax-free, and are operated on a commercial basis by the banks and building societies.

Each individual over 18 is allowed one TESSA lasting for five years, following which a new TESSA can be opened under the regulations then in force. A total of £9,000 can be placed in a TESSA, either by monthly deposits of £150, or by lump sum payments of up to £3,000 at the start of the first year, followed by annual payments of up to £1,800 in the three succeeding years and up to £600 in the final year.

On the maturity of a TESSA on its fifth anniversary the full capital amount — a maximum of £9,000 — can be transferred into a new TESSA. The accrued interest cannot be reinvested if it brings the total above the £9,000 limit.

Interest accrues during the five year period and is credited net of basic rate tax. At the end of the five years a bonus of the basic rate tax is credited to the account so that in effect the deposit interest is tax-free. During the life of the TESSA up to the full amount of the net income can be withdrawn but any repayment of capital will bring the account to an end, without the bonus. Interest on a TESSA will not need to be declared on tax returns.

Any investor with cash savings, and especially the higher rate taxpayer, should consider a TESSA in combination with his or her other deposits. Although there is a five year life to the account, he can withdraw his capital and net accrued income at any time (but losing the right to the tax bonus), so the position is not dissimilar to an ordinary deposit account. However, except in cases where the accrued income has been continually withdrawn, an investor thinking of closing his account early should give consideration to the fact that all accrued income will be deemed to have been paid at the time of closure and may increase that year's income tax liability (see **20.2.1**).

2.3.16   Certificates of tax deposit

Certificates of tax deposit are not strictly speaking a form of investment but a scheme operated by the Inland Revenue whereby future tax liabilities can be provided for in advance. The deposits are therefore guaranteed by the government.

Certificates are available to any taxpayer — individual, trustee or corporate — and can be surrendered to meet tax liabilities of any kind, except PAYE income tax or income tax deducted from payments to subcontractors. Different rates apply to deposits below £100,000; there is no maximum deposit.

Interest is paid for a fixed maximum period at a rate specified by HM Treasury when purchased, but the rate varies in line with money market rates. If the deposit is not used to meet tax liabilities but is instead withdrawn for cash, interest is paid at a much lower rate. Interest is paid gross and is subject to income tax.

These certificates are suitable only for taxpayers facing known future tax liabilities, although such taxpayers should consider whether a better return could be obtained by investing elsewhere until such time as the liability has to be met.

Deposits are made by applying to any Collector of Taxes, who issues a certificate specifying the date of receipt and the amount of the deposit. Any request for a deposit to be withdrawn for cash should be made to the Collector of Taxes, accompanied by the relevant certificates.

2.3.17   Treasury bills

Treasury bills are bearer documents issued by the Bank of England and guaranteed by the government. There is a £5,000 minimum holding.

A Treasury bill is initially a 91-day loan to the Bank of England. No interest is paid but bills are issued at a discount. The difference between the discounted price and £100, the redemption price, is the capital gain accruing to the investor, and the annual rate of discount which it represents is called the Treasury bill rate. Although the holder may not encash the bills at the Bank of England before the due date, they can be sold through the discount market at any time at the prevailing market price.

The difference between the discounted price and the price at which the bills are redeemed at the Bank of England or sold in the market is subject to tax. In the unlikely event of a private investor holding a Treasury bill, the gain would be liable to income tax. Treasury bills are suitable for companies rather than individuals and confer total security on short-term deposits.

Tenders for Treasury bills must be made on printed forms (available from the Chief Cashier's Office, Bank of England) and must be submitted through a London clearing bank, discount house or stockbroker. The value of bills tendered for and the price at which the investor is prepared to buy them must be specified. On the day tenders are received the Bank notifies persons whose tenders have been accepted in whole or in part. Since Treasury bills are bearer documents, they should be held in safe custody.

2.4 Comparing different types of security

The investor, in making a choice between different types of security, should take into account not only the relative importance to him of income and of capital gain but also:

(1) the degree of security against default;
(2) the expected rate of return;
(3) the tax advantages or disadvantages attaching to the security (see also Chapter 20);
(4) the convenience and cost of dealing in the particular security;
(5) the ability to realise the investment; and
(6) the prevailing rate of inflation.

2.4.1 Security against default

The British government has the power to levy taxes and to print money and it is in the highest degree unlikely that it would ever default on any of its borrowings, which include national savings certificates, National Savings Bank deposits, premium bonds and government guaranteed fixed interest stocks. It is generally assumed that the government would stand behind borrowings of local authorities, which in any event have the power to levy local charges. All these securities, therefore, have an intrinsic safety which the private sector cannot emulate.

2.4.2 Rate of return

The rate of return on securities may be specified and fixed, as it is for conventional national savings certificates, local authority deposits, Treasury bills and fixed interest stocks issued by public and private sector organisations. In most other cases the rate of return is specified initially but may be subject to variation to reflect the general movement of interest rates. Returns on some investments may be linked to the prevailing rate of inflation.

2.4.3 Tax advantages

Certain securities carry tax advantages, which may be of particular benefit to higher rate taxpayers. Examples are National Savings Bank ordinary accounts (up to a specified limit), national savings certificates, index-linked national savings certificates and prizes on premium bonds. British government guaranteed stocks are free of capital gains tax (see also Chapter 20).

2.4.4 Convenience and cost of dealing

The securities described in this chapter can (with the exception of certificates of tax deposit and Treasury bills) be negotiated conveniently through high street outlets such as the Post Office, banks and building societies. In many cases no commission or other dealing costs are incurred.

2.4.5 Ability to realise the investment

With the exception of Treasury bills and certificates of deposit, the securities covered in this chapter cannot be sold to third parties. Thus the investment can be realised only by withdrawing the money from the borrowing organisation. This can be done on demand or at fairly short notice in the case of National Savings Bank accounts and certificates, national savings index-linked certificates (after one year if indexation is required), premium bonds, government stock and bank, Girobank and building society accounts. In other cases the capital initially invested is tied up for a particular period: this applies to local authority deposits and building society term investments as well as national savings income bonds. If certificates of tax deposit are encashed instead of being used to meet tax liabilities, a lower rate of interest is paid. Early withdrawal in these cases will either be impossible or entail a financial penalty. This disadvantage also applies to commitments to save regular amounts through yearly plan schemes.

2.4.6 Maintenance

The investor should retain safely all documents (particularly bearer documents) relating to the investments covered in this chapter. If the investor changes his address he should notify the appropriate body.

2.5 Preview of 1995

The forecast for the public sector borrowing requirement for 1995/96 is £18bn, but with the economy growing faster than predicted, and tax income rising while unemployment spending falls, the figure might need a number of downward revisions during the year. Funding through the gilt-edged market will naturally cover the greater proportion of this, but National Savings will be expected to play its part; the last four financial years have each produced net funding of around £3.5bn, but raising money through this source might prove a little more difficult this year.

With an election due in 1997 at the latest, the government will be hoping to see the feel-good factor returning for the voter. House prices may not help much in 1995 and unemployment, though still falling, may not be moving fast enough to put more cash into people's pockets. Earnings growth will not be sufficient in itself, so perhaps the only hope is a further fall in the savings ratio — the amount of free cash which is saved rather than spent — to fund an improvement in consumer spending. If this is the case, then it is possible that National Savings may find either that net new investment starts to slide or, possibly, rates are set gently to deter new investment so that money is spent, rather than saved. The gilt-edged market would be expected to make up the slack.

Two products — the Yearly Plan and the Save As You Earn scheme — are being dropped in 1995 due to lack of interest in the former, and duplication with the building societies in the latter.

February 1995 would also see a rise in the rates of commission charged by National Savings on the purchase of gilt-edged stock on the National Savings register across Post Office counters. The dropping of the two products, and the raising of commission rates, were expected to save £2m in costs in 1995 and £2.5m in subsequent years.

Some useful addresses can be found at the end of Chapter 3.

3 Listed investments

John Smithard, of James Capel & Co

3.1 Introduction

This chapter is concerned with securities created when bodies such as the government and individual companies wish to raise money. These securities can be traded on The Stock Exchange, where they are listed. However, this chapter does not deal with shares in private companies. Unlisted securities are covered in Chapter 2.

This chapter contains an introduction to The Stock Exchange and also deals with the distinction between market-makers and agency dealers, the mechanics of dealing in listed UK and overseas securities, as well as those traded on the Unlisted Securities Market, and sources of information.

Sections **3.5** and **3.6** cover fixed interest borrowings ('stocks'); section **3.5** deals with those issued by the public sector and which are traded on The Stock Exchange, and section **3.6** with analogous private sector stocks. The purchaser of either kind of stock knows precisely what interest payments he will receive during the life of the stock, since, with very few exceptions, these are fixed. He also knows what he will receive if he retains the stock until redemption, and since this amount is normally more than the purchase price, he will realise a known capital gain. He also has the option of selling in the market before redemption, although the price obtainable in the market fluctuates from day to day.

Section **3.7** covers companies' ordinary shares traded on The Stock Exchange. Shareholders normally receive dividends the total of which may vary from year to year, reflecting the changing profitability of the company. In addition, the market price of shares may also fluctuate from day to day. There is thus no certainty as to the level either of income return or of capital gain, although the hope is that over a period of years the general level of share prices will rise to reflect inflation and growth in the economy.

3.2 Review of 1994

Even in 1987, the year of the stock market crash, equities and gilts ended the year higher than the levels at which they had started it. Unfortunately, at a time of improving economic growth, and with inflation and interest rates at modest levels, neither market managed a year-on-year improvement in 1994. The stock market, measured by the widely based FT All Share Index, fell by 9.6 per cent while the FT-SE Index, which measures the movement in the largest 100 shares, fell by 10.3 per cent; in the meantime, gilts fell by 14 per cent on average, with longer dated stocks down by 18.5 per cent. It was not a good year for investors, who would have fared a good deal better by keeping their money on deposit. Indeed, it was only the second year since 1976 that equities had produced a negative return.

Most of the damage was done in the first six months of the year. The catalyst came from the US where capacity restraints were leading to worries of an overheating economy and a rise in inflation. Short-term interest rates turned in January, the world's bond markets saw this as a worrying development, and equity markets soon followed them down. The FT-SE Index reached an all-time high in early February at 3,520; the lowest depths were hit towards the end of June, 18 per cent down. A recovery of sorts started in the UK as base rates began to move up again, fears of inflation being the reason for the rise. However, as this move indicated that the Bank of England was continuing its drive against the UK's seemingly perennial problem of keeping inflation under control, the longer-dated end of the gilt-edged market was able to breathe a sigh of relief and start to show some stability, helping to underpin share prices. With hindsight, shares had looked expensive earlier in the year and were now beginning to show much better value.

Stockbrokers are always happy to talk about how share portfolios should be able to reflect the underlying growth in any given economy, especially the UK. So what are the explanations for the fall? Difficult to answer when the economy grows by 4 per cent, inflation ends the year at around 3 per cent, and we have no balance of payments-induced sterling crisis. Certainly, the rise in long-term interest rates around the world, measured by the yield on longer dated bonds, was part of the explanation. Perhaps the truth of it is that shares had risen too fast, too soon in 1993 on the first signs that the economy really had started to pull itself out of recession. Shares are valued by the relationship between their price and the earnings of the company; this P/E ratio was around 23 times in January 1994, much higher than the longer-term average and needing a massive rise in corporate earnings during the year to sustain share prices at that level. Earnings were set to grow, but at an insufficient rate to support share prices. Problems in government were no help at all, and perhaps part of the fall could be put down to a readjustment of values before the possible arrival of the next Labour administration.

Turning to the individual sectors of the market, the best performance was seen from the oil stocks — broadly Shell and BP — helped by an oil price rising from the depths and continued restructuring-induced recovery at BP. Printing and packaging also fared well as the industry was able to put through price rises. Mineral extraction, a sector dominated in size by RTZ, benefited from rising raw material prices brought about by improving economies around the world. Electricity stocks seemed to be let off relatively lightly by the industry regulator at the time of the pricing review, and improved further towards the end of the year as the RECs tried to pass some of their cash balances back to shareholders in the way of special dividends and share buy-backs. Food retailers recovered from the oversold position of 1993. Broadly speaking, the rest of the market fell, with building related stocks worst hit on worries over the effect of higher base rates. Insurances lost out on US pollution scares and, for the life companies, the continued fall-out over the mis-selling of pensions. Property stocks, which had performed so well on recovery hopes in 1993, turned back as interest rates started to rise again. General retailers were de-rated with the consumer unwilling to pay up, and the stores having to cut selling prices to the bone. Kingfisher, the Woolworth's holding company, was the worst-performing FT-SE share; British Steel was the best.

Highlights for the year included the take-overs of Westland by GKN, the Scottish supermarket group William Low by Tesco, and London Weekend Television by Granada. Failed bids included that of Enterprise Oil for LASMO, while merger talks between Warburg, the largest UK merchant bank, and Morgan Stanley of the US, hit the rocks fairly soon after they were announced. Bids for the submarine manufacturer VSEL by British Aerospace and GEC were referred to the Monopolies Commission. Lloyds Bank's proposed acquisition of the Cheltenham & Gloucester Building Society was put on hold. SmithKline Beecham became the world's leading over-the-counter drug maker by buying businesses from Eastman Kodak; Reckitt & Colman took a major step in household products through a large US acquisition, while selling its UK foods and drinks businesses. BAT finally received the go-ahead for the $1bn purchase of American Tobacco. In terms of new issues, the largest was the £4.4bn value given to BSkyB.

Gilts were yielding around 6.5 per cent at the start of the year at the longer end of the scale, about 5 per cent at the shorter. Aggressive selling in the futures market by hedged funds started the slide as US short rates turned, and this led to selling of gilts by institutions which were not natural holders but which had enjoyed the ride in 1993 as interest rates fell. The economic fundamentals were fine for the gilt market, with a growing economy led by export markets and not by consumers, inflation kept at low levels, and an improving trade balance. This background exerted itself later in the year and helped stabilise the gilt market, but the damage had been done. By the end of the year long gilts were yielding 8.5 per cent, with the shorter end at over 7 per cent.

Following the sharp fall in mid-March, Wall Street put in a resilient performance for the rest of the year even though interest rates were rising slowly and constantly. The economy grew at around 4 per cent, but corporate earnings growth matched investors' expectations. It proved one of the better stockmarkets in 1994, although it could not match Tokyo which performed better, certainly in sterling terms. Japan was a year of two halves, rising strongly until mid-June as indications of the economic recovery started to be seen, then drifting off for the remainder of the year. The index is still way below its all-time high. Apart from Scandinavia, the continental European markets broadly moved as one — downwards on balance. Australia was poor, as were many of the Far Eastern markets, especially Hong Kong on property values fears, although Taiwan and Korea managed an improvement in 1994.

The graphs on pages 39–41 illustrate:

(1)   the performance of ordinary shares measured by the FT-SE 100 Share Index;
(2)   the performance of government securities (gilt-edged stocks), measured by the FT Actuaries All Stocks Index;
(3)   the movement in UK interest rates and the inflation rate;
(4)   the movement of sterling on a trade-weighted basis;
(5)   the sterling-adjusted performance of New York, Tokyo and continental European equities.

3.3   Comparing different types of security

The investor, in making a choice between different types of security, should take into account not only the relative importance to him of income and of capital gain but also:

(1)   the degree of security against default;
(2)   the expected rate of return;
(3)   the tax advantages or disadvantages attaching to the security;
(4)   the convenience and cost of dealing in the particular security; and
(5)   the ability to realise the investment.

Figure 3.1 FT-SE 100 index

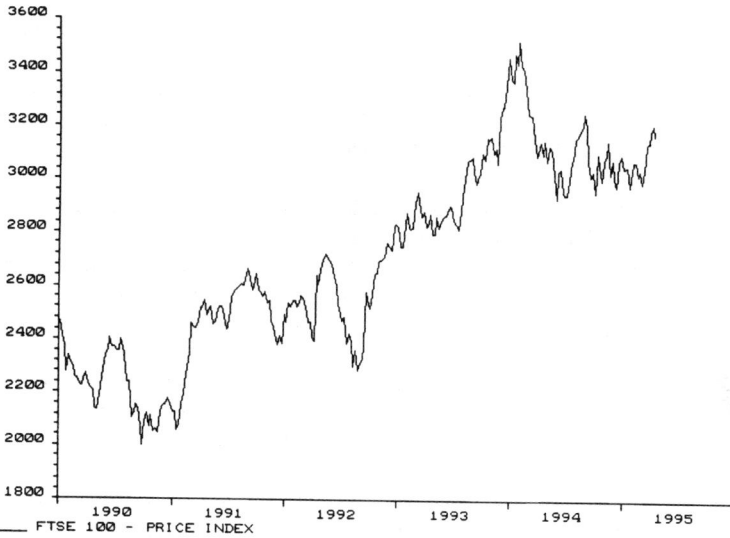

FTSE 100 - PRICE INDEX

Source: *Datastream*

Figure 3.2 London FTA Government all stocks index

FTA GOVERNMENT ALL STOCKS - PRICE INDEX

Source: *Datastream*

Figure 3.3   London clearing banks base rate and UK inflation rate

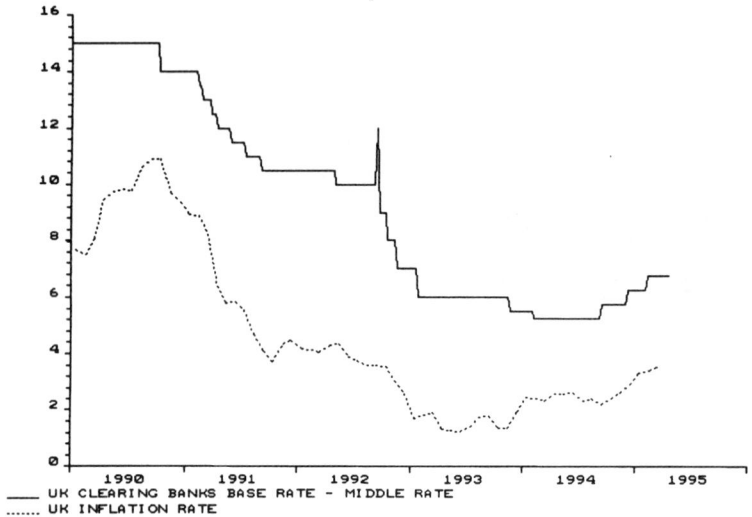

UK CLEARING BANKS BASE RATE - MIDDLE RATE
UK INFLATION RATE

Source: *Datastream*

Figure 3.4   Bank of England trade weighted sterling index

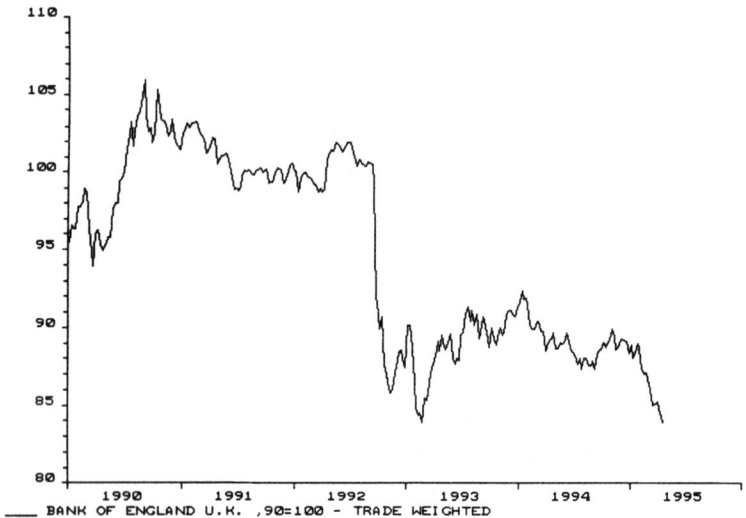

BANK OF ENGLAND U.K. ,90=100 - TRADE WEIGHTED

Source: *Datastream*

Figure 3.5 New York, Tokyo and Continental indices in sterling (rebased to 100)

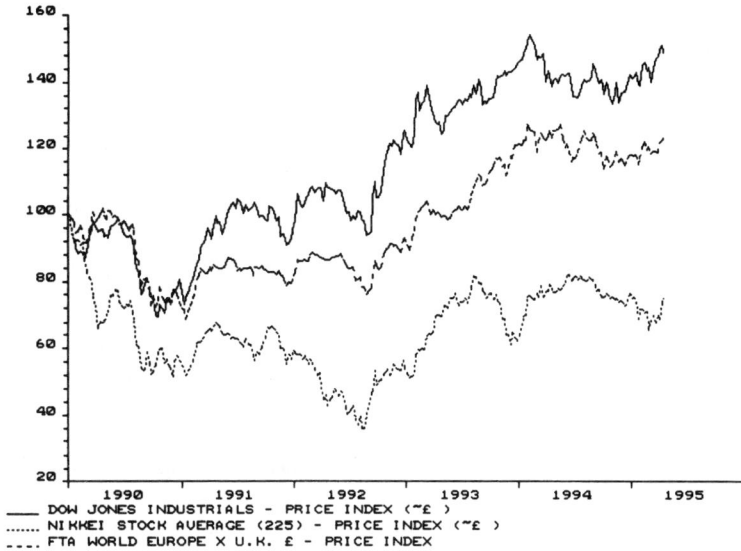

```
DOW JONES INDUSTRIALS - PRICE INDEX (~£ )
NIKKEI STOCK AVERAGE (225) - PRICE INDEX (~£ )
FTA WORLD EUROPE X U.K. £ - PRICE INDEX
```

Source: *Datastream*

3.3.1 Security against default

The British government has the power to levy taxes and to print money and it is in the highest degree unlikely that it would ever default on its borrowings whether as National Savings (see Chapter 2), gilt-edged securities or Treasury bonds. It is generally assumed that the government would stand behind borrowings of local authorities, which in any event have the power to levy rates and the council tax. All these securities, therefore, have an intrinsic safety which the private sector cannot emulate. The safety of private sector borrowing lies in the reputation, integrity, viability and good management of the body concerned.

3.3.2 Rate of return

The rate of return on securities may be specified and fixed, as it is for fixed interest stocks issued by the government and by public and private sector bodies. In many other cases the return is specified initially but may be subject to variation to reflect the general movement of interest rates. Returns on some investments may be linked to the prevailing rate of inflation. Finally, the return may be dependent, as in the case of ordinary shares, on confidence in and the performance of the company. The more uncertain the return, the more attractive it has to be to compensate for the risk of underperformance. On the other hand, the investor should beware of overvaluing the certainty of return in money terms, since the real value of such returns can be eroded by inflation.

3.3.3   Tax advantages

The basic rate income tax payer is likely to find little tax advantage in individual forms of listed security and he must choose whether the emphasis in his portfolio is to be on high income, the prospect of capital gain, or a balance between the two. Naturally, both among fixed interest stocks and ordinary shares, the investor will find a range of income yield from which to choose, and a stock which offers a good net return to a basic rate investor may not appeal so much to an investor who pays the higher rate. In terms of capital gains tax, British government stocks are exempt, no matter how long they have been held, and individuals will find that they have an exemption also for the first £6,000 of capital gains on disposals in the 1995/96 tax year, after the indexation of book cost. Now that separate taxation of married couples has been introduced, each spouse has his or her individual capital gains tax allowance. Most trusts have an exemption of the first £3,000 of indexed capital gains on disposals in this tax year. In equities, including unit and investment trusts, each individual can also take advantage of a personal equity plan, in which dividend income is free of all income tax and capital gains are exempt from capital gains tax.

3.3.4   Convenience and cost of dealing

In general, investments listed on The Stock Exchange are liquid within reason and no investor should feel tied into any holding unless it is of unmarketable size. Dealing on The Stock Exchange, whether direct through a stockbroker, or indirect through an agent, will generally involve the payment of commission and other expenses (see pp 47 and 48).

3.4   The Stock Exchange

3.4.1   Constitution and regulatory role

Historically, the burden of supervision of the securities industry has lain with The Stock Exchange. However, under the Financial Services Act 1986, Stock Exchange member firms must now be monitored by a self-regulatory organisation (SRO) which, in turn, is approved by the Securities and Investments Board (SIB). In the SIB's hands rests the responsibility, delegated by the Department of Trade and Industry, for the entire securities industry — this includes Stock Exchange business, life assurance, unit trusts and commodities — both to regulate and to defend standards. Rules of any SRO must be equivalent in effect to those of the SIB and the remainder of the industry.

From its earliest origins in the coffee houses, through the establishment of an elected membership at the beginning of the nineteenth century, practice and regulation have developed together. The rules had evolved to meet changing circumstances and to deal with abuses. Under the Financial Services Act 1986, the position has now changed in that the Securities and Futures Authority (as SRO) has taken over a number of the regulatory roles, such as the authorisation of members, their conduct of business with clients and compliance matters. The Stock Exchange (as the Recognised Investment Exchange) remains responsible for the dealing rules, the listing of new securities and the provision of market related information services amongst many other matters. There is a close working relationship between the two bodies.

3.4.2   The primary and secondary markets

The Stock Exchange provides the main securities market in the UK, representing both a new issue and a trading market. The new issue, or primary, market provides the mechanism for the raising of capital by means of the issue of securities. Users of capital, be they government, local authorities or public companies, all seek funds of a long-term nature, and a large part of these funds is obtained by the issue of securities through the primary market.

Suppliers of capital, whether they are institutional or individual savers, need to invest their money in such a way that it is readily realisable. Hence the existence of the secondary, or trading, market in which it is possible to deal in several thousand securities listed on The Stock Exchange. It is also possible to deal in traded options (see **3.7.2**). The overall market capitalisation of securities listed on The Stock Exchange at 31 December 1994 was £3,339bn, of which gilts accounted for £222bn and UK equities for £762bn. The balance was made up by overseas stock with a London listing and eurobonds.

3.4.3   The Unlisted Securities Market and other markets

In November 1980 the Council of The Stock Exchange established the Unlisted Securities Market, to provide a market for smaller or less mature companies for whom a full listing is inappropriate. Securities of companies admitted to this market are not officially listed for statutory purposes, so that there are restrictions on the extent to which they can be purchased by certain investors, such as investment and unit trusts. This market is regulated by The Stock Exchange but in general the requirements for companies admitted to the USM are less onerous than those for listed companies. The future of the USM is currently under discussion.

Permission may also be obtained from the Council of The Stock Exchange under Rule 4.2 for specific bargains in the securities of some companies which are neither officially listed on The Stock Exchange, nor admitted to the USM. This makes it possible for a shareholder in such a company to sell his shares through The Stock Exchange (subject to prior permission) and, for an investor wishing to do so, to take an interest in an unlisted company which may be known to him from a local or other source. Companies whose securities are dealt in under Rule 4.2 have not been subjected to the same critical examination as that which has been undergone by listed companies and by those admitted to the USM; there is no formal relationship between The Stock Exchange and such companies. Accordingly, The Stock Exchange will not allow a 'market' to develop in such securities and restricts the number of bargains allowed. Deals are done on a 'matched bargain' basis.

3.4.4   Overseas securities

This chapter is primarily concerned with UK securities, but British investors should remember that they can also deal in foreign securities, not only those listed on The Stock Exchange in London, but also those listed on foreign exchanges (see Chapters 4 and 5).

Residents of the UK are no longer required to deposit all foreign currency securities with an authorised bank or other authorised depositary in the UK, although on grounds of security and to protect the investor's interests on dividends and stock issues, it is still advisable for some foreign stocks, in particular those which are in bearer form, to be held by a bank or agent, either in the UK or overseas. Neither should investors overlook the withholding tax of the country in which they invest, since this is not always allowable against UK tax. Should bearer bonds be lost, the expenses incurred and work involved in obtaining duplicates can be considerable.

3.4.5   Dealing on The Stock Exchange

Following Big Bang in October 1986, the distinction between firms acting as stockbrokers and stockjobbers became blurred. Formerly, a member firm of The Stock Exchange would deal only as one or the other: as a broker it would advise and transact business for its clients, either individuals (private clients) or institutional, with a jobbing firm whose role was to buy, and to sell securities owned by it, for its own profit. Investors could not deal direct with a jobber, but were obliged to deal through a stockbroker who would charge a commission for this (the amount being laid down by The Stock Exchange). This commission also covered ancillary services such as advice, valuations and tax calculations.

The current position is that broking and jobbing (now called market-making) subsidiaries can belong to the same parent. Institutional investors can now deal direct with market-makers. However, many institutions, and all private clients, will continue to use the broking arm of a firm exercising both roles, or a firm which concentrates solely on broking. Broking continues in the same manner as before: advice, recommendations, dealing at best price, settlement and protection of benefits accruing to the investment until registration.

The minimum rates of commission (formerly set by The Stock Exchange) have been abandoned and firms have been left to charge their own rates. For the private client, it may be that the commission charge has changed very little, and firms are now moving towards charging for ancillary services in order to keep dealing commissions competitive.

Generally, the method of dealing in stocks and shares is as shown in Figure 3.6 on p 46. The client will speak or write to the stockbroker looking after his affairs and is likely to discuss what he wishes to do. The initial contact might alternatively have been made by the stockbroker. At this stage, if a sale is intended, it may be necessary for the broker to estimate potential tax liabilities as this may have some bearing on the discussions — many brokers will keep a running record of earlier transactions for the client to help them. By referring to sources of information to hand, primarily the screen-based price service, the broker will be able to give some indication of the current trading price. If an order is given by the client, it will be attempted immediately unless an unobtainable price limit has been set.

The broker then contacts his dealing staff whose function is to deal with the market-maker in that share who is offering or bidding the best price in the size (number of shares) required by the client. The change from face-to-face encounters on The Stock Exchange floor to a screen-based system means that the agency dealer needs only to look at his monitor to find the best price available in the most frequently traded stocks where market-makers' two-way quotes are firm; but those shown for the smaller-capitalised stocks are often indicative only and are not necessarily true dealing prices. The dealer will complete the order, occasionally with reference to the private client executive if there is some difficulty in dealing, with one or more market-makers including, in many cases, the in-house market-making side. The dealer should always try to improve on the prices quoted by the market.

Figure 3.6   Dealing on The Stock Exchange

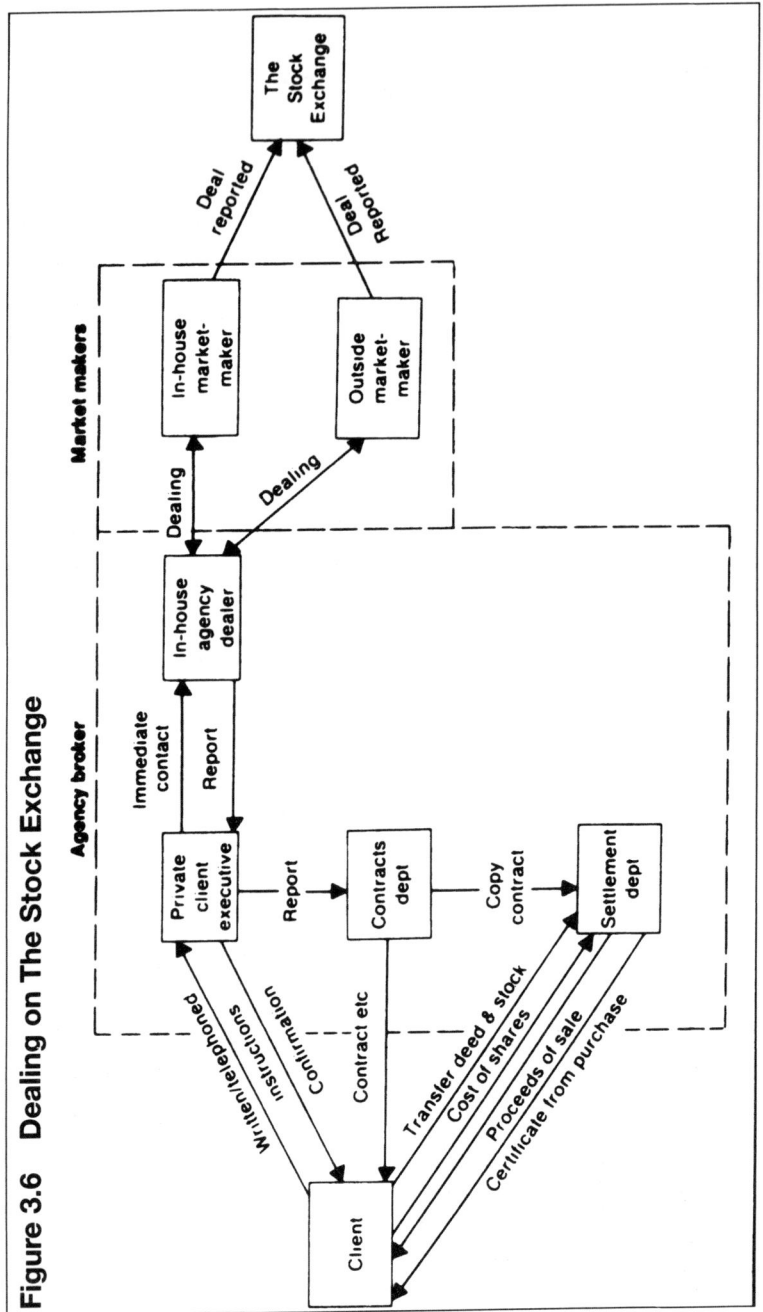

Figure 3.7 Contract note

Name and address
of stockbrokers

Bargain ref:

Bargain date:
Time of deal:

As agents we have bought for Mr J Smith

20,000 United Sprockets ord 25p at 56p

         £11,200.00

Commission at 1.5%	£168.00	
Stamp duty	56.00	
PTM levy	1.00	
		225.00
		£11,425.00

Bargain effected with connected company

Settlement date:

Subject to the rules, customs, usages and
interpretations of The Stock Exchange

(Signature of stockbrokers)
Members of The Stock Exchange

With investor protection being of paramount importance, any deal for a client transacted through the in-house market-maker has to be done at the best price available in the market at that time, whether made by the in-house team or others. It will often be the case that the in-house team will match the best available price elsewhere, when they are not making it themselves, as the private client order is on average relatively small set against the size of institutional orders.

The dealer, having completed the bargain, will report to the private client broker who in turn, if requested, will contact the client with oral confirmation. The time of dealing will appear on the contract note so that no confusion will arise as to price, especially important in shares whose prices are volatile. The contract note, which will indicate whether the bargain has been made with a connected party, will then be produced together with any other documentation required to cover a sale. An example of a bought contract note appears on p 47 (Figure 3.7) — a sold contract note would not include stamp duty, and the costs would be deducted from the sale consideration, rather than being added.

The settlement date appears on the contract note. Generally, settlement for a gilt is made on the next working day although delayed settlement can be agreed in advance.

Rolling settlement for equities, the greatest change in Stock Exchange settlement practice in 200 years, was introduced on 18 July 1994. The settlement date was set for a ten working-day basis (T+10). The cost of purchases, and the proceeds from sales, should then be available on this fixed date after dealing (sales, of course, only if the paperwork has been returned to the broker). Rolling settlement will move to a five working day period (T+5) in June 1995 and perhaps, in a few years, to same day settlement through the use of direct debit facilities with clients' banks.

Special provisions will be available for settlement for any date between T+0 and T+30 in order to tie in with clients' requirements, although the dealing price may reflect this change to the normal pattern. This will help investors wishing to close a position already opened just a few days earlier.

When selling, a client can expect to receive immediately in the post the contract note, which should be kept for tax purposes, and a transfer form. The transfer must be signed by the registered holder of the investment and returned to the brokers (together with the certificate representing the holding). The transfer form for sales of gilts eventually shows both seller and purchaser, although only the seller's name appears initially. Sales of unit trusts are covered by the same type of form, or through endorsing the reverse of the certificate. As to UK registered shares and corporate loans, a different transfer form is completed allowing settlement through the TALISMAN system.

TALISMAN was introduced in 1979 to speed up and simplify the transfer of shares from sellers to buyers. It uses a centralised settlement system in which shares from all sellers are transferred into The Stock Exchange's own nominee company, SEPON Limited, which holds them until the correct form is lodged to transfer the shares to the buyer's name. The earlier system linked buyers and sellers on the same transfer form, causing lengthy delays in cases where sellers could not produce certificates or did not sign the transfer in time. TALISMAN has been extended to cover actively traded South African, Australian and Irish shares.

Transfer of bearer shares — mostly overseas companies — passes on good delivery. North American shares are in bearer form once the registered holder has signed the pre-printed form on the reverse of the certificate.

The buying client will not see a transfer form but will immediately receive a contract note. This should be kept for taxation purposes. If so arranged, he may also be sent a dividend mandate form, to be signed and passed to his bank, which will authorise the company (or the Bank of England for a gilt) to pay all dividends direct to his bank account instead of his registered address. There is little more for him to do, except to arrange payment to his broker on settlement day. Depending on the speed of registration (usually out of the broker's hands) he would expect to see a certificate for his new holding within eight weeks of purchase. The company's registrars must be informed of any change of the investor's address.

Dividends

When a company intends paying a dividend, it must temporarily halt the registration of new shareholders in order to produce dividend warrants and tax vouchers in time for the dividend date. The registration process for that dividend stops on the 'record' or 'books-closing' date. Dealings in cum-dividend form include the right to the forthcoming dividend; dealings in ex-dividend form do not include the right to the dividend and it belongs, when paid, to the seller. Even under the TALISMAN system, shares bought cum-dividend are occasionally not able to be re-registered in time for the record date and the company is obliged to pay the seller, as his name still appears on its books. It is then for the seller's broker to claim the dividend from his client and for the buyer's broker to pay the dividend to his client. The dividend will be passed from selling broker to buying broker.

Capitalisation and rights issues

If a company makes a capitalisation issue (often called a scrip, bonus or free issue) or a rights issue, a record date is used once again, although The Stock Exchange will not usually mark the shares ex-entitlement until the working day immediately after new certificates or documents of title are posted. It is the buying broker's duty to claim from the selling broker any entitlement received by the seller which belongs to the buying broker's client. Where a seller is unable to produce documents of title for a rights issue by the time that new shares have to be accepted, then his broker must protect the buyer's entitlement so that those new shares do not lapse.

Stamp duty

Stamp duty is payable on purchases of shares, warrants and convertible loan stocks: it is collected by the buying broker and accounted for on the bought contract note. The current rate is 0.5 per cent on the consideration after rounding up to the next £100. There is no stamp duty payable on purchases of gilts or corporate loan stocks. For unit trust purchases, the stamp duty is covered by the initial charge. Stamp duty at differing rates may be charged on purchases of overseas shares. In certain transactions, eg purchase and sale by an investor of the same shares for the same settlement date or purchase of renounceable letters of acceptance or allotment, stamp duty reserve tax is payable at the rate of 0.5 per cent on the amount or value of the consideration.

Commission

The scale of minimum commissions set by The Stock Exchange has now been abolished and brokers are able to charge competitive rates. A new client should ensure that he knows what rate of commission will be charged on his dealings; firms have started to charge non-advisory clients, requiring only a dealing service, different rates from those charged to clients needing advice and periodic valuations.

PTM levy

Deals showing consideration of £10,000 or more also attract a flat £1 levy to help fund the costs of the Panel on Take-overs and Mergers. This is only charged on dealings in UK equities and UK registered convertibles.

3.4.6   Stockbroker services

Stockbrokers, market-makers, licensed dealers in securities and all others in the industry are subject to regulation by self-regulatory organisations, answerable to the Securities and Investments Board with wide-ranging powers.

Stockbrokers provide a variety of services in addition to buying and selling on behalf of clients. Brokers act on the specific instructions of their clients and give advice when called on to do so. They can also provide valuations of a portfolio at regular intervals and make recommendations. Alternatively a client may choose to give his broker discretion to manage his investments on his behalf, buying and selling when the broker considers it to be advantageous and reporting his actions to his client. Charges, if any, for these services (over and above the commission that they charge for dealing) vary from firm to firm.

The stockbroker, with access to economic and analytical material, often produced by his own firm's research department, is able to advise on investment policy and help in the choice of securities which best match his client's objectives. The investor can approach a firm of stockbrokers direct, or can instruct his bank, accountant, solicitor or other financial adviser to approach a stockbroker on his behalf.

3.4.7 Sources of information

Every weekday the previous day's dealing prices and closing quotations of listed securities are published in The Stock Exchange Daily Official List. The last recorded marks are also shown for securities traded in the Unlisted Securities Market. The *Financial Times* and other newspapers also give a list of closing prices — generally the middle market price of each (ie the average of the buying and selling prices).

A number of indices are published, of which the FT-SE 100 Share Index is the best known: it is widely quoted in the press and used as a barometer of price movement of shares. More sophisticated indices are published in respect of government securities, fixed interest and gold mining shares. The FT-SE 100 Share Index is an arithmetically weighted index of 100 leading UK shares, revalued each minute, giving an immediate picture of market movements. The companies appearing in the index are, in general, the largest in market capitalisation terms and account for almost 70 per cent of the total capitalisation of the UK equity market.

The most representative indices for ordinary shares are the FT-SE Actuaries Share Indices, covering at present around 920 shares and 38 different sections of the market. These are compiled daily. To give a broader picture of equity price movements the *Financial Times* and the Institute of Actuaries also produce daily indices for the next 250 highest capitalised companies after the components of the 100 Share Index, an index for the top 350 companies, a Small Cap index and a Fledgling Index.

Daily indices of government securities, corporate fixed interest securities and gold mining shares are published in the financial press, together with indices of overseas markets.

Apart from primary sources of information such as political and economic news and statements, and annual accounts and other reports and circulars issued by companies, a wide range of information and comment is available from financial columns in newspapers, financial journals and newsletters. In addition, the results of stockbrokers' research covering both individual companies (most of which have been visited by the stockbroker) and sectors of the market are published together with economic forecasts, and various publicly available statistical services provide immediate access to relevant information. All this information provides the raw material for what is termed 'fundamental analysis'.

Technical analysis — the use of charts — provides data expressed in three forms: line, bar and point-and-figure charts. It is not the purpose of this chapter to explain these three forms of chart in detail, still less to comment on methods of interpreting them. However, charts are often a useful source of further information, for instance, apart from displaying the levels of the main markets, they can also be used to show a price level of a particular share or stock in relation to an appropriate index and how the performance of the particular investment has changed over a period of time in relation to the market generally.

Information issued by The Stock Exchange, such as the total number of daily bargains and the volume of equity turnover, has for some time been used as a measure of the current level of activity in the market. Other more sophisticated charts, such as confidence and over-bought/over-sold indicators, are now increasingly used and from these and many others the technical analyst tries to assess what is likely to happen in the future. In essence, chartists use technical analysis as a tool for demonstrating the existence of complex interrelationships between events and expectations, with a view to determining from established trends and patterns the direction in which the market generally, or a particular share, will move.

3.5 Listed public sector securities

3.5.1 British government stocks

Legal nature

British government stocks (also called 'British funds' or 'gilt-edged securities' or simply 'gilts') represent borrowings by the British government or borrowings of certain nationalised industries which are guaranteed by the government. The investor can be entirely confident that interest will be paid and the principal repaid in accordance with the terms of the loan. A number of names are used for specific stocks — Treasury, Exchequer, Funding, Gas, etc — but these have no practical significance for the investor.

Pre-conditions

Gilt-edged securities listed on The Stock Exchange may be held by all categories of UK investor — governmental, personal, corporate or trustee. However, friendly societies or trustees acting without specific investment powers in their trust deeds must observe the Trustee Investments Act 1961.

Characteristics

British government stocks, with certain limited exceptions, carry a fixed rate of interest (the 'coupon') which is expressed as an annual rate on £100 nominal of the stock. Thus the holder of £100 nominal of Treasury 8¾ per cent 1997 will receive £8.75 per year until that date (subject to deduction of income tax at the basic rate), irrespective of the price which he may have paid or of the market price from time to time. In March 1981 the first issue of an index-linked gilt-edged stock was launched on which both capital and interest were linked to the RPI and currently stocks are available with redemption dates ranging to 2030. With the exception of Consols 2½ per cent, on which interest is paid quarterly, interest on all British government stocks is paid at six-monthly intervals.

In addition to paying interest during the lifetime of the stock, the government has an obligation to redeem its stock, ie to repay each loan at the nominal, or par, value of £100. The precise nature of this obligation is different for different stocks: it may be to redeem either:

(1) on a fixed date (eg Treasury 8¾ per cent 1997 must be redeemed on 1 September 1997); or

(2) within a specified range of dates (eg Treasury 8 per cent stock 2002/06 must be redeemed at some time between 5 October 2002 and 5 October 2006); or

(3) on a small number of low coupon stocks (eg Consols 2½ per cent, Treasury 3 per cent and War Loan 3½ per cent) at any time chosen by the government.

The government is unlikely ever to redeem the stocks in the last category unless the general level of interest rates falls below the coupon. They are purchased mainly for the interest payments, which give a high level of fixed income; but capital growth on them depends on interest rates falling rather than on the passage of time to a certain redemption date. The government is also unlikely to redeem a stock in category (2) above before the last date for redemption if the general level of interest rates remains higher than the coupon.

The period still unexpired before redemption is used to classify government stocks, as follows:

(1) Short-dated stocks ('shorts') are defined as stocks with less than five years until redemption.
(2) Medium-dated stocks ('mediums') are stocks with between five and 15 years still to run to redemption.
(3) Long-dated stocks ('longs') are stocks with over 15 years until redemption.
(4) Undated or irredeemable stocks are those with no final date specified for redemption.

Although all the irredeemable stocks have low coupons, there is a wide choice of different coupons in the other categories, ranging from 3 per cent to 15 per cent. The investor should therefore be able to find a stock which combines the redemption date which he is seeking with his preferred rate of coupon.

The two benefits of buying gilt-edged stocks are (1) the interest received; and (2) the capital profit which can be made when a stock bought below par is repaid at par or when a stock is sold through The Stock Exchange at more than the purchase price. Two kinds of yield can be calculated to help in assessing the benefits: running yield and redemption yield.

The running, flat, or interest yield ignores the possibility of capital profit and takes into account only the interest. It is calculated by dividing the coupon by the price paid by the investor, ignoring any accrued interest, and multiplying by 100 to produce a percentage.

The redemption yield takes account of both the interest and the capital gain (or, in some cases, loss) which would occur if the stock was held until redemption. The most common form of redemption yield is the gross redemption yield, which ignores the effect of income tax. Redemption yields cannot of course be calculated for undated stocks, since there is no realistic prospect of redemption.

The price of gilts is determined by such factors as the amount of new stock which the government might have to issue to fund its borrowing requirement, the amount of new money flowing into the institutional investors (such as pension funds), and the attractiveness of gilts compared with other investment opportunities. Thus, if the general interest rates and yields on other investments rise, the yields on gilts will also rise, ie the price of gilts will fall. With the probable exception of index-linked stocks, gilt prices will also fall if inflationary expectations rise. Any kind of political, economic, financial or industrial news may affect gilt prices, in so far as it affects the market's expectations about inflation, interest rates or the government borrowing requirement.

Although gilt prices do not tend to fluctuate as much as those of ordinary shares, the timing of both purchases and sales still requires careful consideration.

Accrued interest

Following the introduction of new rules in February 1985 designed to prevent 'bond-washing' or the substitution by investors of tax-free capital gain for taxable income, the market price of all gilts excludes the interest which has accrued since the last interest date and a separate payment is made in respect of this. In a 'cum dividend' transaction (one where the purchaser will receive the next dividend payment) the purchaser pays to the seller the amount of interest which has accrued to the date of sale since the last interest payment, as the purchaser will later be receiving interest for the full six-month period. In an 'ex dividend' transaction (where the seller will receive the next dividend payment) the seller pays to the purchaser the amount of interest which will accrue between the date of sale and the next interest date.

Index-linked gilts

In March 1981, the government made its first issue of an index-linked gilt, whose redemption value and annual income return were linked to the change in the RPI in order to compensate the holder to maturity for the effects of inflation. Since this date, and with inflation at lower levels, these stocks have been a cheaper method of finance for the government than conventional higher-coupon fixed interest gilts and a number of further issues have been made.

Income from index-linked stocks is relatively low as the main advantage to a holder is through the inflation proofing afforded to the invested capital. The income payments increase every six months to reflect changes in the RPI.

The timing of market purchases and sales requires consideration since dealing prices do not necessarily reflect the underlying value of the stock.

A comparison might here be made with index-linked national savings certificates which increase in value each month in line with the change in the RPI (see **2.3.3**).

As with conventional gilt-edged stocks, the market price of index-linked stocks will not include interest which has accrued since the last payment date.

Taxation

Interest is paid net of basic rate income tax, except in the case of War Loan 3½ per cent and any stock bought through branches of the Post Office. Interest received by individuals is treated as investment income and is subject to higher rate income tax, where appropriate.

With some exceptions, overseas holders of gilts who are both resident and ordinarily resident outside the UK are exempt from all UK taxes on a large number of British government securities.

For transfers of certain interest-bearing securities made on or after 28 February 1986, the provisions of the accrued income scheme, introduced by the Finance Act 1985, apply. The securities affected include any loan stock or similar security (but not shares in a company) whether of the UK government, any other government, any public or local authority in the UK or elsewhere, or of any company.

Where such securities are transferred, the scheme provides for apportionment of interest on a daily basis with the result that, for tax purposes, the seller is treated as having received interest accruing up to and including the settlement day and the purchaser is treated as having received the interest accruing thereafter. Interest is therefore deemed to have been received by the seller on a sale 'cum div' and by the purchaser on a sale 'ex div' and, in each case, there is a corresponding rebate for the other party to the transaction. The charge to tax is calculated by reference to interest periods which will usually end on each normal interest payment date. If deemed interest exceeds rebates for a given interest period, the difference is chargeable to income tax under Schedule D, Case VI (or, where the securities are non-UK securities, Schedule D, Case V).

No charge will arise if the taxpayer concerned is an individual and at no time in the year of assessment in which an interest period ends, or the previous year of assessment, does the nominal value of securities held by him exceed £5,000. Husband and wife are treated separately for this purpose.

Stamp duty is not payable on purchases of British government stock.

Suitability

Investment in British government stocks is a convenient way of providing for future commitments, the timing and size in money terms of which are known or can be confidently predicted. On the other hand, if the size of the commitment is uncertain because of the impact of inflation in the intervening period, the investor should consider a portfolio comprising both fixed interest stocks, index-linked stocks and ordinary shares.

Because default is virtually inconceivable and interest and redemption value are both fixed, with the exception of the irredeemable issues and the index-linked stocks, gilts are also ideal for the investor for whom security is paramount. Most investors through The Stock Exchange will place some value on security and are therefore well advised to include a proportion of such stocks in their portfolios. Trustees, if they have not been given express powers by their particular trust deed, are obliged by the Trustee Investments Act 1961 to invest a proportion of the trust funds either in this sector of the market or in other fixed interest stocks carrying 'trustee' status.

Further, the advantages of ready marketability and reasonably high yields should not be overlooked.

Mechanics

There are four ways of dealing in gilt-edged stocks:

(1) by a direct approach to a stockbroker;
(2) by an indirect approach to a stockbroker;
(3) through the Post Office; or
(4) by application for newly issued stock direct to the Bank of England.

Direct approach to a stockbroker

An investor may place his order to buy or sell with a stockbroker who will execute the transaction on The Stock Exchange for a commission. For information on dealing see **3.4.5**.

Indirect approach to a stockbroker

The investor can instruct his solicitor, accountant, bank or other financial adviser to place the order to buy or sell on his behalf with a stockbroker. The stockbroker may share the commission earned from an agent's client with that agent.

Dealing through the Post Office

Members of the public can buy all stocks (on the National Savings Stock Register) through branches of the Post Office, from which application forms can be obtained, or by direct application to the National Savings Stocks and Bonds Office in Blackpool. Interest on stocks purchased in this way is paid gross. The maximum amount that may be invested in any one stock on any one day is £25,000, but there is no limit to the total amount of stock which may be held. Execution of orders takes longer than if they are placed direct with the stockbroker, leaving the price paid or received more open to chance. Moreover, the Post Office, unlike stockbrokers, will accept orders to buy or sell only at the best price obtainable, and it cannot give advice, manage portfolios or take orders to buy and sell when prices reach particular levels. On the other hand, fees charged by the Post Office on both purchases and sales may be considerably lower than Stock Exchange commissions. See also **2.3.10**

The Post Office maintains a separate register from the Bank of England Register. Any stock on the National Savings Stock Register may be transferred to the Bank of England Register, but only £5,000 nominal of a particular stock may be transferred by any one investor from the Bank of England Register in a calendar year.

Purchase of newly issued stocks

The above methods of dealing in stocks concern those already issued and trading on The Stock Exchange. When a new stock is first issued by the Bank of England, application forms (obtainable from the Bank of England, banks or stockbrokers or cut out from newspaper advertisements) must be sent to the New Issue Department of the Bank of England.

The names of holders (other than those who bought through branches of the Post Office) are registered with the Bank of England, and holders receive certificates which are evidence of registration.

The direct cost of dealing is limited to the commission charged by the stockbroker, the Post Office or other agents. For dealing on The Stock Exchange see **3.4.5**.

As a rule, prices per £100 nominal of stock are quoted in multiples of £$\frac{1}{32}$. Three months before redemption, prices are quoted in pounds and pence.

Safe custody

The contract note, which constitutes evidence of a sale or purchase, is relevant, *inter alia*, for taxation purposes and should be kept in a safe place.

For stocks where a register is maintained, certificates are evidence of title and should also be kept in a safe place. If certificates are lost, duplicates can be obtained only against an appropriate form of indemnity.

3.5.2 Other public sector stocks

Certain public boards are entitled by Act of Parliament to borrow on the security of their revenues without government guarantees, stated or implied. Examples are the Agricultural Mortgage Corporation, the Metropolitan Water Authority and the Port of London Authority.

Commonwealth stocks carry no British government guarantee and are the obligation of the issuing authority.

Commission on both public board stocks and Commonwealth and overseas government stocks is likely to be charged by the stockbroker. In most respects they are similar to debenture stocks (see **3.6.1**). For dealing on The Stock Exchange see **3.4.5**.

3.6 Listed company fixed interest securities

3.6.1 Legal nature

Fixed interest stocks issued by companies are a form of borrowing. There are three basic types of security:

(1) debenture stocks;
(2) loan stocks; and
(3) preference shares (which are not borrowings).

Debenture stocks

These are either mortgage debentures, secured by a fixed charge on the company's properties, or debentures secured by a floating charge on some or all of the company's assets.

For all debenture stocks (and, nowadays also, all listed unsecured loan stocks), a trustee is appointed to supervise the performance of the company's obligations and to act for the holders in the event of default. The trust deed sets out the rights of the lenders, including limitations on the company's freedom to act in ways which might undermine their security (eg borrowing limits are imposed and changes in the nature of the business and substantial disposals of assets are restricted).

Loan stocks

Loan stocks are unsecured obligations. If the borrowing company fails to meet its obligations, loan stockholders are in the same position as other unsecured creditors: they can sue for their money, but if the company's assets remaining after creditors ranking ahead of the unsecured creditors have been paid off are insufficient to meet the claims of all unsecured creditors, stockholders receive only that proportion of the remaining assets which the outstanding principal amount of the loan stock bears to the company's total unsecured debts.

An important variant is convertible loan stock, which carries the right of conversion into the company's ordinary shares (see further **3.6.3**).

Preference shares

Preference shares are not debts but are part of the share capital of the company, issued on terms which are usually set out in the company's articles of association. Before any dividend is paid to ordinary shareholders, preference shareholders are normally entitled to receive a fixed dividend, provided that sufficient profits are available to cover it. If the company is wound up, preference shareholders rank ahead of ordinary shareholders up to the nominal value of their capital, but have no further rights unless expressly provided for in the articles.

An important variant is convertible preference shares, which carry the right of conversion into the company's ordinary shares (see **3.6.3**).

3.6.2   Pre-conditions

Fixed interest stocks listed on The Stock Exchange may be held by most categories of UK investor, although friendly societies and trustees acting without specific investment powers in their trust deeds must observe the Trustee Investments Act 1961.

3.6.3   Characteristics

Like dated government stocks, dated debentures, dated loan stocks and redeemable preference shares carry a fixed rate of interest for a specified number of years, at the end of which the principal amount becomes due for repayment. However, unlike the government, the company may have the right to repay before the stated redemption date and may do so if general interest rates fall substantially below the coupon. Thus the actual life of the investment may prove to be shorter than the originally stated term.

Private sector securities are less easily marketable than gilt-edged stocks and, with the exception of most convertible stocks, can normally be purchased on higher yields than government securities paying the same rate of interest over the same number of years. This yield differential also reflects the value given by the market to the weaker level of security offered by the loan stock.

Convertible stocks

Convertible stocks, sometimes referred to as 'deferred equities', have certain additional characteristics. Essentially they are securities issued with a fixed interest payment and fixed redemption date, but conferring the right to convert on a certain date or dates into a stated number of ordinary shares of the company.

Convertible stock usually provides a much higher running yield than the ordinary shares of the company concerned, in addition to being slightly more secure, although an investor who exercises his conversion right will not share in any capital gain achieved up to that point by an investor who had originally invested in the ordinary shares. Until the first conversion date, the market price of convertible stock tends to maintain a fairly steady relationship to the market price of a corresponding block of ordinary shares. However, the price of the convertible stock will not fluctuate to the same extent as the share price, since it will also be influenced by the general level of yields on non-convertible fixed interest securities.

Holders of convertible stocks will receive notification of the conversion option and advice should be sought at that time. It is most important to take action by the final conversion date, either exercising the conversion option or selling the convertible stock. Once the right to convert is lost, the stock will then be valued as a straightforward fixed interest security, which often results in a sharp drop in value.

The decision to exercise the right to convert on one of the conversion dates will largely depend on whether the income on the stock is likely to be less than the prospective return, in the form of dividends, on the holding of ordinary shares into which the stock can be converted.

The majority of the convertible securities in issue are convertible loan stocks, but some convertible debenture stocks and some convertible preference shares exist (see **3.6.1**).

3.6.4 Taxation

Stamp duty is not payable on transfer of debentures and non-convertible debenture or loan stocks, but it is payable (by the purchaser) on transfer of convertible stocks and on preference shares, whether convertible or not.

Fixed interest non-convertible stocks bought after 13 March 1984 and fulfilling the requirements for 'qualifying corporate bonds' in s 64 of the Finance Act 1984 are treated in a similar way to government securities (see **3.5.1**) and disposal or redemption gains are exempt from capital gains tax. Losses are not offsettable.

Gains on disposals of convertible stocks and on disposals of shares received following conversion of convertible stocks are subject to capital gains tax.

Interest on loan stocks is paid after deducting income tax at the basic rate. Holders not liable to tax may reclaim it, while those liable at the higher rate will be assessed on the gross amount of the interest, credit being given for the tax already deducted at source. The provisions of the accrued income scheme described in **3.5.1** may apply to the transfer of loan stocks.

In the case of preference shares, the 'imputation system' results in a slightly different treatment. The dividend paid is not subject to deduction of tax; instead it carries a 'tax credit'. The recipient's tax liability is calculated on the total of the dividend and the tax credit, with the result that for a basic rate taxpayer there will be no further liability to tax after allowing for the credit. Those not liable to tax may claim back the tax credit, while higher rate taxpayers will be liable to tax on the total of the dividend and the tax credit, the credit satisfying the basic rate part of their liability.

3.6.5   Suitability

Fixed interest stocks are suitable for investors who have known future commitments to meet or who want to maximise the return on their invested capital through a mixed portfolio of stocks and ordinary shares. Private sector debentures or loan stocks may represent a cheaper route to these goals than gilts if the investor is prepared to forgo the additional security offered by gilts.

Convertible stocks are a means of keeping the investor's options open as between investing in ordinary shares or in fixed interest stocks.

3.6.6   Mechanics

The method of dealing is shown at **3.4.5**.

3.6.7   Safe custody

The contract note, which constitutes evidence of the sale or purchase, is relevant, *inter alia*, for taxation purposes and should be kept in a safe place. Certificates are evidence of title and should also be kept in a safe place, although if certificates are lost, duplicates can usually be obtained against an appropriate form of indemnity.

3.7 Ordinary shares

3.7.1 General

Legal nature

A company is a legal person, capable of perpetual succession and distinct from its proprietors, namely the persons who contributed the original capital, or their successors. Ownership of a company takes the form of 'shares' in the capital of the company. All companies listed on The Stock Exchange, or the subject of trading in the Unlisted Securities Market, are limited liability companies, and the shareholders usually have no liability to creditors if the company defaults on its obligations.

Shareholders are the proprietors (or members) of the company. Subject to a company's memorandum and articles of association, and to whatever dividends the company in fact pays, ordinary shareholders have the right to all profits after payment of prior charges on the company's revenue, such as interest, wages, other running expenses, taxes and dividends on preference shares. In the same way, if the company is wound up they are entitled to all assets remaining when prior claims have been met. Thus they own the residual assets or 'equity' of the company — hence the term 'equities' to describe ordinary shares.

Ownership of most shares listed on The Stock Exchange is established by registration; the name of the owner is entered on a share register by the company's registrars (sometimes an agent office of the company and sometimes a bank or other specialist organisation), which then issue share certificates.

Extensive and up-to-date information is required from companies when they seek an initial listing on The Stock Exchange (or permission for trading on the Unlisted Securities Market), issue new shares or other securities for cash, make a take-over offer, or seek to effect a merger or reconstruction. Such information requirements may be prescribed by legislation, by The Stock Exchange or by the Panel on Take-overs and Mergers.

Pre-conditions

Shares listed on The Stock Exchange can be held by most categories of UK investor, although friendly societies and trustees acting without specific investment powers in their trust deeds must observe the Trustee Investments Act 1961.

Characteristics

Ordinary shares are a company's risk capital; the investor expects a reasonable and rising level of dividend income and a rise in the share price, but there can be no certainty about this. If his expectations are fulfilled or exceeded, he is rewarded for taking the risks that dividends might have been low or non-existent and that the share price might have fallen.

Dividends are paid out of profits, normally following the recommendation of the directors.

The market price of a company's shares will fluctuate from day to day and will in part reflect objective data such as its past records on profits and dividends and its assets; but prices will also be affected by subjective judgements about the company's probable future performance. News about the company (including its regular profit announcements) will influence the price, but so too will news concerning the sector or sectors in which the company operates and, indeed, news affecting the political situation and/or economy as a whole. Prices are also influenced by the amount of new money which the institutional investors, in particular, have to invest, some of which is likely to find its way into company shares, the proportion depending on how attractive shares are considered by comparison with other investments.

Scrip Dividends

In order to conserve cash flow and to give shareholders a method of accumulating more shares, many companies now allow their shareholders to elect to take dividends in the form of shares in lieu of cash. This is commonly known as a scrip dividend. As the company is issuing new capital direct to its shareholders there are no brokers' costs nor stamp duty, but there are no tax savings for the recipient. Although the individual is treated as having received gross dividend income of an amount which, when reduced by basic rate income tax, is equivalent to the 'cash equivalent', this latter figure (the net dividend on his holding) only is used to acquire new shares at a pre-ordained pricing formula. The tax credit on the dividend cannot be reclaimed where a shareholder does not have sufficient annual income to pay income tax at the basic rate. A higher rate taxpayer must also eventually find the difference between the tax credit deemed to be his and the tax liability on the dividend's gross equivalent out of cash from other sources as he will have received no cash from the company, save perhaps for a small balancing item. The active share investor ought also to bear in mind before accepting scrip dividends that records will need to be kept completely up to date for the purposes of capital gains tax as each new allotment of shares requires an updated book cost.

Some companies now offer enhanced scrip dividends, to a value greater than the underlying cash dividend, and may offer a cheap broker option for selling the dividend shares at a premium value to the underlying cash dividend.

Taxation of income and capital gains

Ordinary shareholders in receipt of dividends also receive a tax credit (corresponding to the advance corporation tax paid by the company in respect of the dividend). Non-taxpayers may claim repayment of the tax credit, while the liability of basic rate taxpayers is satisfied by the credit. For those liable to tax at the higher rate, tax is calculated on the total of the dividend and the tax credit, and the tax payable is reduced by the amount of the credit.

Capital gains realised from the sale of shares may be liable to capital gains tax, and capital losses can be used to offset other gains. As a general rule capital losses can only be carried forward, but they may be used to offset earlier capital gains where they all occur in the same fiscal year.

Capital gains tax considerations are important and investors should try to make full use of the annual exemption for capital gains tax available in each tax year to individuals. This implies that an investor should endeavour either to switch from investments where the income or growth potential has run its course to others where the return is likely to be greater, or to increase the base costs of his shares (within the capital gains tax exemption) by the action widely known as 'bed and breakfasting'. This entails a sale of shares one afternoon and their repurchase the next morning in the expectation that the share price has not moved. As these transactions are completed for the same settlement date and as the investor's name need not have to be deleted from the company's share register, it is not necessary for him to provide a share certificate to the broker or to sign a transfer deed. However, the Inland Revenue has the ability to see through transactions made purely for the avoidance of tax, and the nervous investor wishing to take a capital gains tax advantage in this way should consider selling the shares and repurchasing them for a later settlement date so that he comes off the company's register of shareholders. He will run the risk of market movements between the sale and purchase. The costs of 'bed and breakfasting' are relatively low, limited only to the stockbroker's commission and the market-maker's 'turn' (the difference between the selling and the repurchase price) together with stamp duty.

Not only can an investor 'bed and breakfast' a gain which would be covered by the annual exemption but he could also 'bed and breakfast' a loss to offset chargeable gains made elsewhere during the tax year.

The Finance Act 1982 provides for indexation relief on capital gains from the 'appointed date'. The 'appointed date' is 6 April 1982 in all cases with the exception of companies, for which it is 1 April 1982. The calculation of the indexation relief, where there has been a single purchase of shares, is straightforward. For shares bought after March 1982, their historic cost is increased by a factor equal to the change in the RPI from the month of acquisition to the month of disposal. For those bought before April 1982, the Finance Act 1988 brings forward the deemed acquisition date to 31 March 1982 and the deemed book value of the holding to the value on that date, as adjusted by capital issues made by the company in the intervening period, provided an election to do this has been made to the Inland Revenue. Some sales will produce indexed gains under the new system where these would have been losses under the old, and *vice versa*, and these will be treated as 'no gain, no loss' situations. Naturally, at the time of disposal, it is impossible to calculate the indexation relief exactly as the RPI figure for that month is not issued until the following month, but an estimated figure can be given by financial advisers or a certain amount of leeway can be left to cover this unknown element. Indexation relief can only be used to reduce a gain, and cannot increase a loss nor turn a gain into a loss.

Where a shareholding has been built up in a company over a period, the calculation of the capital gains tax position on disposal including any indexation relief can be extremely complicated, and accurate records of dates of purchase should be kept by all investors. This is especially the case where scrip dividends have been taken in lieu of cash.

Suitability

Ordinary shares are suitable for the investor who is able to accept an element of risk and is looking for rising income and a hedge against inflation, particularly if he follows attentively the fortunes of companies in which he invests.

For the investor who needs to estimate with a degree of confidence the timing and size in money terms of his future commitments, shares are not as suitable as fixed interest stocks.

Unlike some of the fixed term savings schemes described in **2.3**, most ordinary shares in public listed companies are readily marketable at a moment's notice. However, since share prices are subject to a considerable degree of fluctuation (greater than that in fixed interest stocks), an investor who is likely to be faced suddenly with unexpected commitments should endeavour not to rely on ordinary shares to meet such commitments.

Mechanics

For the mechanics of dealing see **3.4.5**.

Safe custody and maintenance

The contract note, which constitutes evidence of the sale or purchase, is relevant, *inter alia*, for capital gains tax purposes and should be kept in a safe place. Share certificates are evidence of title and should also be kept in a safe place, although if certificates are lost, duplicates can usually be obtained against an appropriate indemnity. Company registrars are likely to make a small administration charge in replacing lost certificates and a bank or insurance company will also charge a fee for 'joining in' the indemnity.

In the case of bearer shares no register is maintained and possession is evidence of title. Bearer shares should therefore be held in safe custody.

The investor is well advised to keep his portfolio under review, either continuously or periodically. Some stockbrokers and other agents will automatically review and revalue the portfolios of their private clients at regular intervals and will be prepared to offer advice. Between these reviews they may also contact their clients to make recommendations affecting individual holdings or the balance of the portfolio between the main investment areas.

In addition to regular reviews, which are essential, the investor who follows the economic, industrial and financial news and who is prepared to buy when a good investment opportunity arises at a reasonable price or to sell a share when its prospects have dimmed or its price is high, will do better than a more passive investor, provided of course that his judgement and the advice that he receives are good.

All registered shareholders will receive the annual report and accounts of the company in which they hold shares. Companies listed on The Stock Exchange or the subject of trading on the Unlisted Securities Market also have to make an interim report, normally containing profit figures for the first six months of the company's financial year and reporting any interim dividends declared. The interim dividend, which is paid at the board's discretion, and the final dividend which is recommended by the directors at the company's year end (subject to the approval of its shareholders at the annual general meeting), normally make up the total dividend for the year. Some major international companies issue interim statements every quarter.

Although annual and interim reports provide natural occasions on which to consider increasing or reducing shareholdings, such action should not necessarily be taken straight away, since the impact of the report will immediately be reflected in the share price. Few tactics can be worse than trying to sell when others are selling and the price is low, or trying to buy when the price is high. Having formed a judgement on whether to buy, sell or merely retain an existing holding, the prudent investor will await a suitable opportunity before acting.

Nominees

Most stockbroking firms offer the use of a nominee facility to their clients. When bought, shares and other Stock Exchange investments (as well as unit trusts) are registered into the name of a nominee company instead of the client's own name. This makes for administrative ease both on the part of the stockbroking firm — which does not then have to chase clients for paperwork following a sale of investments, merely producing a contract note as proof of the transaction — but, more importantly, for the client. Using a firm's nominee company does not mean giving the firm discretion over one's investments; a client will often retain an advisory relationship, although in most cases firms will require the use of their nominee services if handling clients' investments on a discretionary basis.

The beneifts to the client are numerous. No longer responsible for the safe-keeping of certificates, nor expected to pay the bank for holding them, the investor also does not need to sign transfer forms when completing sales. This becomes very important under rolling settlement, especially as the settlement period comes down to only five working days from June 1995. It becomes the brokers' responsibility to advise on rights issues and other corporate actions relating to the client's holdings, for which the documentation is handled by the nominee company. Dividend income can be mandated direct to the investor's bank, either straight from the investment company if 'designated' nominees are used or, at intervals, from the stockbroking firm when investments are held in 'undesignated' nominees. Brokers can produce a composite tax voucher, acceptable to the Inland Revenue, at the end of each tax year, listing all dividends received by the nominee company on behalf of the investor during that year and can provide capital gains tax calculations.

It is important, however, to ensure that the security of the nominee company is of the highest order and, especially, that the company has adequate backing over and above any investors' protection schemes in case of fraud within the nominee company.

Personal equity plans

PEPs were introduced in the 1986 Budget and allow investors to commit in 1995/96 up to £9,000 in a tax-efficient form of saving.

A new plan can be entered into each tax year. Investment changes within the plan are allowed. The tax advantages continue until the investor ends the plan.

UK registered shares listed on The Stock Exchange or dealt on the Unlisted Securities Market may be included in the plan as direct equity holdings, but the full £6,000 of a general PEP may be initially invested in investment trusts or authorised unit trusts which themselves are at least 50 per cent invested in UK and EU equities. To reflect the advent of the single European market, the PEP rules are in the process of being changed to allow direct investment of up to £6,000 in equities of EU companies. From the 1995/96 tax year, it is expected that certain preference shares and convertible preference shares will also be included as acceptable investments, allowing an element of fixed 'interest' into PEPs. Cash may be held in a PEP and interest is credited net of basic rate tax, which is reclaimable by the PEP manager to produce a gross figure, provided the cash is eventually invested in qualifying shares or unit trusts.

Since January 1992, individuals have also been able to invest £3,000 in a single company PEP issued either by a listed UK company (in which case only shares in that company are acceptable) or by a recognised Plan Manager (allowing switches from time to time between shares of differing companies).

Shares arising from new issues, including privatisations, can be transferred into a PEP within 42 days of the announcement of allocation, at the issue price. This issue value will count towards the annual investment limit. There is no liability to income tax at basic rate or higher rate on dividends on shares held in the PEP, nor is there any liability to capital gains tax on any disposal in the duration, or at the end of the plan. PEPs are therefore an advantageous method of saving through risk investment for all equity investors, but especially so for those on the higher rate of income tax or who generally have an annual capital gains tax liability. The advantages to basic rate or non-taxpayers who do not pay capital gains tax are not so obvious, especially if management charges are high.

PEPs can be held by anyone aged 18 or over who is resident and ordinarily resident in the UK or, though non-resident, is a Crown employee serving overseas.

Each plan must be managed by an investment adviser, authorised under the Financial Services Act 1986, and registered with the Inland Revenue. The manager will arrange for investors to receive annual reports of each investment, although often charging a fee for this service, and ensure that all rights of that shareholder are made available to him. All records, dealing and other paperwork will be the responsibility of the manager, who should liaise on the investor's behalf with the tax authorities (see also Chapter 20).

3.7.2   Warrants and options

Legal nature

An alternative to buying a security outright is to purchase the right to buy a security (see also Chapter 6). There are three ways of doing this:

(1)   Warrants give holders the right to buy a particular company's ordinary shares at a fixed price. The right can normally only be exercised between two specific dates in the future.

(2)   Conventional options confer the right to deal in a specified number of company's shares at a fixed price (the 'striking price') at any time during the option period (normally three months). To obtain an option the investor pays a price ('option money' or 'premium'), often expressed in pence per share. A 'call' option confers the right to buy at the striking price. A 'put' option confers the right to sell at the striking price. A 'double' option entitles the investor either to buy or to sell at the striking price.

(3)   Traded options — 'calls' or 'puts' — are available in a limited but increasing number of leading companies, the FT-SE Index and the Euro-FT-SE Index, and, in the case of company shares, take a standardised form, each unit normally representing 1,000 shares in the underlying equity. At any time before the expiry date (either three, six or nine months after the commencement of the option), the holder can exercise the option. Alternatively, he can sell the option on The Stock Exchange, where another investor can buy it.

Pre-conditions

Before dealing in traded options it is essential for the investor to have read the brochures prepared by The Stock Exchange which cover in detail this specialist area of the market. The investor will also need expressly to authorise the stockbroking firm in writing before they can transact traded options business on his behalf. There are no other special pre-conditions to investment in warrants or conventional options over and above those applying to ordinary shares. However, such investment would not ordinarily qualify under the Trustee Investments Act 1961.

Characteristics

There are clearly two sides to any option transaction. On the one hand, the purchaser of the option is paying a premium in the hope that the underlying share price will rise or fall depending on the type of option. Since the premium will be low relative to the share price, the investor is able to obtain gearing (buy the option to acquire or sell more shares than if he dealt in the underlying shares). At the same time, should the share price decline substantially, his risk is limited to the option money (which can be lost entirely).

On the other hand, there must be a writer of such an option, who will take the option money and any dividends on the underlying shares (if he is a covered writer and already holds the stock) in exchange for an agreement to supply to, or take up the shares from the option buyer if the price rises or falls sufficiently. This role will appeal to the shareholder who wishes to hedge.

Taxation

The short-term nature of transactions in traded options may involve their being treated for taxation purposes as trading rather than capital transactions or even possibly as transactions falling within Case VI of Schedule D. The full cost of acquisition is taken into account in the capital gains tax computation. The abandonment of a traded option is treated as a disposal.

Suitability

Options are suited to the active investor, prepared to risk a small premium on his judgement about likely movements in share prices over the short-term. If he has little capital to invest, he might well consider traded options. The longer-term investor wishing to back a judgement that a particular company's shares will improve might consider purchasing warrants, although the number of companies with warrants is limited.

Mechanics

The mechanics of investing in options are similar to those applicable to private sector stocks (see **3.4.5**), except that for traded options the London Clearing House supervises the registration and settlement of transactions.

Safe custody

Warrant or option contract notes should be kept for tax purposes and certificates for warrants should be kept in a safe place.

3.7.3   Offers from companies

Whereas earlier sections were concerned with dealings by an investor in the market on his own initiative, this section is for the most part concerned with opportunities which may arise suddenly and may require an investor to respond rapidly to them. However, as will be seen, an application for shares under an offer for sale has often, though not always, to be actively sought out by an investor, and a take-over offer comes not from the company in which the investor has invested but from some other company.

It is a common feature of all the transactions referred to below that strict time limits are laid down for the taking of decisions by the investor, who should therefore allow adequate time for taking advice.

Offers for sale

Although there are several ways in which a company may obtain an initial listing of its shares, only one of them, the 'offer for sale', normally involves the private investor, although very occasionally the private investor is given an opportunity to participate in a private placing of shares on an initial listing or on entry to the Unlisted Securities Market.

In the most normal type of offer for sale, an unlisted company seeks an initial listing (or permission for trading to take place in the Unlisted Securities Market) for all its shares and makes a substantial proportion of its issued share capital (normally not less than 25 per cent) available to the general public. The shares may be made available either by means of a sale by existing shareholders of part of their holding or by the offer of subscription for new shares, the subscription moneys being paid into the company. Sometimes an offer for sale combines a sale and a subscription.

The offer is made by means of a prospectus, usually prepared by the company in conjunction with an issuing house or a firm of stockbrokers and with the help of professional advisers. The prospectus and accompanying application form are available from the issuing house, the stockbrokers acting for the company and selected branches of banks, and are also advertised in newspapers. If members of the public wish to participate in the offer, they must take steps to obtain a copy of the prospectus and complete and lodge the application form, with the application moneys, within the (very short) period prescribed by the prospectus.

Occasionally investors receive an opportunity to participate in an offer for sale by reason of a holding of shares in another company which is 'floating off' a subsidiary.

Rights issues

A company wishing, subsequent to obtaining its initial listing or permission to enter the Unlisted Securities Market, to raise capital by the issue of new shares or of securities convertible into shares will normally have to do so by means of an issue by way of rights to its existing shareholders. If it wishes to issue shares to third parties for subscription in cash, it will normally, in accordance with the requirements of The Stock Exchange, have to seek the prior approval of shareholders.

An issue by way of rights will almost invariably be made on terms considered to be favourable to the shareholders, with a view to persuading them to take up the offer. Generally, a shareholder who does not wish to take up the whole of the offer (whether because he does not have available funds or for some other reason) may sell, prior to the payment of subscription monies (ie nil paid), the rights subscribed, either through the market or privately, or simply fail to accept the offer, leaving it to the company to sell the rights on his behalf and account to him for any premium. He may, if he wishes, accept the offer in part.

However, there has been a discernible move towards a form of disguised rights issue, known as a placing with clawback, where a company making an acquisition will raise sufficient funds, subject to agreement by its shareholders in general meeting, by placing new shares with institutions while allowing current shareholders to apply for these shares in proportion to their present holdings. Entitlements not taken up by shareholders may be transferred but cannot be sold through the stock market in nil paid form. The higher the level of acceptance shown by shareholders, the greater the clawback from the institutional placees.

A rights issue is made by means of a prospectus, which typically consists of a provisional allotment letter and an accompanying, or earlier, circular. The provisional allotment letter is a temporary bearer document of title, which is negotiable for the period during which the offer is open for acceptance (a minimum of three weeks) and for a further period of weeks when the shares are dealt in on these documents. Thereafter, the shares become registered.

Capitalisation issues

From time to time companies also make capitalisation issues — from the company's viewpoint, merely a book-keeping exercise, reflecting the incidence of accumulated and undistributed profits and/or the effects of inflation. Although shareholders receive 'free' shares, which can be dealt in on a temporary bearer document of title (either a fully paid renounceable allotment letter or a renounceable certificate) for a period of weeks, the issue of these shares represents no more than a rearrangement of existing shareholdings and any disposal of the new shares may give rise to a liability to capital gains tax. Special rules apply for arriving at the acquisition cost for capital gains tax purposes, depending on whether all or part of the underlying holding was acquired before 5 April 1982.

Demergers

The growth of companies through acquisition is occasionally reversed by demerger, allowing a subsidiary to be managed more effectively without centralised control. In terms of shareholder value, it is probable that the sum of the demerged parts initially will be more than the consolidated holding prior to the demerger. The separated companies will subsequently pay to their shareholders (who on demerger will be the same) dividends recommended by their own boards. Dealings on The Stock Exchange in the demerged companies will commence, with the share price of the parent company adjusted downwards to take into account the distribution of assets. The book cost of the original holding is apportioned between that holding and the demerged company in accordance with their first day values so that the book cost of the demerged company is equivalent to the reduction in cost in the original holding. It is deemed to have been acquired at the same date or dates as the original holding for capital gains tax indexation purposes.

Take-over offers

From time to time shareholders in a particular company may receive offers from another company wishing to acquire their shares in exchange for cash and/or shares and/or other securities of the other company. Most take-over bids are conditional upon a reference not being made to the Monopolies and Mergers Commission. Under the Fair Trading Act 1973, the Director General of Fair Trading has the power to recommend to the Secretary of State for Trade and Industry that a proposed merger be referred to the Monopolies and Mergers Commission if (*inter alia*) (1) the value of the assets being taken over exceeds £70m, or (2) he believes that the merger involves the national or public interest, usually due to the combined enterprise having more than 25 per cent market share of a defined class of goods or services. Whether the take-over proposal has or has not been agreed with the directors of the target company, the directors of that company will have to give to shareholders a recommendation as to whether to accept the offer. Shareholders can expect to receive not only that recommendation, but also offer documents and (particularly in the case of a contested take-over offer) a flood of circulars. The prudent course for the shareholder is to take careful note of the timetable for accepting the offer prescribed in the offer document and to delay taking any decision or action until a day or two before the closing date under the offer, in the hope that a higher offer may be forthcoming either from the original offeror or from a counter-bidder. If a higher offer is made by the original offeror, an earlier acceptance of the offer at the lower level will not preclude the shareholder from accepting the higher offer, and if a competing offer is made by a third party, an earlier acceptance of an offer can be withdrawn in certain circumstances.

Maintenance

The investor should retain safely all documents (particularly bearer documents) relating to the investments covered in this chapter. Each time he changes his address the investor should notify the appropriate body.

3.8 Preview of 1995

While 1994 brought strong corporate earnings rises, the fall in the equity market came through a devaluing of that earnings growth, the catalyst being the rise in shorter-term interest rates and some nervousness over the quality of the growth. That de-rating seemed overdone by the start of 1995, and with earnings growth expected in double figures for the year, the prospects for the UK equity market seem quite attractive, even without any re-rating of shares. The improvement should also be intact notwithstanding the expected further rise in interest rates. Politics will enter the equation, with investors focusing on the timing of the next election, although the political dimension had been within the market for some time before the start of the year.

Political concerns will have an impact on one or two sectors in particular. A change in government could bring about a more difficult background for the banks with worries over windfall taxes, and some of the utilities, especially if industry regulators are given further powers. More positively, however, the areas of out-performance may remain for the time being with the secondary sectors such as the heavy goods manufacturers, the commodity-related primary sector having put in a good performance in 1994. It is here that temporary bottlenecks may appear, allowing companies to increase their margins and produce a good boost to profits. It is probably too early to become excited with the consumer-related sectors, especially as individuals may struggle with the rise in mortgage rates and increased indirect taxation. However, a tax-cutting budget in November might make the consumer stocks more attractive but, until then, it is likely that retailers will have to remain competitive to ensure sales. Quantity of sales, rather than margins, might be the important factor for retailers again in 1995. A good deal depends on the housing market, which may stay in the doldrums for another year.

In the US, long-term interest rates may stay quite stable although shorter rates will continue to rise if the economy, which has considerable momentum, does not slow down. Corporate earnings growth will stay strong, although not at peak levels. The greatest risks — and, of course, any sharp weakness on Wall Street inevitably flows through to other markets — are that growth and inflation continue to exceed expectations, or that we see large redemptions of mutual funds (equivalent to our unit trusts) driving down the market in order to take advantage of better returns on cash on deposit.

The Japanese economy seems to have bottomed out and there should be good corporate earnings growth, although the rating already given to Japanese shares does not seem to give much scope for a sharply rising market. The returns to UK holders might be reduced by a weakening yen. There are worries over the possible repatriation of money to Japan to help pay the costs of the earthquake at the start of 1995, and the effect that this may have on other world markets.

Earnings growth in Germany should be strong, but the market started the year already quite expensively rated. The Far East still looks attractive on a medium-term view, as do the emerging markets although, as always, they will be volatile and are not for the faint-hearted.

Back in the UK, the successful introduction in 1994 of rolling settlement on a ten working day basis — commonly known as T+10 — leads to an expected further shortening in late June 1995 to T+5. Crest, the continuation of the ideas introduced, unsuccessfully, through Taurus to reduce settlement costs through a paperless system, and to reduce risk through more prompt settlement of transactions, will start tests in 1995 with a view to its introduction towards the end of 1996.

We should also have seen the launch of the Alternative Investment Market in 1995, designed to meet the needs of growing entrepreneurial companies wanting access to equity capital. Although still on its last legs, 1995 may prove to be the end of the Unlisted Securities Market, with companies either moving up to a full listing or perhaps using the AIM for their requirements.

3.9   Conclusion

Historically, listed investments have presented a good means of saving with the flexibility of choice between income or growth, or a balance of the two. However, potential investors must give full regard to the detrimental effect that inflation can have on the return on fixed interest securities, and the damage to capital values that a decline in the general level of a stock market can create even to a quality list of blue chip equities. Most investment is on a long-term basis, regard being given to the real economic growth potential of the chosen investment area, and provided that the individual can accept the risks involved in this form of investment, balanced against the twin benefits of the potential for reward and the ease of encashment, if necessary, listed investments would seem an excellent place for savings over and above more immediate cash requirements. The spate of privatisations during the 1980s has done a lot to draw back the veil of mystery over equities in particular; they can now be accepted as part of the savings of all individuals as, especially in the case of personal equity plans, the level of entry is now within the reach of so many more people. No longer can equity investment be thought to be limited to the very rich.

Sources of further information

Bibliography

Admission of Securities to Listing (looseleaf), The Stock Exchange
The Stock Exchange Unlisted Securities Market, The Stock Exchange, 1994

The City Code on Take-overs and Mergers, and the Rules Governing Substantial Acquisitions of Shares (looseleaf), The Panel on Take-overs and Mergers, 1985

Self-defence for Investors, Securities and Investments Board, 1986

Financial Services — A Guide to the New Regulatory System, Securities and Investments Board, 1986

An Introduction to The Stock Market, The Stock Exchange, 1986

An Introduction to Buying and Selling Shares, The Stock Exchange

Introduction to Traded Options, The Stock Exchange

The Unlisted Securities Market, The Stock Exchange

What's the Form?, The Stock Exchange, 1990

The International Stock Exchange Official Yearbook, The Stock Exchange, 1994

Investing in Gilts, Bank of England, 1993

Allied Dunbar Tax Handbook 1995–96 (3rd edition), FT Law & Tax

Professional and Impartial Investment Advice, APCIMS, 1993

Useful addresses

The Public Relations Department
The Stock Exchange
Old Broad Street
London
EC2N 1HP

Tel: (0171) 588 2355

Director of Savings
National Savings Bank
Boydstone Road
Glasgow
G58 1SB

Tel: (0141) 649 4555

The Director
Department of National Savings
Bonds and Stock Office
Preston New Road
Blackpool
FY3 9XR

Tel: (01253) 766151

The Director of Savings
Savings Certificate and SAYE
   Office
Milburngate House
Durham
DH99 1NS

Tel: (0191) 386 4900

National Girobank
Bridle Road
Bootle
Merseyside
G1R 0AA

Tel: (0151) 928 8181

The Securities and Investments
   Board
Gavrelle House
2–14 Bunhill Row
London
EC1Y 8RA

Tel: (0171) 638 1240

Inland Revenue
Public Enquiry Room
West Wing
Room 62
Somerset House
London
WC2R 1LB

Tel: (0171) 438 6622

The Building Societies
   Association
3 Savile Row
London
W1X 1AF

Tel: (0171) 437 0655

Finance Houses Association
18 Upper Grosvenor Street
London
W1X 9PB

Tel: (0171) 491 2783

Bank of England
Threadneedle Street
London
EC2R 8AH

Tel: (0171) 601 4444

The Association of Investment
   Trust Companies
8–13 Chiswell Street
London
EC1Y 4YY

Tel: (0171) 588 5347

The Securities and Futures
   Authority
Cottons Centre
Cottons Lane
London
SE1 2QB

Tel: (0171) 378 9000

The Panel on Take-overs and
   Mergers
PO Box 226
The Stock Exchange Building
Old Broad Street
London
EC2P 2JX

Tel: (0171) 382 9026

Association of Unit Trusts and
   Investment Funds
65 Kingsway
London
WC2B 6TD

Tel: (0171) 831 0898

Association of Private Client
   Investment Managers and
   Stockbrokers
112 Middlesex Street
London
E1 7HY

Tel: (0171) 247 7080

4 Major overseas markets

Malcolm Baker, of Threadneedle Investment Managers Ltd

4.1 Introduction

One of the earliest acts of the first Thatcher government, in October 1979, was to suspend exchange controls. Investing overseas, hitherto a cumbersome operation, suddenly became much easier, leading to a substantial growth in London's investment management and broking activities.

This rapid growth is illustrated overleaf; Figure 4.1 shows the amounts invested each year by banks, by financial institutions such as insurance companies and by other residents, usually individuals. A typical pension fund will now hold possibly 30 per cent of its assets in foreign securities whereas this figure would have been perhaps only 5 per cent in 1979.

It is possible to distinguish two motives for this surge in overseas investment. One, which might be called the 'passive' reason — though this is not to decry it in any way — is the desire to further diversify the risk in a portfolio by reducing its dependency on one country's market alone. The other motive, the 'active' one, is quite simply the belief that overseas assets are going to do better than those in the UK.

4.2 Opportunities overseas

The range of possibilities when investing overseas is wide, from the large well developed markets of the US to the fledging entities of what used to be the Soviet Union and its satellite nations. Excluding the 'emerging markets', which are dealt with in Chapter 5, the UK-based investor can divide the world into five main areas. The relative importance of each of these markets within the 'global' stock market is as follows: the US 36 per cent; Japan 28 per cent; Continental Europe 17 per cent; the UK 10 per cent; and other Far Eastern markets 6 per cent.

Figure 4.1   Portfolio investment overseas

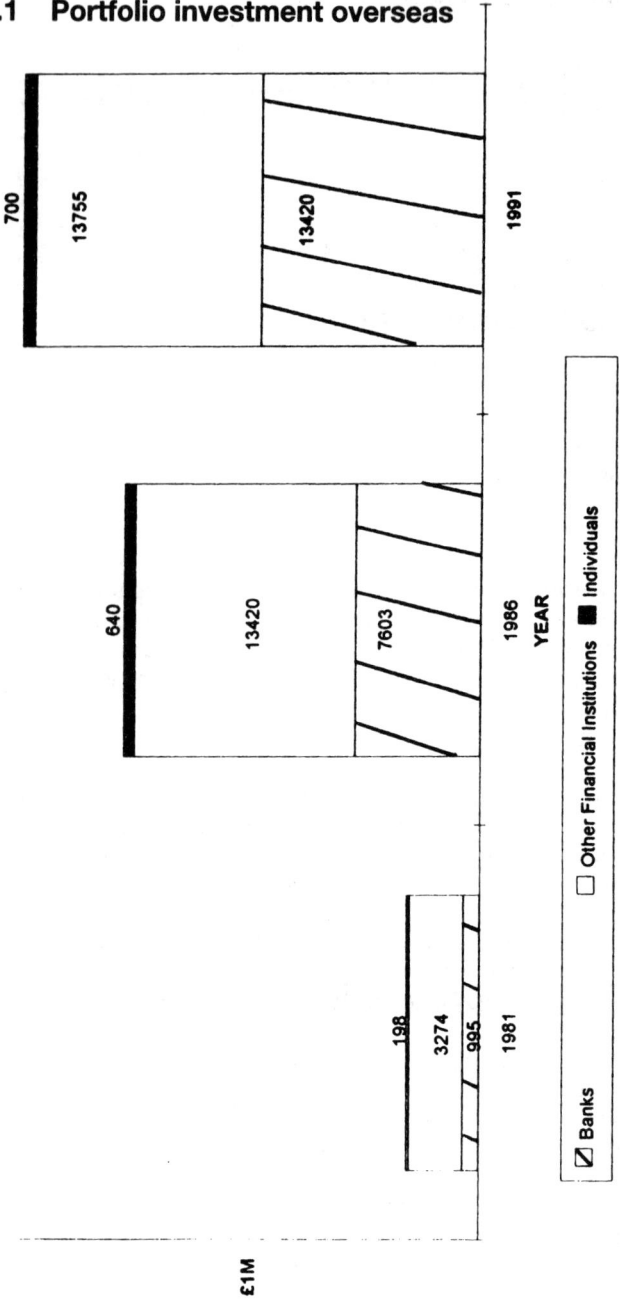

Figure 4.2   United States

```
          THE U.S.MARKET                    26/1/95
500
450
400
350
300
250
200
150
100
      1986    1987    1988    1989    1990    1991    1992    1993    1994
——  THE U.S. MARKET
---- US RELATIVE TO UK
```

Source: *Datastream*

It can be seen that the US market dominates in terms of size, though it was only a few years ago that this title went to Japan. The percentage taken up by Continental Europe might seem surprisingly small, given that it contains several economies larger than or as large as the UK: a similar point might be made about the other Far Eastern markets which comprise not only Hong Kong and Singapore, but also Australia and some of the rapidly growing smaller economies such as Taiwan and Korea. Below, the characteristics of each of these main areas are considered.

4.2.1   United States

The solid line in Figure 4.2 shows the performance of the US stock market as measured by the Standard and Poors Composite Index. The dotted line shows the performance of the US market, adjusted for the sterling/dollar exchange rate, against the British market; it gives an accurate picture of what an investor would have gained (rising trend) or lost (falling trend) by investing in the US rather than the UK.

Over the period as a whole, there has been little to choose between the two markets. However, there have been substantial swings of up to 30 per cent in the intervening period. This shows how important it is to get the timing of one's investment right.

There are in fact a number of exchanges in the US. In the case of the New York Stock Exchange (NYSE), companies quoted are generally large and to obtain a quotation they must have sound finances and a good record. The American Exchange and the over-the-counter market exist primarily

Figure 4.3   Continental Europe

EUROPEAN MARKETS   26/1/95

—— EUROPEAN MARKETS
---- EUROPE RELATIVE TO UK

Source: *Datastream*

for companies not qualified for the NYSE, but many large and good quality companies choose to remain on one or the other, finding the service perfectly adequate.

Apart from being the largest stock markets in the world, the US markets are probably the most sophisticated. Companies are closely analysed and many portfolios are run on an extremely rigorous mathematical basis. A great deal of company information is published and is readily available in printed form or on screens. Business is strictly regulated by the Securities and Exchange Commission. There are well developed options and futures markets, though these are principally designed for the institutional investor.

4.2.2   Continental Europe

Once again, in Figure 4.3, the solid line shows the actual performance of the European markets, while the dotted line tracks their performance relative to the UK.

The European stock markets performed extremely well in the mid-1980s, a result of their 'discovery' by international investors after a long period of somnolence. Then followed a period of under-performance as economic growth began to slow and, following the crash of 1987, international investors drew in their horns. Another sharp upward movement was precipitated by the fall of the Berlin Wall in November 1989 and the subsequent reappraisal of growth prospects for Europe. In the event, this vision was interrupted by the global recession which began to bite in Europe in 1991, against a background of high interest rates. European markets performed relatively badly during this period and it was not until 1993, when interest rates fell convincingly, that they began to do better.

Stock markets in Europe have traditionally played a less important part in national life than in the UK or the US. Historically, companies have turned to the banks rather than The Stock Exchange when looking for finance and this goes some way to explaining why their stock markets are smaller and less developed than elsewhere.

Although changes have occurred in the last ten years, the managers of European companies tend to place greater emphasis on the well-being of employees and customers than is the case in English speaking countries. Shareholders, therefore, come lower down the list of priority, with the result that they are treated less well than in some other markets and information is more difficult to obtain.

The main markets, in terms of size, are France and Germany, followed by the Netherlands and Switzerland. Among the Mediterranean countries, Italy and Spain figure largest though there are also bourses in Portugal, Greece and Turkey. All the Scandinavian countries are represented.

4.2.3   Japan

Strong economic growth and financial deregulation created a substantial pool of liquidity in the mid-1980s. Much of this money found its way into the property market, though substantial sums were also invested in the stock market, giving rise to the now notorious 'bubble' of 1986 to 1989. The bubble finally burst when the authorities began to worry about asset inflation feeding through into more general price increases and, indeed, the stability of the whole financial system. The ensuing period of monetary retrenchment was followed more recently by a sharp slowdown in the rate of economic activity: both of these factors lay behind the significant under-performance by the Japanese market between 1989 and 1992. The recovery has been frustratingly slow; however there are now signs that the worst is over.

There are eight stock exchanges in Japan, although only the ones in Tokyo, Osaka and Nagoya handle large volumes of transactions. There are over 2,500 listed companies and these are split into three categories. The first category comprises nearly 1,300 large companies; the second, some 760 smaller companies; and the over-the-counter market, around

Figure 4.4   Japan

THE JAPANESE MARKET   26/1/95

THE JAPANESE MARKET
JAPAN RELATIVE TO UK

Source: *Datastream*

450 recently listed entities. In general, companies graduate from the over-
the-counter market to the second category and then to the first category
as their sales and profits reach the appropriate levels.

In addition to ordinary shares there is a wide range of convertible bonds
and equity warrants traded in Japan. These instruments are a common
means of raising capital, since straightforward rights issues are rare.
There is also a very large Japanese warrants market in Europe which
trades while Japan sleeps.

Japanese companies report business results every six months and the
degree of information disclosed to investors is improving year by
year, although sometimes falls short of standards experienced in the
West.

An unusual feature of the Japanese stock market is the presence of large
'cross shareholdings' in which one company will hold shares in a selection of other companies with which it has business or other relationships.
About 30 per cent of the market is held in this fashion and this tends to
inhibit take-over activity.

The individual investor is still an important force in the Japanese market
accounting for around 30 per cent of daily volume. However, buying and
selling by individuals tends to be driven by the large broking houses, with
the result that certain types of company will be in vogue for a period and
then fall from favour.

Figure 4.5 Far East

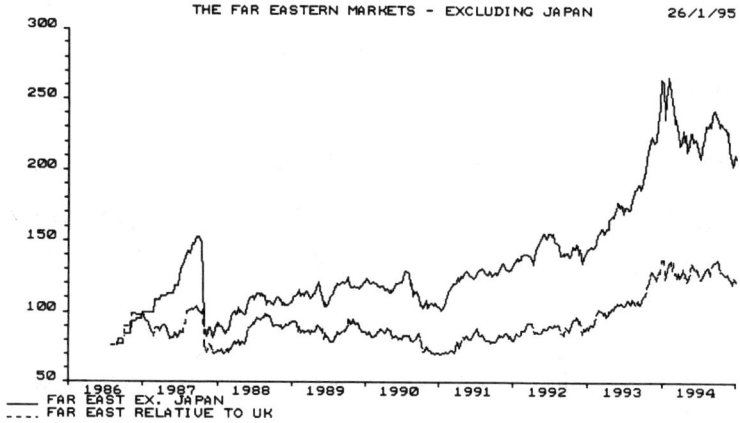

THE FAR EASTERN MARKETS - EXCLUDING JAPAN   26/1/95

FAR EAST EX. JAPAN
FAR EAST RELATIVE TO UK

Source: *Datastream*

4.2.4 Other Far Eastern markets

The performance of the Far Eastern markets in relation to the British market has been mixed. Between 1986 and 1990 the record was dull, though this had much to do with the weakness in the US dollar which is the key currency for many of these markets. From early 1991 onwards performance has been much better, reflecting the improvement in the dollar and, more importantly, a growing appreciation of the potential in the Far East, particularly in China.

The Far Eastern markets include, by convention, Australia and New Zealand in the south, Hong Kong, Malaysia, Singapore and the smaller but fast growing areas such as Indonesia, Thailand, as well as Taiwan and Korea, and the Philippines. Increasingly China, with its own stock markets in Shanghai and Shenzhen, is attracting direct investment; and India is expected to become a major market in the region. The smaller markets are covered more fully in Chapter 5 (Emerging markets).

While Australia and New Zealand are relatively mature economies, showing all the signs of that condition, the rest of the area is seeing rapid expansion. As an example, national income in Thailand, Indonesia and Taiwan has grown in real terms by between 5 and 10 per cent over each of the last five years. In Europe, 3 per cent growth is thought to be good! These economies benefit from well-trained, low cost labour forces and good connections with the huge consumer markets of the US and Japan. In addition to traditional commodity-based industries, these countries are seeing rapid growth in manufacturing and tourism.

Stock markets are echoing the economy in terms of rapid development. However, local investors tend still to dominate activity and these markets are more prone to speculative excess than is the case elsewhere. This volatility is exaggerated by the fragility of the political regimes in some areas.

While Australia and Hong Kong offer a broad range of investments, the other markets tend to consist of a limited number of blue chip stocks, particularly banks, and a large number of small stocks that are not so easily traded.

4.2.5   Emerging markets

In addition to these well established homes for international investors, there are the emerging markets such as Mexico, Turkey, or India. These are covered in Chapter 5.

4.3   Choosing a market

4.3.1   Economic activity

It would seem common sense to argue that, since stock markets have something to do with the creation of wealth, choosing a market is a matter of picking the country with the best economic prospects. In the long term, this is generally true. However, it is not an infallible guide. For example, between 1975 and 1985, at a time when the German economy was growing substantially faster than that of the UK, the German stock market rose at an annualised rate of 10.4 per cent, while the British market went up by an annualised 15.6 per cent. Over a shorter-term horizon, it is generally true that the stock market of a country that is about to emerge from a recession is more likely to perform well than one where the economy is beginning to cool down.

4.3.2   Interest rates

Interest rates are important too, and these will generally shadow the rate of inflation. As a rule of thumb, a market where interest rates are falling should generally do better than one where interest rates are rising.

4.3.3   Valuation

We now come to the vexed question of valuation. In the UK market, stocks can be evaluated against their earnings or their asset backing or their dividend yield, and the same thing can be done for individual stock markets. However, it is debatable whether international comparisons of this sort are particularly useful. Certainly, given the substantial variations in both accounting systems and the perceived role of the stock market in the economy, it is difficult to compare the valuation of one stock market against another. What may be useful is to look at each individual market against its own historical averages, but even here there are so many different measures that may be used that the results are often contradictory.

4.3.4 Currency

One of the most important considerations in investing overseas is that the investor is not only buying into the shares or bonds of a foreign country, but also its currency, and currencies can fluctuate substantially against one another. It is perfectly possible for the gains made by investing in one market in preference to another to be wiped out by adverse currency movements. For instance, between June 1991 and August 1992, the US market rose by around 12 per cent, far outstripping that of the UK, which fell by 5 per cent. However, during that period the dollar fell by over 20 per cent against sterling so that for a UK-based investor the overall return from the US market would have been a fall of 9 per cent, in other words worse than if the investor had left his money at home. Hence it is absolutely vital to take the effects of likely movements in currencies into account.

To summarise, then, the major factors that should be considered when choosing where to invest are:

(1) the likely performance of the economy;
(2) the level of interest rates and likely changes in their direction;
(3) the valuation of stock markets; and
(4) the likely movements in the foreign exchange rate.

The correct choice of stock market involves a thorough command of these factors, judgement and, let it be said, a certain degree of luck. No-one — not even the most experienced professional — expects to get it right all the time. If all this seems too intimidating, bear in mind that we shall be looking later in the chapter at how to gain the advantages of investing overseas without having to make these choices.

4.4 The mechanics of investing overseas

4.4.1 Direct investment

Despite the seemingly cumbersome arrangements for transferring stock, running a portfolio invested in British shares is not a particularly daunting task. This is certainly not the case when investing directly overseas.

Consider, first, the information needed to make a decision about which shares to buy. Aside from the obvious language difficulties, companies in many overseas markets place little emphasis on their shareholders, so that even the annual accounts may yield significantly less information than would be the case for a British company. In addition, the accounts are likely to have been prepared under different accounting conventions, which further complicates analysis.

Then comes the nitty gritty; the buying, selling and holding of stock. Stock is often still held in bearer form, so that the share certificates are the only evidence of title. In this case, dividends are not paid out automatically by the company, but have to be claimed by the shareholder. The same applies to capital issues. Hence the administrative work starts to build up and this can only be avoided by employing a custodian bank to hold the shares on the investors' behalf. At this stage the costs of owning shares begin to rise quite considerably. By extension, the whole process can be made much simpler by dealing through a British bank or broker who will look after the administration, but in this case a fee will be payable to the British company in addition to any local custodian or brokerage charges.

On top of this comes the question of local taxation which, even when a double taxation agreement is in operation, involves substantial extra work or administrative fees.

It is apparent, then, that investing directly in overseas assets is not an attractive route for most. It is therefore necessary to think about the various types of collective investment schemes which are available.

4.4.2 Collective investment schemes

A major advantage of any collective investment scheme run by a well resourced, professionally run investment management house is that the investor gets access to a broadly diversified pool of assets that are under continual review. However, in the arena of overseas investment, collective schemes funds offer further advantages:

Administration

The complexities of the mechanics of investing overseas have been outlined above; by investing through a collective investment scheme, the burden of all this administration is borne by the managers. Buying and selling overseas investments through a collective scheme is as simple as buying domestic funds.

Flexibility

The complexities surrounding the decision of which market to invest in were discussed earlier. The great advantage of a collective investment scheme is that it offers two different approaches to international investment — the global route and the country specialist.

Global funds

In general these funds will invest all around the world, changing their exposure to different markets as the managers see fit. The difficult decision about which markets to invest in is taken by the fund managers rather than the individual. The investor can therefore gain exposure to overseas markets with none of the agonising involved in the country allocation decision.

Specialist geographical funds

These funds are limited to investing in one specific area, generally one of those in **4.2** above. These are for investors who want to make their own decisions about country allocation, but want all the other advantages of collective schemes.

Whichever route is chosen, the international fund or the country specialist, the investor has a substantial array of vehicles to choose from. Most of the funds quoted will be general funds, in the sense that they will tend to invest in the larger stocks in each market. However, as in the UK, there are a number of specialist funds, invested in smaller companies, asset-backed stocks or particular sectors such as commodities.

The characteristics of each type of collective scheme — unit trust, offshore fund or investment trust — are discussed in Chapters 7 and 8. However, there are a few points to make about each of them in the context of international investment.

4.4.3 Unit trusts

These are probably the most accessible category of collective scheme for the overseas investor; most trusts tend to be generalist funds offering either particular regions or a wholly global portfolio. (See chapter 8).

4.4.4 Offshore funds

These are broadly similar to unit trusts, except, of course, that income is received gross of tax. From the perspective of an overseas investor, the offshore fund sector tends to offer more specialist investment vehicles as well as the 'bread and butter' funds found elsewhere. For instance, one management house has no less than six funds specialising in different aspects of the US stock market.

One obstacle to an understanding of investment in offshore funds is that the fund may be valued in a currency that is neither the investor's own currency nor that in which the investments were originally denominated. For instance, the price of many offshore funds will be quoted in US dollars, even though the fund may have sterling-based investors and may itself be invested in the Tokyo stock market. A common mistake in this case would be to assume that, since the fund is denominated in US dollars, movements in the dollar will affect the value of the investments to the sterling-based investor. Not so; what affects the value of the investments in this case is the level of the stock market and the yen/sterling exchange rate — nothing else.

4.4.5   Investment trusts

The stock market value of an investment trust will usually be at a discount or, more rarely, a premium, to the value of the underlying assets. This discount to net asset value is a very useful indicator of investors' sentiment towards a particular stock market; the discount will tend to narrow as the market becomes more popular and conversely will widen as it falls from favour. For the contrarian investor, who likes to invest in areas that are out of favour in the belief that sentiment will improve at some point, the level of the discount is a useful indicator; in other words the contrarian buys when the discount is large and sells when it narrows. The advantage of investment trusts is that the investor not only benefits from the rise in the value of the underlying assets but also from the narrowing discount to net asset value. For those who fancy their ability to pick the winners among global stock markets this is an attractively geared way of backing their judgement.

4.5   Conclusion

To summarise, investing overseas is most easily done through one or other of the collective schemes. Those looking to diversify their portfolios may feel attracted towards a global fund, where all the country allocation decisions are taken by the fund managers. Those going abroad because they feel that prospects are better than in the UK may well have more specific ideas and are more likely to be tempted by a fund specialising in a particular region or country. A key factor to remember is that returns on investments overseas can be significantly affected by fluctuations in exchange rates.

5 Emerging markets

*Douglas W Adams, Marketing Director, Templeton Investment
Management Ltd*

5.1 Introduction

Do you ever look at where things are made? If you do, you may have
noticed the growing number of products that have their origin outside
the major Western economies. This is just one aspect of the changing
nature of the world economy. Companies in many developing nations
now compete successfully with the best in the world, combining skilled,
but low cost, labour with up-to-date technology. In turn, these trends are
opening up opportunities for investors to participate in the development
process and spread of prosperity.

Are these opportunities only for professional investors or should anyone
constructing a portfolio to meet long-term objectives include emerging
markets in their range of possibilities? As the arguments set out below
show, there are good reasons to include a degree of emerging market
exposure in most equity portfolios. With young, ambitious populations
the probabilities are that a number of emerging economies in Asia, Latin
America and Southern and Eastern Europe will become economic
powerhouses in the next 10 to 20 years.

5.2 What are emerging markets?

'Emerging markets' is the term commonly applied to financial markets in
the developing nations of the world. This definition includes most of Asia
(with the exception of Japan), all of Central and South America, parts of
Southern and Eastern Europe, and all of Africa. Not all countries covered
by this definition possess equity markets, and some that do will not permit
investment by foreigners. Prominent among emerging markets that have
attracted substantial funds from Western investors in recent years are
countries as diverse as the Philippines, Turkey and Brazil; and states
better known for economic success, such as Hong Kong, Singapore and
Korea also often feature in emerging market portfolios.

5.3 World of change

Thoughts of developing nations often conjure images from television news bulletins of famines, civil wars, coups and deprivation. Problems do exist, but an exclusive focus on the problem areas blinds us to the more generalised, if less newsworthy, progress that most countries are making. A number of factors contribute to this progress. Improving standards of nutrition and education, the application of technology and the liberalisation of economies are judged by many to provide the real driving force for improvement.

Better nutrition

The world has never before enjoyed such an abundance of food. This growth in food supply provides a much more nutritious diet for the fast growing populations of the developing world. For example, according to World Bank statistics, daily calorie supply per capita in developing countries grew by 17 per cent between 1965 and 1990, from 2,320 to 2,706. This compares with a UK figure of 3,149. Moreover, individual countries enjoyed even faster increases. In China calorie supply rose by 40 per cent over the period, catching up with the average for developing nations as a whole. Indonesia saw an even more impressive rise of 47 per cent in its catch-up process.

Improved healthcare

At the same time, the quality and availability of medical care shows substantial gains, even if it does lag the standards we enjoy. Statistics show that the number of doctors per 1,000 of population in developing nations rose from 0.47 in 1965 to 1.11 by 1991. This rise of 136 per cent compares with a rise of 43 per cent in the UK to 1.64.

Increased Life expectancy

Putting better nutrition and healthcare together results in dramatic increases in life expectancy. An Indian born in 1960 had a life expectancy at birth of only 43 years. By 1992 this expectancy had grown to 61. Similarly for a Brazilian life expectancy improved from 55 to 66 years over the same 30 years. Since the years from 16 to 65 tend to be the most economically productive, this increase in life expectancy boosts the economic potential of the developing nations. By contrast, in the developed economies, slowing population growth and an increase in the retired population will act as a damper on growth potential as we enter the 21st century.

Figure 5.1 Annual GDP growth developed v developing countries December 1988 to December 1994

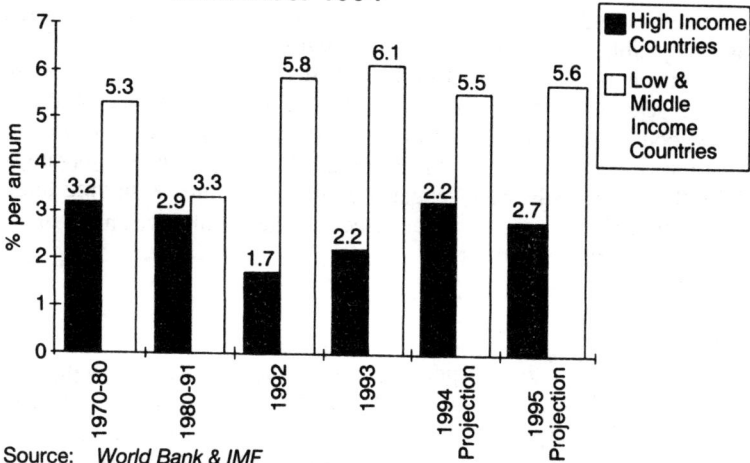

Source: *World Bank & IMF*

More education

Learning and experience are further aspects of longer life spans. An individual finds it more worthwhile to learn skills the longer expected life is, and he or she also becomes much more productive through work experience. Moreover, educational standards have been rising in many of the developing nations. For example, in 1950 under 50 per cent of Brazilian adults were literate. By 1990 this proportion stood at over 81 per cent.

Technology transfer

Better standards of education give greater capacity to absorb and adapt new techniques and ideas. And as technology advances so it becomes more transportable. Thus it is now commonplace for companies in emerging economies to apply the state-of-the-art techniques to their businesses.

Faster growth

Taken together, these socio-economic changes have helped to boost growth in the developing nations as a group, leading to improved living standards for their populations. As Figure 5.1 shows, annual growth in developing nations has been outstripping that of the developed economies over an extended period, and the IMF predicts (September 1994) that this outperformance will continue. They anticipate that, even allowing for the problem cases, developing nations will grow by 5.6 per cent in 1995, compared with expected growth of 2.7 per cent in the industrial nations.

This fast growth translates into an opportunity for investors only if there are accessible equity and fixed interest markets where transactions can be carried out cost effectively, preferably without intervening taxes and exchange controls. Moreover, the extent to which shares or bonds represent good value for the future must be considered. If the enthusiasm of other investors has bid up the price of shares, then faster economic growth may already be discounted in the marketplace. In this sense emerging market investment has direct parallels with investment disciplines in the major markets.

Liberalisation

While many shares in emerging markets have shown exceptional gains in recent years, the trend towards economic liberalisation and privatisation has provided a dramatic increase in the number, width and depth of those markets which are open. Increasingly the governments of developing nations view investment by foreign portfolio investors as a means of attracting much needed capital to fund growth. Experience shows that these inflows tend to speed up considerably following the introduction of open market policies. In addition, removing government control in many areas of developing economies often acts as a spur to growth, with Latin American countries providing an excellent example. Thus a virtuous circle develops with investment flows raising the sustainable growth rate, which in turn adds to the attractiveness of the country to further investment.

Volatility spells opportunity

Often the euphoria that accompanies this process carries share prices to levels of extreme overvaluation, making them vulnerable to any bad news or shock and, as is typical in all markets, periods of excess optimism are usually followed by bouts of excess pessimism. Thus individual emerging markets may prove highly volatile. This is both the danger and the opportunity of emerging markets. Events in Mexico at the beginning of 1995 provide a clear example. Astute investors prepared to sell at times of extreme optimism, but then to buy again when pessimism reigns, can reap handsome rewards from the long-term progress of developing countries.

Markets in context

One way of putting these developments in context is to compare the overall size of the emerging markets with those of the developed world. At the end of November 1994 the International Finance Corporation

Figure 5.2   Emerging markets, UK and World share index movements compared 1988–1994 (£)

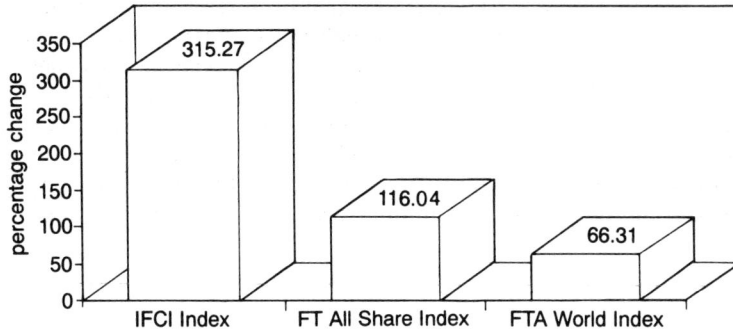

Source: *IFC & Templeton*

(IFC) calculated that emerging markets were capitalised at £1,200bn. This compares with the Morgan Stanley Capital International (MSCI) estimate of developed market capital capitalisation of £8,200bn, and a figure of £740bn for the London market.

Market catch-up

A striking example of the growth of emerging markets is given by the near 16 fold expansion of the total value of emerging market shares over the last decade. The November 1994 figure of £1,200bn contrasts with a figure of only £57bn in 1983. Put another way, in 1983 emerging markets as a group were only equivalent to around one third of the total value of the UK market. At the end of November, they were nearly 60 per cent bigger than London — the world's third biggest equity market.

5.4   Performance

The IFC, an arm of the World Bank, has been at the forefront of encouraging institutional investment in developing nations, and provides a series of indices which show the performance record of emerging markets individually and as a group. Of particular use are the series of investible indices tracking the performance of those markets and shares that are available to foreign investors. As Figure 5.2 shows, the IFC Investible Composite (Total Return) rose by 315 per cent in sterling terms in the period from its first calculation at the end of 1988 to December 1994. This compares with rises of 116.04 per cent for the FT

Figure 5.3   Six year index price performance to December 1994 % (£)

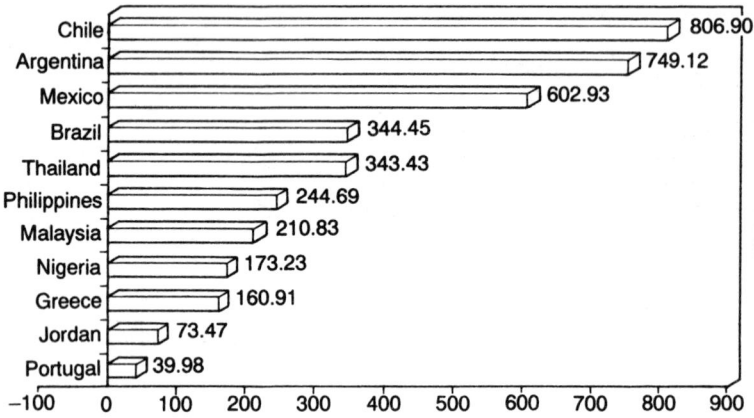

Market	Value
Chile	806.90
Argentina	749.12
Mexico	602.93
Brazil	344.45
Thailand	343.43
Philippines	244.69
Malaysia	210.83
Nigeria	173.23
Greece	160.91
Jordan	73.47
Portugal	39.98

Source: *IFC*

All Share Index (an average of UK share prices) and 66.3 per cent for the FTA World Index (a measure of average share price movements world-wide) over the same period.

Variation

This average picture masks much variation. For example Chile, the best-performing market according to the IFC, shows a rise of 807 per cent since the end of 1988, compared with a rise in Portugal of 40 per cent, considerably behind the UK and World averages.

Big swings

Breaking down the longer-term picture into annual slices shows that the progress of individual markets is anything but smooth. Table 5.1 gives the year-by-year movements in sterling for some typical examples. There may be strong long-term returns, but the ups and downs can be severe in comparison to the developed markets.

Diversification gives stability

Another feature of emerging markets suggested by Table 5.1 is a tendency for them to move out of sync. Analysis of the correlation between these markets does confirm that their month-to-month movements are

Table 5.1   Share price movements by country by year (£%)

	1990	1991	1992	1993	1994
Argentina	−47.0	412.6	−9.2	76.3	−30.2
Greece	70.6	−16.7	−9.8	24.8	−6.3
India	−0.8	22.1	51.9	21.5	0.3
Korea	−37.6	−13.2	28.0	23.8	9.5
Philippines	−61.5	63.9	46.2	140.4	−16.3
Turkey	−18.8	−39.9	−41.6	242.1	−45.8
UK	−14.3	15.1	14.8	23.4	−9.6

Source: *IFC & Templeton*

much more out of step than is the case for the developed markets. This is an extremely important attribute. As a consequence, a portfolio exposed to a wide range of emerging markets will suffer from much less volatility than a portfolio invested in one market. In other words, in a diversified emerging market portfolio, losses in one area are likely to be offset by gains in another. This may not give the spectacular returns available when a portfolio is concentrated in a sharply rising market, but it does provide a much more stable route to long-term gains. Indeed, in recent years, the volatility of emerging markets as a group has been broadly in line with the London market.

5.5   Individual markets

As would be expected with such a diverse set of economies there is considerable variation among emerging markets in terms of size, whether measured by market capitalisation (total value of shares quoted on a market) or number of shares listed. India has by far the greatest number of shares quoted, 6,800, roughly ten times the next largest market Korea, which has 693. But the capitalisation of the Indian market is relatively modest at £82bn (end November 1994). This is just two thirds the size of Mexico (£125bn) (end November 1994), the largest market in terms of value. Yet there were only 190 Mexican shares listed at the end of 1993. Nigeria has almost as many listed shares as Mexico, but its market capitalisation is a tiny £1.7bn (end November 1994).

While the situation shows great improvement in recent years, the degree of openness of markets varies too. For example Chile, India and Korea still impose administrative or fiscal barriers of varying degrees of severity to foreign portfolio investors.

The data in Table 5.2 shows that 1994 was a bad year for emerging markets, with many more markets losing ground than yielding positive returns. And Brazil, the best performer among the larger emerging markets in 1994, has since seen a sharp set-back as a result of the Mexican financial crisis. But this poor result in 1994 has to be seen in the context of very strong returns in 1993, that leave the IFC Investable Index up by 46 per cent in the two years to December 1994.

5.6   Where next?

In the mid-1980s, when diversified emerging market funds first began to appear, it was commonplace for the portfolio to hold shares from as few as five or six countries, including Hong Kong and Singapore. And even then, portfolio managers would often include shares quoted on the major markets, where the choice could be justified by the companies' trading or business links with the developing world. Now as many as 20 to 25 countries can be represented in a diversified portfolio. This increase in diversity should, in the long term, help to lower the risk of global emerging market funds.

Changing attitudes

The sharp increase in interest in emerging markets by Western investors, and the resulting flow of capital, provides a tempting example to governments of countries short of capital and where equity markets either do not exist or where restrictions keep out foreign investors. It is hardly surprising therefore that a new wave of developing nations are now seeking ways in which they can overcome these hurdles to attract their share of this capital flow.

At the same time investment managers faced with the challenge of maintaining strong performance records strive to be first to invest in a new market where shares may still be bought very cheaply. These mutually supportive forces will see a growing list of markets appearing in portfolios in the years to come.

New markets

For example, in 1993 the potential of China held the focus, while in 1994 possibilities for investment in Russia and Vietnam began to emerge. More managers are now talking about the potential to be found in some African countries, largely because of the cheapness of shares, rather than

Table 5.2   Market statistics

Latin America	Market Capitalisation £bn (November 1994)	Number of Issues (December 1993)	Six year price performance (to December 1994)	1994
Argentina	26.6	180	749.1%	–30.2%
Brazil	121.8	550	344.4%	56.2%
Chile	45.5	263	806.9%	34.4%
Colombia	9.5	89	n/a	19.0%
Mexico	125.3	190	602.9%	–42.9%
Peru	5.4	233	n/a	39.4%
Venezuela	2.4	93	n/a	–20.9%
Total	336.5	1,598	570.1%	–15.8%

Asia	Market Capitalisation £bn (November 1994)	Number of Issues (December 1993)	Six year price performance (to December 1994)	1994
China	29.9	183	n/a	–67.0%
Korea	126.4	693	n/a	9.5%
Philippines	34.8	180	244.7%	–16.3%
Taiwan	139.0	285	n/a	15.1%
India	81.8	6,800	n/a	0.3%
Indonesia	30.9	174	n/a	–24.3%
Malaysia	132.8	410	210.8%	–25.0%
Pakistan	7.7	653	n/a	–10.8%
Sri Lanka	2.0	200	n/a	–8.2%
Thailand	83.5	347	343.4%	–24.1%
Total	668.8	9,925	85.2%	–6.5%

Europe, Middle East & Africa	Market Capitalisation £bn (November 1994)	Number of Issues (December 1993)	Six year price performance (to December 1994)	1994
Greece	9.0	143	160.9%	–6.3%
Hungary	1.1	28	n/a	–13.9%
Jordan	2.9	101	73.5%	–14.3%
Nigeria	1.7	174	173.2%	154.2%
Poland	2.1	22	n/a	–45.7%
Portugal	10.1	183	40.0%	0.6%
South Africa	139.5	647	n/a	n/a
Turkey	14.7	152	n/a	–45.8%
Zimbabwe	1.3	62	n/a	14.5%
Total	182.4	1,512	37.0%	–33.8%

Total emerging markets	Market Capitalisation £bn (November 1994)	Number of Issues (December 1993)	Six year price performance (to December 1994)	1994
Total	1,187.7	13,035	254.6%	–18.4%

Source: *IFC, Datastream & Templeton*

the anticipation of an economic miracle. Kenya, Zimbabwe, Botswana and Ghana all probably fall into this category, while the transition to democracy in South Africa provides the possibility of investing in a relatively developed market. The Arab nations of northern Africa — Morocco, Tunisia and Egypt — all possess small equity markets which could become popular in time.

In Eastern Europe, Poland and Hungary have attracted most interest to date. Equity markets are also developing in the Czech Republic and the Ukraine. And the privatisation process is moving at a whirlwind pace compared with that undergone in the UK — according to *The Economist* by late 1994 14,000 big and middle-sized enterprises, employing 86 per cent of Russia's industrial workforce. This gives Russia a smaller state-owned sector than Italy.

More than anything, it is this potential for new markets to blossom that adds credibility to the view that emerging markets will be a long running theme rather than a fad of the early 1990s.

5.7   Factors to consider

If you feel that you wish to take advantage of the opportunities available in emerging markets how should you go about it?

5.7.1   Direct investment

Direct investment in emerging markets will not prove straightforward for the private individual or even for smaller institutions. Apart from Hong Kong, and perhaps Malaysia, Singapore and Mexico, it would probably prove difficult to find a private client stockbroker with the experience and inclination to deal directly in emerging markets. Thus, direct dealing requires either purchase of those emerging market shares that are listed on developed markets or contact with a broker operating in the markets chosen. Then difficulties of time zone, language, currency, settlement, delivery of share certificates and cost of contact all arise. For example in Turkey settlement the day after dealing is required, hardly sufficient time for the paperwork to have reached the UK even by fax. Tracking direct investments in emerging markets would also prove difficult for the intrepid private investor. Coverage of individual shares in emerging markets is almost non-existent in the daily press, and even reporting of market movements is patchy. A final consideration is the risk inherent in investing in a single share in these new markets. If the markets themselves are volatile the movements at the level of individual shares can be extreme.

5.7.2 Funds

As a result of the recent popularity and strong track record of emerging markets a wide range of funds suitable for the private investor now exists. These fall into a number of categories. Both closed-ended and open-ended funds are available, and in each case global, regional and country-specific varieties can be found.

Investment trusts

In the UK closed-ended funds are more usually known as investment trusts, and have a fixed number of shares in issue. This means that the fund manager has a given amount of assets to manage and if new investors buy the trust the fund manager receives no additional assets to manage, rather the share price rises reflecting the buying pressure. (See Chapter 7).

Unit trusts

Open-ended funds are typically unit trusts, although very similar vehicles called Sicavs, usually registered in Luxembourg or Dublin, have appeared in recent years. As the name implies, these funds are open to new assets, and new buying of the fund results in new assets for the fund manager to look after, but has no direct impact on the valuation of units. (See Chapter 8).

57 Varieties

Global emerging market funds enjoy the freedom to invest in developing nations worldwide and so may move assets between countries as conditions dictate. Regional funds are more constrained in their investment scope, and are limited to a particular geographical area of the world, such as South East Asia or Latin America. Country funds limit their exposure to a specific economy.

5.7.3 Open versus closed-ended

As with many investment decisions, there is no right or wrong answer on which is the best route to take. It all depends on circumstances. Broadly speaking, open-ended funds allow an investor to purchase units at a price equivalent to his share of the net assets of the fund, after initial charges. And in most open-ended funds currently available in the UK no charge is made for the sale of units back to the manager. Thus an investor in an open-ended fund knows that units may be sold at any time at a price that is based on the value of the assets in the trust.

Watch the premium

The price paid for shares in an investment trust depends on the balance of supply and demand in the marketplace at a given point of time. Typically, investment trusts trade at a price per share which is below the net assets attributable to a share. This gap is termed 'discount to net asset value'. The opposite phenomenon of a premium to net asset value is much less common. In 1993 and 1994 the popularity of emerging market investment trusts drove many on to a premium. In other words, even taking dealing costs out of the calculation, investors seem prepared to pay more than the value of their share of the trust's assets when making purchases of the investment trust.

The Mexican crisis at the beginning of 1995 saw these premiums evaporate, illustrating the argument that investors who paid a premium run the risk of facing a discount when they come to sell.

In such a case the return realised is below the underlying return on the trust's assets. An investor paying £1.10 for shares with an underlying net asset value of £1 and selling them later for £1.80, at a time when the net asset value per share stands at £2, realises a profit of 63.6 per cent. However, the assets in the trust have risen by 100 per cent over the same period. An investor in an equivalent open-ended fund would have achieved a return of around 95 per cent, even taking account of typical initial charges. And it is interesting to note that a number of emerging market specialists offer both open and closed-ended versions of their funds, utilising the same investment team, disciplines and shares. When a premium exists on a closed-ended fund and an open-ended alternative is available it may prove beneficial for the investor to sell shares in the investment trust and buy units in the open-ended fund. Of course the opposite can also occur, giving a distinct advantage to investment trust purchasers in depressed market conditions.

Long-term advantages

Proponents of closed-ended funds point out that in the case of volatile markets like those of the developing world, investment trusts possess a clear advantage for the long-term investor. The manager of a closed fund does not have to worry that an inflow of new cash will appear at times of optimism, forcing him to buy shares that may have already risen to unattractive price levels from a long-term perspective. Nor does he face sudden calls for cash to meet the liquidations that often accompany a market setback, forcing the manager to sell shares that offer sound long-term prospects. Thus, it is argued that an investment trust manager can take a more objective long-term view, buying and selling shares according to his own judgements, rather than finding that investment decisions are driven, at least in part, by the money flows that the fund experiences.

Micropal, the performance measurement service, provides comprehensive data on all the emerging markets funds available in the UK. An examination of these performance tables, an extract of which is shown below, suggests that for the short period during which both open and closed-ended emerging markets funds have co-existed no category of fund has a clear upper hand. Variations in performance driven by other factors remain more important.

Table 5.3   Global funds available in the UK: performance by type

Global Fund	*3 year performance to December 1994*	*Type**
Beta Global Emerging Markets Investment Trust	43.4%	CE
Foreign & Colonial Emerging Markets Investment Trust	59.0%	CE
Gartmore Emerging Markets Fund	38.2%	OE
Genesis Emerging Markets	72.5%	CE
GT Emerging Markets (A Shares)	55.2%	OE
Prosperity Emerging Markets	77.5%	OE
Templeton Emerging Markets Investment Trust	82.4%	CE
IFCI Composite Index	62.9%	—

*Open-ended (OE) or closed-ended (CE)

Source: *Micropal Emerging Markets Fund Monitor*

5.8   Country versus geographically diversified funds

Among the emerging market funds available to UK investors, some have the freedom to invest in all the emerging markets of the world, some focus on particular regions such as South East Asia, or Latin America, while yet others concentrate on single countries. Generally the more specific a fund, the more risky it will be.

Choosing a fund investing in the next market to enjoy popularity from domestic and international investors alike can give spectacular returns. But being sucked into a fund in a market that has already risen a long way can prove an expensive mistake. As illustrated by events in Mexico, falls of 50 per cent or more can occur rapidly in these markets, with little that the fund manager can do if the objective of the fund requires the assets to be invested in that country. For most investors a more diversified approach is appropriate.

Diversity equals safety

The main advantage of more widely spread funds is the safety that comes from diversification among economies with different structures, business environments, and political conditions. These differences mean that a change that affects one market adversely may have no effect, or even a beneficial impact elsewhere. This is most true for those funds that have the freedom to invest in any emerging market in the world. While regional funds do have an advantage over individual country funds, there is a tendency for markets within regions to move in step, reflecting the similarities often found among neighbouring countries and their degree of economic integration from trading links. This message was driven home to investors in Latin American Funds in early 1995 as the markets in Brazil and Argentina tumbled on the back of problems in Mexico.

5.9 Choosing a fund manager

For emerging markets the criteria for choosing a fund management group are no different from those that apply for choosing managers for the developed markets. First, does the manager's literature demonstrate a coherent strategy to the challenge of investing in emerging markets? Many different approaches exist — some focusing on individual shares, others on economic and political fundamentals, and yet others on a mixture of the two. A good manager will be able to articulate clearly the approach adopted. A poorer manager will be less capable of explaining how the task is carried out.

Resources

Secondly, can a manager show that the resources are available in terms of experience, people, technology and contacts to put the chosen strategy to work? For example, even professionals find good information on emerging market companies harder to find. So if a manager professes a stock by stock approach then a global team will be required to carry out the necessary research.

Consistent success

Thirdly, can the manager demonstrate a consistent record of success in emerging markets? While performance in isolation provides an unreliable guide to the future, when examined in conjunction with other criteria it can provide greater insights. A good record but no clear strategy may just reflect good luck in the past which may not be repeatable in the future.

Diversify managers

Don't just look for one manager. Except for the smallest portfolios it makes sense to choose two or more managers with contrasting approaches. This adds to your overall diversification, as the pitfalls of one strategy are likely to be avoided by another.

5.10 Timing

As with all equity investment there is no certain means of knowing the best time to invest.

Many who committed money to emerging markets in early 1994, following the strong performances in 1993 bitterly regretted their decision a year later. But to sell on short-term disappointments flies in the face of equity market experience. All equity markets can be volatile in the short-term, but the long-term rewards usually outstrip the returns available from other forms of investment and saving. Remember that the arguments in favour of emerging markets rely on the long-term structural changes that are under way in the world economy. Patient investors who let these powerful trends work for them over an extended period of time are likely to reap the greatest benefits and, as in developed markets, regular investment through one of the many savings schemes linked to emerging market funds provides an excellent means of reducing the risk of committing funds at a short-term market peak.

5.11 Conclusion

Emerging economies will exert a major influence over the rest of our lives, with a strong probability that they will provide the most dynamic economic performance in terms of growth and progress in living standards. For investors they will provide the potential for strong long-term returns. However, the path will not be smooth and any investor in these markets must be prepared for the ups and downs. Don't invest money that you may need in the short or medium-term in these markets, ie money you might want to call on in the next five to seven years to meet living and other expenses. As a general rule, the younger or wealthier you are the greater the exposure you can afford to have in these markets, but it is probably wise to place an upper limit of 20 per cent of an equity portfolio in these markets. Also remember to include in your decision the exposure you may have to emerging markets via more generalist international unit or investment trusts. Finally remember to update your thoughts on what markets are in the emerging category. Japan was an emerging market 25 years ago. Perhaps Mexico, South Korea and Turkey will count as developed markets in 2020, replaced by nations such as Peru, Cambodia and Ukraine in the truly emerging markets portfolios.

6 Derivatives de-mystified

Michael J. Box—Threadneedle Investment Managers Ltd

6.1 Introduction

The aim of this chapter is to record what futures, options and swaps are, indicate how they are priced, and give a few examples of when they are used. Derivatives enable asset management decisions to be undertaken cheaply and quickly, with, moreover, an infinite spectrum of possible risk/return profiles, most of which happen to be fairly simple in concept. The fact that the correlation between the returns from a traditional asset and a derivative of it may vary from 0 per cent to 100 per cent or even to −100 per cent, depending on how the underlying asset moves, means that the derivative often does not fit into standard accountancy pigeon-holes, perhaps being both an asset and a liability, and with both equity and fixed income characteristics. Derivatives are in the ascendancy, and will certainly not go away! (See also 3.7.2).

6.2 'Surely derivatives are very risky?'

Let us reflect on an equity fund that is measured against some equity index benchmark. Such a fund will generally be more or less fully invested in equities on the basis that although there might be a stock-market crash at any time, steady appreciation of capital and especially income is the more likely norm. In short, the expectation of tripled income after 20 years is of more importance than the possibility of temporarily losing one third of capital value in the next six months. Thus such funds should feel fairly indifferent to a crash, but if the fund fell by 'only' 18 per cent when the benchmark fell 20 per cent, then the fund's trustees would doubtless be pleased. We accept the possibility of full exposure to a crash because we know that the alternative of hedging on a regular basis, spending perhaps 2.5 per cent each quarter on put options, will in the long run lead to very significant underperformance.

These considerations lead us generally to undertake derivative trades in such a way that the fund would *always* be able to meet any obligations arising from those trades, could never become insolvent, and would have a value of zero only if the whole equity market in fact fell to zero.

The essence is to *avoid gearing*. It is gearing that could cause a modest market movement to lead to insolvency. It is gearing that is dangerous, not derivatives *per se*. Dangerous gearing can be entered into by borrowing and investing in blue chips or gilts, without going anywhere near an option or a future.

Derivatives modify the traditional x-axis asset value/y-axis portfolio value 45 degree line sloping up to the right.

6.3   What is a future, and how is it priced?

Let us consider the FT-SE futures contract based on the FT-SE 100 share index of 100 leading UK equities, and which is a cash-settled contract for differences.

A *buyer* of one FT-SE futures contract will gain/lose £25 for every point that the FT-SE 100 index moves above/below the price paid until the contract expires — three of the Mar/Jun/Sep/Dec expiries exist at any time.

Conversely a *seller* of one FT-SE futures contract would lose/gain £25 for every point that the FT-SE 100 index moved above/below the price received throughout the period.

The exposure to the equity market represented by one FT-SE futures contract is £25 × price paid. Thus with the FT-SE around 3,000, the value of the market exposure represented by one futures contract would be around £75,000. This is the amount that would be lost by a buyer of one contract if the equity market fell to zero, the same as for an investor who bought actual stocks for £75,000 in the proportions that make up the FT-SE index.

Similarly if the market doubled, any investor who had bought/sold one contract would gain/lose £75,000.

For every FT-SE futures contract traded, initial margin of £2,500 — a figure that is increased in periods of high volatility — needs to be put up to the clearing house, and maintained. Whether the futures have been bought or sold, losses must be made good each day, and correspondingly profits may be withdrawn. Such daily cash flows are termed 'variation margin'.

Since an investor need produce only £2,500 of initial margin to trade £75,000 of market exposure, the potential for highly geared (30 times!) speculation is obvious. It will be seen that the marginning system protects the clearing system against the first

£2,500/£25=100 points

of any adverse movement, should a speculator be unable to meet his daily margin call. If this occurred, as a first step the speculator's position would be closed out by his broker.

Having acknowledged the speculative possibilities of the instrument, and how the marginning system works to constrain them, the principal advantages of futures, namely cost and speed will be discussed.

6.4   Dealing in futures and stocks compared

If FT-SE futures did not exist, an institutional fund manager making a short term foray into/out of the UK equity market would typically incur the following expenses:

a)	*on buying*	
	middle price to offer spread	0.2%
	commission	0.2%
	stamp duty	0.5%
b)	*on selling*	
	bid price to middle spread	0.2%
	commission	0.2%
	Total	**1.3%**

Thus taking FT-SE to be 3,000, a movement of 40 points would be necessary before any possibility of profit from the trade would exist.

With FT-SE Futures, the bid-offer spread may be taken as one index point, plus slightly less for the total round-trip commission including clearing of just £14 per contract.

Hence for round-tripping each £75,000 of exposure, dealing in futures would cost £40 as compared with £1,000 when dealing in actual stocks.

Additionally visualise a desire to significantly change UK equity exposure quickly. With futures the trade could be done in a few minutes, with just one deal ticket. Effectively all the stocks would be dealt in at the same time. The problems posed by the alternative of dealing in 100 individual stocks (in what sequence?) at times of rapidly changing prices — plus the effort of booking, checking and settling all these trades, registering and perhaps claiming dividends, scrip issues etc — are obvious.

Moreover the required change in UK equity exposure might involve a compensating change in exposure to gilts or some specified overseas equity market(s). Appropriate futures can be used for the other side of such asset allocation switches also.

6.5   Fair value for futures

An investor who buys FT-SE futures will make or lose capital depending on market movement just as an investor who buys actual stocks. However, the futures purchaser will be able to earn interest, say at 6 per cent, on most of his cash, although he will not receive the stock dividend yield of say 4 per cent. Accordingly the use of futures saves the cost of carry of

6%–4%=2% p.a.

For FT-SE futures with three months to expiry, this amounts to 0.5 per cent, and so with FT-SE at 3,000, the fair value of the three month FT-SE future contract would be 3,015. If futures were not at such a premium to the spot/cash market, then in principle arbitrage would be possible.

Departures of the FT-SE futures price from fair value generally amount to a very few points, vastly less than the cost of 40 points for a round-trip in physical stocks, as indicated earlier.

6.6   What is an option?

Options *are of two types,* calls *and* puts.

A *buyer* of a call option has the *right*, but *not* the *obligation*, for a specified term to buy an agreed quantity of a particular asset at a stipulated price.

A *buyer* of a put option has the *right*, but *not* the *obligation*, for a specified term to sell an agreed quantity of a particular asset at a stipulated price.

Thus an investor who buys an option, whether a call or a put, can *never* lose more than the option premium paid, since he need not exercise the option if the asset price moves in the opposite direction to that antici-pated. His potential profit is unlimited.

The counterparty from whom an option is bought is said to *write* the option. An option writer can *never* make more profit than the option premium received, which of course happens if the option is not exercised. An option writer's potential losses are unlimited.

A distinction is drawn between *writing an option*, which involves its cre-ation, and *selling an option* which involves closing out an option bought earlier.

Two classes of options are recognised. So-called 'American-style' options which can be exercised *at any time* up to the expiry date, and 'European-style' options which can be exercised *only* at the expiry date. These terms have no relationship to the geographic area to which the options relate or from which they originate.

Exercise of options may involve the transfer of ownership of the asset, such as BAT shares, or it may be cash settled, as in the case of FT-SE options.

Marginning of (combinations of) written options is a complex business frequently using the so-calling 'Span' system. Unlike futures, the buyer of an option cannot ask to receive his profit to date on a daily basis. The writer of an option can put up collateral in the form of discounted stocks and bonds, and not simply as cash, as is required for futures variation margin.

The books on option pricing by Cox & Rubinstein and Hull cited in the references are highly commended, but here something rather shorter than their combined 840 pages will have to suffice.

6.7 The Black-Scholes fair value for European-style options

The commonest valuation and pricing tool for options is the *Black-Scholes model*, which gives the fair price of a European-style call option as

$$C = S.N(d_1) - X.exp(-rt).N(d_2)$$

where
$$d_1 = (\ln(S/X) + (r + \sigma^2/2)t)/(\sigma.sqrt(t))$$
$$d_2 = d_1 - \sigma.sqrt(t)$$
$$S = \text{current stock price}$$
$$X = \text{exercise price of option}$$

t   =   time to expiry of option
r   =   risk-free interest rate
σ   =   standard deviation volatility of stock

and   N(x) is the cumulative probability distribution for a standard-ised normal variable (ie it is the probability that such a variable will be less than x).

The fair value, P, for a European-style put option can be priced using the *put-call parity* relationship

$$S+P=C+X.\exp(-rt)$$

which notes the equivalence of buying stock and a put now, and buying a call *now* to be exercised at some specified later date.

The Black-Scholes formula is thus seen to be a closed form solution which can be readily implemented using well-known accurate approxi-mations to the standard normal cumulative p.d.f.,N(x).

6.8   Problems with the Black-Scholes formula

The derivation assumes that the asset is non-dividend paying. To some extent this short-coming can be handled by fudging, using a discounted value of the dividend to amend the option price, and by looking at the ex-dividend date as a discontinuity.

When pricing an option on a *bond*, it will be realised that a change in bond price would represent a change in the bond's yield, when presumably the risk-free interest rate used in the formula would not remain constant.

However, the real problem with the Black-Scholes formula is that it does *not* apply to American-style options.

In the case of calls, this problem is not too severe, since the holder of an American-style call option will usually not exercise the option prior to expiry, naturally preferring to keep his money on deposit for as long as possible since the right to the asset has been secured. Thus most holders of American-style call options will find it logical to behave as if the options were European-style, and accordingly the pricing of the two call option styles are generally very similar.

However, the rights of the asset do not apply to the *option* on the asset, so the investor may wish to exercise his option so as to obtain for example a dividend or perhaps voting rights. Because the price of an option comprises the option's *intrinsic* value plus time value, it will usually be more efficient to *sell* the call option and *buy* the stock rather than *exercise* the call option, since upon exercising an option any time value is forfeited.

In the case of puts, the price of European-style and American-style options can be significantly different. For example, suppose an investor owns six month options which give him the right to sell an asset at 400p which now stands at 1p. The American-style option can *and would* be exercised to give 399p now, and thus would be priced at 399p. By *not* exercising, the maximum possible extra gain would be 1p, whereas by exercising a definite 12p interest could be earned. Even on the basis of giving the full 400p in six months' time, the price of the European-style put could not exceed 388p now.

The mathematics of producing an analytic formula for evaluating American-style puts is seemingly intractable.

American-style puts are evaluated using numerical methods involving decision trees. These methods demand extensive computing power, and can handle in principle any option however complex. An example would be a *path-dependent 'knock-in'* option, where the pay-off from the option will only occur if the daily closing price of the asset has breached some specified level at some time during the option's life, and is *not* solely dependent on the asset price at expiry.

The critical inputs required by the Black-Scholes model, namely interest rates and most especially asset price volatility assumptions, pose severe problems in their collection and assessment.

When an investment manager requires an option, it is normally to back some perception that future movements of the asset's price will not (or may not) follow a theoretical log-normal distribution based on recent history. Accordingly, the fact that the option is priced slightly above its fair value — supposing that we can agree what that is — is a fairly academic matter. Thus the fact that a Broker tells us that a Glaxo put is 3p dear is hardly going to matter if the Glaxo share price is going to fall 100p in the next fortnight. Rather an option should be regarded as a commodity, to be bought at the cheapest price available if its utility to us so warrants.

6.9 Arbitrage

Arbitrage between FT-SE futures and the underlying stocks is not of practical interest to ourselves. Firstly a large number of futures traders would see any possibility long before ourselves, perhaps on the back of other business that they had to conduct. Also the market-makers can deal in stocks free of the half per cent stamp duty, which would seem to terminate the possibility for us. Moreover, which of the funds for which we have stewardship actually would expect us to employ very large amounts of their capital to make small arbitrage profits anyway? Incidentally, the concept of 'risk-free' arbitrage is dependent on the forecast amounts of dividends due, and also significantly on their dates of payment, both factors which have been subject to increased variability of late. (Of course departures from expectation on these counts will not necessarily always be adverse, but it is not risk-free arbitrage.)

6.10   The relationship between options and futures

The general perception of 'futures and options' couples them together although they seemingly are as dissimilar as chalk and cheese, eg:

	Maximum Profit	**Maximum Loss**
Buy or sell futures	unlimited	unlimited
Buy options	unlimited	premium paid
(calls or puts)		
Write options	premium received	unlimited
(calls or puts)		

However the <u>combination</u> of *buying a call option* <u>and</u> *writing a put option* with the same strike price and expiry date behaves like a future, and is termed a *synthetic future*. It can be seen that the asset will be acquired at the strike price regardless of what the actual asset price is at expiry; if the asset is above the strike price we will exercise our call, whilst if it is below, then the person to whom we have written the put can be relied upon to exercise it. Since we are *guaranteed* to acquire the asset at a pre-determined price at a specified future date, we are long of a future. Possible movement of the asset price means that our potential profit and loss are both unlimited.

Popular perception of derivatives is that to gain exposure to a market an investor 'buys the futures or buys call options'. However it is again stressed that these are very different types of exposure, with futures giving exposure to *both the upside and the downside* with no cost other than borrowing/cost-of-carry, whereas buying a call option gives exposure only to the upside, but at a real cost of paying an insurance premium. If an investor has been swayed by an argument that exposure to an asset is desirable, then logically he should first think in terms of buying futures rather than buying calls. In the case of exchange-traded futures, almost all the liquidity is invariably in the nearest expiry contract. With options, the concentration of liquidity in the nearest expiry, whilst still very pronounced, is less severe. Accordingly a synthetic future using options represents the practical way of entering into a futures position of slightly longer duration. Also a long or short synthetic future position can be executed in any *stock* — as opposed to just indices — for which options exist. This is a very great advantage, since futures do not exist on individual stocks.

The concept of a synthetic future is not merely a clever relational academic nicety. It can offer a very attractive way of quickly committing long-term funds to the market. For example, on one occasion when the market was in a very depressed state, not surprisingly calls were cheap and puts were dear. The Investment Director judged that there was more risk in continuing to allow cash to build up than in putting it into the market. Accordingly an 11 month synthetic FT-SE future trade was executed, as an alternative to investing directly. Most of the available cash was invested in 11 month CDs, since the fund in question was not gearing up at all. It was calculated that as compared with buying stocks, in 11 months' time the fund would be 2.25 per cent better off through adopting this route — actually £900,000 on the £40m investment in question — after deducting dividends foregone from the interest earned. (This ignores the substantial saving on expenses as compared with buying stocks, which would increase the advantage by 1.25 per cent if market exposure was not required outside the period in question.)

6.11   'Over-the-counter' trades

Options trades on recognised exchanges are restricted to specified assets, strike prices and expiry dates, with most liquidity in the contracts nearest to expiry and with strike prices close to current market levels. With 'over-the-counter' trades — colloquially OTC — not only can all these variables be chosen to meet the fund's requirements, but inherently more complicated pay-off parameters can be set depending on for example exchange rates, interest rates and bond yields as well as equity indices or stock prices. The more restrictions that are placed on the option's pay-off, the cheaper it becomes. Thus if an investment manager strongly believes that a whole string of events will all take place, then he can obtain 'cheap' options to benefit from this view, because the market will be somewhat sceptical of his judgement that all these events will in fact occur.

Option activity can of course be driven by concerns over the *liabilities* and not just the assets. Thus if the actuary fears that some combination of exchange rates, interest rates and equity market levels, albeit unlikely, would disproportionately affect the liabilities, then an option with a pay-off dependent on these outcomes could prove a cheap way of improving solvency. Essentially in this situation an asset would have been added to the portfolio to improve the asset-liability matching.

The pay-off schedule of an OTC option can be anything that the invest-ment manager wants it to be, and several investment banks will be keen to quote for any structure required.

Options of course do not give any 'free lunches', and indeed the wide-spread use of the phrase 'using options for *income enhancement* through writing covered calls' is a misnomer — the fund is being paid in return for being prepared to give up all the upside of the asset above a certain level, and it must be remembered that from time to time such 'income enhancement' will prove to be a poor alternative to capital appreciation foregone.

An investment manager will frequently see no reason to change the current relationship of his portfolio to his benchmark or liabilities. However, whenever he has strong convictions concerning a possible future economic scenario, involving either the extent, limit or direction of absolute or relative movement (or non-movement) of some (or all!) of asset prices, indices, interest rates and currencies, and is prepared to live with the consequences of being wrong, then there will be a derivative strategy from which he can benefit.

With derivatives, the possibilities available to an investment manager are no longer restricted to just 'buy, sell or hold' assets. For example, in 1988 (the year after the crash), the UK equity market stayed in a very tight trading range, so that the option strategy of regularly writing both short-dated 'out-of-the-money' calls and 'out-of-the-money' puts proved highly popular and rewarding, serving to emphasise to some of the scep-tics that options offered profitable opportunities that were not available in the pre-derivatives age.

Also outperformance options enable a fund manager to back a view that asset A will outperform asset B, even if it is unclear in which direction the assets will actually move over the term in question.

The pay-off performance of any OTC derivative is *not* guaranteed by any exchange or clearing house, but is solely dependent on the continued financial health of the selected counterparty.

6.12 What is a swap, and how is it priced?

Swaps are based on just one simple proposition, namely that the cost of money is a floating rate, and money can be used to buy an asset and thus secure the total return of capital gain (OR LOSS!) plus any income that the asset may produce.

Thus to secure the total return of any asset class — equity, bond, property, commodity or whatever — an investor needs to pay a floating rate to an investment bank for that bank to borrow money so as to acquire the asset, and hence be able to pay the ensuing total return. If an investor wishes to reduce his exposure to the UK equity market say, then he can *offer* the total return of the FT-SE index to an investment bank in return for *receiving* a floating rate. Although he holds the asset he will not enjoy any capital gain (or loss) and income that the asset produces over the specified period of a few months to several years, since this will be passed over to the investor paying the floating rate. Thus by entering into the swap agreement, or 'swapping out' of the asset, the investor's return over the period will be the same as if he had sold the asset, and placed the proceeds on deposit. The expenses of sale and re-purchase will have been avoided however.

The investment bank is remunerated by actually paying marginally less than Libor flat, say Libor minus 20 basis points. This difference represents an exceedingly cheap and efficient method for a fund manager to temporarily exit from a market.

The swaps market is highly competitive, since investment banks are very keen to make a small margin on a large trade, if they can satisfactorily hedge their risk. Why do we accept their intermediary role? Answer: we do not have a presence in any options and futures pits, do not monitor positions round the clock, nor have access to the necessary huge client base worldwide or indeed sufficient capital or adequate computer systems.

If a fund manager wanted to buy the total return of FT-SE, a market-maker would look to see how he could most cheaply hedge himself — in stocks, in futures or in options. Indeed instead of offering the swap at Libor plus 20 bp, he might offer it at Libor *minus* 15 bp if he had just paid Libor minus 20 bp to an investor who wanted to *sell* the FT-SE return for the period!

An investment bank may also offer very attractive swap terms through going on risk and not hedging immediately in anticipation of being able to hedge more cheaply later. Or it may offer attractive terms because it knows where it can obtain offsetting business.

Sources of further information

Bibliography

Options Markets, John C. Cox & Mark Rubinstein, Prentice-Hall, 1985

Options, Futures and other Derivative Securities, John Hull, Prentice-Hall, 1989

7 Investment trusts

Jeremy Burnett Rae, MA (Oxon), Barrister,
Investment Secretary, Threadneedle Investment Managers Ltd

7.1 Introduction

Collective investment media enable investors to pool their resources so as to create a common fund for investment by professional managers. The two great benefits of this collective approach to investment are (1) more efficient and economical investment management; and (2) greater security through the spreading of risk over a diverse range of investments.

To meet these needs, various different media, such as investment trusts, unit trusts and offshore funds (see Chapter 8) and insurance bonds (see Chapter 14) have evolved from separate legal and financial origins, subject to varying regulation and tax treatment. The choice between the different media in practice may depend on the investor's convenience as much as the features of the collective media, which are increasingly given a 'level playing field' by regulations. Nevertheless there are still some marked differences in the ways these investments are marketed, priced and taxed, quite apart from the management of the underlying assets.

The most straightforward and flexible of these media is the investment trust, which is actually not really a trust, but simply a limited company in which investors buy shares and other securities so as to benefit indirectly from its assets and income. An investment trust is constrained by its authorised capital, which cannot readily be changed or repaid to shareholders, and the shares are generally bought and sold by investors on The Stock Exchange at market prices determined only by supply and demand.

7.2 Historical background

The first investment trust to be established in England was the Foreign and Colonial Government Trust, which was created as a trust in 1868 and in 1879, owing to doubts concerning the legality of its original structure, was reorganised as a public limited liability company under the Companies Act 1862. The original objective of this trust was, in the words of its initial prospectus, to provide '. . . the investor of moderate means the same advantage as the large capitalists in diminishing risk in foreign and colonial stocks by spreading the investment over a number of stocks'. By the early 20th century a number of other investment trust companies had been incorporated in England and Scotland and the investment trust had become firmly established in the UK as an investment medium. Some of these early trusts (including 'The Foreign and Colonial Investment Trust plc') still exist today despite two World Wars and many serious economic crises. During the last 100 years, investment trust companies have provided much new capital for UK businesses by underwriting or subscribing for public issues of securities and accepting private placings, thus giving important support to capital investment in the UK.

Investment trusts are probably the most flexible of the collective media, free to invest in any kind of assets, and the individual companies and the securities that they issue vary widely. In comparison with the other media, two distinctive characteristics are their ability to 'gear-up' their sensitivity to the markets by borrowing, and the fact that the shares are generally priced by supply and demand in the market at significantly less than the value of the underlying assets of the investment trust. Both these factors tend to make investment trusts more sensitive to movements in the markets as a whole, while still spreading the specific risks of investments in individual stocks.

As explained in **7.7**, certain capital gains tax concessions are given to those investment trusts which have been approved by the Inland Revenue. In order to obtain approval the investment trust must, among other requirements, be resident for tax purposes in the UK and have its ordinary share capital listed on The Stock Exchange. This chapter deals primarily with investment trusts which have been so approved for tax purposes and which have been incorporated in the UK. Unapproved investment trusts can generally be treated like any other company.

7.3   Recent developments

Investment trusts ('ITs') constantly attract innovative uses and developments in the best traditions of the City. As well as over 250 existing investment trusts available in the stock market, a continual stream of new issues and additional tranches provides opportunities for both general and specialist investment of all kinds.

3i, the UK's largest investor in unquoted companies, and a member of the

FT-SE 100 Index, overtook the mighty general IT, Foreign and Colonial, as the largest investment trust immediately at its introduction in September 1994, and is now capitalised at about £2 billion. The top ten trusts together account for over a third of the total market capitalisation of the 124 constituents of the FT-SE Actuaries Investment Trust Index, but this preponderance must not obscure the immense diversity of the ITs available to investors.

'C' or Conversion shares have now become the standard method for investment trusts to issue additional capital in a fluctuating market without diluting the interests of existing holders in a fully invested IT. Basically, the newly subscribed 'C' capital is managed and invested in a separate pool until its portfolio is fairly comparable to the original investment pool, when the pools are amalgamated at a fixed date and the 'C' shares converted to ordinary at the then fair prices determined by the market.

As a final note, the Edinburgh Investment Trust after over a century made history by becoming the first IT to elect a trade unionist to its Board. As an ex-director of the Bank of England, Gavin Laird, the general secretary of the Amalgamated Engineering and Electrical Union, was presumably seen as the ideal candidate to demonstrate that the industry moves with the times.

7.4 Legal nature

7.4.1 Constitution

An investment trust is a limited liability company with a share capital, and is a legal entity separate from its shareholders or managers. In practice the trusts are often promoted and managed by fund management groups who run a number of investment trusts and other funds, which, in some cases, own the management group or control its Board. However, the shareholders are always entitled to vote to replace the management, and there has been much take-over activity.

Like any limited company, an investment trust company is constituted by the contract with its shareholders contained in its memorandum and articles of association. The memoranda of investment trusts usually contain wide powers to invest the funds of the company in securities and property and to borrow, but, for tax reasons, commonly prohibit trading (as opposed to investing) in securities or property; and their articles of association normally contain a provision prohibiting the distribution of capital profits by way of dividend. However, approved status for tax purposes (see **7.7**) requires certain practical limitations on the exercise of these wide investment powers.

An investment trust itself is not permitted to advertise its shares for sale except by reference to Listing Particulars, registered with the Registrar of Companies and complying with the Financial Services Act. However, managers will eagerly respond to enquiries, and increasingly advertise schemes to facilitate investment. Further advice and information are available from stockbrokers, through whom the shares are often bought, and from the Association of Investment Trust Companies (see page 140).

7.4.2   Investment trust securities

Investments are made by buying stocks, shares and warrants of the trusts. Apart from ordinary shares, a trust may issue debenture stock (secured by a charge on its assets), unsecured loan stock, preference shares or warrants. The holders of such securities are entitled to receive interest or preference dividends at the applicable rate before any dividends are paid to the ordinary shareholders. These securities may, in the long run, prove less profitable, but are more secure since, on a winding-up of the company, the ordinary shareholders are entitled only to any surplus assets remaining after payment of all other liabilities, including the repayment of principal and income due to holders of loan capital or preference shares. If an investment trust has a high proportion of its capital in the form of loan capital and preference shares, major fluctuations in the value of the underlying assets attributable to the holders of its equity share capital can result. This topic is discussed in more detail at **7.6.5**. (Debenture stocks, loan stocks and preference shares are discussed at **3.6**.)

Warrants are securities which give the holder the right (without obligation) to subscribe for shares subsequently on fixed terms: in the meantime the warrants are themselves listed investments whose market price will change rapidly according to the prices of the underlying shares, but without yielding an income. For example, suppose a warrant entitles the holder to subscribe for certain investment trust shares at 95 pence each. If the shares are currently worth £1, the warrant will trade at about 5 pence. If the shares rise by 10 per cent to £1.10, the warrants should rise 200 per cent to 15 pence; conversely if the shares fall by 10 per cent to 90 pence, the warrants would be practically worthless. Warrants clearly offer a more volatile capital investment in the success of an investment trust than its ordinary shares (see also **3.7.2**).

7.4.3 Split capital trusts

As well as issuing all the usual company securities, investment trusts can also go further and, instead of ordinary shares, issue their capital split into different issues tailor-made for different kinds of investors.

In most ordinary companies, directors generally have considerable freedom as to how much dividend to distribute out of profits, and are only expected to manage their dividend policy to provide growing dividends indefinitely; such companies are not expected to be wound-up, and shareholders' rights in a liquidation are largely academic. Investment trusts must distribute most of their income and none of their capital profits for tax reasons, although to some extent they can manage what proportion of profits are receivable as income.

However, some 30 split capital trusts are constituted with separate classes of shares which will be repaid (or at the least, the question will be put to a vote of shareholders) at a fixed date. Each class of share capital has specified entitlements to dividends in the meanwhile and to capital distributions, in a stated order of priority between the classes of shares, and the directors have very little discretion as to the application of whatever profits they make. While the total performance of the investment trust will always depend on the success of its investment managers, each class of shares will have relatively more or less predictable expectations, designed to be particularly valuable to certain kinds of investors. These benefits can make the total value of the trust's securities higher than if it simply issued one class of ordinary shares.

The earliest split capital trusts have capital shares, which provide no dividend income at all but the right at liquidation to all capital gains within the trust, and income shares, which distribute the entire trust's net income, but will be repaid at the liquidation date at only their fixed nominal value. The prices of each share will reflect the demand from investors, taking account of the specified rights of *all* prior classes of shares and other securities. Thus, the income shares offer a very high running yield, suitable for PEPs or for trustees paying a widow's annuity, while the capital shares would attract a higher rate taxpayer approaching retirement, or anyone who has not used his valuable tax-free capital gains tax allowance.

7.4.4 Specialised split capital investment trust securities

Investment trusts are free to create any kind of securities for their investors, and the principle has been used to design shares with sophisticated characteristics, which require individual analysis of exactly what is offered and the security that will be obtained. These securities can be superbly efficient investments, but it is quite inadequate and highly dangerous merely to rely on the names of such specialised securities, and investors must consider the rights of both their own intended shares and all other securities which will have priority in any situation, together with current circumstances which change after the securities are issued. Some kinds of income shares have no capital entitlement at all, and others have index-linked or other formula based income. Each class of security will have its own profile of risk and reward, ranging from a preferred stock many times covered by assets, to highly speculative zero coupon shares. Needless to say, the value of these securities will ultimately depend on the success of the managers' investment policy, but to very differing extents. The only real rule is that, inevitably, the sum of the rights of all classes of issued capital is equal to the total net capital and income of the trust. Thus, at the end of the queue on each distribution, one class of shares will have the most uncertain outcome, in effect securing all the prior entitlements; and naturally such risky securities will be priced to earn, on average, the highest expected rewards.

Amongst these more sophisticated securities are:

Zero dividend preference shares

A low risk investment suitable for financing future capital sums without income tax liability in the meanwhile, such as school fees. The risk can be assessed by measuring how many times the capital repayment is covered by net assets, or in other words how much the managers can lose without affecting the repayment at all.

Capital entitlements: a fixed capital return payable on liquidation.
Income: nil.

Income shares and annuity shares

It is essential to check exactly what type of share is being considered. These shares can be particularly appropriate for non-taxpayers, in PEPs, or for non-working spouses. In many cases, a gross redemption yield can be calculated and compared with that on the nearest equivalent gilt-edged securities, taking account of the different levels of risk.

Capital entitlements:
(1)   the original split capital trusts repay a fixed amount on liquidation, and their income share price will fall towards this value as this date approaches;
(2)   some more recent issues are also entitled to part of any capital

appreciation, after prior classes of shares are satisfied;
(3) a very different type, sometimes called annuity shares, have no capital entitlement at all beyond a nominal 1p.

Income: these shares have exceptionally high running yields, benefiting from the gearing from other classes of capital such as zero coupon shares.

Stepped preference shares

Another low risk security having priority over ordinary shares and most other classes, giving a known growing income and capital return if held to redemption (hence redemption yields can be calculated and compared with government securities).

Capital entitlements: a fixed capital return payable on liquidation.
Income: a predetermined dividend rising at a specified rate such as 5 per cent per annum.

7.5 Conditions for purchase

There are in general no limitations on the purchase of UK investment trust shares. Investors must of course satisfy any restrictions imposed by their own powers (eg as trustees), or any foreign laws to which they are subject. Investment trusts are normally a wider-range investment under the Trustee Investments Act, and collective investment media generally help to satisfy trustees' duty of diversification.

Personal Equity Plans can invest freely only in qualifying investment trusts, which are those that keep at least half of their portfolio in EU ordinary shares. PEPs can invest only up to a limit of £1,500 in 1994/95 (instead of the standard £6,000) in non-qualifying investment and unit trusts.

7.6 Characteristics

All investment trusts have the same legal structure in common, but its flexibility gives an enormous range of very different investment vehicles, both as to the underlying investment management of the trust and the interests that investors can take. As well as traditional general trusts directly comparable with conservatively regulated unit trusts and insurance bonds, there are highly specialised issues tailor-made for particular purposes and suitable only for sophisticated or expertly advised investors of the appropriate type (see **7.4.4**).

7.6.1 Spread of risk and flexibility

An important feature of investment trust shares, like other collective investments, is the spread of risk which can be achieved by the investor. Investment trust shares represent an indirect interest in all the underlying assets of the trust, which can give the small investor a well balanced portfolio with a good spread of risk which would be too expensive and impracticable to obtain and manage by direct investment. But larger investors (personal or corporate) also invest through investment trusts in order to obtain professional or specialised investment management, currency management or gearing, and their attention to the trust's management of their interests may benefit all shareholders.

The wide investment powers of most investment trusts enable them, subject to the limitations acceptable for tax purposes, to follow a reasonably flexible investment policy. In response to changes in investment or fiscal conditions, they can adjust the emphasis in their portfolios on income or capital appreciation or on a particular sector of the market or geographical location. In addition, they are able, within limits, to invest in real property (although usually through the securities of listed property companies), in shares of unlisted companies and in other assets and, although they do not trade in securities themselves for tax reasons, they may establish dealing subsidiaries to take short-term positions in securities. Due to SIB regulations, an authorised unit trust must necessarily have a less flexible investment policy than that of an investment trust.

The basic investment characteristics of any investment trust are stated in its prospectus and may be indicated in its name. However, since investment trusts are flexible vehicles and investment conditions are constantly changing, a better indication of an investment trust's current policy can be obtained from its latest report and accounts.

As well as its investment objectives and financial record, another vital characteristic of an investment trust is its size. A small investment trust may be able to out-perform a larger one by adopting a more flexible investment policy, but its shares could be less marketable than those of a bigger trust, with a greater spread between buying and selling prices.

7.6.2 Income and capital gains

The total returns from an investment are traditionally assessed as income and capital gains, but in an inflationary age the distinction is rather artificial, and the balance between the two can be deliberately adjusted (eg by selling securities cum- or ex-dividend). However, in general, dividend income is usually more predictable than capital performance, not least because it is often actively managed for consistency. Income and capital gains from investments are taxed differently and may be separately owned, so the balance between the two is very significant to many investors. Some markets, particularly in the Far East, offer negligible dividend yields and correspondingly greater expectations of gains, but investment trusts may be chosen with a wide range of dividend policies.

As previously mentioned, warrants yield no income at all, which can be useful for instance to parents who would otherwise be liable to income tax on investments given to their children.

Most investors are free to adjust the 'income' they draw from their investments, either by reinvesting surplus net dividends, or by regularly selling shares to supplement the dividend yield. So far from being improvident, this is often a very sound strategy: up to £5,800 capital gains per year can be taken free of tax, in addition to the income tax allowances. Provided that the withdrawals do not exceed the capital gains (often profits retained within the trusts), the value of the investment will not be eroded. Some investment trusts offer facilities for such standing arrangements.

7.6.3 Investment overseas and currency management

Although most investment trusts adopt a flexible investment policy and are not rigidly committed to maintaining a particular proportion of their investments in any one geographical area, some of them specialise in one or more overseas areas in which they maintain special knowledge and investment expertise. These trusts provide a useful medium for overseas investment which often presents practical difficulties for direct investors.

Many trusts use foreign currency loans for overseas investment, so that the exposure of the trusts to the foreign exchange markets can be managed independently of the investments made in any country. At the same time the trust may be geared-up (see **7.6.5**), but whenever the managers choose to reduce the exposure of the trust to the market they can simply make a sterling deposit to remove the gearing.

For example, a foreign investment which gains by 20 per cent in local currency terms would still show a 20 per cent sterling loss if the exchange rate fell by a third. However, if the managers borrow the amount of the investment locally and the exchange rate falls, the liability to repay is reduced along with the assets. At the same time the trust's original capital remains intact, and could also be invested in any market.

Another, sometimes cheaper, way of hedging against exchange rate exposure is the 'currency swap' under which a UK investment trust swaps an amount in sterling with, say, a US company for an equivalent amount of US dollars. The US dollars received by the investment trust are used for portfolio investment. At the end of the agreed period the investment trust simply hands back the same amount of dollars to the US company in return for the sterling amount agreed at the outset. The risk of a default by the other party is limited to the possible exchange loss and attributable expenses, and both companies avoid the expenses of using a bank as intermediary.

The investment trust has always been a useful medium for overseas investment by UK residents because such investment is a difficult matter for most private investors, having regard to the distances involved, foreign market and settlement practices and the taxation and other problems which may arise in the overseas territories concerned. The average UK investor does not have sufficient resources to manage his UK investments effectively, let alone a portfolio of overseas investments.

7.6.4   Stock market price and underlying net asset value

An investment trust incorporated in the UK in general cannot usually purchase or redeem its own shares. Consequently, investment trust shareholders can normally only realise their investment by selling their shares through the stock market to other investors, or if the trust is wound-up or taken over. The market prices of investment trust shares are dictated by supply and demand and for many years have generally stood at a discount to the value of their underlying net assets. These discounts and valuations are regularly published for most trusts. Investment trusts still often stand at a price in the stock market which is 15 or 25 per cent lower than the estimated amount per share which would be paid to shareholders on a liquidation of the company. The obvious explanation for these substantial discounts is a lack of demand for investment trust shares in the market. It is due, in part, to lack of publicity, competition from pension and insurance funds and unit trusts (whose managers are free to advertise their units for sale and to offer commissions to selling agents), and the fact that investment trust shares are often held by long-term investors. All these factors have contributed towards a comparatively low level of regular dealing activity in investment trust shares and so reduced their marketability.

In order to realise the profit inherent in the discount on net asset value, a number of investment trust companies have been reconstructed by their managers, taken over by other companies, placed in voluntary liquidation or 'unitised'. Unitisation is a scheme under which the shareholders pass a special resolution to wind up the investment trust and transfer its investments to an authorised unit trust in exchange for units of the unit trust.

Subject to Inland Revenue clearance, unitisation does not of itself involve the investment trust shareholders in any liability to capital gains tax and on a subsequent disposal of units in the authorised unit trust, the acquisition cost of those units for capital gains tax purposes is the original acquisition cost of the shares in the investment trust from which the units arose. Following the unitisation, the former shareholders in the investment trust can sell their new units in the authorised unit trust at a price based on the underlying assets of the unit trust (see Chapter 8) and so the discount will have been effectively eliminated.

The discount on net asset value has also been eliminated for some investment trust shareholders by take-over offers being made for their shares at prices near their underlying net asset value. Some of these take-over offers have been made by predator companies, while others have been made by institutions, such as pension funds, which see the acquisition of an investment trust company as an inexpensive means of acquiring a 'ready-made' investment portfolio and perhaps eliminating a competitor. However, a take-over, unlike a unitisation, may unexpectedly crystallise a liability to capital gains tax.

If the discount is eliminated in one of these ways, or simply narrows as a result of increased market demand, it will be beneficial to holders who bought their shares at a discount and can sell at a price nearer to the net asset value. When the investor comes to sell his shares, so long as the discount is not larger than when he bought them, he should not suffer loss solely by reason of its existence and in the meantime will have benefited from the income on the assets.

Another factor which will affect the stock market price of investment trust shares is the market-maker's turn, ie the difference between the higher offer price (at which the market-maker is prepared to sell to the investor) and the lower bid price (at which the market-maker is prepared to buy from the investor). The spread between the market-maker's bid and offer price will usually be wider in the case of shares of the smaller, less marketable trusts.

This assumes that there is a sufficient market for the shares to enable them to be sold at all. In practice, a small investor in most of the larger investment trusts should not experience any difficulty in disposing of his shares, subject to the applicable discount on net asset value.

7.6.5 Gearing

In addition to its equity share capital, an investment trust may raise further capital by issuing debenture or loan stocks or preference shares and borrow money in sterling and foreign currencies. On a liquidation of the investment trust, holders of such stocks or preference shares and lenders of funds to the investment trust are entitled to repayment of fixed amounts of capital or principal from the assets of the trust in priority to equity shareholders. Only the surplus assets remaining, after discharge by the investment trust of all its other liabilities, are distributable to the equity shareholders. In effect, any increase or decrease in the value of the assets of the investment trust is primarily attributable to one or more classes of its equity share capital. An overall increase or decrease has a greater effect on the underlying value of its equity share capital in the case of a trust which has raised most of its capital in the form of loans or preference shares than in the case of a trust which has raised most of its capital by issues of equity shares. In UK securities terminology, if the proportion of a company's capital which has been raised in the form of loans and preference shares is large in relation to its equity capital, the company is described as 'highly geared' and, if small, the company's 'gearing' is said to be low; the US term is 'leverage'.

The following examples will illustrate the consequences of gearing; taxation and other factors have been ignored in the interests of simplicity.

Example 1:   Ungeared trust

A new ungeared investment trust raises £1m by an issue of equity shares and invests the proceeds of the share issue in a portfolio of securities. If the value of the portfolio doubles to £2m, the assets of the trust attributable to the equity shareholders will increase 100 per cent. If the portfolio halves, the net value for ordinary shareholders will, likewise, decrease by 50 per cent.

Example 2:   Geared trust

Suppose a new geared investment trust raises £1m by (a) issuing 500,000 preference shares at £1 each and (b) issuing equity shares at an aggregate price of £5m, and then invests the total proceeds of £1m in a portfolio of securities. If the portfolio doubles in value to £2m, on liquidation the investment trust will have to pay £5m to the preference shareholders; but, after this payment, the amount attributable to the trust's equity shares will have increased by 200 per cent from £5m to £1.5m. On the other hand, if the value of the portfolio halves, the preference shareholders will be repaid £5m, leaving nothing for the ordinary shareholders; a 100 per cent loss.

The ability of investment trusts to gear their portfolios in this manner is one of the principal differences between investment trusts and unit trusts. The latter have only very limited powers to borrow money without gearing up.

The examples given above illustrate the effect of gearing on the capital assets of an investment trust, but, if the lenders of money to an investment trust or its preference shareholders are entitled to payment of interest or dividends at a fixed rate, gearing will also have an effect on the income of the trust from its investments which is distributable to its equity shareholders. An increase (or decrease) in the income arising from a geared trust's investments will have a greater impact on the amount of income available for distribution to equity shareholders of the trust by way of dividend than will a similar fluctuation in the income of an ungeared trust.

Equity shareholders of investment trusts will benefit from investing in highly geared investment trusts when the assets in which those trusts have invested are rising in value but they are at greater risk when such assets are falling in value. One of the more difficult tasks of a professional investment manager is to utilise gearing successfully. The investment manager must decide when to gear up the trust and when to undertake a rapid 'de-gearing' exercise by repaying borrowings or turning substantial portions of the investment portfolio into cash or assets which are not likely to fluctuate significantly in value.

7.7 Taxation

7.7.1 Approval of investment trusts

This chapter deals with 'approved' investment trusts as opposed to 'unapproved' investment companies. Only approved investment trusts (and authorised unit trusts) attract the capital gains tax exemption outlined below. An approved investment trust is one which is not a 'close company' and which, in respect of an accounting period, has been approved by the Board of Inland Revenue. The Inland Revenue appear to have discretion to withhold approval, even in the case of an investment trust which would otherwise qualify, but they will approve a company that can show that:

(1) it is resident for taxation purposes in the UK;
(2) its income is derived wholly or mainly (which in practice means approximately 70 per cent or more) from shares or securities;
(3) no holding in a company (other than another approved investment trust or a company which would qualify as such but for the fact that its shares are not listed as required by (4) below) represents more than 15 per cent by value of its investments;
(4) all its ordinary share capital is listed on The Stock Exchange;
(5) the distribution as dividend of capital profits on the sale of its

investments is prohibited by its memorandum or articles of association; and

(6)   not more than 15 per cent of its income from securities is retained unless legally required.

It is expressly provided that an increase in the value of a holding after it has been acquired will not result in an infringement of the 15 per cent limit referred to in (3) above. However, the holdings of an investment trust in its subsidiary companies are treated as a single holding for the purposes of this limit, as are its holdings in other companies which are members of the same group of companies. In addition, any loans made by the trust to its subsidiaries are treated as part of its investment in the subsidiaries for the purposes of ascertaining whether the limit has been infringed.

7.7.2   Approved investment trusts — capital gains

Investment trusts are corporations and their income is subject to corporation tax in the same manner and at the same rates as other corporations, but capital gains accruing to approved investment trusts are wholly exempt from capital gains tax in the hands of the trust. Thus active management of the trust's investments need not be constrained by tax on realising gains and the investor may only be subject to tax on disposing of his investment trust shares.

7.7.3   Approved investment trusts — income

The taxation of the trust's own income, and of the income and gains of investors in the trust, is exactly the same as for other limited companies (see Chapter 3). The corporation tax system is complicated and a detailed explanation of it is outside the scope of this handbook but a brief summary may help.

Income

Franked income

This is income received by a trust in the form of dividends paid by a UK company in respect of which that company has paid advance corporation tax (ACT). ACT is effectively a payment by a UK company on account of its own corporation tax liability and is made in respect of dividends paid by it. The rate of ACT is expressed as a fraction of the dividend paid. The current fraction is 20/80, which means that if a company pays a dividend of £80 to a shareholder it must pay £20 ACT in respect of that dividend; the shareholder will receive a tax credit of £20. The amount of the dividend plus the ACT is known as a 'franked payment'. A trust is itself liable to pay ACT on paying dividends to its own shareholders, but franked income received by a trust can be passed on by way of dividend to its own shareholders without any payment of ACT by the trust. Further, the franked income is not liable to corporation tax in the hands of the trust.

Unfranked income

This is all other income (such as interest on gilt-edged securities, bank deposit interest and dividends paid by foreign companies) which does not carry a tax credit indicating that ACT has been paid in respect of it. Unfranked income is less favourably treated, being subject to corporation tax. However, interest paid by the trust and the fees paid to its investment managers are set primarily against unfranked income, reducing the amount liable to tax.

7.8   Unapproved investment companies

Unless an investment company has the status of an approved investment trust (see **7.7.1**), it is subject to ordinary forms of corporate taxation and will not qualify for the capital gains tax exemption mentioned in **7.7.2**. Thus both the investment income and capital gains made by such a company will be taxed, under the terms of the Finance Act 1987, at the corporation tax rate. Under the Taxes Act 1988, a close investment holding company does not qualify for the small companies' rate. In addition, if an investment company disposes of its assets and is then liquidated there is effectively a double capital gains tax charge, because (1) the company will be liable to corporation tax on capital gains realised by it on the disposal, and (2) its shareholders will be liable to capital gains tax in respect of any capital gains realised by them on the disposal of their shares in the investment company, which will occur by reason of the distribution of cash proceeds to them in the liquidation. (Considerations affecting investment in a private investment company are discussed in Chapter 13 at **13.4**.)

Having regard to these disadvantages and to the fact that, so long as the investment company continues in existence, profits on the sale of investments may only be distributed to its shareholders by way of comparatively highly taxed dividends, the investment company has become unpopular as an investment medium. In fact, in order to mitigate this unsatisfactory taxation position, many unapproved investment companies have been 'unitised' (see **7.6.4**). The advantage of unitisation is that it defers the capital gains liability on the company shares until the ultimate disposal of the units issued on unitisation, which may be spread over several years to take full advantage of the annual CGT exemptions.

7.9   Suitability

Investment trusts are a suitable investment medium for small and large investors who are resident in the UK for tax purposes, who wish to spread their investment risk and who do not have the expertise or the resources to make direct investments. However, the investor in investment trusts should be aware of the possible advantages and disadvantages which may result from the existence of the discount on net asset value (see **7.6.4**) and from the ability of investment trusts to gear their portfolios (see **7.6.5**). If the investor is unwilling to accept the risk involved for the sake of the possible greater rewards, the unit trust is probably a more suitable investment medium. On the other hand, investment trusts have frequently shown better long-term returns. Split capital trusts are highly suitable for the investors for whom they are designed, but more care must be taken accordingly.

7.10   Mechanics

Investment trust shares may be bought in new issues or acquired on The Stock Exchange through stockbrokers, banks and other investment advisers. A number of stockbroking firms specialise in the investment trust sector and will be able to provide detailed information relating to individual trusts, including analyses of past performance, level of discount on underlying net asset value and investment policy. The Association of Investment Trust Companies freely offers excellent literature on investment trusts generally, and its members in particular. Information on individual trusts can be obtained from Extel cards (available in large public libraries), or directly from the managers, who may also offer shares for sale through 'savings schemes'.

Investment trust savings schemes are operated by managers to avoid some of the restrictions on marketing shares. Typically they offer lump sum, regular savings and dividend reinvestment options. The contributions are pooled by the managers and used to buy shares on The Stock Exchange, and the saving in transaction costs may reduce the investor's brokerage as low as 0.2 per cent, although some schemes provide for the payment of substantial commissions to intermediaries, the cost of which is ultimately borne by the investor.

Costs of both acquisition and disposal on The Stock Exchange will normally include stockbrokers' commission, which is subject to negotiation, but for a private investor is likely to be something between 1 per cent and 1.65 per cent, depending on the extent of the service the client requires from the broker; there will usually be a minimum, perhaps £25, and a lower rate for large deals. On purchases, there will also be stamp duty at 0.5 per cent and the spread between bid and offered prices may be around 1.5 per cent, though it will usually be less on the freely traded shares of large companies. There is no initial charge payable to the managers, but further brokerage will be payable on final realisation of the shares by sale.

7.11 Maintenance

Running costs vary from one investment trust to another, but management fees, often in the region of 0.5 per cent per annum on the value of the portfolio, are usually payable by the trust at half-yearly intervals in addition to its day-to-day operating expenses. New and converted specialist trusts, such as those involved in providing venture capital, often pay higher fees, perhaps 1.5 per cent. Economies can often be achieved in cases where the managers act as managers for several investment trusts and are therefore able to spread the burden of management and administrative expenses among a number of different trusts. These management fees and expenses are normally deductible from the income of the trust for corporation tax purposes, whereas the management fee of a private portfolio manager generally has to be found out of his client's after-tax income. In the case of investment trusts, the level of management fees and the extent to which operating expenses may be charged to the trust are not controlled by any external regulation and generally trusts are lightly regulated without the expensive compliance arrangements required of unit trusts.

Like any other investment, holdings in investment trusts should be periodically reviewed by the investor or his adviser. Performance of the investment trust may be monitored by observing its quoted stock exchange price in the daily newspapers and the changes in its underlying net asset value, and by reading the half-yearly financial statements and annual directors' reports and audited accounts, which will be sent to registered shareholders and are generally available free on request. The annual report and accounts will contain detailed financial and other information relating to the trust and will usually include details of its investment portfolio as at the date of its balance sheet. The trust will also convene an annual general meeting of shareholders to adopt the annual report and accounts and to conduct other business. Any registered shareholder may attend and vote on the resolutions proposed at these meetings or, if he does not wish to attend, he may appoint a proxy to vote on his behalf.

7.12 Preview of the year ahead

The flexibility of a limited company as a collective investment vehicle always offers a simple starting point for continual market developments. In addition, however, this year there should be two hybrid structural developments from investment trusts ('ITs'): the venture capital trust ('VCT'), a cross between the IT and the former Business Expansion Scheme, announced in the November 1993 Budget; and the open-ended investment company (OEIC), a cross between an IT and a unit trust, modelled on the variable capital companies common elsewhere in the European Union.

A venture capital trust, like an IT, will itself be exempt from capital gains tax, so that VCTs themselves will be broadly tax neutral; but in addition investment in a VCT, like a PEP, will be free of income tax and capital gains tax; and investors will receive income tax relief on subscriptions into new VCTs, and capital gains which would otherwise be chargeable on other investments can be rolled over into a VCT investment within six months before or after realisation. The limit of £100,000 per annum is far more generous than for PEPs.

The legislation for VCTs is now basically fixed, although not finalised at the time of going to print, and in practice Inland Revenue and Stock Exchange requirements can substantially affect the final form of the new investments. A VCT, like an IT, will be a listed public company, specially approved by the Inland Revenue, which must derive its income 'wholly or mainly' (in practice, at least 70 per cent) from securities; but which must also within three years of approval invest at least 70 per cent of its assets in 'qualifying holdings' in unquoted UK trading companies.

At least 30 per cent of a VCT's investments overall must be in ordinary shares, with the balance in other share capital or long-term debt.

A VCT may invest a maximum of £1 million per year in any one trading company, which may not be larger than £11 million immediately after the investment, and must not be controlled by the VCT or anyone else. No holding may exceed 15 per cent of the VCT. The detailed requirements for the trading companies are comparable to those for the Enterprise Investment Scheme, such as the requirement for the investment to be used in trading within 12 months.

All the VCT's investments must be new, ie initial subscription of shares or debt, and no securities of the trading company may be listed or quoted on the USM at the time (although listing on the Alternative Investment Market is allowed, as is subsequent admission to listing). Like an approved investment trust, a VCT must distribute 85 per cent of its income; but it may also choose to distribute capital profits.

Stock Exchange requirements are likely to be comparable to those for ITs, including a majority of directors independent of the sponsoring investment house, and other precautions for transactions between a VCT and its sponsors; other regulatory requirements should also be modelled on ITs. Inland Revenue approval may be granted provisionally, and subject to withdrawal for breach of the conditions or limits.

Regulations to permit open ended investment companies have been developed by HM Treasury at the instance of investment managers who believe that Continental investors are deterred from UK unit trusts because they are unfamiliar with trust law. The project has become entangled in the separate question of simplifying the only permitted system for determining fair prices for investing in and realising units in unit trusts. Whatever the outcome of these debates, and it remains to be seen whether the new systems are actually more attractive or economical than the old, the companies will undoubtedly take advantage of the extensive publicity when any changes are made.

7.13 Conclusion

While the market prices of investment trust shares are below their underlying asset values, investors can take the opportunity to profit from this discount, either on a reconstruction, take-over or winding-up of the trust, or if rule changes or market conditions increase demand for (and so prices of) investment trusts. Predators continue to give every incentive for good performance to trust managers, who have started to respond with 'poison pill' measures such as investment in unquoted shares or the issue of warrants which make a take-over expensive or unattractive. The freedom of investment trusts to issue innovative securities using sophisticated financial structures, and to invest with new techniques and instruments which are largely denied to other collective media, is of increasing importance as other differences are reduced. For example, because investment trusts do not have to contend with fluctuating capital flows, they are particularly suitable for index-matching investment policies: the first conversion of a trust into a fully indexed fund was not a success, but other trusts may do better. The flexibility of investment trusts in the hands of their professional managers will ensure they remain efficient and attractive investment vehicles for small and large investors alike.

Sources of further information

Useful addresses

Association of Investment Trust
  Companies
8–13 Chiswell Street
London
EC1Y 4YY

Tel: (0171) 588 5347

S G Warburg Securities
1 Finsbury Avenue
London EC2M 2PP

(This firm does not deal directly
with private investors, but
publishes an annual *Private
Investor Guide to Investment
Trusts*, which includes a list of
some suitable brokers.)

8 Unit trusts and offshore funds

David Ballance, MA (Oxon), Investment Manager, Threadneedle Investment Managers Ltd

8.1 Introduction

Another form of collective investment medium (see Chapter 7) is that of unit trusts. A unit trust is a trust fund, in which the investors hold direct beneficial interests. It is normally open-ended, meaning that units are created or redeemed at the current fair prices, and so the managers buy and sell units as required by investors (see **8.7**).

Obviously the honesty and competence of the managers of such trusts is of fundamental importance, and the constitution, management and marketing of trusts are all regulated in the UK, primarily under the Financial Services Act 1986. These powers are exercised by the Securities and Investments Board (SIB) and a number of self-regulatory organisations with delegated powers over member firms. Only authorised persons may conduct investment business. The European Community Directive on Undertakings for Collective Investment in Transferable Securities (the UCITS Directive) requires all member states to assimilate their regulations for certain collective schemes, which may then be sold throughout the European Economic Area.

8.2 Historical background

Units in the first unit trust in the UK were offered to the public in April 1931 by the M&G Group, which still exists today as one of the leaders of the industry. Allied Investors Ltd, now Allied Dunbar Unit Trusts plc, followed in 1934 and is now the third largest unit trust group. The first trusts were 'fixed' trusts and offered virtually no flexibility in investment policy once the trust deed had been executed. Each new subscription was invested in the fixed portfolio and each unit was thus unchanged in its composition. Each unit was normally divided into sub-units for sale to the public.

The first 'flexible' trust (the type of trust which is marketed today) was not offered to the public until 1936. When the Prevention of Fraud

(Investments) Act 1939 came into force, supervision of the new industry was made the responsibility of the (then) Board of Trade. Under that Act, revised and re-enacted as the Prevention of Fraud (Investments) Act 1958, the Department of Trade and Industry (DTI) laid down regulations for the conduct of unit trusts, supervised charges and 'authorised' unit trusts complying with its requirements until 1988. The power of authorisation for new unit trust schemes then passed from the DTI to the Securities and Investments Board (SIB).

8.3   Authorisation

The main requirement for authorisation of a unit trust by the SIB is that a trust deed conforming with the Board's regulations is executed, between a company performing all management functions for the trust (the managers) and an independent trust corporation (the trustee) to hold the trust's investments and supervise the managers. Both the managers and the trustee must be incorporated under the law of, or of some part of, the UK or any other member state of the EU, must maintain a place of business in Great Britain and must be authorised persons to conduct investment business and so subject to the regulators' rules for conduct of business. The persons who are to be directors of a unit trust management company must be approved by the SIB. The trust deed and regulations must provide for, *inter alia*:

(1)   managers' investment and borrowing powers and limits on investment of the trust's assets;
(2)   determining the manner in which prices and yields are calculated and the obligation of managers to repurchase units at the 'bid' price;
(3)   setting up a register of unitholders, with procedures for issuing certificates and dealing with transfers;
(4)   remuneration of the managers and trustees;
(5)   periodic audits of the trust and the issue of financial statements to unitholders, with reports by the managers, trustees and auditors;
(6)   meetings of unitholders under certain circumstances.

Authorisation makes it possible for unit trust managers to advertise units for sale to the public and carries with it tax privileges for the trust. These taxation aspects are discussed in detail in Section **8.9**. This Part deals only with unit trusts which have been authorised by the SIB, and the expression 'unit trust', when used in this Part, means an authorised unit trust unless otherwise indicated. (As to unauthorised unit trusts, see **8.12**.)

8.4   Highlights of the previous year

Sales of unit trusts in 1994, compared with the previous two years, were as follows:

	1992 *£m*	*1993* *£m*	*1994* *£m*
Industry sales	9,560.2	18,739.9	19,672.0
Industry repurchases	8,914.6	9,604.5	11,423.0
Net new investment	645.6	9,135.4	8,249.0

At 31 December 1994 the total funds invested in authorised unit trusts were £92.116bn.

Thirty-one new trusts were launched in the year making a total of 1,559, operated by 162 management companies, compared with 156 at the end of 1993, and 151 at the end of 1992. One encouraging feature of 1994 was a sharp rise in the number of unitholders. At the end of 1994 there were 6.12 million unitholders, compared with 5.04 million at the end of 1993.

After the very strong returns achieved by equity investors in 1993, 1994 proved to be a much more difficult year. While consumer price inflation remained subdued through the world, continued strong industrial recovery in the USA, a sharper-than-expected bounceback in European economic activity, and sharp rises in certain commodity prices re-ignited investors' fears of rising inflation and interest rates. Short-term interest rates began to rise in the USA in February 1994 and have continued to rise, and UK base rates began to rise towards the end of the year. The recovery in Germany also forced investors to re-think their forecasts as to how low German interest rates could go. The effects of the above were felt first in global bond markets, and the collapse in bond values spread to equities.

Against that background the only major equity market to rise during the year was that of Japan. With the Japanese economy still very weak, and inflation virtually non-existent, Tokyo was to some degree immune to the worries of elsewhere. In all the Japanese equity market rose 8.3 per cent, a rise of 14.6 per cent in Sterling, aided by the strong yen. Elsewhere it was a story of declining markets, with the US market down by 7 per cent, the UK market by 9.5 per cent and those of France and Germany by 16 and 7.5 per cent respectively. There were some bright spots in Europe; the smaller markets of Sweden, Italy and Finland all achieved positive returns, the latter of 24 per cent as the economy recovered from deep recession.

Some of the weakest areas were in the Pacific Rim and emerging markets, areas that had sparkled during 1993. With such areas more dependent on funds flow from the US, the rises in American interest rates have choked off liquidity, leading to sharp falls in share values. 1994 saw a fall of 33 per cent in Hong Kong, 12 per cent in Thailand and 26 per cent in Malaysia, whereas in emerging markets the Mexican crisis of December 1994 set off domino effects elsewhere.

8.5   Pricing of units

Since 1 July 1988, unit trust managers have been free to choose whether to deal on 'forward prices', ie at the next price to be calculated, or at prices already calculated and published, as had been usual. Many management companies have availed themselves of this opportunity. With forward pricing, a buyer does not know exactly how many units he will receive, but he does know that he will deal at a fair, up-to-date price. If, on the other hand, a management company is dealing on historic prices and the value of a trust is believed to have changed by more than 2 per cent since the valuation on which the company is offering to deal, a new price must be calculated (using an index if the trustee agrees). Alternatively, the company can change to forward pricing.

More information now has to be given with the unit prices published in newspapers. In addition to bid and offer prices, the initial charge and the cancellation price must now be shown. The cancellation price is that at which the company can cancel units that it has created or bought back from the public. If the trust is on a bid basis, the bid and cancellation prices will be the same.

The Financial Services Act 1986 became effective in 1988 (see Chapter 21) superseding the Prevention of Fraud (Investments) Act 1958. As a result, much of the regulation of unit trusts, including authorisation, will be transferred from the DTI to other bodies. The regulation of borrowing powers and permitted investment remains with the DTI, and the constitution of unit trusts is regulated by the DTI and the SIB, but the management of trusts is regulated by the Investment Management Regulatory Organisation (IMRO) and the marketing by the Life Assurance and Unit Trust Regulatory Organisation (LAUTRO) and the Personal Investment Authority (PIA).

The Budget of 1994 made no change to the limits on annual investment in unit trusts and investment trusts via personal equity plans, which stayed at £6,000. Investors continued to be able to invest in trusts which held more than 50 per cent of their assets in EU countries, a reform introduced in 1991 (see also pp 69 and 389).

However, the Budget of 1994 made one important change to the structure of personal equity plans, by making corporate bonds and preference shares eligible for inclusion. Given the high yields available from such instruments, such a change may be attractive for income-oriented investors, and one would expect the number of unit trusts in this area to increase to meet that need.

8.6 Legal nature

As mentioned in **8.3**, a unit trust scheme is constituted by a trust deed which is made between the managers, who are the promoters of the scheme and who will subsequently be responsible for the conduct of the investment and for administration, and the trustee (usually one of the clearing banks or major insurance companies), which is responsible for ensuring that the managers act in accordance with the provisions laid down in the trust deed and which holds the assets of the trust on trust for the unitholders. Regulations determine the content of the trust deed and other binding requirements, and both the trustee and the management company are subject to the Conduct of Business Rules.

The underlying securities are registered in the name of the trustee or, if in bearer form, held in the custody of the trustee, which also holds any cash forming part of the fund. The trustee, as the legal owner of the underlying assets for the unitholders, receives on their behalf all income and other distributions made in respect of such assets.

The trust deed and regulations also lay down a formula for valuing the trust to determine the prices at which units may be sold to the public by the managers and at which units must be bought back by the managers from the public (see below). Additional units may be created to meet demand from the public or existing units may be cancelled as a result of the subsequent repurchase of units from the public. A unit trust is thus 'open-ended' and can expand or contract depending on whether there is a preponderance of buyers or sellers of its units.

Three prices are quoted for unit trusts. These are the 'offered' price, at which units are offered for sale to or subscription by the public, and the 'bid' price, at which the managers buy back units, and the cancellation price, at which the managers may arrange for units to be redeemed out of the assets of the trust. These prices are, broadly speaking, ascertained in the following manner:

(1) the offered price is calculated by reference to the notional amount which would have to be paid to acquire the underlying assets held

by the trust, to which are added the notional acquisition costs (such as brokers' commission and stamp duty) and the preliminary management charges (see **8.11.1**);

(2)   the bid price is calculated by reference to the notional amount which would be received on a disposal of the assets held by the trust, from which are deducted the notional costs of the disposal, ie brokers' commission and contract stamp.

An investor must never be required to pay more for his units than the offered price as calculated under the trust deed, nor may the unitholder on a sale of his units be paid less than the bid price as so calculated. When an investor buys units, the managers may either create them or sell units that they have previously repurchased. The spread between the offered and bid prices under the DTI rules is normally between 8 and 11 per cent, but in practice most unit trust managers quote spreads for their own dealings in units between 5.5 and 7.5 per cent, which may be positioned anywhere between the maximum offered and minimum bid prices applicable on subscription for new units and cancellation of existing units.

Managers normally base their buying price for units in a particular trust on the strict bid valuation if they are buying back more units than they are selling, since this is the price at which units must be cancelled. Conversely, if the managers are selling more units than they are buying, their selling price is normally based on the full offered price, at which units must be created.

A unit trust cannot 'gear' its portfolio by borrowings, either unsecured or secured on the assets of the trust. The only circumstances in which borrowing is permitted are to anticipate known cash flows (such as dividends due) or to hedge against currency losses on holdings of foreign securities. The gearing effect of hedge borrowing is almost eliminated by the requirement that a matching sterling deposit must be made (see **8.8.2**).

The trust deed, which takes effect subject to any regulations under the Financial Services Act, may make provision for the trust to be terminated and also specifies circumstances in which the approval of unitholders at a general meeting needs to be sought. Such approval is required, among other things, for proposals to vary the provisions of the trust deed, to change the investment objectives of the trust or to amalgamate it with another trust. Unitholders' interests are thus protected despite the fact that no annual general meeting is held, since certain material changes affecting their interests may be effected only with their approval in general meeting.

8.7 Conditions for purchase

Any individual, corporate body or trustee may acquire and hold unit trusts without any condition or restriction, subject to any limitation which may be imposed on its own investment powers.

Unit trusts are specifically mentioned as approved 'wider range' investments under the Trustee Investments Act 1961. Unit trusts whose portfolios consist exclusively of investments suitable for 'narrow range' investments under the same Act may themselves be included in the narrow range investments. Trustees should, however, satisfy themselves of their powers to invest in unit trusts by reference to their trust instrument.

Nearly all unit trust managers specify a minimum investment, usually in the range of £250–£1,000. Certain specialist funds have higher minima. These minima do not apply to monthly saving schemes, where amounts from £10 per month may be invested on a regular basis.

Since a unit trust is open-ended, there is no maximum holding, though a corporate or trustee unitholder may be restricted by his own investment limitations.

In the case of some 'exempt' unit trusts, purchasers will still have to satisfy the managers that they enjoy tax-exempt status (eg they are pension funds or charities) (see **8.13**), despite the fact that 'exempt' unit trusts' fiscal privileges have been outmoded by the exemption of all authorised unit trusts from tax on their capital gains.

Persons resident outside the UK may acquire and hold unit trust units, subject to the local exchange control rules in their country of residence or domicile. However, for reasons of taxation, it is usually preferable for such people to invest in 'offshore' funds (see **8.15**).

8.8 Characteristics

Unit trusts must invest the greater part of their portfolios in securities listed on recognised stock exchanges. Trust deeds usually contain power for unquoted investments having an aggregate value not exceeding 5 per cent of the value of all the investments of the trust to be held. Depending upon their trust deeds, trusts may also be allowed to hold a proportion of their investments in shares on the London Unlisted Securities Market.

The investments of the majority of unit trusts are usually in equity shares. Preference shares are, however, occasionally held for reasons of yield, since the income from these, unlike interest on bank deposits or gilt-edged securites, is 'franked' investment income (see **8.9.2**). Following the Finance Act 1980, fixed interest funds (ie those investing in gilt-edged and other bonds) became increasingly common (see **8.9.2**), but some have lost a part of their attraction now that the taxation of income on an accrual basis has removed much of their tax efficiency compared with direct investment.

As mentioned in **8.5** above, the reforms announced in the 1994 Budget, whereby corporate bonds and preference shares are now eligible for personal equity plans, will obviously have implications here.

Traditional authorised unit trusts may, in general, invest only in securities, although new classes of unit trusts are now authorised to invest in other financial instruments, or property, and mixed funds invest in several different classes, including commodities. These new schemes may have separate regulations of investment and borrowing powers, and may have a separate tax regime. All trusts, including traditional schemes, may use certain traded option techniques for hedging purposes. Call options written and put options bought must be covered by the relevant securities held in the trusts.

It is not, at present, possible for a unit trust to adopt the 'split form' whereby all the income accrues to one class of holder and all the capital appreciation to the other.

The specific investment characteristics of unit trusts will vary depending on the stated objective of any particular trust. However, all unit trusts share certain general characteristics.

8.8.1   General characteristics

Spread of risk

By acquiring an interest in a portion of all the investments in the underlying portfolio of a unit trust, an investor can achieve a much wider spread of risk than he could himself achieve economically with limited resources. By spreading his investment across a large number of companies in a wide variety of industries in a number of different countries, the investor can much reduce the risks inherent in a holding of shares in only one company or a small number of companies. The result is likely to be a much more even progression of capital and income growth. Regulations covering the maximum investment of a trust's assets in a single company or issue, ensure that a wide spread of risk is achieved. In practice, unit trusts usually hold something between 30 and 100 investments, considerably more than the required minimum.

Professional management

By committing his investment funds to the purchase of a holding in a unit trust the investor is in effect delegating the day-to-day management of his portfolio to the managers of the trust. Virtually all unit trust management companies employ a team of investment specialists whose aim is to maximise capital and/or income performance, and who are given a wide discretion within the limitations imposed by the trust deed to increase or decrease the liquidity of the trust or to switch investments as they consider appropriate. The advantage to the investor is that his investments are under the continuous supervision of people whose business it is to keep abreast of economic, political and corporate developments at home and abroad.

Simplicity and convenience

The sometimes tedious paperwork associated with owning a portfolio of securities is largely eliminated. Day-to-day decisions on such matters as rights and scrip issues, mergers and take-overs are all taken by the managers. Dividends are received by the trustee and distributions of the trust's income are made, usually twice a year, to unitholders together with a report on the progress of their trust during the preceding accounting period.

Marketability

In view of their open-ended nature, as a result of which units can be created or cancelled to meet the requirements of investors, unit trust units can be regarded as a totally liquid investment, with none of the constraints on marketability sometimes encountered in connection with investment in some of the smaller listed companies. As a result of the pricing structure, referred to in **8.6**, purchases and sales of units take place at prices which reflect the underlying value of the trust's assets.

8.8.2 Types of unit trust

While all unit trusts share the investment characteristics listed above, there are a very wide range of trusts which offer different investment objectives designed to suit different categories of investors. The main types are described below.

Balanced trusts

These invest in a portfolio which is usually composed of leading 'blue chip' shares with the aim of achieving a steady growth of both capital and income. These trusts are designed for the investor who wishes to invest in a wide spread of ordinary shares. They are suitable for the first-time investor in equities, who wishes to hold the units for longer term investment or saving.

Income trusts

These aim to achieve an above-average yield to the investor whose primary need is for a high and growing income. Normally, such trusts give a yield between 1.2 and 1.5 times that available on shares generally. These trusts are most suitable for retired people, widows, or others who depend on investment income. Such trusts may purchase convertible shares as a way of achieving their yield objectives.

As a group, income trusts generally performed well through the 1980s, as the UK economy recovered from recession and dividends grew ahead of inflation. However, in 1990 and 1991 these trusts markedly underperformed their balanced and capital trust counterparts, again proving their greater dependence on conditions in the domestic UK economy. Following the departure of sterling from the ERM in September 1992, and the subsequent sharp falls in UK interest rates, these trusts recovered a lot of that lost ground, as investors sought stocks which would benefit from economic recovery in the UK.

Capital trusts

These are designed to seek maximum capital growth. The income from such trusts is usually low. These characteristics make them particularly suitable for those who want to build up a nest-egg.

Fixed Interest trusts

These generally invest in a portfolio of government bonds, corporate bonds and convertible shares and may be either income or capital trusts. Such trusts may be suitable for those requiring a high income, although prospects for income growth are unlikely to be as good as in equity trusts.

Overseas trusts

These aim to provide the investor with an opportunity to invest through stock markets in other countries of the world. Investment overseas is a particularly complex and difficult task for the private person, but can be rewarding in times when sterling is weak against other currencies or when economic conditions in some region overseas are particularly buoyant. The sharp depreciation of sterling in 1992 proved again the merits of investing in these trusts, as a hedge against devaluation. For these trusts, the 'back to back' loan can be a useful investment tool to neutralise currency fluctuations while preserving the exposure to the stock market in the chosen country. The term 'back to back' is used to describe the need for unit trusts to make a sterling deposit equivalent to the amount of foreign currency borrowed. The need to make this deposit arises from the restrictions on gearing by unit trusts (see **8.6**, and see chapters 4 and 5).

Specialist trusts

Certain trusts, sometimes referred to as 'specialist trusts', are promoted to invest in particular sectors of the securities market (eg commodities or smaller companies). These trusts are suitable for the larger or more sophisticated investor who wishes to concentrate on a particular sector while still achieving a spread of risk. The specialist nature of such trusts means that the investor may be somewhat more at the whim of fashion; UK smaller companies' unit trusts, for example, after many years of above-average returns, markedly underperformed their more balanced counterparts from 1989 to 1991. UK smaller companies' unit trusts, like UK income trusts (qv) are very dependent on conditions in the domestic UK economy; as with income trusts, this class of trust has seen a very strong revival in its fortunes since September 1992. Within the category of specialist trusts, one of the major areas of growth in the last two years have been emerging markets. Here investment via unit trusts is clearly much to be preferred to direct investment, given the greater need for spread of investment in areas where markets can be extremely volatile.

Accumulation trusts

Certain trusts within all the categories referred to above are structured and promoted on the basis that they will accumulate the net income within the trust rather than distribute it to unitholders. This income is nonetheless subject to taxation as if it had been received by unitholders.

'Tracker' trusts

Certain trusts are structured to imitate a stock market index and so achieve a performance matching that market. Because of their essentially passive nature, with investment managers taking fewer active decisions, such trusts normally have lower management charges. These trusts are also referred to as indexed trusts.

8.9 Taxation

8.9.1 Introduction

Section **8.3** of this chapter dealt with 'authorised' unit trusts, as opposed to 'unapproved' investment companies and 'unauthorised' unit trusts.

Only approved investment trusts and authorised unit trusts attract the capital gains tax concessions outlined below. This section on taxation also refers briefly, by way of comparison, to the tax treatment of unauthorised unit trusts.

Authorised unit trusts

An authorised unit trust for taxation purposes is a unit trust which, for any accounting period, is a unit trust scheme that has been authorised by the Securities and Investments Board, in accordance with the Financial Services Act 1986. The conditions which must be fulfilled before the SIB will confer authorisation have been discussed in **8.3**. By virtue of the Income and Corporation Taxes Act 1988, s 468, for taxation purposes an authorised unit trust is effectively treated as a company, its unitholders are treated as shareholders in a company, and any distributions of income made to its unitholders are treated as dividends paid by a company to its shareholders. The exception is fixed interest trusts (**8.8.2**), which are taxed as trusts. Following the 1990 Budget, the corporation tax payable by all unit trusts that come within EC rules has been, from 1 January 1991, at a rate equal to the standard rate of income tax. This removed a discrimination against unfranked income in the hands of trusts other than fixed interest trusts (see below). An authorised unit trust and its unitholders are given the same capital gains tax concessions as equity shareholders in other vehicles.

8.9.2   Taxation of approved and authorised unit trusts

Taxation of the trust

As mentioned above, authorised unit trusts (other than fixed interest funds) are effectively treated as corporations for taxation purposes and are granted the same capital gains tax concessions as approved investment trusts. The corporation tax system is complicated and a detailed explanation of it is outside the scope of this guide, but a brief statement of the position as it relates to the income and capital gains of approved investment trusts and authorised unit trusts is set out below.

Income

Franked income   This is income received by a unit trust in the form of dividends paid by a UK company in respect of which that company has paid advance corporation tax (ACT). ACT is effectively a payment by a UK company on account of its own corporation tax liability and is made in respect of dividends paid by it. The rate of ACT is expressed as a fraction of the dividend paid. Prior to March 1993 this fraction was 25 per cent, which meant that if a company paid a gross dividend of £100 the shareholder would receive £75 net dividend and an ACT credit of £25.

However, the first Budget of 1993 announced a far-reaching and complex reform of ACT, primarily in response to the pattern of surplus ACT built up by UK companies. In essence the rate of ACT was reduced from 25 per cent to 20 per cent, but in two stages, such that for tax year 1993/94 the rate of ACT was 22.5 per cent. However, the tax credit granted to shareholders in respect of dividends paid, was reduced to 20 per cent from 6 April 1993, with a consequent loss in net income, albeit small. This net income loss was also mitigated by the fact that several UK companies brought forward the paying of dividends to beat the 6 April 1993 deadline, and by the fact that several companies chose to pay enhanced scrip dividends. In 1994 when the ACT rate was reduced to 20 per cent, this income loss disappeared.

The amount of dividend plus the ACT is known as 'franked payment'. A trust is itself liable to pay ACT on paying dividends to its own shareholders, but if its dividend is paid out of franked income, it can deduct the amount of the tax credit received from the paying company from its own ACT liability. It is this difference between the ACT rate of 22.5 per cent and the tax credit rate of 20 per cent for tax year 1993/4 which caused the income loss referred to above since, in contrast with previous years, and indeed with the proposals from 6 April 1994 onwards, the trust had a residual liability for ACT. Franked income remains not liable to corporation tax in the hands of the trust. More generally, the Finance Act 1994 makes provision for further alterations to the system of ACT. In particular there are proposals to introduce a system of Foreign Income Dividends, whereby UK companies making distributions out of foreign income earned, would be able to achieve a more generous system of ACT offset than heretofore.

Unfranked income   This is all other income (such as interest on gilt-edged securities, bank deposit interest and dividends paid by foreign companies) which does not carry with it a tax credit indicating that ACT has been paid in respect of it. Certain unfranked income received by certain unit trusts (not investment trusts) is treated differently, as described in **8.9.1**. Unfranked income was less favourably treated for tax purposes, being subject to corporation tax (currently at 35 per cent or 25 per cent if the smaller company rate is applicable) in the hands of a trust (other than an authorised unit trust established especially to invest in UK government securities). However, interest paid by the trust and the management fees paid to its investment managers are set primarily against unfranked income, thereby reducing the amount of income which will be subject to corporation tax. However, following the 1990 Budget this discrimination against unfranked income was removed from 1 January 1991. From that time the rate of corporation tax for all unit trusts that come within the EC rules for undertakings for collective investment in transferable securities (UCITS) has been equal to the standard rate of income tax.

Income received by authorised unit trusts complying with the provisions of the Income and Corporation Taxes Act 1988, s 468(5) Section 468(1) of the Income and Corporation Taxes Act 1988 provides that authorised unit trusts are to be treated as if the trustees were a company resident in the UK and the rights of the unitholders were shares in the company. However, if the terms of the trust deed require that the trust fund must be invested only in assets which produce income which would be taxable under Schedule C (interest on gilt-edged securities) or Case III of Schedule D (interest on deposits, debentures and loan stocks), subs (5) of s 468 provides that the general treatment under subs (1) will not apply. The effect of this is that such trusts are liable only to income tax at the basic rate. This provision, introduced in the Finance Act 1980, effectively removed the disadvantages previously suffered by unit trusts set up to invest in fixed interest securities and allowed the creation of a new range of unit trusts. On the other hand, the management expenses of such trusts cannot be set against their income for calculation of their tax liability. However, as mentioned above, as from 1 January 1991 all unit trusts that are UCITS within the EC rules have been able to do so, as well as paying corporation tax at a rate equal to the standard rate of income tax. The Finance Act 1994 contains provisions for the introduction of an asset test, for trusts that derive their income primarily from interest-bearing assets. Under these provisions trusts that have more than 60 per cent of their assests will pay corporation tax at 25 per cent, rather than the normal rate of 20 per cent. Such provisions are an attempt to equalise their treatment with that of bank and building society accounts, which are deemed to be their main competitors. The corporation tax of 25 per cent will still be recoverable in the hands of non-taxpayers.

It will be seen from the above that income accruing to a trust in the form of dividends on ordinary and preference shares in UK companies (ie franked income) was, until 1 January 1991, treated more favourably for corporation tax purposes than other forms of income. Subject to any relevant double taxation treaties, the amount of any foreign withholding tax borne by the trust in respect of income received from its overseas investments may be deducted from the corporation tax payable by the trust in respect of its income. This may prevent full set-off of ACT paid by the trust on the distribution of that income.

Capital gains

Capital gains accruing to authorised unit trusts are exempt from capital gains tax.

Taxation of the trust's shareholders

Income

The shareholder in a trust (other than an authorised unit trust established to invest wholly in UK government securities) who receives a dividend in respect of his shares will receive a tax credit for the ACT attributable to that dividend. As in **8.9.2**, the reforms to ACT proposed in the 1993 Budget have implications for shareholders in a trust. The reduction in tax credit to 20 per cent meant that non-taxpayers, who formerly received a full tax credit of 25 per cent in respect of an ACT rate of 25 per cent, suffered an income loss equivalent to the difference between 20 per cent and the net ACT rate of 22.5 per cent. A unitholder liable to income tax at the higher rate of 40 per cent whose liability to extra tax used to be 15 per cent, being the difference between the tax credit rate of 25 per cent and 40 per cent, saw that liability rise to 20 per cent, given the new tax credit rate of 20 per cent. For basic rate taxpayers the position is more complex, given that unearned income will be deemed to be liable for tax at the new 20 per cent lower band of income tax. Only basic rate payers whose unearned income exceeds £3,000 suffer an increased tax liability.

Capital gains

Capital gains made on units in authorised unit trusts or shares in approved investment trusts are treated exactly the same as gains made on any other type of security; ie the gain, after allowing for indexation, is added to the taxpayer's income for tax purposes.

For 1995/96, capital gains up to £6,000 are exempt from tax. In addition, acquisition costs for capital gains are adjusted for changes in the RPI from March 1982 or the date of purchase, if later, under the Finance Act 1982, ss 86 and 87 and the Finance Act 1985, s 68. Gains and losses accruing on the disposal of assets held on 31 March 1982 may be computed on the basis that those assets were acquired at their market value on that date. This rebasing cannot, however, increase either the amount of a gain or the amount of a loss as compared with what the gain or loss would have been under the previous capital gains tax regime.

The concessions given to trustees of settlements by the Finance Act 1978 (now contained in the Capital Gains Tax Act 1979, Sched 1) in relation to capital gains tax are more restrictive. Where the settlement was made before 7 June 1978 the trustees will not be liable to capital gains tax, if the net gains made by them in 1989/90 do not exceed £2,500. For settlements made after 6 June 1978 this limit may in certain circumstances be reduced. For certain disabled persons' trusts there is an exemption which is the same as for individuals, ie £6,000 of gains in 1995/96.

8.10 Suitability

Unit trusts are suitable for investors, large or small, whether trustees, corporations or private individuals who wish to invest in a portfolio of either general or specialist securities in the UK or overseas, but who do not wish, or are not investing sufficient sums, to run their own investments.

Because the income from and the value of all securities can fluctuate, investors should understand that unit trusts are risk investments. 'The value of the units as well as the income from them may go down as well as up' is the caveat which must appear in all unit trust advertisements and literature soliciting purchases of units issued by managers who are members of the Unit Trust Association. However, the fact that unit trusts cannot, by law, gear up and that present regulation ensures a reasonable level of diversification within the trust, considerably reduces the inherent risk of the investment.

8.11 Mechanics and maintenance

8.11.1 Mechanics

Unit trust units may be acquired through any professional adviser (stockbroker, bank, accountant, solicitor or insurance broker). Many have departments specialising in advice on the selection of unit trusts. There are also several firms which offer unit trust portfolio management and advisory services. If there is any doubt as to the suitability of unit trusts to the investor's needs, professional advice may be desirable in any case.

Alternatively, unit trusts' units may be acquired directly from the managers on either telephoned or written instructions. The disposal of units can be achieved in exactly the same way.

The names, addresses and telephone numbers of unit trust managers are given in many leading newspapers, together with a list of the current prices of the trusts they manage. All managers will supply more comprehensive information and copies of recent reports on particular trusts on request.

The Association of Unit Trusts and Investment Funds can supply a comprehensive list of members and other general information about unit trusts on request. (See end of chapter for details.)

When units are purchased, an initial charge payable to the managers is usually included in the unit price. There is no restriction on the initial charge, but the trust deed must contain a figure for the maximum permissible charge and all advertisements or literature must give details of the actual current charge. Initial charges are normally in the region of 5 per cent to 6 per cent.

Most managers pay commission to accredited agents. This is borne by the managers from the permitted initial charge.

The unitholder receives a contract note giving details of this purchase and subsequently receives a certificate showing the number of units of which he is the registered holder. Payment of the proceeds of sale is normally made by the managers within a few days of their receiving the certificate signed on the reverse by the unitholder.

8.11.2 Maintenance

Annual management fees based on the value of the trust are deducted by the managers from the income of the trust. As in the case of investment trusts, these fees are deductible from the income of the trust for tax purposes. The exception is the type of gilt or fixed interest trust made possible by the Finance Act 1980 (see **8.9.2**), in which fees can only be deducted from net income after tax. From the annual charge the managers must meet the costs of trustees' fees, audit fees, administration and investment management. The maximum permitted level of annual management fees must be laid down in the trust deed and the actual level charged set out in all advertisements and literature. If managers wish to increase the fees to a level not exceeding the maximum figure, unitholders must be given three months' notice in writing. Increases in the maximum figure must be approved by unitholders at an extraordinary meeting. Fees charged usually vary between 0.75 and 1.5 per cent per annum, although management charges for certain indexed trusts may be as low as 0.5 per cent.

Certain other costs, including agents' fees for holding investments in safe custody overseas and the cost of collecting foreign dividends, may be charged to the income of the trust. These costs are usually small in relation to the total income.

The stamp duty and brokerage on the purchase and sale of underlying investments are borne by the trust but are reflected in the pricing structure (see **8.6**).

Like any other investment, unit trust holdings should be periodically reviewed by the investor or his adviser. The investor should be able to monitor the performance of the managers by reading the half-yearly (or sometimes annual) reports which they are required to send him. These reports should contain:

(1)   a statement of the capital and income performance of the trust during the period, compared with appropriate indices;

(2)   an assessment of portfolio changes during the period or any change in investment philosophy;

(3)   the managers' view of the forthcoming period;

(4)   a list of the current investment holdings;

(5)   the figures for the income distribution; and

(6)   a ten-year capital and income record.

8.12   Unauthorised unit trusts

Unauthorised unit trusts are unit trusts which have not been authorised by the Securities and Investments Board (see **8.3**). In some circumstances, authorised status for a unit trust may, for somewhat technical reasons, carry with it certain taxation disadvantages. In particular, if an authorised unit trust (other than one established specially to invest in UK government securities) is to receive a substantial proportion of its income other than by way of distributions from companies which are tax-resident in the UK (ie in unfranked form), it will have income which is liable to corporation tax because of the rule deeming an authorised unit trust to be a company for taxation purposes. In these circumstances an authorised unit trust would have to pay corporation tax on a substantial proportion of its income, thus reducing the amount of income available for distribution to unitholders. This may be contrasted with the position where an authorised unit trust is in receipt solely of dividends from UK companies, in which case all the income which it receives will be 'franked investment income' and thus not liable to corporation tax. Accordingly, in cases where a material proportion of foreign income or other income liable to corporation tax is to be received, a unit trust may be established in unauthorised form in order to ensure that its income is liable only to ordinary income tax at the basic rate (presently 25 per cent), the payment of which is reflected in distributions to the unitholders. The treatment for income tax purposes of an unauthorised trust which receives a high proportion of its income in unfranked form will be more favourable than that of an authorised unit trust which receives a like proportion of unfranked income. But usually the advantage is small compared with the disadvantage relating to capital gains (see **8.9.2**), and it was negated, from 1 January 1991, by changes announced in the 1990 Budget (see **8.9.1**).

An unauthorised unit trust does not benefit from the capital gains tax exemption of authorised unit trusts. Capital gains tax will therefore be payable in full, putting such a trust at a disadvantage in comparison with an authorised trust so far as capital gains tax is concerned, unless the unauthorised trust is an exempt trust.

8.13 Exempt unit trusts

Exempt unit trusts are unit trusts designed for particular types of unit-holders. While many such funds exist, their rationale was destroyed by the exemption of unit trusts from tax on chargeable gains in the Finance Act 1980. Exempt unit trusts may be in authorised or unauthorised form.

8.14 Preview of the year ahead

1994 proved to be a very poor year for forecasters, the present writer included. While it proved correct to continue to be optimistic on inflation, forecasts invariably failed to foresee the large slump in bond values and the consequent impact on equities. At the present time of writing it seems clear that short-term interest rates in the UK and US have not yet peaked, and those in Germany will probably start to rise during this year, and with that rates elsewhere in Continental Europe. The Kobe earthquake in Japan has also delayed the return to economic growth in Japan to some degree. All of these factors are not totally helpful for equities, however strong profits recovery is under way and history has shown that at this point in the investment cycle markets can progress despite rising short-term interest rates, provided profits growth remains robust. At the risk of compounding last year's error, the present writer would expect equity markets to rise this year, especially as the present cautious investor sentiment contrasts sharply with the euphoria that greeted the start of 1994.

8.15 Offshore funds

The expression 'offshore fund' is applied loosely to any investment medium, whether it be a unit trust or an investment company, which is based outside the UK in one of the many tax havens around the world and which is designed to produce a common fund for investment by professional investment managers on behalf of a number of investors. Offshore funds are usually based in jurisdictions where their activities attract little or no local tax, such as the Channel Islands, the Isle of Man, the Bahamas, Bermuda, the Cayman Islands, the British Virgin Islands and Luxembourg. The exact taxation effects will depend on several factors, including where the trust is resident, where it invests, and the existence, or otherwise, of relevant double tax treaties. As a general rule, such funds do not benefit from double tax treaties on dividends received but, at the same time, no corporation tax is payable within the fund and no withholding tax imposed on distribution of income to investors. The activities of offshore funds tend, in general, not to be as strictly regulated as those of UK investment trusts and unit trusts and are regulated by local authorities. Potential investors should therefore check carefully the structure, charges and credentials of the managers of such funds before making investments.

Recently there have been cases, for example, where the very high yields being advertised on certain offshore gilt funds, were only being achieved by funds paying out of capital, with corresponding adverse implications for investors. Offshore funds may or may not be recognised by the Securities and Investments Board and contact with the management company in question or with a reliable newspaper should be able to furnish such information.

There are many different types of offshore funds, investing in different forms of assets and operating under different jurisdictions. As with unit trusts (**8.8.2**) they may be general or specialist, be invested in UK or overseas equities or fixed interest securities. They may, subject to tax or exchange controls in investors' countries of residence, be a suitable medium either for persons temporarily or permanently resident outside the UK for tax purposes, or for investors of non-UK domicile, who are resident in the UK who wish to take advantage of remittance basis taxation. Such investors will wish to ensure that their investment income and realised gains arise outside the UK's tax jurisdiction. Offshore funds may also be attractive to UK residents, especially those requiring an investment medium where distributions are paid gross, perhaps because they are non-taxpayers, but any UK residents considering investing in offshore funds should seek expert advice on taxation implications before making such an investment.

8.16   Unauthorised property unit trusts

Direct investment in property and investment in property shares is covered elsewhere in this publication. However, there are also a number of property unit trusts all of which, until recently, have been unauthorised (see **8.2**, **8.3** and **8.17**) and which were initiated to allow tax-exempt pension funds to have a stake in property with the benefits of diversification provided by a large property portfolio. The operation of an unauthorised property unit trust is free from statutory control to a similar extent to a private investor, being governed primarily by the terms of the trust deed (see **8.3**). As these unit trusts are tax-exempt funds both in terms of capital gains tax and income tax, allocation of units is limited strictly to investors in a similar exempt situation. Section 81 of the Finance Act 1980 provided that gains accruing to all authorised unit trusts, irrespective of their investors' tax status, should be exempt from capital gains tax, and thus the distinctive position of property unit trusts limited to exempt investors is no longer as important as it was before 1980.

Property unit trusts raise funds through subscription by certificate holders. The value of the units is assessed by independent valuation of the property assets within the fund, usually on a monthly basis. The annual reports and accounts normally provide extensive information on the content of the property portfolio.

8.17 Suitability

Property unit trusts are suitable for small pension funds and other tax-exempt funds seeking a stake in property but without sufficient capital to create a properly diversified direct portfolio. The main drawback in practice is the lack of flexibility in making withdrawals, particularly on a substantial scale, as these are dependent on similar subscriptions from other investors or a sale of underlying assets. However, the main advantages of these unit trusts are the wide spread of investments for an investment of relatively small sums of money and the fact that the investor can 'buy' property expertise in the form of property unit trust managers in several different trusts.

8.18 Authorised property unit trusts

Until recently, all property unit trusts were unauthorised (see **8.12** and **8.16**); however, moves were made, following both the Financial Services Act 1986 and activity by the DTI and SIB, to allow the creation of authorised property unit trusts. In December of 1990 the DTI published its latest consultative document on Authorised Property Unit Trusts and in July 1991 published the marketing rules and legal framework within which authorised property unit trusts will operate. These rules took effect from 1 August of 1991. The trusts would operate under an identical framework to other authorised unit trusts (see **8.3**) and will be open to investment from private investors and not just tax-exempt bodies such as pension funds and charities. However, given the less liquid nature of the underlying property assets, the regulations make clear that investors may not always be able to realise their units immediately, and that in such cases the managers will indeed have the right not to repurchase the investors' units. It needs also to be borne in mind that property values, unlike those of equities or bonds, are often a matter of a valuer's opinion, and that therefore greater volatility should possibly be expected from property unit trusts. Two authorised property unit trusts have been launched, both of which were re-launches of previously unauthorised property unit trusts, and at the time of writing the first authorised property unit trust to invest solely in residential property is in the process of being launched.

8.19   Other developments

The DTI has also been exploring the feasibility and desirability of warrant trusts and futures and options trusts which as the names imply will invest solely in warrants or futures and options contracts. As with authorised property unit trusts (see **8.18** above), the consultation period ended in March 1991 and the regulations for such trusts also came into operation on 1 August 1991. Given the nature of the underlying assets, investors should bear in mind that such trusts will have a higher than average risk profile, and while returns from them could be very large, such trusts should probably be used only as part of a well-diversified investment portfolio. At the time of writing, around 25 futures and options trusts and one warrant fund have been launched.

1992 saw the end of the consultation period for open ended investment companies (see also **7.12**). No such schemes are as yet operational, but if such schemes are set up it is conceivable that they could prove competitive *vis-à-vis* unit trusts.

8.20   Conclusion

After the strong returns of 1993, 1994 proved an object lesson to forecasters and investors alike that share values can fall as well as rise. The investment cycle is undeniably more mature than two or three years ago, and at some point more cautious investors may move back towards deposits. However with the market economy making ever more progress in the world, there remains the intriguing possibility, as yet unproved, that we are entering a business cycle that is longer than what we have been used to, in which steady economic growth is coupled with low inflation. The equity world has also increased, with areas, admittedly risky and volatile, available for investment that would have been unthinkable even only five years ago. The main lesson to be learnt from recent experience is that in practical terms no investor is ever able to buy at the bottom of the investment cycle; such facilities as savings plans and pound-cost averaging, as offered by the unit trust industry, therefore perform a valuable function especially for small investors. Another growing feature of equity markets is increased globalisation and speed of reaction to events; when markets turn they can do so at sufficiently high speed that again unit trusts are a most efficient vehicle for all but the most sophisticated investors. In addition, the collective nature of unit trusts means that a spread of investments can be provided to small investors which would normally be beyond their financial means, and the present writer furthermore believes that the 20 per cent rise in the number of unitholders in 1994, in a year of poor returns, bears eloquent testimony to the continued popularity and efficiency of unit trusts. This is even more true for specialist areas and emerging markets, where unit trusts can often provide exposure that would otherwise be prohibitively expensive or impossible for smaller investors to obtain. For all these reasons unit trusts can continue to represent a core element in most private investors' equity portfolios, providing an efficient route whereby investors can benefit from the resources of professional investment management.

Sources of further information

Legislation

Capital Gains Tax Act 1979
Companies Act 1985
Finance Act 1980
Finance Act 1982
Finance Act 1984
Finance Act 1985
Finance Act 1986
Finance Act 1987
Finance Act 1988
Finance Act 1989
Finance Act 1990
Finance Act 1991
Finance (No1) Act 1992
Finance (No2) Act 1992
Finance Act 1993
Finance Act 1994
Finance Act 1995
Financial Services Act 1986
Income and Corporation Taxes Act 1988
Prevention of Fraud (Investments) Act 1958

Bibliography

Unit Trusts: What Every Investor Should Know (3rd edition), Gilchrist, Woodhead-Faulkner, 1982

Unit Trusts (FT Guide series), Stopp, Financial Times Business Information

Unit Trusts and the Financial Services Act, Unit Trust Association/ Touche Ross, 1988

Various explanatory leaflets available on request from the Unit Trust Association and the Association of Investment Trust Companies

Unit Trusts: A Guide for Investors, Williams, Woodhead-Faulkner Money Guides

Useful addresses

Association of Unit Trusts and
 Investment Funds
65 Kingsway
London
WC2B 6TD

Tel: (0171) 831 0898

Association of Investment Trust
 Companies
8–13 Chiswell Street
London
EC1Y 4YY

Tel: (0171) 588 5347

Department of Trade and
 Industry
Companies Division
10–18 Victoria Street
London
SW1H 0NN

Tel: (0171) 215 5000

The Association of Corporate
 Trustees
43 Surrey Road
Bournemouth
BH4 9HR

Tel: (01202) 761112

The Securities Association
Cottons Centre
Cottons Lane
London
SE1 2QB

Tel: (0171) 378 9000

Securities and Investments Board
Gavrelle House
2–14 Bunhill Row
London
EC1Y 8RA

Tel: (0171) 638 1240

9 Real property

Geoffrey J Abbott, Dip FBA (Lon) FRICS, Head of Sales and Purchases and Investment Partner of Smiths Gore (Chartered Surveyors)

9.1 Introduction to real property

This chapter is a general introduction to the subject of real property and to Chapter 10 (dealing with residential property), Chapter 11 (on agricultural land and woods) and Chapter 12 (on commercial property). Readers should appreciate that the subjects covered are vast and complex. All matters referred to have been condensed and investors must take independent professional advice.

Real property is a legal interest in land and/or buildings of four principal types:

(1)   residential;
(2)   commercial;
(3)   farmland;
(4)   woodlands.

In the case of vacant farmland and woodland it may also include growing crops as well.

Investment in property falls into two main categories:

(1)   Direct investment: by purchase of an interest in a property.
(2)   Indirect investment: by purchase of units in property bonds and other unit linked schemes, or by the purchase of shares in a property company.

These chapters deal with direct investment.

Property is generally considered one of the most secure forms of investment as it is almost totally indestructible and immovable (it cannot be lost or stolen) and usually produces an income. However, an investment in property is complicated and a thorough understanding of all its implications is necessary to ensure optimum results are obtained from the investment selected.

Today, ownership of land and property is in many hands. The principal types of owner are:

(1)   private individuals;
(2)   trust funds;
(3)   public and private investment and trading companies;
(4)   the institutions; and
(5)   national and local government and various bodies under them.

The owner of a property, or the freeholder (superior), may have others with lesser interests in the whole or parts of his property. The owner of these lesser interests will normally be either a lessee, a tenant or a licensee (vassels/feuers) depending on the nature of their interests. There can also be third party rights over property. These may vary from a right of the general public to use a footpath for instance, or a statutory undertaking to lay a water pipe or electricity on, under or over the owner's or lessee's land, or the right of an individual to cross another person's land to gain access to his land.

An interest in property may satisfy three separate needs: enjoyment, investment and security. Enjoyment in its broadest sense might be considered as the actual use of that land, whether agricultural, a place to live, a place to manufacture, a place from which to extract minerals or a place of employment or entertainment. Enjoyment and investment are commonly combined, eg owner-occupiers of residential property rarely consider their home as an investment, although for the great majority it is the largest single investment that they will ever make.

Many forms of ownership of an interest subject to a letting do not entitle the investor to any direct enjoyment of the land but simply to participate in an agreed share of the income or produce obtained from it, usually in the form of a cash rent.

All readers must appreciate, however, that where investments are made for maximum financial gain the most important factor is timing. All markets are cyclical. Whatever the care in initial selection and subsequent management, if a purchase is made at the top of a market cycle short-term performance will inevitably be disappointing. Alternatively, almost all purchases made at the bottom of a cycle will ultimately perform well. Investment based on this strategy is known as counter cyclical.

9.2   Legal, taxation and cost factors of real property

9.2.1   Legal

The legal root of English and Welsh property law is fundamentally different from that in Scotland. Whilst legislation is commonly drafted to give similar effects, it does not always do so in practice. Historically, the main purpose of property laws and legislation was to establish ground rules by which owners, landlords and tenants should behave to each other and their neighbours. However, recent legislation to protect the wider community's interests with planning and other legislation, has tended to restrict the owner or tenant's right to do what he likes with his property. The body of law is substantial but its application to any individual property varies. An experienced property lawyer is therefore an essential member of any property investor's team.

9.2.2   Taxation

As with all forms of investment, owners of real estate are liable to pay revenue, capital gains and inheritance taxes in one way or another. The impact of these taxes on the owners of different types of property varies significantly and may determine the type of property invested in and even whether to choose property or non-property investments. Finally, business rates apply on occupation of most commercial property, and council tax on residential property.

The body of taxation law is again substantial, detailed and complex. An experienced property tax adviser should be consulted.

9.2.3   Costs

The purchase, ownership and the eventual sale of any interest in real estate will normally incur costs. When property is held for investment they will affect the net yield achieved. The level of costs will reflect the particular nature and circumstances of the property or portfolio held and will typically be in the form of acquisition, management or disposal costs.

Acquisition costs

The purchaser of any real estate should be prepared for costs of 2.5 to 3 per cent on top of the purchase price (costs associated with a lease may be substantially different). These costs are made up of 1 per cent stamp duty on properties having a value of £60,000 or more, 1 per cent for agents' fees and 0.5 per cent for solicitors' fees. There may be an additional charge on the solicitors' account for search fees and VAT is payable on both agents' and solicitors' fees. The VAT status of many forms of commercial property investment should also be checked out before an offer is made.

Investors should also consider certain other additional costs, eg a structural survey on older buildings or a planning appraisal for potential development situations. The investment may also involve a mortgage or other form of borrowing and the associated valuation and commitment fees are normally paid by the borrower/purchaser.

Finally, the purchase of vacant farmland usually also involves the purchase of growing crops and the payment of tenant right. Professional fees for the valuation and negotiation of agreement on these will normally be in the 2.5 to 5 per cent range.

Management costs

Stocks and shares are essentially a passive investment, whereas most forms of property investment call for active management. Property management costs are very variable. Over the years most property will need to be repaired, insured, altered, re-let, improved or perhaps even redeveloped. It is only by good management that the asset can maximise its rental and capital value in a changing marketplace.

Examples of typical management costs are:

(1) Fully let office on full repairing and insuring (FRI) lease — 2 to 3 per cent of gross rent.
(2) Small market town shop on standard repairing lease — 5 per cent of gross rent.
(3) Substantial arable farm on FRI lease — 7 per cent of gross rent.
(4) Complex traditional let estate — 10 per cent of gross rent.
(5) Short-term furnished residential letting — 20 per cent of gross rent.

Agents' property management fees are usually agreed at the outset, as a package to reflect the range of services needed, and paid out of rental income when received. Fees for farm and forestry management services will depend on whether the agent is merely used on a consultancy basis or is responsible for the day-to-day running of a trading business. Where a surveyor is instructed to negotiate or advise on a rent review, lease renewal or re-letting, fees range from 7.5 to 10 per cent of either the first year's rental obtained, or of the increase over the previous rent, depending on the circumstances of each case, plus VAT and expenses.

Disposal costs

The costs of selling are as variable as the types of property involved. Agents' fees vary from 1 per cent of the price achieved for a large commercial property investment, up to 2.5 per cent for a smaller residential property, with the associated solicitors' fees normally in the 0.5 to 0.75 per cent range. VAT is also payable on professional fees.

Local advertising costs at the lower end of the residential markets are normally borne by the agent. National advertising and higher quality particulars, professionally printed, are usually met by the vendor, who also carries the cost of all advertising and printing for most other forms of property sale.

An owner may wish to dispose of just part of his property interest for a certain period. This would normally be dealt with by granting a lease, tenancy or licence. Agents' fees will typically be up to 10 per cent of the first year's rent plus VAT and direct expenses, including marketing costs. Solicitors' fees will depend on whether a standard lease/agreement is used or whether a document has to be specially drafted to meet the circumstances.

9.3 Property valuation

The diversity of property types and reasons for ownership produce a wide range of approaches to property valuations. The location, accessibility and setting of a property will always influence its value.

The capital value of a vacant house is an equation of demand and supply in the relevant market at the time. Reference to sales of comparable properties is the only guide. However, a specific purchaser may pay a premium for a particular property for no better reason than that he wants to live in it.

In other sectors, such as sporting estates, the market seeks to quantify a purchaser's potential pleasure of ownership by relating value to past bag or catch records. Similarly the value of amenity woodlands is linked to the purchaser's anticipated pleasure in ownership. In commercial woodlands, however, the value is based on capitalisation of future income flows from timber sales, perhaps many decades ahead.

It is only in the markets for let properties that value is linked to the capitalisation of rent passing. Indeed in many sectors of the commercial property markets a well-let property is worth significantly more than its vacant equivalent.

In most commercial property markets the rental income is capitalised over a term of years or in perpetuity (depending on whether the property is leasehold or freehold) at an investment rate set by the market. This will reflect the risks associated with that property (security of income, obsolescence of the building, economic factors and the cost/inconvenience of management). The capitalisation rate will also reflect the expectation of future rental growth.

9.4   Role of advisers

Real property should never be acquired, sold or developed without the investor first obtaining competent professional advice. For most investors the advisers will comprise:

(1)   A chartered surveyor: for his knowledge of the relevant market, his ability to appreciate and value potential properties, his negotiating skills and finally his ability to manage the property over the years and maximise its end value.
(2)   A solicitor: with appropriate property experience to advise on legal matters generally, convey properties on purchase and sale and draw up leases and other legal documents throughout the life of the investment.
(3)   A chartered accountant/financial adviser: to advise generally on funding/sources of capital and methods of minimising the impact of revenue and capital taxes over the years.

Dependent on the nature of property investments actually made, some investors may also require the services of other advisers from time to time. They might include architects, quantity surveyors, farm and/or forestry management consultants.

10 Residential property

Geoffrey J Abbott, Dip FBA (Lon) FRICS, Head of Sales and Purchases and Investment Partner of Smiths Gore (Chartered Surveyors)

10.1 Highlights of the past few years

Since the Autumn of 1988, problems have rippled up through the tiers of the residential property market, from starter homes to luxury homes, and from the south up to the north. Values are now typically down by over 30 per cent from the peak in the summer of 1988. The downward adjustment was not an even process across the country nor in the different sectors in the market.

With the fall in interest rates and signs of economic recovery, turnover has increased significantly in London and parts of the south in particular over the last 18 months and values have stabilised at around 60 per cent of the peak levels of August 1988 with limited recovery in values in selected areas. Unfortunately perceptions of values are still too high in the minds of many potential vendors.

10.2 The alternatives

10.2.1 Personal homes

The purchase of a home is probably the largest investment which the great majority of us make without ever considering it an investment. It is the only form of property investment where capital gains are normally tax free. The owner, if he has more than one home, may elect which is his 'principal residence' and may vary this from time to time subject to notifying the Inland Revenue. A person required to reside in employer-provided accommodation may acquire a house and enjoy capital gains tax exemption on it, provided he intends in due course to live in it.

The capital gains tax exemption usually applies to a house and up to one acre of grounds, but exceptions exist above and below this amount and professional valuation advice should be sought.

In spite of the recent past, the purchase of a home has long been considered the safest and soundest form of property investment. The purchaser enjoys absolute control over his investment and may obtain tax relief at 20 per cent (and 15 per cent from the tax year 1995/96) in respect of interest on loans up to £30,000 for house purchase. Funds for purchase are traditionally obtained on mortgage from building societies and insurance companies. The major clearing banks also entered this field in 1981.

Houses are normally sold by private treaty, but investment or let houses, and increasingly mortgage repossessions, are sometimes sold by auction. Factors to consider on house purchase include:

(1)   style, location and potential planning factors;
(2)   structural condition;
(3)   availability of main services (gas, water, electricity, telephone, drainage);
(4)   the local rate of council tax.

The length and cost of journeying to work is an increasingly important factor. Unmodernised houses may be eligible for local council improvement grants.

At the end of the day, however, the most important question is whether you and your family actually wish to live in the house. First and foremost it is to be your home.

Insurance of property should usually be on the estimated cost of replacement (equivalent reinstatement cost) which may exceed the market value of the property. It should normally be index-linked to increase the sum insured in line with inflation of building costs.

10.2.2   Let houses and flats

Let houses and flats are occupied by tenants and produce a rental income. They are often referred to as 'investment' houses or flats and most postwar legislation has been viewed as favouring tenants. As a result the market shrank dramatically though recent tentative legislation to restore the market has had some effect.

Rent Acts

Most let houses and flats are covered by the Rent Acts under which the tenant has security and the rent is fixed from time to time by the rent officer (an official of the local authority) at a 'fair rent' level which is generally well below market levels. Increases set by the Rent Officer may only be phased in over a period of years.

Protected shorthold tenancies (one to five years)

Under the Housing Act 1980, protected shorthold tenancies were introduced for new lettings of more than one year but less than five years, under which the landlord can regain possession upon expiry, provided certain conditions are fulfilled. Whilst the initial rent may be agreed between the parties, the tenant may apply to have the rent fixed by the rent officer at any time.

Assured and assured shorthold tenancies

These were introduced under the Housing Act 1988 for new lettings after 15 January 1989 at market rents, subject to a right of appeal to the Rent Assessment Committee who will look to comparable market lettings in the area. Both give the landlord greater rights to possession at the end of the term, but in the case of assured shorthold tenancies the landlord or his successors have the right to a court order for possession.

Corporate tenants

Corporate tenants are excluded from the security of tenure provisions of all the Acts, though tenancies predating 15 January 1989 are subject to the rent officer's assessment of a fair rent. Care must be taken to ensure that all sublettings to company employees are genuine, as 'sham' arrangements may result in a secure sub-tenancy.

Long leasehold houses (over 21 years)

Houses let on long leases were very common, particularly in the major cities. Under the Leasehold Reform Act 1967 the lessees of the majority were granted the right to enfranchise or purchase their freeholds.

Under the Leasehold Reform, Housing and Urban Development Act 1993 these rights of enfranchisement, subject to a number of conditions and exceptions, were extended to higher value leaseholders previously excluded from the 1967 Act.

General

In the case of old regulated tenancies, a 100 per cent or more increase in capital value can be released if vacant possession is gained.

Let houses and flats are considered a safe and secure form of investment if the location is selected carefully, management standards are high, and the investor understands the nature of the tenancy. Subject to the inevitable political risk of socialist legislation reversing the more favourable 1980s legislation, let houses and flats are now worthy of consideration.

10.2.3 Blocks of flats

The investment considerations in respect of blocks of flats are similar to those for let houses and flats. However, the market in blocks of flats has tended to be determined by their 'break-up' value rather than by the income produced. This break-up value arises through an investor being able to acquire a complete block of flats at a figure which will enable him subsequently to dispose of the flats either to the occupying tenants or with vacant possession, if obtained, and so realise an overall capital gain.

In the late 1980s the competition for blocks of flats having a break-up value was dramatic. However, it is a high risk form of investment, as there is no guarantee of obtaining vacant possession, having regard to the high degree of security of tenure enjoyed by most tenants. Recently tenants have formed their own associations to try to control their landlords' operations, and the political risks and social problems for an investor operating in this market are considerable.

The situation is confused by the fact that tenants of flats were granted, amongst other things, under the Landlord and Tenant Act 1987, a right of first refusal if the landlord decided to sell his interest.

Further, the Leasehold Reform, Housing and Urban Development Act 1993 gave tenants, subject to complex rules and criteria, the right to initiate either the purchase of the freehold of their block of flats or an extension of their leases.

10.2.4 Holiday homes and time sharing

With increasing leisure time, the demand for holiday homes in the UK (which vary from a site on which to park a caravan to a substantial secondary house) has increased very considerably. The value of these properties is very much related to the personal choice of the purchaser, who is greatly affected by the ease of access to and from the major conurbations and the environment when he gets there. Lettings of these properties for holiday purposes are exempt from Rent Act protection. They can be good investments, with the added advantage that they can provide holiday accommodation for the family as well.

Holiday homes may also be purchased abroad. Specialist advice needs to be taken with regard to such matters as local exchange control, the mechanics of purchase and availability of services. Good agents and lawyers are even more essential abroad than in the UK.

Partly as a result of this, a new concept of property ownership known as 'time sharing' has become popular. In essence, this provides for the investor to acquire an interest for a stated period (a week or a month) in each year in perpetuity or for a period of years. It effectively widens the spectrum of investment to encompass the smaller investor who can secure holiday accommodation with the added potential of capital growth.

It is sometimes associated with questionable sales techniques and even fraud, but it is an interesting concept for those who have limited funds which would otherwise be insufficient to purchase a holiday home. If the owner does not wish to use the accommodation each year, the property can often be exchanged if the location is in a major resort.

The method of sale varies according to the country, some properties being sold freehold and others on long leaseholds. An annual service payment is payable by the owner, together with the cost of electricity, water and other services used during a vacation. There are a number of companies specialising in this market who advertise nationally.

Holiday homes can be a sound investment but location is critical. If abroad, there are many possible pitfalls, not the least of which can be guaranteeing sound title.

10.3   Preview of the year ahead

Turnover started to pick up again in a few selected areas about two years ago. At the present stage of the cycle generalisations are dangerous as some areas and/or sectors of the market are still dormant whereas others have seen sufficient turnover for long enough for values to be rising modestly again.

Otherwise in the year ahead we will see turnover picking up in wider areas with further growth in values in areas of strongest activity — with the South generally benefiting more than the North and Scotland.

11 Agricultural land, woodlands and miscellaneous

Geoffrey J Abbott, Dip FBA (Lon) FRICS, Head of Sales and Purchases and Investment Partner of Smiths Gore (Chartered Surveyors)

11.1 Introduction

The last 15 years have been a period of dramatic change for the land using industries, in perceptions of desirable land uses generally and in the pressures on rural land of our predominantly urban population. Since 1939, pressure to increase self-sufficiency in both agricultural and forest products had led to significant changes in crop and livestock selection/husbandry and the rapid incorporation of modern technology into the rural industries.

During the 1980s, the Green lobby and 'conservation interests' became increasingly significant, overlaid by international concerns such as damage to the ozone layer and the long-term effects of clearance of the tropical rainforests. The issues underlying these pressures for change are complex yet, because the great mass of our urban population has little direct contact with the countryside, the problems in the countryside are often seen in oversimplistic terms and the positions taken up can be illogical and/or inconsistent.

Further, few have yet acknowledged that the achievement of these desirable objectives will ultimately have a dramatic effect on the life-styles and work practices of our urban populations. The majority of gasses which attack the ozone layer and cause acid rain emanate from urban chimneys, heating systems and exhaust pipes. Similarly much of the pollution in our rivers is the result of discharges from urban factories and sewage works.

The countryside is about diversity. An investment primarily in one form of land use will often directly or indirectly involve other land uses as well. Houses and woods are an integral part of farmland and all often overlay mineral deposits and are the natural habitat of the sportsman's quarry.

Throughout this chapter we seek to indicate typical cash yields on the various forms of land use but obviously many of the benefits of owning country property, which influence its value, do not come in the form of annual income.

Many purchasers of a vacant farm also get a nice house to live in and perhaps an interesting shoot as well; development possibilities (whether in the form of houses, golf courses or mineral workings) or favourable capital or inheritance tax treatment in the future earn no income today; the surrender of the tenancy of a house or farm in due course can release significant latent capital value; and the mere ownership of a certain stretch of countryside can give the owner great personal satisfaction.

It is these factors and the post-war investment track record of country property which explain the historically relatively low initial yield typically earned on most forms of investment in land.

As we run up to the 1996 review of the Common Agricultural Policy in Europe, the perception is that there will be little direct impact on farming profitability though, increasingly, support is swinging from production to conservation objectives.

11.2   Agricultural land

11.2.1   Background

Usable agricultural land in Great Britain totals approximately 45,000,000 acres of which about 66 per cent is owner/occupied or vacant, and 33 per cent is subject to tenancy. They form two very separate markets with significant valuation and yield differences for otherwise physically similar properties. Within these overall totals there is an enormous diversity of soil types, topography, climate and physical location to which individual farmers apply their financial resources and technical/managerial skills. The result is the diverse range of land uses and end products still found in the countryside today.

Investors are strongly recommended initially to quietly reflect on Table 11.1 (see p 180). Whatever the financial resources and skills he has to bring to bear on the property he buys, its many physical and climatic characteristics will rule the uses to which it is suited. Field scale bulb growing is only economic on the better soils and hardwood trees simply will not survive on solid rock at high altitudes. Finally, a good livestock farmer is seldom a good arable farmer and *vice versa*.

Within both the vacant and let (often referred to as 'investment') land markets there are therefore many sub-markets within which properties suited to different principal agricultural uses are grouped.

Investors should also appreciate that a farmer runs a business. Like any other business, the actual financial results on any individual farm, however well the farming system is suited to the property, will reflect his managerial/technical skills and commercial judgements. As reflected in the rental market, the profit potential of a good farm is significantly greater than a poor farm. However, managerial skills on the individual farm remain critical to that unit's actual profitability. There are plenty of examples of poor farmers on the best land going out of business and good farmers on the poorest land making good money.

All investors should make a firm policy of sitting down with their advisers regularly to review whether this property or that one should still be owned or sold or perhaps passed down to the next generation. As part of these regular reviews, the potential of all land for higher value alternative uses should also be considered together with actions which might help to ensure its eventual release.

Could that droughty field cover potentially valuable gravel deposits, or might the field by the village be developed in 20 years' time? If the answer is yes, consideration should then be given as to whether you will need that money in due course or whether it would make more sense to pass the land down to the next generation at purely agricultural value. Finally, a well-screened site is more likely to receive planning consent in due course than a prominent one out in the open. Should a belt of trees be planted now?

11.2.2 Highlights of the previous year

The farmland markets have experienced a strong recovery in demand at a time of very limited supply. The result has been a further strong recovery in values by between 20 to 30 per cent with the previously unfashionable best quality soils (Grade I and II) benefiting particularly from improved potato prices. The Mormon Church in particular bought two large port-folios of commercial vacant farms in East Anglia.

Gross yields on let land have fallen by a further 0.5 per cent over the year and typically now lie around 5 per cent.

Demand for residential estates has also shown similar strength, though the importance of a balanced property has been well demonstrated.

11.2.3 Vacant possession land

As vacant farmland represents over two-thirds of all farmland in Great Britain it is obviously the principal land market. By definition it is free-hold land offered for sale with vacant possession or available for the purchaser to physically occupy. Over the years between 1 per cent and 2 per cent is offered for sale on average each year in packages from five acres

Table 11.1   Approximate distribution of soil grades and land uses

Soil Grade	England Percentage	England Acres 000s	Wales Percentage	Wales Acres 000s	Scotland Percentage	Scotland Acres 000s	Great Britain Percentage	Great Britain Acres 000s	Principal Farming/Forestry Uses	Principal Alternative Uses
I	3.3	806	0.2	8	0.3	49	1.9	863	Intensive arable cropping eg bulbs, vegetables, roots & cereals. No forestry.	Coarse fishing in drainage channels and lowly valued pheasant shooting.
II	16.7	4,083	2.3	96	2.3	383	10.2	4,562	Arable cropping/intensive grassland eg cereals with roots and/or dairy cows. Limited forestry.	Principally 'dull' flatland but greater potential on poorer Grade II land out of Fens and similar areas
III	54.0	13,203	17.5	729	13.6	2,175	36.1	16,107	Extensive arable cropping, rotational grassland eg cereals, oilseed rape & beans or grass leys for dairy cows, beef, sheep. Hardwood forestry mainly.	Pheasant/partridge shooting/roe deer stalking. Game fishing if suitable rivers/streams. Limited B&B, pony trekking etc.
IV	15.7	3,838	44.2	1,842	10.2	1,631	16.4	7,311	Permanent grassland/rough grazing eg beef and sheep rearing with limited dairying & cereals. Commercial softwood forestry.	Grouse shooting. Red deer stalking on open hill. Roe deer stalking in softwood plantations. Game fishing where suitable water.
V	10.3	2,518	35.8	1,491	73.5	11,775	35.4	15,784	Rough grazings often with rock outcrops, eg principally summer grazing with hardy sheep breeds & hill cattle. Limited softwood forestry.	Extensive B&B, pony trekking, hill walking, rock climbing etc.
TOTAL	100	24,448	100	4,166	100	16,013	100	44,627		

of bareland to 5,000 acres fully equipped with houses and buildings. However, offerings in recent years have been well below both their historic levels and demand.

The principal buyers of most commercial farmland are normally farmers who buy the land to farm, though many others buy from time to time for various reasons. The market for particularly attractive stretches of countryside with high quality houses or for Scottish sporting estates is dominated by the wealthy, and in some cases the international wealthy, for reasons unlinked to the income which they may be able to earn from ownership of the property. In the case of land overlying potentially valuable minerals or which may be developed over in the future, the more imaginative investors or mineral operators and developers will normally compete to purchase.

Vacant possession land has been a very satisfactory investment since the Second World War, but values have fluctuated over the years and timing, as in all investment, has been a major factor for the most successful.

Given the diversity of the markets and understandable regional variations over time, reliable statistics about past land value trends are very difficult — and potentially dangerous if used for short-term comparisons. Indeed, the continuing fall shown for 1994 totally contradicts the experience of the market generally. The only series which stretches back over the whole of the post-war period is the Oxford Institute/Savills series but it is based on averaging vacant land sales *at auction* reported in the *Farmer's Weekly*. It can therefore make no allowance for properties withdrawn 'in the room' and subsequently sold privately. It remains, however, the best guide to value trends over time and is set out in Table 11.2 on p 182.

When selecting in which part of the country to buy, the private investor is understandably usually influenced by his background. As a general rule, investors in straight farmland should seek to acquire the best land in the chosen area, because history shows that given a competent level of farm management, the best land generates the greatest profits over the years.

Further, outside of the wholly commercial areas of farming such as the Fens, farmland with an attractive appearance has always tended to sell for a premium value. As conservation considerations become increasingly influential, the land markets are reflecting the conservation value of otherwise well-farmed land. Enhancing the wildlife value of a property, by well-planned hardwood tree planting, pond maintenance and sensitive

Table 11.2   Average vacant land values at auction

With Possession £/acre		With Possession £/acre	
1951	88	73	757
52	76	74	636
53	73	75	539
54	75	76	734
55	80	77	991
56	78	78	1,327
57	73	79	1,769
58	85	1980	1,726
59	101	81	1,729
1960	123	82	1,844
61	124	83	2,082
62	134	84	1,978
63	168	85	1,935
64	214	86	1,697
65	235	87	2,001
66	242	88	2,178
67	258	89	2,654
68	280	1990	2,568
69	299	91	2,431
1970	245	92	2,202
71	262	93	2,208
72	596	94	2,035

management of ancient pastures, should be an on-going management consideration of all investors. In recent years an increasing level of grants and subsidies has been available for such conservation policies.

CAP reform has also established the form of agricultural support for the future — away from encouraging ever increasing output per acre and towards fixed payments per acre cropped or breeding livestock maintained, with 12 per cent or more of arable land being put to set aside.

Remembering what was said earlier about the importance of management to the actual financial results (see **11.2.1**), and that some of the benefits of owning vacant farmland do not come in the form of cash income, the monetary benefits may be expected typically to work out as shown in Table 11.3 opposite, for a well run unit.

These overall yields, being an amalgam of the secure return to the investor as landowner (in the form of rental value of around 50 per cent of the net profit) and the higher risk return to him as a trading farmer,

Table 11.3 Monetary benefits of farm ownership

	Intensive Arable	Extensive Arable	Dairy (inc. Quota)	Livestock Rearing	Hill Farming (inc. Sheep Quota)
Land Value, say	£2,250	£1,750	£1,500	£1,200	£700
Working Capital, say	500	400	3,000	600	300
TOTAL CAPITAL	£2,750	£2,150	£4,500	£1,800	£1,000
Net Profit, say (inc. rental value)	£150	£130	£200	£60	£25
Annual Return, say	5.45%	6.05%	4.44%	3.30%	2.25%

Source: *Smiths Gore Farm Management*

reflect the fact that farming is passing through a difficult phase. Also the vacant value of the farm is typically 200 per cent of its let land value.

There are many options open to the investor for the management of his vacant farm or land and he should take professional advice. He may manage his farm personally, or farm in partnership with another farmer, or he may have a contractual or profit-sharing arrangement with another farmer. The method will depend on the investor's income requirement, managerial ability and capital situation. The choice will affect the amount of farming capital required, the level of return obtained, and the extent of involvement in the day-to-day running of the investment.

When structuring management by a partnership or contractual arrangement, special care is needed so as not to convert vacant possession land into tenanted land, thereby losing the premium (which currently can be around 50 per cent of vacant value).

'Intensive livestock' is a specialist form of farming and is restricted mainly to pigs, poultry (chickens and turkeys), veal, barley, beef and salmon or trout. These enterprises are usually capital-intensive in buildings and equipment and are restricted to small acreages (two to 20 acres). The investment can be speculative and the return is very dependent on expert management in a volatile market.

11.2.4 Let or investment land

'Let' or 'investment' land comprises about 33 per cent of the total usable agricultural acreage of Great Britain, having declined from around 90 per cent at the turn of the century. The land is let to a tenant who pays a rent and the investor may therefore not be able to live on the property or to farm it himself.

Traditionally, let land was worth two-thirds or more of its value with vacant possession. However, in the post-war period, legislation affecting the landlord/tenant relationship was seen as favouring the latter, and taxation policy has tended to favour the owner-occupier. As a result, let land is now generally worth nearer half of its vacant value.

From September all new lettings of farms (not being succession tenancies under the old Agricultural Holdings Act) will be in the form of Farm Business Tenancies covered by the new Act which passed through both Houses of Parliament last winter and spring. Subject to the length of the tenancy granted, the value differential between vacant and let land should be less.

However, as this new legislation will have little initial impact, this chapter deals with existing agricultural investments let under the old agricultural holdings legislation.

Investment opportunities vary from single let farms to large residential estates; from 10 acres up to 5,000 acres or more.

Agricultural land is usually let on what are technically annual tenancies but which actually give security for life, indeed often with rights of succession, subject to certain rules, for up to three generations. However, an interesting recent court case (*Saunders v Ralph*) suggests that the succession rights under the 1976 Act may be retrospective. Let farms which have passed down through the family for a number of generations may therefore have no succession rights attaching to them.

Because of the security of tenure provisions of the past Agricultural Holdings Acts, landlords have tended, whenever land has come in hand, to enter into various management and contract farming arrangements for the future to avoid the Agricultural Holdings Acts and preserve their vacant possessions premiums.

Leases for terms of years revert on expiry to annual tenancies unless the parties agree otherwise. Lettings are mainly the subject of written agreements but otherwise are governed by the Agricultural Holdings Act 1986.

The tenancy agreement must be examined by a professional adviser, since it forms the basis for all matters affecting the investment in the future. Tenancy agreements vary but the most important clauses are:

(1)   a prohibition against sub-letting and assignment;
(2)   the allocation of the repairing and insurance liability;
(3)   a requirement for the tenant to occupy the farmhouse; and
(4)   the right to recover possession for the use of some or all of the land for non-agricultural purposes at less than one year's notice.

Rent is customarily paid half-yearly in arrears, but newer agreements may require it to be paid quarterly in advance. Either the landlord or the tenant may initiate a rent review each three years to a definition of rental value outlined in the Acts.

Rent levels vary. Rents fixed under the Acts may be 40 to 50 per cent below the rents obtainable from those rare vacant farms offered for letting on the open market by tender. Examples of sitting tenant rents per acre compared to tendered rents might be:

(1)   for well-equipped Grade I or II soil arable farms in the Fens: £70 as opposed to £100 or more;
(2)   for well-equipped Grade II or III soil arable farms (not Fens) and well-equipped dairy farms; £50 as opposed to up to £100; and
(3)   for poorer land or poorly equipped farms: £35 as opposed to £50.

Under most older tenancy agreements the landlord is responsible for insuring and for a major part of the cost of repairs to the houses and buildings though full repairing and insuring tenancies are now common for new lettings.

Most let land is owned by private families as part of substantial estates passed down through the generations or is held by traditional institutions such as the Crown, the Church and numerous colleges and charities, most of whom buy for the long term.

Tenanted land may be one-third of the total stock of farmland in Great Britain but, because of this ownership pattern, only represents a very small part of the total farmland market each year. Supply to the market obviously varies but last year only 20,000 acres passed through the open market. This is only about a third of what was typical in the 1970s.

Currently, buyers of let farms are a broadly based group comprising tenants buying in their farms, private investors, family trusts, certain charities and both traditional and a few financial institutions. Management is customarily undertaken by professional firms of chartered surveyors, with land agency departments, or by resident agents on larger estates.

Investors should be aware that there is no fixed relationship between gross and net yields. A typical gross yield today of 5.5 per cent might net back on a full repairing and insuring let farm to 4.5 per cent whereas on a traditional landlord repairing and insuring let estate it might be under 3 per cent in the short term. However, that let estate may well have latent potential to be released by active management which may compensate for the lower initial net yield. Each investment opportunity must be viewed on its own merits.

11.2.5   Finance

The basic rule for the investor in farmland is that he should have the majority of the funds available in cash. Except in special circumstances farmland investments should not be made on the back of borrowed money. The gross initial return to a typical investment in a let farm is currently only 5 to 6 per cent. Investment in a similar vacant farm is typically twice as high so the return to his investment in land (being the rental value of that land) is currently 2 to 3 per cent. A significant proportion of the purchase price therefore borrowed at say 7.5 per cent cannot be funded by the farm.

Within the agricultural industry, facilities for short-term borrowings of working capital are commonly provided by the clearing banks. Merchants' credit can also be taken but, when allowance is made for the discounts which may be lost, it can prove very expensive. Medium-term finance for machinery purchases, etc may also be provided by the clearing banks and various finance/leasing houses.

Long-term finance to the industry has traditionally been provided by the Agricultural Mortgage Corporation and the Scottish Agricultural Securities Corporation with the main clearing banks participating more recently. Subject to the borrower's ability to service the loan, up to two-thirds of the agricultural value of a farm can usually be borrowed at competitive rates which may be variable or fixed and be for up to 40 years. Interest is normally tax allowable and repayment of principal is commonly by way of linked life policies.

11.2.6   Preview of the year ahead

Many questions overhang the agricultural industry but over the last couple of years interest rates have fallen, short-term farming profitability is far better than expected and one effect of set aside has been to encourage farmers back into the market to buy additional land.

As demand considerably exceeds supply, vacant land values generally can only rise further.

Currently there is a particular shortage of quality residential estates, Scottish sporting estates and agricultural investments.

11.3 Woodlands

11.3.1 Background

Woodlands cover just over 5 million acres or about 10 per cent of the surface area of Great Britain. This compares with between 20 to 30 per cent in most EU countries. Ninety per cent of UK timber consumption is imported, at a cost of £7.2bn in 1990. Annual timber production in Great Britain grew from about 3.5 million cubic metres in 1980 to 5.35 million cubic metres at the end of the decade. It is forecast to grow to 10 million cubic metres by around 2000. However, consumption is also expected to rise over the period.

Of the national forest, some 25 per cent is made up of hardwoods (often also referred to as deciduous woodlands) and 75 per cent is made up of softwoods (often also referred to as coniferous or evergreen — though beware of the deciduous larch!). Woodlands and forests take three principal forms.

Amenity and sporting woods and copses

These are normally found in lowland Great Britain in the form of hardwoods or mixtures. They are usually relatively small and can be politically sensitive locally, often being covered by Tree Preservation Orders. Whilst individual trees may be substantial and of significant value, these woods have little to do with commercial timber production. However, they can provide great enjoyment and satisfaction to the buyer.

Larger blocks of hardwoods

Typically found in lowland Britain, they can have a significant value but day-to-day management is often influenced by sporting and conservation considerations. Originally they formed parts of larger estates and can prove a very worthwile investment.

Commercial softwood plantations and forests

These are commonly found in the higher rainfall areas of the country, principally in the hills of Wales, the north of England and Scotland, with other pockets such as the Breckland Sands around Thetford on the Norfolk/Suffolk borders and the New Forest in Hampshire. Being based on fast-growing trees well suited to both the pulp industry and the sawwood market they are the backbone of commercial forestry.

Conifers grow in western Britain almost twice as fast as in Scandinavia, Russia and most of North America, thus providing shorter rotations and a long-term competitive advantage.

Of the national forest approximately 40 per cent is owned by the Forestry Commission and 60 per cent by private investors/estates. The Forestry Commission was established in 1919 to encourage private owners to restore the productivity of their 3 million acres of woodland ravaged by fellings during the First World War and to create a State Forest of 1.75 million acres. The Commission's current estate is just over 2 million acres and principally made up of softwoods. As part of the wider privatisation programme, the Forestry Commission has had a target of selling 250,000 acres, or just over 10 per cent of its forestry portfolio by the end of the decade. A recent review of the Forest Enterprise part of the Forestry Commission came out against the wholesale privatisation of the Commission's owned forests. However a continuation of the existing selective sales programme seems inevitable.

Whilst the privately owned forest is more balanced overall between hardwoods and softwoods, the former tends to be owned by farmers and estate owners in lowland Britain. Much of the latter is in the hills having often been established by investors during the 1960s, 1970s and 1980s, with substantial incomes from other sources motivated by tax planning considerations available at the time.

Forestry planting still attracts substantial grants though forestry costs can no longer be offset against other income. The ownership of woods still has other valuable advantages:

(1) income from productive woodlands is tax free;
(2) assets comprising forestry business qualify for 100 per cent relief from inheritance tax after two years' ownership;
(3) the land element can attract capital gains tax rollover relief.

Investment in woodlands is essentially about investing in relatively low value land with a growing crop on it with a rotation life which may typically range from 40 years for some fast-growing conifers to 100 or 200 years for slower growing hardwoods. Normally, the first 20 years or more are about outgoings to establish the crop and manage it through to production age. From the commencement of thinnings, income may be expected to pick up from humble beginnings every five years for softwoods and ten years for hardwoods through to the bulk of the income from the felling of the final crop. A softwood crop planted today may be expected to show an internal rate of return of around 5 per cent per annum over the life of the crop.

Alternatively an investor may acquire an established plantation already in production and obtain a tax-free income. Such a wood would typically be valued on the basis of a discounting of the expected net income stream in the 5 per cent to 7 per cent range.

The underlying economic argument for investing in forestry is that the world has been consuming its forests at well in excess of sustainable growth rates for many decades. A significant shortfall of timber is therefore likely in the future. However, as much of the world's timber reserves are in the Third World, which is primarily concerned with short-term survival, the supply of timber on to the world markets may continue at in excess of growth rates. Conservationists were able to halt felling over a large area of the US in 1992 to protect the habitat of the Spotted Owl. This directly affected the supply and price of timber in 1992/93.

11.3.2   Market trends

Demand for attractive amenity woods and established commercial woodlands with a positive cash flow remains strong. The value of the former is currently underwritten by various conservation bodies and the attractions of a tax-free income from the latter are likely to increase over the years.

The market for bareland in the hills with forestry approval, once worth up to three times its alternative hill grazing land value, died with the 1988 Budget statement. There are signs that the introduction of the Beef/Sheep Livestock Quota (under the CAP reform package), grants under the Farm Woodland Premium Scheme and Better Land Supplement Payments may be starting to encourage the planting of lowland livestock rearing farms valued in the £400 to £700 per acre range.

Generally, demand for young softwood plantations many years off economic production remains uncertain but demand is showing signs of recovery.

11.4   Miscellaneous land uses

11.4.1   Accommodation land

Accommodation land refers to small areas within a farm or estate which do not naturally fit in with the main land uses. They are often held for alternative use at a later date or as grazing land for conservation purposes (for instance a small area of permanent grassland). The expression can also be taken to mean those small areas of farmland which come up for sale from time to time, typically on the edge of a village or town.

Because of the limited acreage, accommodation land often appeals to the smaller investor with limited funds available, although it is usually more expensive to buy per acre than normal farmland. For the investor prepared to take on the problems of management and supervision they can sometimes generate a significant income from pony grazing. A portfolio of such units can give outstanding performance over the years if planning consent for an alternative high value use (eg residential development) is granted on one or more areas of accommodation land.

Accommodation land with vacant possession is sometimes held unused, but more often let on short-term arrangements outside the security of tenure provisions of the Agricultural Holdings Acts. Professional advice should always be taken over such arrangements as they can all too easily become secure agricultural tenancies.

The principal forms of short-term lettings are:

Grassland

Grazing lettings or grass keep sales are licences for a fixed period of less than one year (and normally from April to October).

(1)   They do not give exclusive possession of the land.
(2)   The grazier's rights are limited to the crop only, either to be grazed by specified categories of stock or mowing for hay or silage.
(3)   The grazier's stock must always be removed from the land at the end of the season.
(4)   There must be no 'understanding' that he will necessarily be granted the grazing in the following year.
(5)   He must be obliged to do nothing whilst in occupation which might imply a continuing interest (eg make any permanent repairs to fences or dig out ditches etc).

Lettings each year may be by private arrangement, by tender or by public auction. 'Rents' achieved for well managed grassland are typically at around 150 per cent of a normal agricultural rental.

Grazing for ponies and horses is normally done on a per head per week payment basis and often generates a premium income. Horses are however choosy grazers and pasture deterioration usually results from horse grazing over the years.

On specialist dairy/beef farms, other people's sheep are often bought in 'on tack' during the winter months to tidy up the pastures. Payment is usually on a per head per week basis.

Arable land

On suitable arable farming soils in areas such as the Fens it is common practice for growers of specialist crops such as carrots to be brought in to take a crop on a licence basis for the appropriate year in the rotation. More normally, short-term lettings of arable land have been dealt with by means of *Gladstone v Bower* arrangements (for more than one year but less than two years) or Ministry Approved Lettings for up to five years. Cereal growing land let in the open market under such arrangements commonly realised rents of around £100 per acre.

11.4.2   Sporting rights

Sporting rights normally form an integral part of any land sale. Over most properties they form a minor element of capital value within the overall transaction. However, on Scottish sporting estates they are often the main constituent of value, assessed by past records of the bag or catch. In such cases ease of access will be a significant factor.

Sporting rights may be divided into three main categories:

(1)   fishing — game and coarse;
(2)   shooting — driven and rough;
(3)   stalking — red and roe deer.

Sporting rights in England and Wales can be a legal estate and are on occasions reserved out of the sale of agricultural land and woods. In Scotland, only salmon fishing rights can form a separate legal estate. They may therefore be acquired separately from the land for personal use or letting, and timesharing of stretches of well-known fishing rivers has become common. Since 1 April 1989 VAT is payable on that element of the value of a land sale which relates to the value of the sporting facility. A transaction will normally only become taxable where a sporting income or value is separately identifiable. There is a further concession that farm tenants will only be expected to pay VAT on the sporting element of their tenancy agreements if it is greater than 5 per cent of total rent.

The recent recession hit demand for sporting rights and values but both are now recovering.

Fishing

Salmon fishing

Capital values of salmon fishing vary enormously according to location and river reputation but can range up to £6,000 a fish or more. Rents can range from £50 to £500 per rod per day. Pollution and salmon disease can have a devastating effect on both rental and capital values. Salmon fisheries cannot be created artificially, and are principally associated with rivers in Scotland and parts of Wales and the West Country.

Trout fishing

This can be on freshwater chalk streams in the south (which command the highest rates and prices), on other rivers generally or on artificial or natural lakes or reservoirs. Demand has been high with rents almost matching salmon river rates on the very best chalk streams. There is evidence of some over-supply of man-made trout lakes in certain areas.

Coarse fishing

Coarse fishing normally occurs in standing or slower-flowing waters in middle England & East Anglia which are usually rented by angling associations or smaller syndicates. Prices and rents vary greatly but old ponds may provide a surprisingly large income close to large centres of population.

Shooting

Shooting rights are, subject to the declining recession, readily lettable to a growing number of field sports enthusiasts. Shoots vary from a well-organised grouse moor in Scotland or the north with accommodation, through to substantial pheasant or partridge shoots in the south or east, perhaps let by the day with beaters and a cordon bleu lunch, down to a rough shoot over a small farm enjoyed informally by friends. Sporting rents vary from significant sums on the very best shoots to a minor additional income to the farm of £1 or £2 per acre. Charges for the best pheasant shoots, mainly in the south, lie in the £17.50 to £25 per bird range with the best grouse moors in the north and Scotland ranging up to £15 per brace after two disastrous breeding seasons.

Deer stalking

Red, Fallow, Roe and Muntjac deer are the quarry, though Red and Roe deer are the principal species. In the UK, Red deer stalking on the open heather hills of the Highlands of Scotland is the most well-known and the most highly valued at a cost of up to £250 per stag. Roe deer stalking is traditionally more highly valued on mainland Europe but commercial lettings in suitable locations are becoming increasingly popular in the UK at between £100 and £200 per buck.

The build up of Roe deer numbers throughout the woods of Great Britain has resulted in professional stalkers shooting from high seats for vermin control purposes and the value of the carcasses. Red deer are also controlled in this way in the Thetford Forest in East Anglia. However, in the south west Red deer, and in the New Forest Fallow deer, are more commonly controlled by hunting with hounds.

Sporting generally

Sound game, vermin and habitat management practices can enhance the holding capacity and sporting qualities of a property but they cannot change the nature of it. For instance, grouse will only survive, let alone thrive, on a well-managed heather moor in the hills of the north or Scotland which benefits from peace and quiet.

Corporate entertaining has increasingly influenced rental levels on the best sporting estates over the last 20 years but the quality of service they demand is also high. Commercial lettings of sporting rights are seldom therefore profitable in their own right but more a means of subsidising the owner's hobby.

Quality sporting rights as a separate investment is normally only for the very wealthy investor who can afford an often substantial capital payment, perhaps millions of pounds, with the prospect of significant annual outgoings. The less wealthy must therefore limit their ambitions to more humble rough shooting, a gun on a syndicate shoot or the purchase of a time share on a suitable river. For most investors, sporting rights will be an indirect benefit of the purchase of a farm, wood or estate.

Market trends

With increasing wealth, leisure time and transport facilities, demand for sporting rights has been increasing steadily. Capital performance has generally been very satisfactory with the market for the very best becoming international. However, they are about enjoying expensive hobbies and the recent recession had affected demand both to buy and rent sporting facilities though most sporting lettings found tenants again last year.

11.4.3   Stud farms and training establishments

Stud farms

Agricultural land may be developed for the breeding of thoroughbred bloodstock, riding horses or ponies. The demand has been increasing with over two million people now members of the various horse societies. For stud farms in the most favoured locations, such as Newmarket, Lambourn and Malton, demand remains relatively strong, although values have fallen and demand has slumped in locations further from the recognised breeding centres where the main stallions stand. The centre of the national bloodstock industry is Newmarket where the National Stud and Tattersalls Sale Paddocks, which have a worldwide reputation, are both based. Stud farms in the favoured areas command a substantial premium over VP farmland.

The environment of a good stud farm is of great importance if the young stock are to grow and develop properly. The type of soil, particularly to facilitate the building of bone, is critical and the best are to be found on free draining chalk soils. A stud farm typically varies in size from 50 to 250 acres and may be a private stud (where the owner maintains his own animals only) or a public stud (where one or more stallions are kept and the mares visit during the covering season and often the foaling season as well). Stables must be of high standard with special boxes and facilities for covering and foaling purposes. The cost of putting up post and rail fencing is high because of the need for small paddocks and double fences.

To establish a stud farm can take up to 20 years for the hedges and shelter belts to mature. Good quality residential accommodation at the stud will be required for the stud groom and other employees: for a medium-sized stud a minimum of five to six houses might be required.

Stud farms usually change hands by private treaty in a limited and highly specialised market. Purchasers will usually be closely connected with the bloodstock industry. It is exceptional for stud farms to be bought as an investment on a tenanted basis.

Training establishments or yards

At various centres in the country, but particularly at Newmarket, Lambourn and Malton, there are established training facilities with extensive gallops and all weather tracks. Training yards usually comprise a trainer's house together with a number of cottages and hostels for stable lads; a minimum of 15 boxes with tack, feed and hay stores; and often special open and covered exercising areas. Business rates are payable on both stud farms and training yards.

Market trends

The specialised markets for both stud farms and training yards had been expanding throughout most of the 1980s with the best being in a truly international market.

However, the recent recession hit the racing industry hard. Most owners of studs are men of substantial wealth who weathered the troubles.

Many owners of training yards, however, increased their facilities during the late 1980s. Values fell significantly, although demand is now recovering.

11.4.4 Mineral bearing land

All minerals other than oil, gold, silver and coal usually belong to the freehold owner of land but may have been reserved to a predecessor in title. On acquisition, purchasers should always check to see if mineral rights are included. The principal minerals are coal, sand, gravel, silica sand (glass), iron-stone, clay (brickmaking or china), limestone and in certain areas other special deposits (tin, copper, etc). With limited exceptions all coal belongs to The Coal Authority and oil/gas deposits to the government.

Strict legislation affects mineral excavation and specified areas are designated in most County Plans. Virtually no excavation is permitted on land classified as Grade I or Grade II. Geological maps will indicate the approximate location of minerals and resistivity surveys and test borings can establish mineral deposit patterns, depths and volumes. Development is usually carried out through a sale or lease to one of the principal operating companies.

The sale of mineral-bearing land incurs capital gains tax on chargeable gains. Profits from the commercial operation of mineral workings are liable to income tax (or corporation tax), with capital allowances (including a depletion allowance of, in general, 50 per cent of the royalty rate of the minerals) available in respect of certain expenditure. Mineral royalties are taxed, broadly, as to one-half as income and the other half as capital.

Tipping, fishing, boating and water skiing rights may be reserved and provide high levels of income and reversionary asset value on completion of excavation. The 'hole in the ground' can be worth more than the original land but there may be an expensive statutory or contractual obligation to restore the land to its original use. The recent Budget introduced VAT on landfill sites.

With the evolving principle that 'the polluter shall pay', the dangers of illegal tipping of noxious substances are an increasing concern. Close control of tipping is essential and the end value of the restored land can be limited.

Minerals are a speculative investment if the land is purchased by an investor other than a mineral operator with mineral exploitation specifically in view. However, some farmland can produce high yields from unexpected mineral excavation. High prices should not be paid merely to hold a speculative 'mineral bank'.

11.4.5   Public leisure/entertainment and retail land uses

Like most subsidiary forms of land use, these categories are all relatively marginal to the whole but potentially significant profit centres on individual properties in the right locations. The managerial skills required are, however, very different from those of a farmer or forester and, if management of the main activity is not to suffer, they are best treated as a separate activity. Their common characteristic is that they are intended to appeal to the general public. They come in three main categories, though they often overlap with each other:

The passive leisure land uses

The obvious examples are leased golf courses, caravan and camping sites and mobile home parks — though the higher the standard of the site and more extensive the facilities (a shop for instance) the less managerially passive they become.

These properties are usually located at or near seaside areas or in areas of scenic beauty. Mobile home parks may be for permanent (all year round) occupation in certain areas specified by local councils. Planning controls are stringent on all large-scale parks or sites. Special facilities are required under the Caravan Sites and Control of Development Act 1960 including washing and toilet facilities, electricity and roads. The Mobile Homes Act 1975 confers on caravan home owners a limited security of tenure. Planning permission is almost always required and not easy to get in areas viewed as being of high landscape value.

An investment of this type can be lucrative but is a high risk, demanding considerable pre-acquisition investigation. The Caravan Club provides information on sites and the pitfalls associated with them. Fashions change and the weather greatly affects the income from holiday parks, particularly in coastal areas, where serious storms can result in large losses. Whilst the recent recession has affected the market, it has been an expanding, if often visually undesirable, area for investment.

The active leisure entertainment land uses

These are typically wild life parks, pleasure gardens, theme parks, riding schools/pony trekking centres and grand houses open to the public. Planning permission is required for wild life parks, pleasure gardens, golf courses and riding schools. Location is of paramount importance since it is essential to be close to urban populations with good road access. Initial development costs are high. It is probable that future legislation and higher design and maintenance standards will further aggravate the position. In the case of country houses, it is specially important to check the building status for planning purposes since 'listed' buildings are graded under the Town and Country Planning Act 1971 and the Town and Country Planning (Scotland) Act 1972 which imposes varying degrees of responsibility on the owner, including the need to obtain listed building consent for demolition, improvements or even minor alterations.

Houses having historic and amenity value are frequently opened to the public as a trading venture, enabling the owner to continue to live in the family home. The trading venture is intended to support the upkeep of the property and its general environment, in addition to the tax advantages of a 'one estate election'. Other large houses have been acquired for institutional purposes, such as research centres, out of town offices, training centres and health farms.

The problems with marketing wild life parks, and more recently golf courses, demonstrate that an investment of this kind is highly speculative in all but the prime locations. It is more often seen as a means to an end by existing owners rather than as the reason for a purchase.

Retail land uses

Farm shops and garden centres are the obvious examples. Farm shops are usually ancillary to farm businesses; they enable the farmer to obtain better prices than he would on the wholesale market by cutting out the middleman.

Garden centres are normally run by individuals or small companies, but in a few cases they are larger enterprises with multiple sites. Planning consent is required.

The location of both farm shops and garden centres is important, the best sites being on main roads and close to large centres of population. The increase in leisure has stimulated the popularity of these enterprises, supplying requisites to the keen gardener and also to the housewife, who is increasingly interested in fresh farm produce, especially for the deep freeze. The 'pick your own' method of sale at certain seasons can be successful and at farms where it is in operation good car parking facilities are essential.

Enterprises of this kind can be a valuable source of additional income and capital if correctly developed out of a farm unit (which is usually owner-occupied) but they are seldom sold as investments.

Sources of further information

Useful addresses

Country Landowners Association
16 Belgrave Square
London
SW1X 8PQ

Tel: (0171) 235 0511

Department of the Environment
2 Marsham Street
London
SW1P 3EB

Tel: (0171) 276 3000

Agricultural Mortgage
  Corporation PLC
AMC House
Chanty Street
Andover, Hampshire
SP10 1DD

Tel: (01264) 334344

Ministry of Agriculture, Fisheries
  and Food
Whitehall Place
London
SW1A 2HH

Tel: (0171) 270 3000

Agricultural Development and
  Advisory Service (ADAS)
Oxford Spires Business Park
The Boulevard
Kidlington
Oxon OX5 1NZ

Tel: (01865) 842742

Royal Institution of Chartered
  Surveyors (RICS)
12 Great George Street
London
SW1P 3AD

Tel: (0171) 222 7000

Incorporated Society of Valuers
  and Auctioneers
3 Cadogan Gate
London
SW1X 0AS

Tel: (0171) 235 2282

National Association of Estate
  Agents
21 Jury Street
Warwick
CV34 4EH

Tel: (01926) 496800

Forestry Commission
231 Corstorphine Road
Edinburgh
EH12 7AT

Tel: (0131) 334 0303

Royal Institution of Chartered
   Surveyors (Scottish Branch)
7–9 Manor Place
Edinburgh
EH3 7DN

Tel: (0131) 225 7078

Scottish Office of Agriculture and
   Fisheries Department
Pentland House
47 Robb's Loan
Edinburgh EH14 1TY

Tel: (0131) 556 8400

Caravan Club
East Grinstead House
East Grinstead
West Sussex
RH19 1UA

Tel: (01342) 326944

Food From Britain
301–344 Market Towers
New Covent Garden Market
London
SW8 5NQ

Tel: (0171) 720 2144

Rural Development
   Commission
141 Castle Street
Salisbury
Wiltshire
SP1 3TP

Tel: (01722) 336255

12 Commercial property

Andrew Bull, ARICS, Partner in Jones Lang Wootton

12.1 Introduction

Review of 1994

To borrow a phrase from the world of football, 1994 was a year of two halves. Property values roared ahead in the first half with the JLW Quarterly and IPD Monthly indices posting returns of 10 per cent and 12 per cent respectively. In the second half values virtually stood still as property belatedly reacted to rising bond yields.

Half time was flagged with exquisite precision by the c£150m issue of BZW's property index certificate, the first derivative widely marketed since the ill-fated Fox futures contract in 1990.

Estimated returns of 12 to 13 per cent in 1994 were less than 1993's returns and absence of rental growth was the principal factor at work here. Throughout the year occupational demand for space grew little if at all, although vacancy rates for well located space began to fall. In the second half of the year we saw some rental growth in prime locations but this was counterbalanced by continued weakness elsewhere.

Debt was replaced by equity in the capital markets. Direct property investment increased from the institutions, notably the life assurance companies (+£2bn) and through new share issues in the property sector. Bank advances to property companies fell by £3.5bn as balance sheet gearing reduced. New construction orders showed a significant increase (+£1.1bn to £5.5bn) but there have been very few speculative schemes initiated. The market remains very cautious in advance of firm evidence of rental growth.

12.1.1 Types of investors

Property investments can be broken down into sub-sectors in which different types of investors will be interested. Properties can be subdivided according to location, type and size. Small industrial units and multimillion pound office investments are unlikely to be of interest to the same investor. Risk-averse investors such as insurance companies and pension funds will prefer to invest in 'prime' properties in established locations let to blue chip tenants on standard full repairing and insuring leases. A factor of considerable importance to these investors is the security of rental income and capital gain. Other investors will, however, be prepared to accept a higher level of risk by purchasing 'secondary' properties if the return on capital is considered to be sufficiently attractive.

The purchase of a commercial property involves the giving up of a capital sum now in exchange for future returns which can be either the benefits of owner-occupation, income flow and/or capital gain. Underlying any property investment decision will be the option of alternative invest-ments, namely stocks, shares, cash, unit trusts and even works of art. In selecting an investment, the investor will seek the highest real rate of return on capital invested but, depending upon the object of the invest-ment, may 'trade-off' a reduced rate of return in consideration for increased liquidity or security of income. The tax status of an investor will also be an important factor.

12.1.2 Property valuation

In its simplest form, the basis of property valuation is the capitalisation of rental income of a property over a term of years or in perpetuity (depend-ing on whether the property is leasehold or freehold) at an investment rate of return which reflects all the elements of risk associated with that prop-erty (security of income, obsolescence of the building, economic factors and the cost/inconvenience of management). The capitalisation rate chosen to value the property will also reflect the expectation of future rental growth and consequently tends to be significantly lower than the yields available from fixed-interest securities. This phenomenon (also illustrated by the div-idend yield of equities) is known as the 'reverse yield gap' and since the 1970s has varied between about 1 per cent and 8 per cent.

12.2   Types of commercial property

Direct investment in commercial property falls mainly into the following categories:

(1)   retail including supermarkets and retail warehouses;
(2)   offices including town centre, out of town and campus;
(3)   industrial including factories, warehouses and hi-tech;

and, to a much lesser degree:

% Yield

Figure 12.1 Property, equity and gilt yields 1965/94

Equities
Property
Gilts

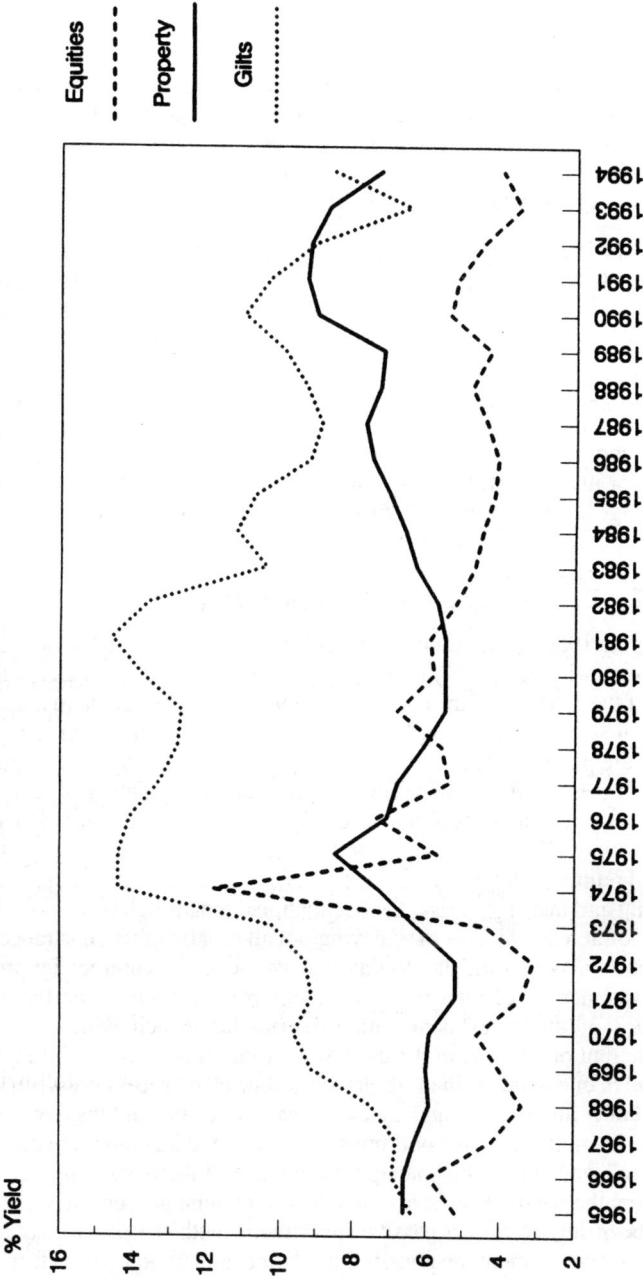

Source: *Datastream, EIU, JLW, Hillier Parker*

(4)   farmland and forestry;
(5)   leisure.

Most investors with a significant long-term investment portfolio will aim to hold the majority of the investments balanced between the retail, office and industrial categories, where there is a well-defined investment market.

12.2.1   Purchase of commercial property

Due to the large amounts of capital required for the purchase of even the smallest commercial property, the commercial property investment market is, like the equity market, generally confined to UK and foreign insurance companies, pension fund and property companies, together with a number of wealthy private individuals or family trusts. UK insurance companies and pension funds began investing in commercial property in the mid-1950s, broadening their asset bases beyond the equities and government securities which had hitherto formed their principal media for investment. UK pension fund investment reached a peak as a percentage of their assets in 1979 and significant net new investment was not then seen until the late 1980s.

12.2.2   Lease of commercial property

During the 1980s commercial buildings were generally leased for a term of 25 years with five-yearly rent reviews to the current open market rental value of the property. During the early 1990s the supply/demand balance has been so radically altered that the market is one in which tenants' desires are paramount. There has been marked owner reluctance to grant shorter leases but the trend to shorter leases and the granting of tenants' options to determine leases continues. At the same time increased incentives by way of cash payments and rent-free periods have resulted in reduced returns to landlords. Under the terms of what is known as a 'full repairing and insuring' lease, the occupational tenant will be responsible for (or for at least the cost of) carrying out all repairs to and insurance of the property. Whilst the day-to-day management of a commercial property investment is of vital importance in terms of maintaining the performance of the investment, and in particular in achieving the best possible rent on review, in the case of a letting of an entire building (as opposed to one which is in multiple occupation) the process is essentially one of collecting the rent and checking that the repairs and insurance are in place. In multi-occupied buildings the repairs and insurance are carried out by the landlord, or his managing agents, with the costs being recovered from the tenants. An investment in commercial property has historically been regarded as a passive investment, with the day-to-day and portfolio management responsibilities being undertaken by a firm of managing agents.

12.2.3 Rent reviews

Investments in commercial property provide regular opportunities for increasing the income obtained from the property through the medium of rent reviews. Since the Second World War the time period between rent reviews has altered. Formerly leases were granted with a period of 21 years between rent reviews, but latterly this decreased to 14 years, then to seven years and is currently five years. Generally, rent reviews result in the rent increasing to the then open market rental value of the property and most institutional leases provide for the rent review to be on an upwards only basis. As mentioned earlier, oversupply and reduced tenant demand resulted in rents falling, increased incentives and shorter lease terms. However, leases granted with terms long enough to have five yearly rent review provisions have on the whole continued to include upward only rent reviews.

12.2.4 Rental growth

As can be seen from the Figures 12.2 and 12.3 on pp 206 and 207 showing rental growth in the three major investment sectors throughout the decade of the 1980s, and also the mean asking yield for the three sectors through the same time period, the rate of rental growth has varied enormously from a peak of about 30 per cent per annum to an actual decline in rental terms. At the same time, yields have altered by as much as 25 per cent.

12.3 Shops

12.3.1 General

Historically, three factors have affected the rental and capital value of shops: location, location and location. Due to the fact that the quality of the location can readily be ascertained, shops have been regarded as one of the most secure forms of commercial property investment. In the past, principal high street locations were rarely subject to major change, except when a town centre redevelopment scheme or a new shopping centre was planned, when it was usually possible to predict the effect that these new centres would have on the existing shopping patterns within the high street. However, the future impact of out of town retail schemes and retail warehouse parks on high street shopping patterns is uncertain. With the announcement of the intentions of major retailers such as Marks & Spencer to set up a number of large-scale operations in out of town locations, the provision of sufficient and accessible car parking and an attractive environment will ensure that retail parks and out of town centres continue to prosper on the same levels as before. Otherwise, traditional town centres will be left to become fashion-dominated, durable-good

Figure 12.2   Rental growth by sector 1973/94

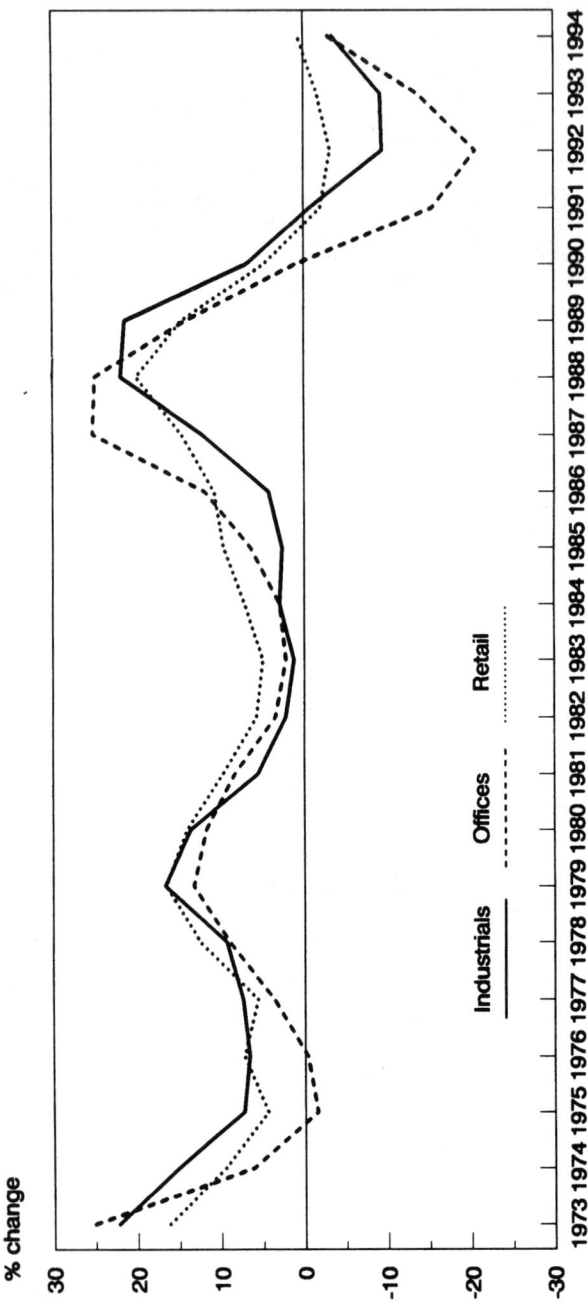

Industrials   Offices   Retail

Source: *IPD, JLW FM Strategy*

Figure 12.3 Property yields by sector

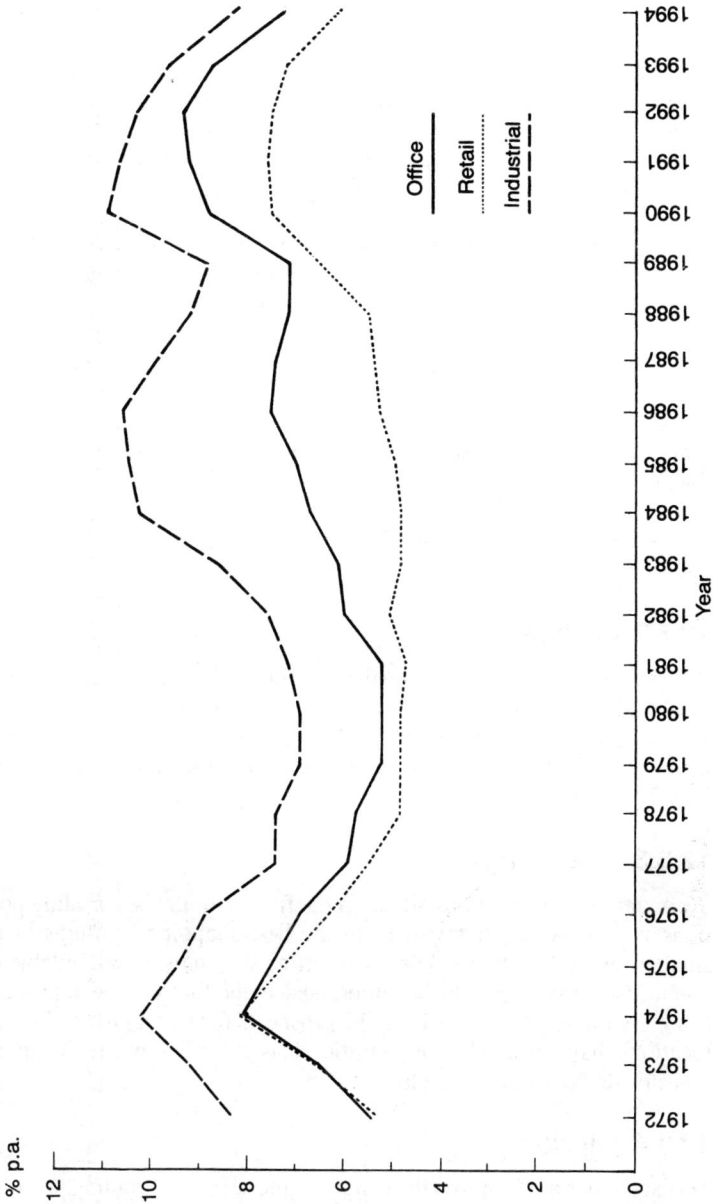

% p.a.

Office
Retail
Industrial

Year

Source *Hillier Parker.* Note: *average yields as at November.*

centres, with food shopping moving out of town. The retailing sector is undergoing significant change, with many retailers repositioning in the market, restyling their outlets and merchandise, and taking over competitors. In addition there was dramatic growth in 'speciality' retailing in the past two years where a number of retailers have been successful in targeting specific markets and responding quickly to changes in consumer demand. Hence the more established chains experienced greater competition for prime pitches in the high street.

A large number of the best shop units in the UK are now owned by the institutions, although a proportion are still owned and occupied by the major retailing organisations. In recent years rental growth has been considerable throughout the retail sector. There has been keen competition to make further investment in this category, whilst the availability of suitable investments is extremely limited in relation to the amount of investment money available. Over the past two years substantial institutional investment has spread out into the best located shops in the smaller towns.

In the property investment market, shops are categorised as prime, secondary and tertiary.

12.3.2   Prime

Prime shops are those situated in the best trading locations along the principal high streets in the larger towns where major multiple retailers, such as Boots, W H smith and Marks & Spencer, are to be found. The rental income obtainable from shop units within these locations varies enormously depending on the importance of the particular town.

12.3.3   Secondary

Secondary shops are shops either on the fringes of the best trading positions within the larger towns or in the best shopping positions in the smaller towns. Due to the shortage of prime shop units now available for commercial investment, the institutional demand for this type of property has grown in recent years. Since the prospects for rental growth in these locations have proved more erratic than those in prime locations, investors expect a higher yield.

12.3.4   Tertiary

Tertiary shops are shops on the fringes of the secondary trading positions and shops in neighbourhood shopping parades, including 'the corner shop'. There is a negligible demand from multiple tenants for representation in these locations. Therefore, covenant strength is poorer and the management load heavier. Consequently, demand for these properties derives principally from private investors. This market is usually very active with sales of all sizes taking place by private treaty or auction.

12.3.5 Out of town shopping

Out of town shopping has evolved through the recognition of the car-borne shopper and may generally be divided into food and non-food retailing. The main DIY specialists (Sainsbury's Homebase, W H Smith Do-It-All, Texas Homecare and B & Q) are often found grouped together and require units of 35,000–50,000 square ft. Out of town food retailers now include most of the major food chains. Good surface car parking and main road prominence are essential criteria.

12.4   Offices

12.4.1   General

In the early 1970s many provincial towns, as well as central London, became seriously over-supplied with office accommodation and rents either remained level or fell. This has started to happen again to a lesser extent in the late 1980s and early 1990s. A factor in the demand/supply imbalance is the lengthy period from planning to completion of a development.

The quality of an office building is of greater importance than the quality of a shop unit. Occupational tenants are setting ever higher standards, requiring good quality finishes, modern lifts, central heating, adequate car parking facilities, the abilty to accommodate a growing range of sophisticated office equipment (notably computers, word processors and communications equipment) and, particularly in central London, double-glazing and air conditioning. The costs of maintaining offices, especially the mechanical services, the unified business rates, and the cost of refurbishing the accommodation, mean that the tenant and investor are subjected to high outgoings. These have increased as a direct result of technological changes having shortened the lifetime of buildings and services.

The most expensive office locations in the UK have historically been the West End and City of London. Since the tenant will be responsible for all outgoings under the terms of his lease, the actual cost of occupation will probably be double the cost of the rent alone. Due to the security and perceived prospects for long-term rental growth offered by buildings within the West End and City of London, there has been a strong institutional demand for investments. Increasingly, foreign investors as well as UK investors have been active in this market although recent oversupply and falling rents in both the City and West End have resulted in more fluctuation and uncertainty as to value leading to reduced investment activity and caution amongst investors.

The other principal office areas in London follow a similar but less expensive pattern to that of the City and West End, although in the late 1980s an upswing in demand coupled with relatively restricted supply resulted in these locations experiencing dramatic growth in rents. Outside London, rents vary from centre to centre, with the towns immediately to the west of London along the M4 corridor being the highest outside London.

12.4.2   Conclusion

Offices form the backbone of most commercial property investment port-folios, due to the amount of money involved and the past performance of rental growth on rent review. They are likely to remain a dominant feature of institutional portfolios and the preferred areas are those in central London and certain selected provincial centres. However, it is becoming necessary to spend large capital sums more frequently to maintain the quality of the investment. Over many years the cost of central London office occupancy and the inconvenience of commuting have encouraged companies to move their operations to suburban and provincial locations.

12.5   Industrial

12.5.1   General investment: factories and warehouses

The declining importance in Great Britain of the industrial and manufacturing sectors, the volatility of the economy and the relatively short economic life of industrial buildings have resulted in investors requiring higher yields for factories and warehouse premises than for shops and offices. In this context, institutional investors tend to prefer warehouse buildings, as opposed to factories, due to the fact that these tend to be less specialised and therefore require fewer remedial works when a tenant vacates the premises. Industrial processes also tend to have a more destructive effect on the actual fabric of the property.

12.5.2   Location criteria

Although the uses of factories and warehouses are different, both in practical and in legislative terms, it is convenient to categorise them together, since the locational and investment critieria are similar. The most desirable investments in this category are situated on well-located industrial estates, close to major conurbations and motorway access points or the national airports. It is interesting to note that proximity to rail services is not an important criterion in the UK, being less important than a good supply of labour and good estate services for the factory owner.

12.5.3 Institutional criteria

The insurance companies and pension funds have developed certain criteria which they look for in modern industrial and warehouse buildings. These criteria relate to clear working height, floor loading capacity, the presence of sprinklers, the proportion of office space to warehouse space within the unit, the number of loading doors, the presence of a concreted hard standing in front of the unit and adequate car parking. Whilst these institutional criteria are often in excess of the criteria required by occupiers, investors would be wise to purchase units meeting institutional criteria, since they will find a wider market in which to sell the property in the future.

12.5.4 Yields

Yields available on prime industrial and warehouse investments are higher than those on prime shops and offices. Rental growth experienced over the late 1970s was, generally, very satisfactory but became static in the early and mid-1980s during the economic recession, and improved again in the late 1980s. Investment in modern industrial and warehouse buildings is a more recent trend than investment in offices and shops but now forms around 25 per cent of a typical portfolio. Opportunities do exist for non-institutional investment where very high yields can be obtained from obsolescent or poorly located properties, but these carry commensurate risk.

12.6 Hi-tech

Whilst many areas of traditional manufacturing industry were affected by the economic recession, the hi-technology field experienced considerable growth. This resulted in a new direction in the design and use of industrial buildings with tenants becoming increasingly discerning as to their preferences in building design and working environment. The most radical change has been the introduction of the building which comprises a two- or three-storey structure designed to permit the interchangeability of functions such as offices, research and development, laboratories or industrial. An out of town location, extensive car parking and landscaping with imaginative and functional finishes both internally and externally create a high quality corporate image. The first and still largest business park in the UK is Stockley Park off the M4 very close to Heathrow airport. Both back office and headquarters type functions are now moving to such business parks.

12.7   Agriculture

Having experienced growth in popularity with institutional investors, at one point forming in excess of 5 per cent of some investment portfolios, farmland and forestry have been increasingly less popular as a result of falling values and the perception of a continued fall in values. In addition, investors have begun to appreciate that in many instances the economic support or tax benefits of these investments have been and are likely to be subject to political tinkering, thus dramatically altering the value of many investments at a stroke.

Smaller, more picturesque farms, especially those with attractive houses have, however, become increasingly attractive and prices have continued to rise for the successful businessman desirous of changing his place of domicile and lifestyle (see also Chapter 11).

12.8   Leisure

Investments in the 'leisure industry' include hotels, marinas, golf courses, sports centres and entertainment facilities. The growing demand for leisure facilities, both home-based and from tourists, is resulting in increasing investment in this field. It is, however, regarded as an investment in management expertise rather than in the property which the particular leisure activity occupies, and great caution is therefore necessary. Quite often an investor's return will be geared to the operator's turnover or profitability rather than to the rental value of the premises, which can sometimes be very difficult to determine.

Whilst the returns from leisure industry investments, in terms of capital gains, can be substantial for the astute investor, the risks are considerable and such investments are not recommended to small investors.

13 Business ventures (without participation in management)

Mike Wilkes of Pannell Kerr Forster, Chartered Accountants

13.1 Introduction

There are always people with experience and no money looking for people with money and no experience. At the end of the day the former sometimes have the money and the latter have had the experience. That is not to say that, in general terms, such arrangements should always be avoided. There are plenty of good ideas which need financing and the rewards to the investor can be substantial, but such investments call for faith in someone else's judgement, nerves of steel and an instinct for gambling. Many ventures have turned out well after being (sometimes more than once) on the verge of disaster. Those who do not like walking along the edge of a precipice should keep to gentler paths.

The seeker after finance will often paint the picture of his prospects in rosy colours, not through dishonesty but because of enthusiasm, and such enthusiasm should always be discounted. Unfortunately it is often highly contagious, so that impersonal, dispassionate, professional advice is essential. The pitfalls should be considered every bit as carefully as the opportunities. It is easier to lose money than to make it; but money is seldom to be made without accepting an element of chance.

In some cases money, once put into a venture, is effectively locked in, come what may. At best it may be possible to withdraw it only at considerable cost. On the other hand, by good judgement and good luck (and any successful venture requires both), there are fortunes to be made. The essential feature of the investments considered in this chapter is that the investor relies wholly on the expertise of someone else — company director, active partner, racehorse trainer and so on — and will probably be involved in matters of which he is ignorant or, at least, inexperienced.

It must never be forgotten that taxation will make inroads into both income and capital gains, and, in this respect, professional advice should always be taken. There may be alternative ways of making investments so that, with this in mind, every scheme requires careful expert consideration. Equally, if losses are incurred, steps should be taken to see that the maximum tax advantage is obtained. The advice of an accountant or a solicitor or probably both can be invaluable, not only in dealing with legal and financial problems that are puzzling the prospective investor but often also in pointing out problems of which the layman may be totally unaware. The effects of taxation are touched on in the following sections, but complex problems can arise which it is impossible to deal with briefly. In every case the solution will depend upon the individual facts.

1981 saw the introduction of the 'Business Start-up Scheme' intended for the encouragement of investment in companies starting new businesses. Provided that the investment complied with the numerous, rigorous and complex provisions set out in no less than 16 sections of and two Schedules to the Finance Act 1981, the amount invested could be deducted from the income of the investor in computing his income tax liability.

The scheme was superseded by the 'Business Expansion Scheme' which, while similar in concept, was more generous in amount, wider in its application and subject to even more complicated legal rules. The scheme was, in many cases, viewed as a tax-saving vehicle rather than a way to take a stake in new ventures and came to an end on 31 December 1993. The 1994 Finance Act introduced a new investment incentive scheme, the Enterprise Investment Scheme, which replaced the Business Expansion Scheme and the 1995 Finance Act will provide for the approval of Venture Capital Trusts (VCTs), yet another investment incentive vehicle. Although the avoidance of tax is the inducement to make such investments, the legislation includes a number of anti-avoidance provisions.

The view is sometimes held that professional advice is an expensive luxury which can be dispensed with. Nothing could be further from the truth. If it seems expensive it is because the mass of all-pervading legislation of recent years has made it dangerous to take any steps in commerce (or indeed in much else) without considering the application of statute law, Statutory Instruments and regulations. Professional advice taken at the outset will often avoid difficulties and disputes at a later stage which may well prove far more expensive in legal costs.

13.2 The current business climate

The recession particularly affected smaller private companies but at last the economy is showing signs of recovery and property values have begun to stabilise. Limited partnerships may be an appropriate way of participating in a business venture without putting one's entire wealth on the line. The need to bear in mind the potential downside has been highlighted by the continuing problems at Lloyd's, where some alarming losses have been experienced by individuals who did not anticipate that they would ever be required to meet substantial cash calls.

13.3 Minority holdings in private companies

13.3.1 Introduction

It was for many years a feature of company law that a private company was one which restricted the transfer of its shares and any company which did not do so was a public company. Under the Companies Act 1980 (a statute enacted largely as a move towards European uniformity) this distinction was swept away and although the words 'public' and 'private' are retained, their meanings are now quite different. A public company is defined in the Companies Act 1985 (a consolidating Act bringing together the provisions of the Companies Acts of 1948, 1967, 1976, 1980 and 1981), and any company not within that definition will be a private company. The principal distinction is that a public company (denoted at the end of its name by the letters 'plc' or by the words 'public limited company') must have an authorised and allotted minimum share capital which is at present £50,000 but which may be altered by Statutory Instrument by the Secretary of State. At least one quarter of that allotted share capital of a public company must be paid up before it can commence business. No such minimum capital requirements exist in relation to private companies. A company need no longer restrict the transfer of its shares to be a private company under the new Act. References in this part of the chapter to 'private companies' are intended, generally, to refer to the smaller family company where control rests in the hands of a few shareholders who are probably the directors or related to the directors. As regards the transfer of shares see **13.3.4**.

A minority holding in a private company may be acquired in a number of ways: it may be inherited; it may be bought from an existing shareholder; it may arise when a company is newly formed to undertake the starting of a business venture; or it may arise on the allotment of shares by a company taking over an existing company or undertaking.

A minority holding is, for the purpose of this chapter, any holding of shares or other securities which does not give the holder control of the company, and thus includes a holding of non-voting shares or debentures. Assuming that a company has shares of one class only, of which each has one vote, a holding of less than 50 per cent is a minority holding.

However, in some companies there are different classes of shares and shares of one class only, for example, might carry a vote, the others carrying no vote or giving the right to vote on certain specified matters only. In other companies there may be one class of shares carrying one vote each and another class of which the shares carry a hundred votes each, so that a holding, in nominal value, of more than half the company's issued capital does not necessarily carry control. Careful scrutiny of the company's capital structure is vital before making an investment in a private company.

13.3.2   Powers of the minority

At general meetings of a company, a vote is first taken by a show of hands (subject to anything in the articles of association), giving each member personally present one vote regardless of the size of his holding. Under common law any one member may demand a poll, the votes then being counted, normally on the basis of one for each share held. The articles may include a requirement that a poll must be demanded by more than one member, but such a requirement is limited by s 373 of the Companies Act 1985 so that, except for certain purposes, an article is void if it requires the demand for a poll to be made by more than five members, or the holders of more than one-tenth of the voting rights, or the holders of more than one-tenth of the paid-up capital entitled to vote.

When a poll is held, each member has (in the absence of any contrary provision in the articles) one vote for each share held. Thus on a poll, one member holding 60 per cent of the issued shares will be able to outvote a dozen members holding the other 40 per cent between them.

An ordinary resolution requires a simple majority of members voting, so that a minority shareholder cannot, in the face of determined opposition, prevent its being passed. However, a special or extraordinary resolution, which is necessary for certain fundamental decisions, requires a majority of three-quarters of members voting, so that on a poll, where each share carries a vote, the holder of 40 per cent of the issued shares, although a minority shareholder, could block such a resolution. An extraordinary resolution is required for, among other things, winding up a company that cannot, by reason of its liabilities, continue in business, and the articles of the company may require such a resolution for various other purposes. A special resolution is necessary for, *inter alia*:

(1)   the alteration of a company's objects (although, in that case, the holders of not less than 15 per cent of the issued share capital may apply to the court to have the alteration cancelled);

(2)   the alteration of a company's articles;

(3)   the change of a company's name (subject to the approval of the

Department of Trade and Industry);
(4)   a reduction of capital (subject to the approval of the court);
(5)   the re-registration of a public company as private or a private company as public under the 1985 Act;
(6)   the re-registration of an unlimited company as limited; and
(7)   the winding up of a company voluntarily.

In addition to considering the effective powers of the majority, it must be remembered that the day-to-day running of the company's business is in the hands of the directors. As a last resort, majority shareholders can remove and appoint directors; minority shareholders cannot. In this connection it is important to note that most companies' articles of association preclude the payment of a dividend in excess of that recommended by the directors. If, therefore, the directors feel it is desirable for any reason to retain the profits, or the bulk of the profits, within the company rather than distribute them by way of dividend, the minority shareholder may find that he is not receiving a satisfactory return on his investment and, even with the assistance of the majority shareholders, there may be little he can effectively do about it.

Arising out of the matters discussed in the previous paragraph, it will be appreciated that the majority could deal with the affairs of a company in a way which might be to the detriment of the interests of the minority, particularly where the minority controls 25 per cent or less of the voting power. The law, however, provides protection for an oppressed minority in two ways. First, the minority may petition the court to wind-up the company on the ground that it is just and equitable to do so. This is, in many cases, an unsatisfactory course to pursue since, at the end of the day, the assets will be sold at their break-up value, the goodwill will disappear and the minority will not have achieved its object, namely that the company should continue to operate but that its interests should be safeguarded. Secondly, the minority may petition the court for relief under s 459 of the Companies Act 1985.

Protection under the 1948 Act was provided where the court was of the opinion that the affairs of the company were being conducted in a manner oppressive to some part of the members (including the petitioner) and that to wind-up the company would unfairly prejudice that part of the members although the facts would justify winding-up on the grounds that to wind-up would be just and equitable. The court, on being so persuaded, could make any order which it thought fit. There is a considerable body of authority as to what constitutes oppression for this purpose.

Under s 459 of the Companies Act 1985, protection is afforded by the court if it is satisfied that the conduct of the company's affairs is 'unfairly prejudicial to the interests' of some part of the members. A petition may also be brought under this provision based on 'any actual or proposed act or omission' of the company. The meaning of 'unfairly prejudicial' is not defined and awaits judicial interpretation.

13.3.3   Liability for uncalled capital

The essential feature of a limited company is that the liability of its share-holders is limited to the capital they put in or agree to put in, and no further demands can be made on them by the company or its creditors except where shares are issued which are not fully paid. The holder of such shares may be called upon by the company to pay up the unpaid balance, and failure to pay on a call may result in forfeiture of the shares. Any holder of partly-paid shares must therefore always bear in mind that a contingent liability attaches to them. If the additional capital is required for development of the business, it will probably be all to the good. It sometimes happens though, that it is needed because the company is in difficulties and may amount to throwing good money after bad.

13.3.4   Transfer of shares

Difficulties may arise in connection with the disposal of a minority holding of shares in a private company. One of the hallmarks of a private company under the Companies Act 1948 was that it restricted transfers of its shares, and if the articles did not so provide, it was not a private company. The usual form, following reg 3 of Table A in Pt II of Sched 1 to the Companies Act 1948, provided that 'the directors may, in their absolute discretion and without assigning any reason therefore, decline to register any transfer of any share, whether or not it is a fully paid share.' It follows that, in such cases, the board must approve the proposed new shareholder and, where the articles are in the form set out above, the court will not inquire into the directors' reasons for refusing to register a transfer if none are given. Thus, whatever the value of the shares might be in terms of the assets and liabilities disclosed in the company's balance sheet, it may well be difficult to find a purchaser at anything approaching that value. The Companies Act 1948, s 28, which made restrictions on transfers essential for a private company, was repealed by the Companies Act 1980. There is nothing to prevent a private company from imposing such a restriction in its articles and in the case of any company whose articles already include it it will remain in force unless the articles are amended. The articles of any company in which it is proposed to invest should therefore be examined with this point in view. The new Table A (under the Companies Act 1985), which sets out a suggested form 8 for the articles of association of a company, does not include any provisions relating to the refusal of directors to register a transfer of fully paid shares, but it is not unusual to see an express provision to the effect included in the articles of association of private companies.

Dealing with shares in a private company is often also restricted by a provision in the articles that a member wishing to dispose of his shares must first offer them to the other members at their fair value which is frequently determined in the absence of agreement between the intending seller and the directors, by the auditors, or an independent chartered accountant. The articles should therefore be examined with this in mind and also with a view to discovering whether, on death, a member's shares may pass to his personal representatives to be dealt with according to his will. In addition a minority shareholder who is an employee might be required under the articles of association to transfer his shares on ceasing to be employed by the company in question.

13.3.5 Loans

An investor may prefer to put money into a company by way of loan rather than by purchasing shares. A loan may be charged on all or any of the company's assets or its uncalled capital, or may be on a debenture, secured or unsecured. The nature of a debenture is difficult to define and Lindley J said in *British India Steam Navigation Co v IRC* (1881) 7 QBD 165, at p 172, '. . . what the correct meaning of "debenture" is I do not know. I do not find anywhere any precise definition of it'.

It is always necessary to proceed with caution when lending to a company. Its memorandum and articles should be inspected to ensure that the borrowing is *intra vires*, and the terms of any loan or debenture must be clearly set out and agreed. Independent professional advice is essential. In particular, where the lender is the settlor in relation to a settlement of which the trustees or a beneficiary are participators of the company, quite unexpected income tax liabilities may arise under s 677 of the Income and Corporation Taxes Act 1988 when the loan is repaid.

Money invested in a company by way of loan will normally entitle the lender to interest at a fixed rate. If the company fails he should not, if adequately secured, be out of pocket: if the company prospers he will receive his interest regularly, and in due course his loan will be repaid, but he will not share in the prosperity of the undertaking.

13.3.6 Taxation

Two applications of taxation must be borne in mind. First, when a dividend is received, a 'tax credit' is given equal in amount to the income tax at the rate of 20 per cent which would be payable on the aggregate of the dividend and the tax credit. The company thereupon becomes liable to pay advance corporation tax on the dividend at a rate of 20 per cent on the aggregate, such advance corporation tax ranking as a credit against the company's corporation tax liability. Higher rate taxpayers will be given credit for the deduction; basic rate taxpayers will have no further tax liability.

Secondly, if and when shares are disposed of and a chargeable gain results, capital gains tax becomes payable. The Finance Act 1988 changed the base date from 1965 to 1982 which favoured many long-term investors, but the Finance Act also unified the rates of tax on income and capital gains so that the maximum rate of capital gains tax increased from 30 per cent to 40 per cent.

Incidentally, a notional capital gain may arise where assets are given away or disposed of for consideration which is less than their full open market value. A person who makes such a gift or sale at an undervalue is treated as if he had received full market value. However, it may be possible for gains arising on such transactions to be deferred or 'held over'. The Finance Act 1989 abolished the general right to hold over gains on gifts, but the hold over provisions continue to apply to gifts of business property (and shares in unquoted trading companies generally fall within this category).

The tax payable on a capital gain arising from the sale of shares will normally be computed as follows:

Sale proceeds	x
Less incidental costs of disposal	x
	x
Less cost/31 March 1982 value	x
Less Indexation (adjustment for inflation based on the increase in the RPI)	x
Less capital losses on other transactions in the year	x
Less £5,800 annual exemption (unless utilised against other gains)	
Less capital losses brought forward (if any)	?
Net gains taxed at either 20%, 25% or 40%	x

13.3.7 Losses

Looking on the gloomy side, it is possible that a loss may arise on the sale of shares in a private company, or on its liquidation. Such a loss may arise because the investor cannot recoup his original investment, but even where he does get his money back, an allowable loss may still arise because of indexation (ie the adjustment made to reflect inflation and calculated as a percentage of the allowable cost reflecting the increase in the RPI during the period in which the investment has been held).

A major change was included in the 1994 Finance Act, which limited the amount of indexation relief which can be claimed for disposals made after 29 November 1993. The initial text of the Bill provided that, for such disposals, indexation relief could only be used to reduce chargeable gains to nil and would not be available to create, or increase, an allowable capital loss.

However, following representations, the Chancellor tabled an amendment to the Finance Bill (now incorporated in the Finance Act 1994), which provided for transitional relief for individuals, and trustees of settlements made before 30 November 1993. For losses realised on disposals made during the period from 30 November 1993 to 5 April 1995, indexation relief will be available up to a maximum of £10,000. This indexation relief must first be used to reduce the net chargeable gains for 1993/94 to the level of the taxpayer's annual exempt amount of £5,800. Any unused indexation losses can be carried forward and used, with any indexation losses on disposals during 1994/95, to reduce chargeable gains for 1994/95. Any such indexation losses which cannot be used during 1994/95, will not be available to carry forward to 1995/96 and later years.

Example 1 — disposals prior to 30 November 1993

An individual invests £10,000 in December 1989. On 14 June 1993 he sells for £11,000. However, the RPI has increased by 18 per cent between 1989 and 1993. Before indexation he has a gain of £1,000 but after taking this into account he has an allowable capital loss of £800.

Example 2 — disposals between 30 November 1993 and 5 April 1995

The circumstances are similar to those in Example 1, but the sale takes place on 31 March 1994. Assuming the RPI has increased by 20 per cent between 1989 and 1994, there is an indexation loss of £1,000. This indexation loss can be set off against other gains arising for 1993/94, which are in excess of the annual exemption of £5,800. Any balance can be carried forward for use in 1994/95. If this cannot be utilised in 1994/95, no relief can be carried forward to 1995/96 and subsequent years. This example also assumes that other indexation losses arising during the period 30 November 1993 to 5 April 1995, when added to this indexation loss, do not exceed £10,000.

Example 3 — disposals after 5 April 1995

The circumstances are similar to those of Example 1, but the sale takes place on 6 December 1995. In this case the indexation relief is limited to the amount of the unindexed gain, ie £1,000 and no capital loss is created.

Reinvestment relief

Reinvestment relief was first introduced in the March 1993 Budget, as a relief for entrepreneurs on the selling of their own business. It was only given real bite in the 1994 Finance Act when the relief was extended for disposals made after 29 November 1993 and became available for *any* capital gain where the gain was reinvested in shares in a qualifying unquoted company. The 1995 Finance Act will contain further extensions to the relief so that it will be available for gains reinvested in Enterprise Investment Schemes and Venture Capital Trusts.

Example

Wendy sells her shares in SAL Ltd in December 1995, for £20,000. She originally purchased the shares in January 1985 for £5,000. In May 1995 Wendy had invested £10,000 in ordinary shares in a venture capital trust.

Wendy's capital gains tax position would be as follows:

	£	£
Proceeds		20,000
Less:		
Cost	5,000	
Indexation relief (say)	3,000	
		8,000
Net gain		12,000
Less reinvestment relief		(10,000)
Net chargeable gain		£2,000

If Wendy was a higher rate taxpayer, her combined income tax and capital gains tax relief could amount to 60 per cent (20 per cent income tax relief for the investment in the venture capital trust, and 40 per cent deferral of capital gains tax)

Capital losses are not normally available to be set against an individual's income, although they do attract capital gains tax relief. However, where an individual has subscribed for ordinary shares in a qualifying trading company and he incurs an allowable loss on disposing of the shares, he may claim relief from income tax instead of capital gains tax. This provision (to be found in s 574 of the Income and Corporation Taxes Act 1988 and generally known as the 'Venture Capital Scheme') applies to disposals on or after 6 April 1980. It must be noted that this relief applies only where the taxpayer has subscribed for the shares and not where he had bought them from another shareholder, unless that other is his or her spouse, and acquired the shares by subscription. It applies only to ordinary share capital and stock and the company must be a 'qualifying trading company' in the terms of the definition provided by the section, that is to say:

(1)   it must exist wholly or mainly for the purpose of carrying on a trade (other than dealing in shares, securities, land or commodity futures);
(2)   it must be resident in the UK from its incorporation until the date on which the shares or stock are disposed of; and
(3)   none of its shares or stock must have been quoted on a recognised stock exchange at any time since 12 months before the date on which the shares or stock were issued.

The relief will be given if the loss results from a sale at arm's length for full consideration, a distribution on a winding-up or a claim that the value has become negligible giving rise to a deemed disposal. Partial claims are not allowed and if the loss exceeds income for the year of claim the excess may either be carried forward or set off against capital gains. Information may be obtained from the Small Firms Service of the Department of Trade and Industry.

13.3.8   Loans

Until recently, professional advisers normally recommended that a person making a loan to a private company should do so on terms which made the loan a debt on a security. This is because such loans constitute an asset for capital gains tax purposes whereas normal loans are outside the scope of capital gains tax (which is fine until the investor seeks relief for a capital loss). As a general principle, losses are available to offset capital gains only if they arise from assets which are chargeable assets for capital gains purposes.

As already stated, as a general principle, a debt on a security does constitute an asset for capital gains tax purposes. This definition is itself obscure.

There is a further problem that even where a loan constitutes a debt on a security, relief may be withheld on the basis that the security is a 'qualifying corporate bond' (in this particular context, a qualifying corporate bond is one where the investor does not qualify for an allowable loss for capital gains tax purposes). It is possible to ensure that a debt on a security does not fall within the definition of a QCB, but it is necessary for the loan to have certain qualities and in particular the loan should normally contain provisions under which it may be converted into ordinary shares or preference shares. Professional advice is essential here.

Loans which are not debts on a security or QCBs

Even where a debt does not fall within the category considered above, it may in certain circumstances entitle the lender to relief as a capital loss if it becomes irrecoverable. The conditions which render the loan a qualifying loan for this purpose are to be found in s 253 of the Taxation of Chargeable Gains Act 1992. These are as follows:

(1)   the money lent must be used by the borrower wholly for the purposes of a trade carried on by him or for the setting up of a trade subsequently carried on by him;

(2)   the borrower must be resident in the UK. The Act does not say at what point the borrower must be so resident and neither does it require the business to be carried on here; and

(3)   the debt must not be a debt on a security. If it is it will fall within the provisions referred to previously.

13.3.9   Relief for financing costs

Interest paid on a loan to an individual is eligible for tax relief only if the money borrowed is used for certain purposes. These include the acquisition of an interest in a close company or in a partnership. In the case of a close company it must be used for the purchase of ordinary shares in a trading or estate company or for the making of a loan to such a company to be used wholly and exclusively for the company's business. The individual will be entitled to the relief if: (1) he holds not less than 5 per cent of the company's ordinary share capital; or (2) he holds some part thereof, however small, and has in the period between the application of the loan and the payment of the interest been personally engaged in the conduct of the business in the case of a partnership, and 'worked for the greater part of his time in the actual management or conduct of the company', in the case of a company. During the same period he must not have recovered any capital from the company or partnership. For details of the complex provisions regarding this tax relief reference must be made to ss 360 and 362 of the Income and Corporation Taxes Act 1988.

13.3.10   Conclusion

It will be appreciated that many problems may arise in connection with company law and tax law. The latter in particular has become a matter of great complexity and specialist advice should always be taken. When all the legal hurdles are overcome, the sky's the limit and, if all goes well, the end result may be that the company 'goes public' or is taken over by a public company, leaving the shareholder with readily realisable shares in a company which may be or become a household name.

13.4 Private investment companies

The first part of this chapter is concerned primarily with trading companies, but much of what has been said applies equally to private investment companies. These are companies which do not carry on a trade but invest, usually either in real property or in stock, shares and similar securities, and receive rents, dividends and interest. The line between property investment and property dealing companies is a difficult one to draw and presents a problem which the courts have often been called upon to solve. Basically, the question is one of intention, but it is not always easy to decide how the available evidence (which may be scanty) should be interpreted. Some of the differences between dealing or trading companies on the one hand and investment companies on the other are dealt with below.

First, when a property is disposed of at a gain, the gain in the hands of a dealing company is part of its trading profit and is taxed at the appropriate rate of corporation tax. Where the disposal is made by an investment company, the gain may be a chargeable gain as defined for capital gains tax purposes and taxed as such. Secondly, an investment company is charged to corporation tax *prima facie* on the full amount of its income and must make a management expenses claim by virtue of which a deduction is allowed for the cost of management. Management expenses (nowhere defined in the legislation) are usually less than the expenses allowable against trading profits. Thirdly, an investment company, if it is a 'close investment-holding company', will be less favourably treated than a trading company as regards distributions.

Because of provisions contained in the 1989 Finance Act, the company will generally be ineligible for the small companies corporation tax rate. This means that it will have to pay tax on its profits at the full 33 per cent rate rather than at 25 per cent. Furthermore, restrictions may apply to repayment claims in respect of tax deemed to be withheld from dividends declared by the company.

In general the capital gains tax treatment of gains and losses arising on shares and loans to private trading companies applies equally to shares/loans involving private investment companies. However, there is one important difference; it is not possible to claim income tax relief under the Income and Corporation Taxes Act 1988, s 574 as described in **13.3.7**.

A further disadvantage which attaches to an investment company (or indeed to any company which makes chargeable gains) is that a double tax liability may arise on capital gains. On the sale of an asset by the company, tax becomes payable (as explained above) on the chargeable gain. That net gain increases the assets of the company and hence the value of the member's shares in it. On a disposal of those shares by him a further chargeable gain may arise.

A private investment company will have larger funds at its disposal than each individual shareholder and may thereby take advantage of opportunities not presented to the smaller investor. Furthermore, the minimum commission charged by a stockbroker may add disproportionately to the cost of investments of the smaller investor. Both these advantages, however, attach to any method by which small investors join together. So long as the basic agreement governing the project is carefully drawn up and fully understood by all those co-operating, a joint co-operative investment scheme may avoid the drawbacks of a private investment company while at the same time possessing many of the advantages. The taxation of unapproved investment companies (whether private or public) and their shareholders is discussed at **7.7**.

13.5   Enterprise Investment Scheme

13.5.1   Introduction

In his Budget in November 1993, the Chancellor announced a new investment incentive scheme, intended to provide a 'targeted incentive' for new equity investment in unquoted trading companies, and to encourage outside investors to introduce new finance and expertise. The Business Expansion Scheme, introduced by the Finance Act 1983, came to an end on 31 December 1993, and provisions contained in the Finance Act 1994 replaced it with the Enterprise Investment Scheme, with effect from 1 January 1994. There are numerous and complex conditions which must be satisfied in relation to the investor, the trade, and the investment. Although many of the rules included in the draft provisions are common to both the Enterprise Investment Scheme and its predecessor, the Business Expansion Scheme, there are some important differences.

For shares issued by a qualified unquoted trading company on or after 1 January 1994, relief will be given at the lower rate of 20 per cent on the amount subscribed for the shares in the year of assessment in which the shares are issued. The maximum investment which may attract relief for 1994/95 and future years will be £100,000 per annum, although for 1993/94 there was a limit of £40,000 which applied to the aggregate of an individual's investment under the Business Expansion Scheme and the Enterprise Investment Scheme. These limits apply to husband and wife separately. It is also possible to carry back up to half of an amount invested by an individual between 6 April and 5 October in any year to the previous tax year, subject to a maximum of £15,000. However, the relief carried back must not take the individual over the limit for the previous year.

Provided that the shares have been held for at least five years, the shares will be exempt from capital gains tax on disposal. Unlike investments in the Business Expansion Scheme however, a loss on the disposal of the shares after the five-year period has elapsed may still attract income tax or capital gains tax relief.

There will be a maximum amount of money which a company will be able to raise in a particular tax year under the Enterprise Investment Scheme. The normal limit will be £1m, but a higher limit of £5m will be available for companies which are engaged in certain shipping activities.

It must be borne in mind that one of the conditions for the granting of this relief is that the company must, throughout the relevant period (see **13.5.4**), be unquoted. If, at the end of the five-year period, the company is still unquoted, the investor may find himself effectively locked in. Of some 500 companies funded under the Business Expansion Scheme in 1983–84 and 1984–85 only about 20 have become quoted companies. If there is no quotation and the investor cannot find a purchaser for his shares he can realise his investment only if the company either disposes of its assets and winds up or sells its undertaking to a quoted company, so that its shareholders finish up with either quoted shares or cash. The directors may, however, be reluctant to accept the loss of directorships which would follow a winding-up and might well follow a take-over.

It must also be remembered that the Enterprise Investment Scheme is being introduced to encourage the investment of risk capital and that that is exactly what such an investment is. Tax benefits may follow an investment under the scheme but there is no certainty that the investment will be successful. Companies in commercial enterprises often have difficulty in producing a prospectus which is of much use to the prospective investor. Projections, by directors, of future profits should be read with caution. The cost of such professional reports as are required for a public flotation will often be prohibitive for new, small and possibly speculative enterprises.

13.5.2 Tax relief available

If all the conditions set out in **13.5.3** are complied with, a claim for relief may be made. It must be accompanied by a certificate from the company (authorised by the Inspector of Taxes) to the effect that it has, at all necessary times, complied with the conditions set out in **13.5.4**. The claim may be made at any time after the company has carried on the qualifying trade or activity for four months and must be made not later than two years after the end of the year of assessment in which the shares were issued. If the four month period expires after the end of that year, it must be made within two years after the end of that period.

If a claim is allowed before the end of the qualifying period (see **13.5.4**) and any subsequent event results in a contravention of any of the conditions, the relief will be withdrawn. If the company fails to carry on the trade for four months by reason of a winding-up or dissolution for *bona fide* commercial reasons and not as part of a tax-saving scheme, the claim will not fail for that reason. Provision is made in the legislation requiring that information leading to a loss of relief must be sent to the Revenue.

13.5.3 Individuals eligible for relief

For an individual to be entitled to the relief under the Business Expansion Scheme he had to be resident and ordinarily resident in the UK at the time of issue. This requirement will not apply to investors in the Enterprise Investment Scheme, and relief will be available for non-residents if they are liable to UK income tax. There will be a further relaxation in that an investor can become a paid director, without forfeiting entitlement to relief under the Enterprise Investment Scheme. This is, however, subject to the proviso that the individual was not connected with the company or its trade prior to the issue of the Enterprise Investment Scheme shares.

The words 'connected with' are given a very wide meaning. An individual is connected with a company if:

(1) he or an associate (defined below) is an employee of the company or of its partner, or is himself its partner or is a paid director of the company or of a company which is in partnership with it;
(2) he possesses (directly or indirectly) or is entitled to acquire more than 30 per cent of the company's issued ordinary share capital, loan capital and issued share capital, voting rights or such rights as would entitle him to more than 30 per cent of the assets available to equity holders on a winding-up;
(3) he has power to secure that the affairs of the company are conducted in accordance with his wishes by means of the holding of shares or the possession of voting power of that or another company or by virtue of any power in the articles or other document regulating that or any other company; or
(4) he is a party to a reciprocal arrangement under which some other person subscribes for shares in a company with which the individual (or any other individual who is a party to the arrangement) is connected.

For the purposes of (1) above, 'associate' means:

(1) the husband or wife, parent or remoter forebear, child or remoter issue or any partner of the individual;
(2) a trustee of any settlement in relation to which the settlor is or was the individual or any of the persons mentioned in (1) (other than a partner), whether living or dead; or
(3) where the individual is interested in any shares or obligations of the company which are (with certain exceptions) subject to a trust or form part of a deceased's estate, any other person interested therein. It may, in this connection, be difficult to ascertain who is an associate and who is not.

The shares must be held in a qualifying company for at least five years and relief will be clawed back if shares are disposed of within the five-year period.

13.5.4 Qualifying companies

Two expressions used in connection with the qualification of a company require explanation.

(1) The 'relevant period'. In relation to 'qualifying companies' and 'qualifying trades' it means the period of three years beginning with the issue of the shares or, if the company was not at the time of such issue carrying on a qualifying trade, the period of three years from the commencement of such a trade.
(2) A 'qualifying subsidiary'. This means a subsidiary company which is not less than 90 per cent owned and controlled by the parent company, no arrangements being in existence by virtue of which it could cease to be so owned and controlled. That condition must be satisfied until the end of the 'relevant period' unless there is an earlier winding-up or dissolution for *bona fide* commercial reasons which is not part of a tax-avoidance arrangement and on which the subsidiary's net assets are distributed not more than three years after the commencement of the winding-up. The subsidiary must exist wholly or substantially to carry on qualifying activities or be a 'dormant' company ie, one which has no corporation tax profits and does not include the making of investments as part of its business.

The conditions to be complied with by the company are as follows:

(1) it must, throughout the 'relevant period', be an unquoted company which must exist wholly or 'substantially wholly' for the purpose of carrying on wholly or mainly in the UK one or more 'qualifying

trades' (see **13.5.5**) or must carry on a business which consists wholly of either:

(a)   holding shares or securities of, or making loans to, one or more 'qualifying subsidiaries'; or

(b)   both (a) *and* the carrying on wholly or mainly in the UK of one or more 'qualifying trades'.

(2)   the company's share capital must not, at any time in the 'relevant period' include any issued shares that are not fully paid up;

(3)   the company must not, at any time in the relevant period, control (whether alone or with any connected person) another company or have a 51 per cent subsidiary or be controlled by another company (whether alone or with a connected person) or be a 51 per cent subsidiary nor must any arrangements be in existence at any time during the relevant period which could bring the company within any of the prohibited situations. An exception is made, however, for companies having subsidiaries which are themselves qualifying companies under (1) above.

(4)   The original rules provided that a company's interest in land could not exceed one-half of its total assets. This condition has however been removed with effect from 29 November 1994, under the provisions of the Finance Act 1995.

Another significant change from the BES rules is that qualifying companies can now include foreign companies. Provided that they trade in the United Kingdom, they will not be required to be incorporated, or resident in the United Kingdom.

13.5.5   Qualifying trades

Some guidance has been given by the Revenue, in a Statement of Practice dated 12 September 1986, as to what, in their view, is meant by carrying on a trade 'wholly or mainly in the United Kingdom' referred to in point (1), above. Each case will be determined on its facts including the 'totality of the activities of the trade'. Thus, regard will be had to such factors as the location of capital assets, and the places where purchasing, manufacturing, selling and other things are done. The carrying on of some activities outside the UK will not disqualify the company if, in the words of the Revenue, 'over one-half of the aggregate of these activities takes place within the country'. The phrase 'over one-half' suggests, that some precise measurement must be possible. The Statement of Practice goes on to say that a company would not be excluded from relief solely because its output is exported, or its raw materials imported, or storage or marketing facilities exist overseas.

A 'qualifying trade' is one which does not to any substantial extent comprise:

(1) dealing in commodities, shares, securities, land or futures;
(2) dealing in goods otherwise than in an ordinary trade of wholesale or retail distribution;
(3) banking, insurance, moneylending, debt-factoring, hire-purchase financing or other financial activities;
(4) leasing, chartering ships, or hiring;
(5) receiving royalties or licence fees;
(6) providing legal or accountancy services;
(7) oil extraction activities; or
(8) providing services of the nature of those set out in (1) to (7) for a trade carried on by any person who controls the trade carried on by the company.

As to (5) above, a trade which consists to a substantial extent of the receiving of royalties or licence fees is not disqualified if the company carrying on the trade is engaged, throughout the relevant period, in the production of films or in research and development and if all royalties and licence fees received by it in that period are in respect of films produced by it or of sound recordings or other products arising from such films or from research and development.

The trade must be carried on on a commercial basis and with a view to realising profits. It must have been carried on by the company for four months before the relief will be allowed and, if not carried on at the time of the issue, must be begun within two years thereafter.

13.5.6 Qualifying investments

For the investment to qualify for relief it must itself comply with a number of conditions:

(1) it must be made by the individual on his own behalf;
(2) the shares must be taken by subscription and not by purchase from an existing shareholder;
(3) the shares must be new ordinary shares which, throughout the five years from the date of issue, carry no present or future preferential rights to dividends, assets on a winding-up, or to redemption; and
(4) the shares must be issued for the purpose of raising money for a qualifying trade or activity carried on, or to be carried on, by the company.

Nor will relief be given to an individual where the company comes to acquire all the issued share capital of another company at any time during the relevant period and the individual (or a group of persons of which he is one) at any such time controlled both companies.

The 1995 Finance Act will amend the current provisions, for shares issued after 28 November, to allow relief to individuals, even where they are involved in the control of another company carrying on a similar trade.

Although the investment, to qualify for relief, must be made by an individual, it may be made through an approved investment fund. Particulars regarding some of such funds are obtainable from the British Venture Capital Association.

13.5.7   Withdrawal of relief

Relief for investment in an Enterprise Investment Scheme will be clawed back if an investor disposes of the shares within a period of five years, unless the disposal arises because the company has gone into liquidation. In these circumstances further income tax or capital gains tax relief may be due to the investor. Where the investor receives no payment as a result of the liquidation, the net amount of his investment may qualify as a capital loss.

The comments set out above should be taken as a guide only. They do not cover every detail of the proposed legislation but should help in identifying most of the difficulties to be faced in crossing this morass of regulations.

13.5.8   Venture capital trusts (VCTs)

In his 1993 Budget the Chancellor announced proposals to create a new relief for investment in venture capital trusts. This announcement was followed by a consultative document, and the 1995 Finance Act will contain provisions which will introduce the relief with effect from 6 April 1995.

VCTs will be companies which are similar to investment trusts and to obtain approval they must meet a number of conditions, in particular:

(1)   The ordinary share capital of a VCT must have been quoted on The Stock Exchange.
(2)   The VCT must not retain more than 15 per cent of the income that it has derived from shares or securities.
(3)   The income received by the VCT must have been derived wholly or mainly from shares or securities.
(4)   The value of investments held by the VCT must consist of at least 70 per cent of qualifying shares or securities.
(5)   At least 50 per cent of the value of a VCT's qualifying holdings must be made up of ordinary shares.
(6)   The value of a VCT's holding in any one company must not exceed 15 per cent of its total investments.

It may be possible for a VCT to be granted provisional approval provided that the 70 per cent, and 50 per cent conditions mentioned in (4) and (5) above, will be met within three years, and the other conditions in the current or next accounting period. This provisional approval will be withdrawn if the VCT fails to meet the conditions within these time periods.

13.5.9 Qualifying holdings

These must consist of holdings in unquoted companies which exist wholly or mainly for the purpose of carrying on a qualifying trade in the United Kingdom. For these purposes a qualifying trade is as defined for the Enterprise Investment Scheme, and the gross assets of the unquoted company must not exceed £10m, immediately prior to the VCT's investment.

Income tax relief

Relief can be claimed by resident individuals aged 18 or over, and is available in two different ways.

Firstly income tax relief at the rate of 20 per cent is given for amounts subscribed for new ordinary shares in the VCT, although the amount subscribed in any one year must not exceed £100,000. The relief will be withdrawn unless the shares are held for at least five years.

In additon, dividends from ordinary shares held in VCTs are exempt from income tax, to the extent that the value of the shares acquired each year does not exceed £100,000.

Capital gains tax

Where investments in VCTs have qualified for income tax relief, disposals after five years will be exempt from capital gains tax.

Reinvestment relief is also available for investments in VCTs, provided that the VCT shares for which the individual subscribes are issued during a period beginning 12 months before and ending 12 months after the date of disposal of the asset creating the capital gain which is to be deferred.

In common with investments in the Enterprise Investment Scheme the deferred gain may be reinstated if the investor disposes of the shares, other than to his or her spouse, or ceases to be resident in the United Kingdom within five years of the issue of the VCT shares.

The relief will also be withdrawn if the company ceases to be a qualifying VCT within three years of the issue of the shares, or within three years of the commencement of trading, if later, or the investor ceases to qualify for the 20 per cent income tax relief.

13.6   Dormant partnerships

13.6.1   Introduction

It is not unusual for a person commencing a trade to find himself short of capital. In such circumstances an investor who is persuaded of the potential viability of the trade may be prepared to put up the capital but not want to play any active part in the carrying on of the business. He will then be a 'dormant' or 'sleeping' partner. Since partners are generally entitled to take part in the running of the business, this arrangement must be the subject of a special agreement.

Unless the business name consists of the names of all the partners, it must comply with the provisions of the Business Names Act 1985. This Act governs names which may and may not be used for business purposes and how and where they must be disclosed. A register of such names was formerly maintained but was closed in February 1982.

13.6.2   Loan creditors

It is important to distinguish a dormant partner from a loan creditor. If the investor receives a fixed rate of interest on his investment he is probably not a partner at all. Under s 2 of the Partnership Act 1890 the receipt of a share of the profits is *prima facie* evidence of partnership, although the receipt of such a share or of interest at a rate varying with the profits does not of itself make the lender a partner. This apparent contradiction was explained by North J, in *Davis v Davis* [1894] 1 Ch 393, and it appears from his judgment that the Act means that all the relevant facts must be taken together, no special weight being attached to the sharing of profits. It is difficult to see how the Act could be intended to mean that, although, in fairness to North J, it is equally difficult to see that it could be intended to mean anything else either. In the majority of cases there will be (and there certainly should be) a written agreement making the position clear. If the agreement so declares and the name of the dormant partner is included in the name of the firm there will be little doubt of the existence of a partnership.

13.6.3   Rights and liabilities

Once it is established that the 'investor' (to use a neutral term) is a dormant partner and not merely a loan creditor, certain rights arise. For example, he will be entitled to inspect and take a copy of the firm's accounts and, in the absence of any agreement to the contrary, to investigate their contents.

A dormant partner is, generally, personally liable for the debts of the firm even if the creditors were unaware of his partnership at the time when the debts arose. This liability extends to the whole of the partner's personal fortune. Such an arrangement can therefore carry considerable personal risk, although this can be curtailed by the formation of a 'limited partnership'.

Under the Limited Partnerships Act 1907 it is possible for a partner to limit his liability to the amount contributed by him to the partnership at its inception, although there must always be at least one partner whose liability is unlimited. The limited partner may not receive back any of his capital so long as the partnership continues, and if any of it is returned to him, his liability up to the amount of his original contribution will remain. He is, of course, entitled to draw out his share of the firm's profits.

A limited partner must always be a dormant partner. Should he take any active part in the running of the business, the limitation of his liability is lost, and it will then extend to the whole of the partnership's debts and to the full extent of his personal assets.

The law relating to dormant partnerships is liberally sprinkled with traps for the unwary, and the law relating to limited partnerships is particularly unsatisfactory. No partnership of any sort should be entered into without taking legal advice, and although the law does not require a partnership agreement to be reduced to writing, it is always desirable that it should be. Whatever the relations may have been at the outset, it is only too easy for the partner entering too readily into informal arrangements to find the whole of his personal estate at risk in respect of liabilities which he played no part in incurring. It is when things start to go wrong that dissensions occur, and by then it may be too late to correct matters which should have been dealt with at the outset.

13.6.4 Taxation

A trading partnership, like any other trader, is normally assessed to tax on the basis of the profits of the trading year ending during the tax year prior to the year of assessment. For example, if the accounts are taken to 31 December, the profits for the year ended 31 December 1993 form the basis of the assessment for the tax year 1994/95. This general rule is subject to various complications relating to the opening years, the closing years, changes in partnership treated as a cessation, and losses. The 1994 Finance Act contains legislation to abolish the 'preceding year' basis of assessment for the self-employed, from 6 April 1996. This change will have immediate effect for businesses starting after 5 April 1994, although existing businesses will not fully change to the current year basis until the tax year 1997/98. There are complicated transitional provisions to ensure that profits are not taxed twice, and special rules will apply where a business changes its accounting date. The assessable profit for the transitional year 1996/97 will be based on a 12-month average of the profits for the two-year period ending in the year ending 5 April 1997. There are however a number of anti-avoidance provisions which are intended to prevent manipulation of trading profits in order to gain a tax advantage.

Having determined the amount of the assessment for, say 1994/95, that amount is apportioned among the partners in accordance with their profit-sharing arrangements for that year regardless of the way in which they actually shared the profit on which the assessment was based. It will be appreciated that this may lead to inequitable results.

Earned income is defined in s 833(4)(*c*) of the Income and Corporation Taxes Act 1988 as income which is 'derived by the individual from the carrying on or exercise by him of his trade . . ., in the case of a partnership, as a partner personally acting therein'. Any partnership income not falling within that definition is investment income. Since a dormant partner (whether with limited liability or not) does not, by definition, act personally in the business, it must follow that any income derived from the partnership will be investment income. This will be of significance in relation to retirement pension schemes.

13.7   Membership of Lloyd's

13.7.1   Introduction

Some 300 years ago Edward Lloyd opened a coffee-house in the City which proved to be a popular meeting place for men with an interest in shipping. In 1692 he moved to larger premises on the corner of Lombard Street and Abchurch Lane, where the financial quarter had become well-established, which soon became known as a centre where ship-owners could take insurance cover. With the increasing size of ships and value of cargoes, the size of the risks grew and individual underwriters were obliged to join in syndicates, so creating the system which still functions today. Lloyd's itself, as in its coffee-house days, does no more than provide accommodation and facilities for the underwriters; it is not, and never has been, an insurer. Lloyd's was incorporated by Act of Parliament in 1871, and that and later Acts regulate the fundamental rules and authorise the making of byelaws by the members. An Act of 1911 authorised the underwriting of non-marine risks, regularising what had already become well-established practice.

Lloyd's of London published a business plan on 29 April 1993, which set out proposals intended to improve the profitability of Lloyd's by increasing capacity, cutting costs and capping losses arising prior to the 1986 account. However, the most fundamental proposal was to allow corporate membership of Lloyd's from the 1994 account. This introduced the concept of limited liability for the first time in the history of Lloyd's.

Members of Lloyd's (called 'Names') are grouped into syndicates and share in the syndicates' profits or losses. As regards losses, each member of a syndicate is liable only for his agreed share (unlike a partnership loss where each partner is jointly and separately liable for all losses) but at present that liability extends to the whole of his assets. Generally, a Name takes no part in managing the affairs of his syndicate. He is thus entirely in the hands of his Underwriting Agent (see **13.7.2**).

Income and gains received by names comprise:

(1)   investment income and capital gains on deposits and reserve funds (see **13.7.2**);
(2)   investment income and capital gains on premiums received and invested by the syndicate; and
(3)   underwriting profits (excess of premiums over claims) if any.

It must not be overlooked that both capital and underwriting losses may also arise. Figures are produced three years in arrears.

Following a series of unprecedented disasters, further problems surfaced in 1991 with claims of fraud and mismanagement, and some syndicates remain open since they are unable to reinsure to close. Names are suffering unprecedented losses.

Membership is reported as being down from 32,400 in 1988 to just over 17,000 in 1994 with many Names being forcibly reminded that their liability is unlimited.

Despite the drop in membership, many Names increased their premium limits for 1994 and with the introduction of corporate members the capacity of the market is estimated at £10.9bn. Many members, however, no longer have the readily realisable wealth formerly relied on (see **13.7.2**) and rely instead on bank guarantees secured against property.

It is suggested that much of the malaise stems from the Lloyd's Act 1982 which ruled that brokers could no longer own agencies managing syndicates. The intention of this was to prevent conflicts of interest but it probably resulted in brokers moving business elsewhere.

Certainly the problems of Lloyd's run deep. As well as many resignations there has been much litigation and constant bad news has tended to scare off potential members. Lloyd's has set up its own reinsurance company but premiums are likely to be so high that some syndicates will not have enough in hand to meet them.

Whilst it may be possible to reduce the element of risk by taking out high level stop loss insurance policies and arranging for the Members' Agent to select appropriate low risk syndicates, one cannot avoid the fact that under the present regime an individual Name accepts unlimited personal liability.

13.7.2   Application for individual membership

The aspiring member must satisfy Lloyd's that he is a proper person to join their number. His application form must be accompanied by a nomination form signed by one member as sponsor and by another to whom the applicant is personally known. The application form is posted in the Underwriting Room and the applicant will then be interviewed by a sub-committee. The sub-committee, whatever other questions it may ask, will always ask whether the applicant clearly understands that he will be trading with unlimited liability. The liability is not limited to the wealth shown (see below) nor to the amount of the deposit (see below). In the event of a substantial claim arising, the whole of the applicant's personal estate is at risk.

It is generally recommended that members should spread their risk among a number of syndicates. Membership of one syndicate only may mean a heavy financial loss in the event of a major disaster.

At an early stage, and certainly before election, the applicant must investigate the syndicate or syndicates which he hopes to join. Assistance in the choice of syndicate may be obtained from a Members' Underwriting Agent (not the same as a Managing Agent, although he may be so in practice). The policy for investing syndicate funds and the likely premium income will be explained by the syndicate's Underwriting Agent (see below) and the result of the last seven 'closed years' will be made available. A 'closed year' is one in respect of which the underwriting account has been closed by reinsuring any outstanding liabilities, usually at the end of the third year. The applicant should also enquire about the establishment of personal reserves, transfer to the Special Reserve Fund, and the form of accounts.

Applications for membership must be approved by the Committee, who apply a means test to the applicant's readily realisable assets which include Stock Exchange securities, life policies at their surrender values, reversionary interests and real property but not the applicant's principal residence. Gold (up to 30 per cent of the total), which must be held by an approved bank in the form of bullion or coins, is valued at 70 per cent of market value. Such things as shares in private companies, jewellery and antiques are not included. An applicant needs to show that he has readily realisable assets worth £250,000.

Where the applicant's wealth comprises items not readily realisable but is in other respects satisfactory, the Committee will accept, in whole or in part, a guarantee or letter of credit from an approved bank, as collateral for which the principal residence may be included. The object of the means test is to ensure that as far as possible, funds will be available at short notice to meet a claim, however large it may be. A booklet entitled 'Membership: the Issues' is obtainable from Lloyd's and sets out all the information which an applicant should know.

13.7.3 Conditions of individual membership

The Members' Underwriting Agent controls the underwriting affairs of the underwriting members of his agency. He maintains the accounts and records and deals with taxation, reserves, investments and other day-to-day matters as well as watching the statistics which give him a guide to current trends. It is also his duty to ensure that the rules laid down by the Committee of Lloyd's are complied with. Every underwriting member enters into an agreement with the agent which sets out the terms and conditions on which the agent acts, including his salary or fee and his rate of commission.

Every individual underwriting member is required to deposit with the Corporation of Lloyd's approved investments or cash which the Corporation holds as trustee. The Lloyd's deposit must be maintained at a minimum of £25,000. For further details enquiries should be made to the deposits department at Lloyd's. The investing of the deposit may be delegated to the Underwriting Agent or may, within the Committee's rules, be dealt with by the member. The income arising on investments deposited remains the income of the member.

A member's premium limit is the maximum premium income which may be underwritten by him in any one year. It is allocated to the syndicate and is then divided among the members in proportions agreed in consultation with the agent. The limit may be increased or decreased according to the market value of the deposit and may be raised if additional amounts are deposited and evidence of sufficient means is produced. If the limit is exceeded the member will normally be required to increase his deposit.

An entrance fee is payable in cash on election and varies according to the category of membership. Entrance fees are not deductible from profits for tax purposes. An annual contribution to Lloyd's Central Fund is also required. The Fund was set up in 1926 for the protection of policyholders in the event of the inability of a member to meet his liabilities out of his syndicate's trust funds, his deposit, his reserves and his personal assets. The reserve is the amount which, under the Rules, has to be set aside each year to meet the estimated cost of winding-up the Name's underwriting accounts.

13.7.4   Taxation

The special provisions covering the taxation of the income of underwriters are currently to be found in ss 450 to 457 of the Income and Corporation Taxes Act 1988, although the Finance Acts for 1993 and 1994 contain further provisions which will change the way in which Lloyd's Names will be taxed from the 1994 underwriting account. The intention is that the profits of the 1994 account will not be assessed for 1994/95, but will be assessed in 1997/98, the year of distribution. This change will create a three-year period for which no profits will be assessable, 1994/95 to 1996/97. These should be carefully considered by the applicant with expert advice. Briefly, the effect of the current legislation for underwriting years up to the 1993 underwriting account is as follows.

Underwriting profits will be assessed on the basis of the profits of the underwriting year ending in the year of assessment and not on the normal basis of the previous year. Thus the profits of the underwriting year ending 31 December 1993 will be assessed for the fiscal year 1993/94 although they are not finally ascertained for three years thereafter. Underwriting profits are profits or gains arising from underwriting business or from assets forming part of a premium trust fund. A premium paid for reinsurance is deductible as an expense. Losses of an underwriting business are allowed against other income of the year of assessment in which they are incurred, and any excess against that of the previous year if the underwriter was carrying on an underwriting business in that year. They cannot, however, be carried forward against general income of a later year but can be set against future underwriting profits.

For underwriting accounts up to and including the 1991 account, relief from income tax at the higher rate is given to underwriters on payments into the Special Reserve Fund, such payments being limited to a sum which, after deduction of tax at the basic rate, does not exceed £7,000 or 50 per cent of underwriting profits for the underwriting year forming the basis period for the year of assessment, whichever is the less. If an underwriter incurs losses which necessitate payment out of the fund, such payments are liable to tax at the higher rate with a credit for the basic rate tax deemed to have been deducted at source. Payments out of the fund are not generally so liable if they are made on death, but are if made on ceasing to be an underwriter. Payment into the fund is treated as an annual charge made under deduction of tax, and payment out as income received after deduction of tax. Changes were made in the administrative arrangements for taxing members of Lloyd's under the Finance Act 1988.

The existing Special Reserve Fund will be abolished after the 1991 Account and will be replaced by a new tax deductible reserve from the 1992 account, although any existing special reserves can be transferred to this new reserve fund. Transfers to fund will qualify for both basic rate and higher rate relief, and it will be possible to transfer 50 per cent of Lloyd's profits into the reserve each year, providing that the value of the funds held in the reserve does not exceed 50 per cent of the Name's overall premium limit. Any income or gains arising from assets held in the reserve will be exempt from income tax and capital gains tax.

Withdrawals from the reserve will be made to fund losses, cash calls, or on resignation or death. This will be treated as underwriting income of the Name at the time of withdrawal. The tax calculation will be based on the actual value of the withdrawal rather than the 'book values' of the assets comprising the withdrawal. In effect the increase in the value of the fund, attributable to income and gains, will not be taxed as it arises, but on withdrawal.

13.8   Investment in another's expertise

The first difficulty in making an investment of this kind lies in discovering the innovator whose expertise is to be given financial backing. The innovator seeking capital has many avenues open to him. He may consult the National Research Development Corporation, the Council for Small Industries in Rural Areas, Investors in Industry Group plc (formerly known as the Industrial and Commercial Finance Corporation) or the Small Business Capital Fund. Alternatively he may look for capital through his bank or a merchant bank, through local accountants, solicitors or insurance brokers, through the Rotary Club or the Round Table, through the local branch of the British Institute of Management or through the Small Firms Council of the Confederation of British Industry. The prospective investor can approach any of these agencies to inquire whether they know of any worthwhile ideas for which backing is sought.

Once the innovator has been located, the prospects of the venture must be carefully examined, not only by the investor's accountant but also by an expert in the technical field where appropriate. Inquiry should be made as to how much of his own capital the innovator is putting into the venture. If he has little he cannot be expected to put a lot in, but his intentions in this respect will indicate his real confidence in the venture. Plans should be carefully prepared and the amount required should be meticulously calculated, all contingencies being taken into account. The information required will include particulars of the product or process, with technical explanations and specifications of patents, if any. Its advantages over existing products or processes must be explained and the costs of development detailed, together with reasoned estimates of future sales. Mere hopes based on speculation will not do.

In general terms, an investor may back another's expertise by means of a private company, a partnership or a loan. A loan will probably be the least attractive method for two reasons. First, adequate security is unlikely to be available. Secondly, the income will be limited to interest at a fixed rate, thus denying the lender any participation in profits should the venture prove an outstanding success — the greatest attraction of this type of investment. As to private companies and partnerships, it will be necessary to determine the appropriate proportionate interests of the investor who is putting in capital and the expert who is putting in expertise. Both may be of equal importance: indeed both are essential, but 50:50 holdings can mean deadlock and are better avoided if possible. This immediately gives rise to a problem which needs professional advice and probably tough negotiating.

Some of the legal aspects of the arrangement (including any liability for taxation on profits or gains arising) have been dealt with in general terms earlier in this chapter. As has already been stressed, every case will present individual problems, and both commercial and professional advice should always be sought. Adequate financial and administrative control is essential for the investor, and he will usually be wise to insist on his own accountant auditing the books and his representative keeping a close eye on the running of the business.

13.9 Racehorses

13.9.1 Introduction

Investing in racehorses is not for the faint-hearted. The rules regulating racing in this country are made by the Jockey Club from whom detailed information may be obtained. Anyone proposing to invest in a racehorse is presumably already well-acquainted with the turf and will know something about horses. Investment may be either in horses in training or in stallions. (Investment in stud farms and training establishments is discussed at **11.4.3**.)

The increase in the cost of buying and running a horse led to an expansion of syndicated ownership regulated (as to horses in training) by the Jockey Club 'rules of racing'. New syndicates are, however, no longer accepted by the Jockey Club and where a horse is owned jointly it must now be by way of a legally enforceable partnership of which each member is registered as an owner. The number of partners is restricted (as it was for syndicate members) to 12. The partnership agreement (which should be drawn up with legal advice) must be registered with the Jockey Club. All partners are jointly and severally liable for entrance fees, stakes, forfeits and jockey's fees. That is to say that any one of them may be held individually liable for the full amount and will then have to recover the due amounts from the other partners.

It is recommended by the Jockey Club that anyone proposing to become a part-owner by way of a partnership should contact them before taking any steps in the matter. The rules governing joint-ownership are complex and the Jockey Club would prefer to advise at the outset rather than unscramble an arrangement that contravenes the rules.

An interest in a racehorse may be bought through the medium of a limited company but it must be realised that the investor is then buying a share in the company and not a share in a horse. There are a number of public limited companies engaged in these activities.

Racing generally is facing severe problems in the coming year as a result of the Horserace Betting Levy Board's forecast of a drop in its funding. It seems likely that prize money levels will fall, the number of meetings will be reduced and some race-courses may be forced to close.

13.9.2 Stallions

As well as investments in horses in training, investments may be made in syndicated stallions. In this case there are no rules of the sort set out in relation to horses in training — *ad hoc* arrangements are made in each case. A stallion may stand at stud until it is 20 years old, but the value of a nomination falls as it approaches that age. A stallion will give about 150 services each season, covering each mare three or four times. Stud fees at present range generally up to about 1,500 guineas, although that figure may be greatly exceeded in special cases.

In a typical syndicate there will be 40 shares, most of which will be held by shareholders with one share each. The agreement usually provides for a committee, including the major shareholder or shareholders, to be set up. The committee will be empowered to decide all matters relating to the management of the stallion and the affairs of the syndicate as agent for the shareholders, although its powers in relation to the disposal of the stallion are usually limited. Generally each shareholder is entitled to one nomination per share for the season. The maximum number of nominations for the season is fixed, and in so far as it exceeds the number available to shareholders, the excess may be sold and the proceeds set against expenses which are borne *pro rata* by the shareholders. The agreement usually provides that the committee must approve mares to be served by the stallion and that a barren mare must also be approved by a veterinary surgeon. A veterinary surgeon will examine any maiden mare before service. Restrictions are usually placed on the disposal of shares and nominations, but it may happen that during the season in question the shareholder has no mare suitable for nomination and in such a case the nomination will be sold.

13.9.3   Taxation

Income tax

It was held in *Benson v Counsell* (1942) 24 TC 178 that receipts from the sale of nominations were receipts of annual income chargeable to income tax under Case VI of Schedule D although they were not trading receipts within Case I. This decision was based on the fact that the taxpayer had not bought the rights to nomination that he sold: what he had bought was an interest in the horse. The sale of the rights merely realised the horse's reproductive faculties and it thus became an income-producing asset. In 1915 the Earl of Derby unsuccessfully contended that a stallion at stud was 'plant' for the purposes of capital allowances (see *Derby (Earl) v Aylmer* [1915] 3 KB 374).

Capital gains tax

The sale of a share in the horse, whether it is a horse in training or a stallion, does *not* give rise to a taxable gain, since s 45(1) of the Taxation of Chargeable Gains Act 1992 takes out of the charge to capital gains tax any gain accruing on the disposal of, or of an interest in, an asset which is tangible, movable property and a wasting asset. There is no doubt that a horse is tangible and movable, nor that it is a wasting asset (ie one with a predictable life not exceeding 50 years).

13.10 Backing plays

It is possible that, somewhere, a playwright has just written a play that will take London by storm and play for years to packed houses. It is, on present showing, most unlikely. It is estimated that only one show in seven put on in the West End will be successful which suggests that somewhere along the line there is a failure to foresee what the public will and will not like. In recent years flops have included *Stop the World I Want to Get Off, Exclusive, Metropolis, Sherlock Holmes, Someone Like You, Look Look, Dean, Barnardo, Can-Can, Fire Angel, King, Top People, Y, Ziegfeld, Troubadour, Bus Stop, Bernadette, My Lovely . . . Shayna Madel, Rick's Bar Casablanca* and *Children of Eden*. Together they have lost millions. The last one, alone, is said to have lost £2.5m.

This is not the place to consider the reasons for this failure rate but those tempted to put money into a play should realise that their chance of making anything out of it are slim. It is statistically more probable that money put in will be lost without tax relief. This is the ideal investment for those who enjoy losing money.

Those who put up the money for a theatrical production — the 'angels' — normally split the profits with the management: the angels usually take 60 per cent and the management 40 per cent, although the proportions are a matter for agreement. The agreement usually also provides for an 'overcall', ie a liability on the part of the angels to put up additional capital should it prove necessary. Before the profits are divided between angels and management there has to be deducted such of the fees and expenses of management as may be specified in the agreement. The agreement should be carefully scrutinised by an adviser familiar with these matters to ensure that the angel is getting his fair share.

Anyone determined to risk this gamble against heavy odds should first become familiar with the track records of various producers. The eager investor should then attempt to force his money on one who seems successful. If a producer makes the approach, consider why his usual sources of finance are not available. There is no central exchange through which investments can be made although assistance may be obtained from the Society of West End Theatre. Whilst not arranging investments itself, the Society will give advice and maintains a list of prospective backers. Since the backer will normally have no opportunity even to read the play he is simply betting on the wisdom of the producer.

The cost of mounting a play will vary enormously. A large-scale musical can cost millions to stage and with production and running costs at their present levels a show has to run for a considerable time before the production costs are covered and anything is paid out. If the production is successful the investor will receive an agreed share of the net profits which will, first, recoup the costs and, thereafter, constitute income for tax purposes.

As a variant of the traditional method of financing, advantage may be taken of the provisions of s 574 of the Income and Corporation Taxes Act 1988 which enables losses on unquoted shares in certain trading companies to be set off against a taxpayer's income. The resulting loss is thus, to some extent, cushioned by income tax relief.

13.11 Options on books

An investor with sufficient faith in a little-known author may back that faith by purchasing an option, exercisable usually for one year, to develop the book into a film or play. A little-known author is suggested as, in the case of a best-seller writer, the option is likely (if it is available at all) to be extremely expensive. It is, of course, much less expensive to buy such an option than it would be to buy the copyright outright.

Once the option is purchased it will become necessary to write or procure a script from the book and then to persuade a film company or theatrical producer to take it up. The time involved in these activities may necessitate the purchase of another year's option.

Would-be purchasers should consult a firm of literary agents for further advice. A list of agents is published in the *Writers and Artists Yearbook.*

13.12 Preview of the year ahead

Despite government assurances that the falling unemployment figures, and other economic indicators point to a substantial recovery, the 'feel good factor' does not seem to have been passed to consumers. After a period of falling interest rates, they have now started to rise once again, and inflation figures, although still within government forecasts, have stabilised and show signs of possible increases in the future.

Lloyd's losses for the 1991 account were even worse than predicted, although hopefully the 1992, 1993 and 1994 accounts will show a marked improvement. Legal disputes continue to cause concern, and it is likely to be some time before Names, still locked into run-off syndicates, feel the benefit of any improvement. It had been hoped that the admission of corporate members would prove to be Lloyd's salvation, but the take-up has been very disappointing and unless the situation rapidly improves the number of Names seems destined to continue to fall.

It remains to be seen whether the tax incentives now being offered to investors in smaller companies will help to provide the kick-start necessary.

Sources of further information

Useful addresses

Registrar of Companies/Registrar
  of Limited Partnerships
Companies Registration Office
Companies House
Crown Way
Cardiff
CF4 3UZ

Tel: (01222) 388588

Lloyd's of London
Lime Street
London
EC3M 7AH

Tel: (0171) 623 7100

National Research Development
  Corporation
101 Newington Causeway
London
SE1 6BU

Tel: (0171) 403 6666

Rural Development Commission
141 Castle Street
Salisbury
Wiltshire
SP1 3TP

Tel: (01722) 336255

Investors in Industry Group plc
91 Waterloo Road
London
SE1 8XP

Tel: (0171) 928 3131

British Venture Capital
  Association
Essex House
12–13 Essex Street
London
WC2R 3AA

Tel: (0171) 240 3846

Development Capital Group
  Limited
21 Moorfield
London
EC2P 2HT

Tel: (0171) 588 2721

Department of Trade and Industry
  Small Firms Service
To obtain address of nearest
  centre, dial 100 and ask the
  operator for Freefone
  Enterprise

British Institute of Management
3rd Floor
2 Savoy Court
Strand
London
WC2R 0EZ

Tel: (0171) 497 0580

Confederation of British Industry
Centrepoint
103 New Oxford Street
London
WC1A 1DU

Tel: (0171) 379 7400

Jockey Club
42 Portman Square
London
W1H 0EN

Tel: (0171) 486 4921

Society of West End Theatre &
    West End Theatre
    Managers Ltd
Bedford Chambers
The Piazza
Covent Garden
London
WC2E 8HQ

Tel: (0171) 836 0971

14   Life assurance

Vince Jerrard, LLB, ACII, Legal Director, Allied Dunbar Assurance plc

14.1   Introduction

Assurance contracts may be divided into three broad types, according to the nature of the primary benefits provided:

(1)   life assurance policies (including single premium bonds) pay out a lump sum on death or on the expiration of a specified period;
(2)   purchased life annuities pay periodic sums as long as the annuitant is alive;
(3)   pension contracts provide pensions and other benefits and are available through one's work or occupation.

Within each of these categories there are further subdivisions. Pension contracts are dealt with in Chapter 15.

14.2   Highlights of the previous year

14.2.1   Life assurance business

1994 proved to be a difficult year for the UK life assurance and pensions industry.

Although results varied greatly from company to company, the overall market was rather depressed, as a result of a combination of factors.

The failure of the housing market to recover and the relatively poor performance of the stock market were two factors, as was the absence of what has been widely referred to as the 'feel good factor', despite an otherwise encouraging economic upturn.

However, one of the key reasons for this lacklustre performance was a certain absence of consumer confidence in the industry. In large measure, this resulted from concern about the possible widespread selling of inappropriate pension schemes over the last few years (further details of which are included in Chapter 15) and the uncertainty and sometimes unfavourable publicity for the industry ahead of the new 'disclosure' regime which has come into effect in 1995 (of which more details can be found in Chapter 21).

14.2.2   Taxation Changes

During 1994 the industry began a consultation process with the Revenue to consider the future direction of the tax regime for life assurance in the UK.

Essentially, there are two broad regimes which could be adopted: the current 'I–E' (Income–Expenses) regime; or a regime based on gross roll-up of income and gains in the life company's funds, with the taxation emphasis shifting almost entirely to the taxation of policy proceeds in the hands of the investor (the GRU approach).

In general, GRU is favoured in most of the EU Countries and the possible threat to the UK industry through the selling of 'foreign' policies into the UK has been one of the factors which has prompted the review. While it seems clear that the current regime will continue for the immediate future, the next year or so should see the finalisation of a plan to take the taxation of the UK industry into the next century.

Ahead of these discussions, a number of changes are currently in progress as a result of ministerial announcement and the 1994 Budget. These measures seek to: improve the UK life industry's position when competing for business in other EU countries (by extending the availability of the Overseas Life Assurance Business Rules); grant 'exemption' from basic rate tax on gains realised by UK residents from policies issued in another EU or EEA country where the insurer has been taxed on investment income and gains accruing for those UK policyholders at a rate of not less than 20 per cent; remove pre-certification for qualifying life assurance policies with effect from 6 May 1996; and implement (also in May 1996) a wider reform of the Policyholder Taxation Rules to simplify them and take account of the European Single Market for Life Assurance.

Of these, it is the review of the Life Policy Tax Rules which may give the greatest cause for concern. The press release which accompanied the 1994 Budget made specific mention of an intention to recast the rules on calculating gains on partial surrenders.

Quite apart from this, the prospect of new Policy Tax Rules taking effect in May 1996 is particularly unappealing if further changes are made shortly after that as a consequence of a decision to move the UK industry to a GRU company tax regime.

14.3   Life assurance policies

14.3.1   Legal nature

Life assurance policies are contracts between the individual policyholders and the life insurance company. The general principle underlying life assurance policies is that the insurance company is the collecting house of pooled risks and investments of policyholders and offers benefits directly to them based on personal contracts.

The life company maintains the underlying investment funds in its own right but, depending on the nature of the policy, undertakes to pay the policyholder either a specified sum, a sum which is increased periodically out of the profits of the company, or one which varies with the value of part of the underlying fund.

An important characteristic of the life assurance policy as an investment is that it does not produce an income, as such, but is essentially a medium-to long-term accumulator. The income and capital gains of the underlying funds accrue to and are taxed in the hands of the insurance company, but the benefit is passed on, to a greater or lesser extent, in the growth in value of the policy. Many types of policy, however, allow regular or irregular encashment of part of the policy (withdrawal plans or encashment of bonuses) to serve as 'income', if required (but see 'Withdrawal plans and policy loans' at **14.3.4** and paragraph **14.3.6** concerning part surrender of single premium policies).

14.3.2   Pre-conditions

In order to take out a life assurance policy an *insurable interest* in the life to be assured must exist, ie a pecuniary interest that would be adversely affected by the death of the life assured. At the time the policy is taken out, the policyholder must have an insurable interest in the life assured commensurate with the sum assured. Individuals have an unlimited insurable interest in their own lives and those of their spouses.

Usually, where life assurance is taken out as an investment, the contract will be applied for and held by a person on his own life or that of his spouse, or on their joint lives, for his or her own personal benefit or for their joint benefit. Policies can, however, be the subject of gifts, in which case they would generally be written in trust for the benefit of the beneficiaries (see **14.3.7**). They can also be assigned, by way of gift, or for value, or as security for a debt (eg as collateral security for a house mortgage or an overdraft).

14.3.3   Divisions and types

Endowment, whole of life and term assurances

All life policies provide life cover — a sum or sums assured payable on death. Most policies, other than temporary assurances, also provide investment benefits — sums payable on surrender or maturity. Life policies may be divided into endowment, whole of life and term policies, depending on the emphasis that is placed on savings or on protection (life cover):

(1)   An endowment policy, which has a high savings element, is one under which the benefits are payable at the end of a predetermined period (the endowment period) or on death, if earlier.

(2)   A whole of life policy is one under which the benefits are in general payable on death, whenever it occurs.

(3)   A term policy is a temporary assurance, the sum assured being payable on death within a specified period only.

Both endowment policies and whole of life policies may be surrendered (ie cashed in) prematurely for a cash lump sum, the size of which will depend on the nature of the contract. Term assurances generally do not have an investment element as far as the individual is concerned, and so rarely have any surrender or cash-in value.

With profit, without profit and unit-linked policies

Within the endowment and whole of life categories, life policies can be of different types, depending on the way in which the sums payable by the company are determined:

(1)   *With profit* contracts are policies under which a minimum sum is guaranteed to be paid by the life company, augmented from time to time by bonuses declared by the company according to its profits. These bonuses may be reversionary (bonuses added to the sum assured, either yearly or triennially) or terminal (bonuses declared at the end of the policy as an increment to the final payment). Reversionary bonuses may be simple or compound: simple bonuses are based only on the sum assured, while compound bonuses are based on the sum assured plus previous bonuses. Reversionary bonuses are usually expressed as a percentage of the sum assured or of the sum assured as increased by previous bonuses. Under a with profit endowment policy the individual will receive at maturity the minimum sum assured plus the bonuses, reversionary and terminal.

A development in recent years has been the creation of what are called 'unitised with profits' policies. These are with profits business but are structured to give the appearance of unit linking, particularly in terms of the policy charging structure. Frequently, unitised with profits business offers a 'smoothed' growth, often with a guaranteed minimum rate, but the guarantee may only apply to maturity and death values and not to earlier surrenders.

(2) *Without profit* contracts are policies under which the life company guarantees to pay an absolute sum and invests the premiums in such a way as to produce that sum, bearing any shortfall in the return or retaining any profit in excess of the guaranteed return.

(3) Under *unit-linked* policies the life company maintains a number of underlying funds, which are divided, for accounting purposes, into 'units'. The company undertakes to pay to the policyholder an amount equal to the greater of the guaranteed sum and the value of the units allocated to the policy. The underlying fund might consist of specific types of investment media often with a choice of geographical spread (such as property, equities, unit trusts, investment trusts, government securities, local authority and bank loans or deposits, or building society deposits) or the fund may consist of a combination of some or all of these ('managed' or 'mixed' funds). Out of every premium a proportion is allocated to the purchase of units which are credited to the policy. The movement in value of the underlying fund is directly reflected in the price of the units allocated to the policy and hence in the value of the policy benefits. Many types of policies give the policyholder himself the right to transfer his policy link from fund to fund at his option, by way of a simple procedure at low cost (eg a policy that is linked to an equity fund may be switched to become linked to fixed interest securities or bank deposits).

A life company generally has full investment freedom as to the type of investments it chooses, subject only to the investments being a suitable 'match' for its liabilities. In the case of unit-linked policies the Insurance Company Regulations only permit linkage to certain types of assets, such as those listed in the paragraph above.

If the contract is one under which a guaranteed minimum or guaranteed absolute amount is provided, the investor knows that he will get at least that sum. At the same time, in the case of with profit policies, he has the advantage of having the guaranteed minimum augmented from time to time by reversionary and terminal bonuses, or, in unit-linked contracts, augmented by the movement of the value of the underlying fund (capital growth plus reinvested income).

Regular premium and single premium policies

A further broad division of life policies (of all types) depends on how premiums are payable:

(1) regular premium policies (also known as annual premium policies) are those under which premiums are payable annually, half-yearly, quarterly or monthly, either throughout the duration of the policy or for a limited premium-paying period of time; and

(2) single premium policies are purchased by way of one single premium or lump sum (although such policies will usually be able to accept further investment at any time).

Qualifying and non-qualifying policies

A brief introduction to qualifying and non-qualifying policies is given at **14.3.6**. The distinction between the two types of policy is important because their proceeds are treated differently for tax purposes in the hands of the policyholder.

14.3.4   Characteristics of regular premium policies

Investment and protection

All endowment and whole of life policies have an investment or savings element as well as a life insurance protection element. The extent to which the policy is slanted towards investment depends on the nature and duration of the policy and the relationship between the premiums payable, the age of the life assured and the extent of the life cover provided.

In general, policies that have a low sum assured relative to the premiums payable over the policy life will have a high savings or investment element, and conversely, high sums assured relative to the premiums payable mean that the policy will be tilted more towards life assurance cover than towards investment. In considering life policies as investments, temporary or term assurances will be excluded, as these generally do not have a surrender value and benefits are payable only on death. They are usually taken out purely for life cover protection, to provide for one's family or to cover a prospective liability such as inheritance tax.

The type of policy that an individual should take out generally depends on his circumstances and objectives, weighing up not only the required degree of investment relative to protection but also the required degree of certainty of result relative to the potential for increased gain.

In general, the incidence of inflation and the conservatism of companies in guaranteeing a long-term return has meant that without profit policies have tended to provide a relatively poor rate of return compared with with profit and unit-linked policies.

A with profit policy gives the prospect of sharing in the company's investment performance where this exceeds that needed to meet the guarantee – but the need to satisfy the guarantee may still lead the company to a more conservative investment strategy.

With no guaranteed investment return a unit linked policy could be viewed as a little more risky but may also offer the prospect of better fund performance.

Withdrawal plans and policy loans

In the past, a feature of many regular premium policies with a high investment content was the facility, after a period of years, to operate withdrawal plans, under which the premium was reduced to a nominal amount, eg £1 per annum and regular or irregular sums could be taken from the policy by way of partial surrender to serve as an income, leaving the balance to accumulate. This withdrawal facility was challenged by the Revenue and withdrawn from qualifying policies issued on or after 25 February 1988. Policies issued before that date may continue as qualifying policies despite the presence of such an option. Substantially the same result may be achieved by taking out a series of smaller policies and cashing in individual policies from time to time while continuing the remainder and it may be possible to take withdrawals from a policy provided it has not suffered such a large premium reduction as was previously allowed. Many policies also give the policyholder the right to borrow from the insurance company at a beneficial rate of interest on the security of the policy.

14.3.5 Characteristics of single premium policies

In the main, the relevant single premium policies for investment purposes consist of single premium 'bonds' which are whole of life assurance policies. For many years these have been, in the main, unit-linked policies often marketed as property bonds, managed bonds, equity bonds, etc by reference to the initial underlying fund to which the policy was linked. There are also single premium endowment policies, but these are less significant.

In recent years, there has been considerable business written as with profit bonds. Although these did not generally incorporate the usual guarantees on future values, they did prove to be attractive in a time of recession and stock market uncertainty.

The main investment characteristic of single premium unit-linked bonds is the high allocation of the premium to investment in the underlying fund, with relatively low life cover. Virtually the entire premium is allocated to 'units', save only for the initial management charges, resulting, in effect, in the investment of most of the premium in the chosen fund. Most companies offer a wide choice of unit funds for the bond linkage.

Subsequently, at no cost or for a small administrative charge, the policyholder may switch his investment to one or more of the other funds and is thereby entitled to select a fund which reflects his own view of market conditions. Switching does not amount to a realisation for tax purposes, which is an important investment advantage.

The income produced by the underlying fund is reinvested, net of tax and annual charges, in the fund. A bond, therefore, serves as an automatic income accumulator as well as giving the investor the benefit of the capital growth from the fund, less a deduction for the insurance company's tax on capital gains.

Where the policy takes the form of a single premium endowment, it provides the policyholder with a guaranteed investment return on his premium over the endowment period.

A case decided (on the hearing of a preliminary matter) in the middle of 1994 raised the question of how much life assurance protection a single premium had to provide in order for it to qualify as a life assurance policy. At first instance the Judge decided that a policy providing a death benefit equal only to the surrender value at the time of death was not a life assurance contract.

It is understood that there is to be an appeal against this decision but, in the meantime, the Revenue and DTI have made it clear that, broadly speaking, if the decision goes against the industry remedial legislation will be introduced to restore the position to that which was understood to be the case, in respect of policies issued before that clarification.

Withdrawals

Most unit-linked single premium bonds allow the investor the right to make regular or irregular withdrawals by way of partial surrender to serve as an income. The same result can be achieved by splitting the investment into a number of smaller policies and encashing individual policies in full from time to time. As these policies are not qualifying contracts they are not affected by the Revenue's attack on withdrawal plans referred to in **14.3.4** but see the section 'Withdrawals' in **14.3.6** below.

Ease of encashment

One of the most important characteristics of single premium bonds is the ease of encashment: there are few formalities other than production of the policy, a surrender form and proof of title. In the case of property bonds, some companies reserve the right, in exceptional circumstances, to defer encashment for a period so as to protect the general body of policyholders by avoiding forced sales of property.

14.3.6 Taxation

Taxation of the life company

The Revenue's review of life company taxation, announced in the 1989 Budget, resulted in a statement by the Treasury in December 1989 and other changes announced in the 1990 Budget. Legislation was included in the Finance Acts of 1989 and 1990 to give effect to these changes. In the main, they took effect from January 1990.

The proposals were less radical than some of those originally canvassed and built on the existing 'I-E' (income-expenses) framework. The following is a brief outline of the new regime.

The life company's management expenses are deducted from the investment income and capital gains of the life fund and the net amount is subjected to tax in the life company's hands at a rate of 25 per cent in respect of the policyholders' share of profits (20 per cent in respect of dividend income, as a result of the March 1993 Budget) and 33 per cent in respect of profits attributable to shareholders in the case of a proprietary company. However, the expenses associated with the acquisition of new business are (after a transitional period) to be spread over a period of seven years. Capital gains on disposals of gilt-edged securities are exempt from tax.

As life companies are generally able to defer realisations of assets for a long period, they usually pass on this benefit in the form of a lower rate of deduction for tax on capital gains from the funds. This is especially true of unit-linked policies.

Previously, deferring gains had also been achieved by investing life funds in units trusts. Much of the investment management could be achieved through the unit trust company selling its underlying assets, these being free of tax from capital gains. However, new rules (with transitional reliefs) have now been introduced to charge tax on unrealised gains in life company holdings of unit trusts and are likely to promote more direct investment by life company funds. See generally **14.2.2** in respect of the current review of life assurance taxation.

Taxation of the policyholder

Qualifying and non-qualifying policies

The income tax treatment of a life policy in the hands of the policyholder depends on whether the policy is a qualifying or a non-qualifying policy. Policy provisions in standard form are usually sent to the Revenue by the life company for confirmation of compliance with the qualifying rules ('pre-certification'). Generally (although the rules do vary for different types of policy) a qualifying policy is one where the premium-paying period is ten years or more and where the premiums payable in any period of 12 months do not exceed more than twice the premiums payable in any other period of 12 months or ⅛ of the premiums payable over ten years. In the case of a whole of life policy, the sum assured payable on death must not be less than 75 per cent of the premiums payable until age 75; and in the case of an endowment policy, the sum assured payable on death must not be less than 75 per cent of the premiums payable during the term of the policy, but for endowments this percentage is reduced by 2 per cent for each year by which the age of the life assured, at commencement, exceeds 55. Taxation of company-owned policies is considered later.

Qualifying policies

Tax relief on the premiums   In the case of a qualifying policy issued before 14 March 1984, the policyholder is eligible for tax relief on the premiums if the policy is written on his life or that of his spouse, if either of them pays the premiums, and if the person paying is resident in the UK for tax purposes. The current rate of tax relief on premiums paid is 12½ per cent. If eligible, the premiums may generally be paid to the life company net of the tax relief and the company will obtain the difference from the Inland Revenue. Tax relief is allowed to the policyholder to the extent to which the total gross premiums paid by him in the year do not exceed £1,500 or, if greater, ⅙ of his taxable income after deducting charges on income but before deducting personal reliefs. Tax relief will not be available if a person other than the life assured or his spouse (such as an assignee) pays the premiums.

No life assurance premium relief is available for policies issued in respect of contracts made after 13 March 1984. For these purposes a policy issued on or before 13 March 1984 is treated as being issued after that date if the benefits it secures are increased or its term extended (either by variation or by the exercise of an option built into the contract) after that date.

Policies intact   While the policies are held intact there is no tax charge to the policyholder.

Tax-free proceeds if kept up for minimum period   If a qualifying endowment policy has been maintained for at least three-quarters of its term or ten years, whichever is shorter, and has not been made paid-up within that period, the entire proceeds will be free of income tax in the hands of the policyholder. For a whole of life policy the appropriate period is ten years. If, however, a qualifying policy is surrendered or made paid-up within these periods, the profit ultimately made on realising the policy (whether by cashing in, death, maturity or assignment for value) will be potentially subject to the higher rate of tax — but not the basic rate — as with non-qualifying policies (see below).

Capital gains tax   No chargeable gain arises on the disposal of either qualifying or non-qualifying policies (note that surrender and payment of the sum assured under the policy are treated as 'disposals' for these purposes) where the disposal is by the original beneficial owner or by an assignee who gave no consideration for the policy (eg received the policy by way of gift).

On the other hand, if an assignee realises a profit on a policy (or an interest under it) that he, not being the original beneficial owner, acquired for value, it will be liable to capital gains tax in the same way as other chargeable assets.

In order to deal with the trade in second-hand policies (which were taxed under the then more favourable capital gains tax regime), anti-avoidance legislation was introduced in 1983 so that, broadly speaking, post 26 June 1982 policies remain in the same income tax regime despite being assigned for money or money's worth. Such policies may give a potential liability to both income and capital gains tax although the Taxation of Chargeable Gains Act 1992, s 37 will prevent a double tax charge arising.

Person liable for the tax charge   See below.

Non-qualifying policies

Tax relief on the premiums   No life assurance premium relief is allowed in respect of premiums paid under non-qualifying policies whether issued before or after 14 March 1984.

Policies intact   As with qualifying policies, while the policies are intact there is no tax charge on the policyholder.

Termination   On final termination of a non-qualifying policy, on death, cashing in, maturity, or sale, the only income tax charge, if any, is to higher rate income tax but not basic rate. To determine whether a charge arises, the gain — basically, the excess of the cash surrender value over the premium paid — is divided by the number of years the policy has been held ('top slicing'). Any previous withdrawals are also taken into account. This slice is then added to the taxpayer's other income for the year (after reliefs and mortgage interest). If the slice, then treated as the upper part of the individual's income, puts him in the higher rate bracket, the average rate of tax on the slice at the higher rate less the basic rate is applied to the whole gain. If the slice does not attract the higher rate of tax, the gain is, similarly, free of tax.

It should be noted that it is only the income in the year of encashment that is relevant. If no chargeable events occur during other years, the individual's income, no matter how high in those years, is irrelevant. Thus, bonds or other non-qualifying policies can be realised tax-effectively in a year when the policyholder's other income is relatively low (eg after retirement).

Example 1 — no income tax charge

A basic rate taxpayer whose income after personal reliefs is £1,000 below the higher rate threshold cashes in a single premium bond that he has held for eight years, for a total gain of £5,000. This gain is divided by eight to produce a 'slice' of £625. The slice, when added to his other income, still does not take him into the higher rate of tax. No tax is payable on the gain of £5,000.

Example 2 — income tax on the gain

If the slice (£625 in the above example), treated as the upper part of the taxpayer's income, falls wholly in the higher rate band of 40 per cent, then the gain of £5,000 will be subject to income tax at the rate of 15 per cent (ie £750) being the difference between the relevant higher rate (40 per cent) and the basic rate of 25 per cent.

Note that, on death, the gain which may be liable to tax is calculated, broadly speaking, as the cash surrender value immediately before death plus previous relevant capital payments under the policy, less the premiums paid. In this way the 'mortality profit' made under the policy at that time is not taxed as part of the chargeable gain.

Withdrawals   Annual tax-free withdrawals or partial surrenders of up to 5 per cent of the premiums paid are permitted up to a total amount equal to the premium or premiums paid. Unused allowances are carried forward. If more than the 5 per cent annual allowance is taken a chargeable excess occurs. The excess becomes liable to the higher rate of tax (but is not liable to the basic rate) if, when added to the taxpayer's other income, it falls into the higher rate.

The 'top-slicing' procedure referred to above applies with some modifications: the first chargeable excess is divided by the number of years since commencement; subsequent excesses are divided by the number of years since the previous excess. The amounts withdrawn are taken into account in computing the gain or loss on final cashing in: the final gain or loss is equal to the cash surrender value, plus previous withdrawals, less the premium or premiums paid, less excesses previously brought into charge.

As mentioned in **14.2.2**, it seems clear that the Revenue intends to change the rules for taxing withdrawals (partial surrenders) from single premium bonds, with effect from 6 May 1996 but the proposals for the new regime have not been published at the time of writing.

Example

Original investment in a bond of £5,000. The bondholder takes withdrawals of six per cent per annum for nine years and cashes in the bond after ten years for £8,000. The final gain on cashing in is £8,000 + £2,700 (ie 9 × 6% × £5,000) − £5,000 − £450 (ie 9 × 1% × £5,000) = £5,250. The 'slice' is therefore £5,250 ÷ 10 = £525. This slice is added to his other income in the year of cashing in to determine if any tax liability exists on the slice and, if so, the rate of charge, after deducting the basic rate. The net rate of charge, if any, on the slice is then applied to the gain of £5,250.

Person liable The person liable for the tax charge is the policyholder if the policy is held by him beneficially, or the individual for whose debt the policy is held as security. Thus, if a policy is assigned by a parent to his or her child by way of a gift and the latter encashes it after attaining majority, the liability, if any, is that of the child regardless of the donor's income and is determined by the child's income at the time of encashment.

Where a policy that is held in trust is cashed in, any chargeable gain is treated as income of the settlor and the tax is his liability, although the settlor can recover from the trustees any tax for which he is liable in this way. If a policy, previously held in trust, has been assigned to the beneficiary in execution of that trust and is subsequently encashed, any gain forms part of the beneficiary's income and is taxed accordingly.

Timing Where the taxable event is the death of the life assured or the maturity, total encashment or sale of the policy, the gain is treated as arising at the date of that event. In contrast, however, withdrawals from policies are treated as happening at the end of the policy year in which they take place. For example, if a policy was effected on 1 June, a withdrawal in February 1994 will be treated as taking place on 31 May 1994 and so will be part of the 1994/95 tax computation for the policyholder and not the computation for 1993/94, the year in which it actually occurred.

14.3.7   Suitability

Life assurance policies are different from the normal run of investments in that they are capital assets that do not produce income as such. All income and capital gains produced by the underlying fund of investments accrue to the life company, while the policyholder receives the benefit in the form of an increase in value of his policy: the net income and gains after tax are taken into account in the value of the units or bonus additions, as the case may be. For this reason, life assurance policies are a very useful means of obtaining capital growth and accumulating income for medium- to long-term investment if immediate income is not required. This can be particularly important for higher rate taxpayers and various types of trust.

Both regular premium and single premium policies (qualifying or nonqualifying) also have the advantage that while they are held intact, the policyholder has no administrative burdens or tax returns to render, as the income and gains are the responsibility of the company.

The medium- and long-term investor

Both single and regular premium policies are ideally suited to the medium- or longer-term investor seeking an institutionally managed investment. Life companies have considerable investment freedom and with profits policies reflect the results of investment across a wide spread of assets. Unit-linked policies offer a choice of property, equity, fixed interest, managed and many other types of unit funds, as well as the ability to switch investments between funds as market conditions change. Indeed, the keynote of most unit-linked policies these days is choice and flexibility to meet changing circumstances, so as to maximise the potential growth and protect the real value of the investment against inflation, particularly over the longer term; while with profit policies offer the relative stability of participation in the company's profits. For the individual who wants a direct link to a managed fund of commercial properties there are few investments comparable with a property bond, or a policy linked to a property fund, or a managed fund with a property content.

Qualifying policies issued pre-14 March 1984 may have the added attraction of tax relief on the premiums — something not available to other comparable forms of investment — as well as freedom from tax on the proceeds if maintained for the required period. The ability of companies to defer realisations and thus make deductions for capital gains liabilities at a rate lower than the life company rate on chargeable gains has been a continuing advantage (but see **14.3.6** in respect of recent changes to unit trusts held by life companies).

Beneficiaries

Life policies are suitable investments for individuals seeking personal investment benefits for themselves or their spouses, or for making gifts to beneficiaries. Since policies are automatic income accumulators, they represent useful investments as gifts for children or for children's own capital. As gifts of policies do not cause chargeable events, a higher rate taxpaying spouse can give a policy to a basic rate (or non-taxpaying) partner before encashment. In this way, any gain otherwise taxable may avoid being taxed by virtue of the new independent taxation regime introduced in April 1990 which no longer aggregates the investment income of married couples. Policies can also be taken out by trustees as investments of the trust, provided the power is given in the trust instrument to invest in non-income-producing property and provided an insurable interest exists, eg a policy on the life of a beneficiary for the ultimate benefit of that beneficiary.

A donor wishing to take out a policy for the benefit of children or other beneficiaries can do so at the outset by completing a standard trust form produced by the life company, at the time of application. Trusts can range from very simple forms for the benefit of named beneficiaries absolutely (under the Married Women's Property Acts or corresponding legislation in Scotland and Northern Ireland, for spouse or children) to more elaborate forms, such as children's accumulation trusts and trusts where the settlor reserves a right to apply the benefits amongst a class of beneficiaries which may include the settlor himself (although to be efficient for inheritance tax purposes the settlor should be excluded from any personal benefit). Similarly, it is relatively simple to make a gift of an existing policy by assigning it to a beneficiary or to trustees for a beneficiary.

The tax considerations described in **14.3.6** should, of course, be taken into account, as well as the taxpayer's potential income and his tax position at the time of prospective encashment (as it is that time that is primarily relevant, not any time during the currency of the policy).

Companies

Companies have frequently found it useful to invest surplus funds in life policies, particularly where providing for a future liability or the replacement of an asset in the future. An insurable interest in the life of the assured must exist. In the past, the only tax consequence of such an investment has been that applicable to a close company in the case of a single premium bond or the premature encashment of a qualifying policy but the Finance Act 1989 contained new provisions so that, broadly speaking, all policies owned by companies (and those assigned to secure a company debt or held on trusts created by a company) are treated, in effect, as non-qualifying policies and taxable to Schedule D, Case VI income.

The new rules apply to policies effected on or after 14 March 1989 and those altered after that date so as to increase the benefits secured or extend the term.

A measure of relief is given in cases where a qualifying endowment policy is used to secure a debt incurred by the company in purchasing land to be occupied by it for the purposes of its trade (or in constructing, extending or improving buildings occupied for that purpose). In such cases, and subject to certain conditions, only the excess policy proceeds over the amount of the debt will be taxable as a policy gain.

14.3.8   Charges

In the case of with profit and without profit policies, the company's charges are implicit in the premium rate for the sum assured. In the case of unit-linked policies, the company's charges consist of a proportion of each premium and charges inside the unit funds. For example, in the case of single premium bonds, typically an initial charge of 5 per cent of the premium is made. This is followed by annual charges in the order of 1.25 per cent of the value of the fund (although this does vary from company to company) deducted from the fund, either monthly or with the same frequency as the fund valuations. These charges cover items such as the company's expenses and profit margins. Such annual charges can become quite significant where the policy has achieved a high value. For this reason some companies have adopted the approach of using a policy charge which is designed to ensure that each policy contributes a fair amount to the company's expenses, irrespective of the size of the policy. In such cases any annual management charge deducted from the funds is reallocated to the policy.

Switching a unit-linked policy between funds can usually be done for a small administrative charge that is far lower than the equivalent cost of switching other investments.

14.3.9 Mechanics

Life assurance policies are generally taken out through the intervention of an intermediary such as an insurance broker or salesman of the life assurance company, or a solicitor, accountant or estate agent acting as agent, or directly with the life company itself. The intermediary, although usually the agent of the policyholder, is generally paid a commission by the life company itself, although some insurance brokers charge the client fees (which are offset against their commission) for the work involved in preparing reports and undertaking financial planning for the client entailing the use of life assurance policies. The Financial Services Act 1986 introduced the concept of polarisation to the industry. This seeks to make clear to the consumer whether he is dealing with a representative of one company or a broker who will survey the market on his client's behalf.

14.3.10 Maintenance

Policies can be held in the individual's own name (usually in the case of policies held for the individual's personal benefit) or by trustees. As long as the policy is not cashed in there are no tax returns and no paperwork. It is only where excessive tax relief is taken on qualifying premiums or gains arise on the happening of a chargeable event (eg a single premium policy that is encashed or a qualifying policy encashed prematurely) that tax considerations arise. It is perhaps largely because of the ease of administration that many individuals with personal share portfolios take advantage of share exchange schemes introduced by life companies enabling them to exchange their shares for single premium bonds at reduced dealing costs.

Holders of unit-linked policies may receive annual fund reports, though the level of useful information provided varies between companies. Because the investment performances of unit-linked single premium bonds are directly related to the underlying funds, it is advisable to review the performance of the respective funds regularly with a view to switching between funds. This can be done with relative ease and at a low cost but for the majority of investors a carefully selected managed fund will satisfy the requirements in respect of a large proportion of their investment.

14.4 Purchased life annuities

14.4.1 Legal nature

There are two broad types of purchased life annuities:

(1) Immediate annuities are contracts under which, in consideration of a lump sum paid to the life company, the company undertakes to pay

an annuity to the annuitant for life, or for some other term, the rate of the annual annuity depending on the age and sex of the annuitant and on the yields prevailing for fixed interest investments at the time.

(2)   Deferred annuities are similar to immediate annuities except that the annuity commences at a future date.

Both annuity contracts are direct contracts with the life company. Some annuity contracts provide for a guaranteed minimum number of payments; some allow the contract to be surrendered for a cash sum that takes into account the growth in the purchase consideration and any annuity payments that have already been made. Other types of annuity contract allow for a cash sum, representing the balance of the original purchase consideration, to be paid on death.

14.4.2   Pre-conditions

There are generally no pre-conditions to investment in purchased life annuities. The purchaser of the annuity will generally be the annuitant himself or someone else who wishes to provide for annual payments to the annuitant.

14.4.3   Characteristics

An annuity contract represents a fixed interest investment providing either regular annual payments for the life of the annuitant (lifetime annuities) or for a fixed period (temporary annuities). These payments represent a partial return of capital plus a rate of interest on the investment. In the case of deferred annuity contracts the initial purchase consideration is accumulated at a fixed rate of interest before the annuity commences. Frequently, deferred annuity contracts are purchased with the object of taking advantage of income accumulation before the annuity commencement date and of cashing in the contract before that time (these are commonly known as 'growth bonds'). In general the life company fixes the rate of the annuity in advance, although cash surrender values may be related to yields on government securities at the time of cashing in. The actual investment yield earned by the life company is irrelevant to the annuitant, as he enjoys a guaranteed benefit.

In the past, two separate purchased annuity contracts were sometimes combined. For example, a temporary immediate annuity for a limited period was combined with a deferred lifetime annuity. This combination, known as a 'guaranteed income bond' (more frequently now written as a cluster of endowment policies), had as its object the provision of a short-term 'income' in the form of the temporary annuity, with the cashing in of the deferred annuity before the annuity commencement date to provide the return of 'capital'. The contracts were so structured that the cash-in value of the deferred annuity generally equals the total purchase price of the two contracts. The tax consequences of this combination have to be closely watched, especially for higher rate taxpayers (see **14.4.4**). Another combination is that of an immediate lifetime annuity, to provide an income for life, and a deferred annuity that can be commenced at a later stage to augment the income or, if the additional income is not taken, to pay a lump sum on death.

14.4.4 Taxation

The life company

In the past, annuities paid represented charges on the income from investments held by the life company for its general annuity business. To the extent, therefore, that the annuities paid equalled or exceeded the interest earned by the company, the interest did not bear tax, and could be passed on to the annuitants gross (although then subject to taxation in the hands of the annuitant).

The Finance Act 1991, however, made the taxation of general annuity business much the same as ordinary life assurance in respect of accounting periods beginning after 31 December 1991 with a generally detrimental effect on purchased life annuities.

The annuitant

Annuities paid are divided into capital content and income content, according to actuarial tables prescribed by the Inland Revenue. For example, if a man aged 70 purchased an annuity of £1,800 per annum payable half-yearly in arrear for a consideration of £10,000, £900 of the annuity might be regarded as capital with the balance of £900 being treated as income for tax purposes. In other words, every annuity is deemed to be partly a return of the original capital invested plus a yield or interest element. The interest element of each annuity payment received by the annuitant is treated as unearned income, although since the abolition of the investment income surcharge for individuals by the Finance Act 1984 this is not currently a significant disadvantage.

Despite this treatment of payments as part capital and part income, the Revenue appear to regard annuities as substantially a right to income so that they cannot be transferred between spouses to take advantage of independent taxation.

In the past, if an annuity contract was encashed or assigned for value, or any capital sum paid on death, any profit made by the annuitant over and above the purchase price of the annuity, unlike single premium bonds, was subject to basic rate tax (as the company would not have paid tax on the income of its general annuity business) and higher rates if applicable. However, as part of the change to the company's tax position, the 1991 Finance Act also brought the chargeable event regime for annuities into line with that for life policies, eg by not charging gains to basic rate income tax.

Higher rate tax is charged in much the same manner as on single premium policies. In other words, the gain element is 'top-sliced' by the number of years the annuity contract has been in existence, and the resulting slice is added to the taxpayer's other income in the year of encashment in order to determine whether or not the higher rate of tax is applicable. The rate on the slice (less the basic rate) then applies to the entire gain. In calculating the amount of the gain the capital element of any annuities paid prior to encashment (but not the interest element) is included as part of the gain.

14.4.5 Suitability

Immediate life annuities are suitable for investors who wish to purchase a continuing income for the rest of their lives by way of a lump sum. Deferred annuities are a means of providing an income to start at a future date, or of accumulating a lump sum with a view to encashment at a future time when other income may be sufficiently low to offset the tax disadvantages of encashment.

14.4.6 Mechanics

Like other life contracts annuities may be purchased through an intermediary or from a life company direct.

14.4.7 Maintenance

As far as immediate annuities are concerned, annual tax returns and tax payments are necessary in respect of the interest element of the annuities. In the case of deferred contracts, no maintenance is required while the annuity contract is intact and not paying an annuity, since the income is income of the life company and not the annuitant. On cashing-in, tax returns are necessary and tax may be payable.

14.5 Preview of the year ahead

Undoubtedly, the life assurance industry is facing a difficult year in 1995: the rate of change in the industry has been at an enormously high rate for several years now and shows no signs of decreasing.

Perhaps the key challenge for the year ahead concerns implementation of the new 'disclosure' regime and the effect which the provision of this extra information will have on clients and salespeople.

There is a general expectation that production levels will fall during the year and the two immediate challenges which will face companies will be in respect of adapting and developing products to meet consumers' real needs and expectations and to ensure that the debate does not become concentrated solely on 'price' but continues to take account of the wider aspects of real 'value for money'.

At the same time as facing these market difficulties, the industry must play a full part in the debate with the Revenue concerning the future of life company and policy taxation. Over the last ten years the Government has set great store by the creation of 'level playing fields' and the life industry must ensure that it is able to enjoy equal opportunities when competing with other EU insurers (for both domestic and foreign markets) and when competing with other investments in the UK market.

14.6 Conclusion

Life policies remain a very simple way of making lump sum or regular investment, although they are best used for medium- to long-term savings.

They act as 'income accumulators' and the life company deals with all tax liabilities while the plan is maintained in force. Withdrawals can often be taken to provide the policyholder with a spendable 'income' and these too can often be taken very simply and with little paperwork. This makes policies easy to administer from the policyholder's viewpoint and they are attractive to many people as a result.

As a pooled investment, they offer a spread of risk normally unobtainable by individual investors, including exposure to the commercial property market. Inexpensive switching between the company's funds, the built-in life cover and the prospect of tax-free proceeds are also attractive benefits of investment through life policies.

The recent tax changes, which have increased liabilities on the industry have already led to many contracts being repriced, but reduced tax rates applying to policyholder income and gains should provide some level of compensation for this.

Sources of further information

Useful addresses

Association of British Insurers
51 Gresham Street
London
EC2V 7HQ

Tel: (0171) 600 3333

National Association of Pension
   Funds
12–18 Grosvenor Gardens
London
SW1W 0DH

Tel: (0171) 730 0585

Inland Revenue Public Enquiry
   Room
West Wing
Somerset House
Strand
London
WC2R 1LB

Tel: (0171) 438 6420

Society of Pension Consultants
Ludgate House
Ludgate Circus
London
EC4A 2AB

Tel: (0171) 353 1688/9

LAUTRO (Life Assurance and
   Unit Trusts Regulatory
   Organisation)
Centre Point
103 New Oxford Street
London
WC1A 1QH

Tel: (0171) 379 0444

Pension Schemes Office
York House
PO Box 62
Castle Meadow Road
Nottingham
NG2 1BG

Tel: (0115) 974 0000

PIA (Personal Investment
   Authority)
Hertsmere House
Hertsmere Road
London
E14 4AB

Tel: (0171) 538 8860

IFA Association
12–13 Henrietta Street
Covent Garden
London
WC2E 8LH

Tel: (0171) 240 7878

Life Insurance Association
Citadel House
Station Approach
Chorleywood
Rickmansworth
Herts
WD3 5PF

Tel: (01923) 285333

Pensions Management Institute
PMI House
4–10 Artillery Lane
London
E1 7LS

Tel: (0171) 247 1452

15 Pension contracts

Stuart Reynolds LLB, Divisional Director, Legal Department, Allied Dunbar Assurance plc

15.1 Introduction

Pension schemes in the UK can be divided, broadly, into three classifications: the State scheme; personal pension arrangements; and occupational schemes. Over the years all three areas have seen far-reaching reform and further changes are likely in coming years as the government responds to the pressures of an ageing population and the requirements of the EU.

Approved pensions schemes have many of the constituents of the perfect investment: tax relief on contributions, tax-free growth, the prospect of a tax-free lump sum and a wide choice of underlying investments in large pooled funds to spread the risk. The major disadvantage is the need to purchase an annuity (taxed) at retirement. Recent changes have removed some of the problems which this can cause.

Not surprisingly, these benefits are carefully guarded by the appropriate authorities through a considerable number of rules and restrictions. This chapter summarises the main benefits and the conditions for their enjoyment.

15.2 Highlights of the previous year

Although the need for individuals to make their own pension provision has never been greater, there is no doubt that the recent bad publicity surrounding the pensions industry has deterred some investors from doing so.

The Securities and Investments Board published in October its long-awaited report into the subject of pension transfers and opt-outs. The report set out a framework for identifying problem cases and laid down a priority order so that the more urgent cases, broadly those nearing retirement, can be dealt with first. There is no doubt that the review process will place considerable demands on pension providers and intermediaries alike. At the time of writing, judicial review proceedings had been started seeking to challenge the legal basis for the review. The major concern is that pension providers and IFAs are being asked to write to their clients and, in effect, initiate complaints which it is felt may, in some circumstances, invalidate the Professional Indemnity insurance held by some providers and IFAs.

Whatever, the outcome of the judicial review proceedings, there is no doubt that the pensions industry must act to restore its credibility and consumer confidence. As the population ages, a trend which will accelerate rapidly into the next century, the need for private pension provision will become ever more pronounced. This is a problem throughout the developed world as State Pension schemes become unable to cope with a falling number of active employees contributing to the pensions of an increasing number of pensioners who are living up to 20 or more years after retirement.

There are respectable arguments for making compulsory some form of private pension provision (either a personal pension or a company scheme). Until that happens, the responsibility for defusing the 'demographic time bomb' will remain with the pensions industry to continue to sell the benefits of approved pension schemes. If the industry fails in this, the social consequences in the next century will be severe. As the 'benefits' of improved health care take effect, retirement may no longer be seen as an opportunity for increased freedom with a degree of affluence, but as an increasingly bleak picture of long years spent in inadequate housing and general poverty.

The new Pensions Act, which started its progress through Parliament in the Autumn, will introduce new safeguards for occupational pensions. The Act implements some of the recommendations of the Goode Committee set up in the aftermath of the Maxwell scandal. However, no amount of regulation will prevent a determined fraudster and some of the Act's requirements (for example, a minimum solvency requirement and increased employee involvement) may deter employers from setting up occupational schemes for their employees.

Finally the government has introduced a new facility, in a move to make personal pensions more attractive. Currently, personal pension planholders must purchase an annuity with the balance of the fund after taking the tax free lump sum. If annuity rates are low when the lump sum is taken the investor is permanently 'locked in' to this rate of return. In future, the purchase of the annuity can be deferred up to age 75. Before then income withdrawals are made, within limits and subject to tax. In theory, this new flexibility will allow investors to purchase an annuity at the best time possible. In practice, timing the purchase to best advantage may prove to be more difficult.

15.3 The State pension scheme

The benefit the State provides to those in retirement falls into two main parts: the basic retirement pension and a supplementary earnings related pension (SERPS). Everyone is entitled to the basic retirement pension payable at State Retirement Age, subject to payment of the necessary National Insurance contributions. For an individual whose earnings have been at the national average level throughout their working life, the State will provide a basic pension of approximately one-third of the final earnings level.

The State Retirement Age is currently 65 for males and 60 for females. The government has announced that it intends to equalise the State Retirement Age at 65 for both males and females. It is intended that this will apply to women retiring after 6 April 2010 with a sliding scale for women retiring over the previous ten years. The effect of the proposals is that for women whose dates of birth are on or after 6 April 1955 the common State Retirement Age of 65 will apply. Women born before 6 April 1950 will benefit from the current age of 60. For those women with dates of birth between those dates the sliding scale applies. For each month (or part of a month) that a woman's date of birth is after 6th April 1950, her retirement date will be deferred by one month.

SERPS was introduced in April 1978 to provide an additional State pension based on earnings (within certain limits) rather than the flat benefit provided by the retirement pension. SERPS also provides a widow's benefit if a husband dies after retirement and also, in certain circumstances, if he dies before retirement. SERPS is funded by the higher rate National Insurance contributions payable by both employers and employees. The self-employed do not contribute towards, or benefit from, SERPS.

In recent years the State pension scheme has come under pressure by increases in life expectancy and larger numbers of retired people in the population. These concerns led the government to reduce the benefits under SERPS so that only those reaching State pension age in the years 1998 and 1999 will receive the original maximum benefits. Those reaching State Retirement Age in or after the year 2010 will receive a pension of only 20 per cent of their earnings (within certain limits) instead of the 25 per cent originally intended, and the relevant earnings to be taken into account will be the average of lifetime earnings and not the best 20 years'

Table 15.1   New State Retirement Ages for women

Date of Birth		Pension age (years/months)	New pension date
Before 6 April 1950		60/0	—
6 April 1950 —	5 May 1950	60/1	6 May 2010
6 May 1950 —	5 June 1950	60/2	6 July 2010
6 June 1950 —	5 July 1950	60/3	6 September 2010
6 July 1950 —	5 August 1950	60/4	6 November 2010
6 August 1950 —	5 September 1950	60/5	6 January 2011
6 September 1950 —	5 October 1950	60/6	6 March 2011
6 March 1951 —	5 April 1951	61/0	6 March 2012
6 March 1952 —	5 April 1952	62/0	6 March 2014
6 March 1953—	5 April 1953	63/0	6 March 2016
6 March 1954 —	5 April 1954	64/0	6 March 2018
6 March 1955 —	5 April 1955	65/0	6 March 2020
6 April 1955 and after		65/0	—

of earnings, as was the original rule for SERPS. A sliding scale will operate for those retiring in the years 2000 to 2009.

15.4 Contracting-in and contracting-out

Those who are participating in SERPS (ie employees earning more than the lower threshold for standard rate National Insurance contributions) are said to be 'contracted-in' to SERPS. Since SERPS was introduced it has been possible to opt-out of the scheme (referred to as 'contracting-out').

Until 6 April 1988, this 'contracting-out' was only possible through an employer-sponsored occupational pension scheme which guaranteed to provide a broadly equivalent level of benefits to the SERPS benefits being lost. Since 6 April 1988, employers have been able to offer contracting-out on a 'money purchase' basis without having to provide the guarantee previously required. In both cases National Insurance contributions are reduced for both the employer and employee but with the loss of SERPS benefits.

However, this change still left the decision whether to offer contracted-out status firmly in the employer's hands. Further changes which took effect on 1 July 1988 gave the individual employee the right to contract out of SERPS on an individual basis, without his employer's consent. The personal pension plans which enable this are also money-purchase arrangements.

Contracting-out through personal pension plans involves the payment of 'protected rights contributions' to the relevant pension contract. The contributions are identified separately from any other contributions paid and create a 'protected rights fund'; it is the 'protected rights benefits' paid out of this fund at retirement which replace the SERPS benefits lost through the decision to contract out. The protected rights contributions are made up of the National Insurance rebate and tax relief on the employee's share of the National Insurance rebate. An age-related incentive of 1 per cent is also payable for those over 30. The incentive only applies to personal pension plans. A move to a system where the rebates vary with age is likely and the government is currently consulting on the details of this proposal.

Contracting-out via a personal pension plan is an annual decision and the individual can contract back into SERPS for the purposes of future benefits.

In general, contracting-out will be of benefit to younger employees but may not match the likely SERPS entitlement for older people and for those on lower earnings. For those contracting-out via a personal pension plan the cut-off ages are currently approximately 47 (males) and 41 (females).

15.5   Types of pension contracts

There are two main types of pension contract in the context of life assurance investment:

(1)   Personal pension plans for the self-employed and individuals who are not in pensionable employment take the form of deferred annuity contracts between the individual and the life company directly and are purchased by single or regular premiums.

(2)   Occupational pension schemes take the form of contracts between the trustees of the scheme (set up by the employer) and the insurance company (in the case of an insured scheme) and provide benefits for employees as a group or on an individual earmarked basis. Controlling directors of director-controlled companies other than investment companies are also eligible for occupational pension schemes.

Since April 1988 individuals have been able to opt out of their occupational pension scheme and provide for their own benefit via a personal pension plan. It is often not advisable to do this if the occupational pension scheme is a good one. Alternatively they will be able to top-up the pension provided by their occupational scheme by making Additional Voluntary Contributions to that scheme or by effecting a free-standing AVC (FSAVC) plan with a pension provider of their choice.

15.6   Characteristics of pension contracts

As with life assurance policies there is a wide variety of types of investment. Companies offer with profit contracts with a level of guaranteed benefits but the right to participate in profits and unit-linked contracts with a wide choice of unit funds and the ability to switch between funds to provide growth on top of any guaranteed benefits. A recent development has been a series of guaranteed equity funds, where investors can benefit from the performance of an index, usually the FT-SE 100 Index, but are protected from stock market falls.

It has become common in recent years for employers to split their pension investment between an insurance company and other investment media by what is known as a 'self-administered scheme'. One of the attractions of such an arrangement is the facility of investing part of the pension fund in the employing company itself either by loans or equity investment (see **15.7.6**).

An attraction of all pension contracts is that the income and capital growth produced by the investment of the premiums accumulate on a gross basis, because pension funds are not generally subject to UK income tax or capital gains tax.

As the contracts provide essentially for retirement annuities and pensions, they cannot generally be surrendered for a cash consideration: benefits must take the form of pensions (part of which can be commuted on retirement) and life cover (including a return of the premiums with reasonable interest, which in the case of unit-linked contracts means the growth in value of the units). An important feature of many of these contracts is the 'open market option' at retirement, enabling the annuitant to use the accumulated fund built up for his pension to purchase an annuity or pension from any other company offering a higher rate. Although funds invested in these contracts generally remain 'locked in' until retirement, a facility offered by many insurers is the availability of loans, on commercial terms, to companies taking out pension schemes or to individual members of these schemes (see **15.7.6**).

15.7 Eligibility, taxation, contribution limits and benefits

15.7.1 The life company

The income and gains attributable to the life company's pension liabilities are effectively free of UK tax, and it is thus able to pass on to its policyholders the entire gross increase in value of the assets and income, after deduction of its charges, without any deduction for UK tax.

15.7.2 Personal pension plans

Personal pension plans (PPPs) were introduced on 1 July 1988 and superseded Retirement Annuity Contracts (often called 's 226 contracts') which ceased to be available for new business after 30 June 1988.

Eligibility

You will be eligible to make contributions to one of these plans if you are in receipt of 'relevant earnings'. This means either earnings from non-

278 *Allied Dunbar Investment and Savings Handbook*

pensionable employments, or from businesses, professions, partnerships, etc. Generally, you are not eligible if you belong to a pension scheme operated by your employer, but you are eligible if it provides only a sum assured payable on your death while in the employer's service. Controlling directors of investment companies are not eligible for any form of PPP in respect of earnings from such a company nor are certain other controlling directors who are in receipt of benefits from their employer's occupational scheme.

Tax relief on premiums and limits

If you have relevant earnings, and pay either single or annual premiums to a PPP within the limits mentioned below, you enjoy full tax relief on those premiums in the relevant years. However, an 'earnings cap' applies so that contributions to a PPP will only be possible in respect of earnings up to £78,600 for the 1995/96 tax year (previously £76,800 for the 1994/95 tax year). The legislation provides that this figure will be increased in future years in line with the RPI (although this did not apply for the tax year 1993/94).

Employees can pay premiums net of basic rate and any higher rate relief is claimed through the PAYE coding. The new 20 per cent band does not affect the rate at which employees can deduct basic rate tax. The self-employed must make contributions gross and claim relief through their annual tax return. The annual limit for contributions to PPPs is 17.5 per cent of your 'net relevant earnings'. This means relevant earnings from your non-pensionable employment or business, etc, less certain deductions such as expenses, trading losses and capital allowances. The limits for older taxpayers are currently as shown below.

An amount not exceeding 5 per cent of your net relevant earnings can be used to provide a lump sum payable from the PPP in the event of your death before age 75. Premiums used to provide this life cover must be included as part of the contributions you are permitted to pay to your PPP.

Age at beginning of year of assessment	%
36–45	20.0
46–50	25.0
51–55	30.0
56–60	35.0
61 and over	40.0

Contributions may be paid to a PPP and a s 226 contract (see **15.7.4**) at the same time but the contribution limits apply to the 'aggregate' of contributions to the two plans (although the 'aggregation' is not always straightforward and paying contributions to both a PPP and a s 226 contract can restrict the overall contribution possible in some cases particularly where contributions are above the earnings cap).

If your employer pays contributions to your PPP, these too must be taken as part of the maximum contribution which can be made to your plan. Employer's contributions are not treated as the employee's income. Protected rights contributions paid to your PPP to enable you to contract out of SERPS can be paid in addition to the maximum permissible contribution calculated as the appropriate percentage of your net relevant earnings.

Years for which relief is granted

Generally, relief is given against net relevant earnings of the tax year in which the contributions are paid. However, you can elect to have any premium you pay treated for tax purposes as if it has been paid during the preceding tax year, or, if you had no relevant earnings in that year, for the premium to be relieved against earnings in the tax year before that; ie there is a 'carry-back' period of one or two years.

To the extent that premiums paid in any year fall short of the permitted maximum of net relevant earnings, it is possible to 'carry forward' the shortfall on unused relief for up to six years and use the shortfall (on a first-in first-out basis) to obtain relief against a premium paid in a subsequent year, to the extent that that premium exceeds the maximum percentage limit of net relevant earnings for the year in which it is paid. The amount of relief which is available in any year as a result of the carry back and carry forward provisions is restricted to the amount of net relevant earnings for that year.

Benefits payable and age at which they may be taken

The PPP scheme established by the pension provider can allow the individual to make more than one contract (or arrangement) under it. The advantages of this are that, as benefits from an arrangement can, generally, be taken only once if they are to include a cash lump sum, multiple arrangements can give the opportunity to take benefits in stages.

Your pension may start being paid at any age between 50 and 75. It is not necessary for you actually to retire before the annuity can commence. In certain occupations the Revenue allow an annuity to start earlier than the age of 50 (eg jockeys, motor racing drivers, cricketers, etc).

In the November Budget, the government announced new rules which are planned to come into force when the Finance Act receives Royal Assent in the Spring of 1995. From then it will no longer be necessary to purchase an annuity when benefits from a personal pension are taken. The annuity purchase can be deferred until age 75. Until then, or the date when the annuity is purchased if earlier, income withdrawals are taken up to a limit broadly equal to the amount of the single life annuity which could have been taken. The amount of income withdrawals has to be reviewed every three years and the withdrawals are taxable in the same way as annuity payments.

Should your PPP incorporate a sum assured, on your premature death the lump sum would be paid and this can be arranged to be free of inheritance tax by writing it in trust where the PPP scheme itself is not set up under trust. The whole of any annuity payable either to you, your spouse or your dependants will be treated and taxed as income (and not, as is the case with purchased life annuities, partly as income and partly as a return of capital, see **14.3.4**). The annuity is currently taxed under Schedule D and income tax is deducted at source. From 6 April 1995, annuity payments will normally be taxed under Schedule E and subject to the PAYE system.

A lump sum may be taken from the PPP, between the ages of 50 and 75, up to a maximum of 25 per cent of the fund then being used to provide you with retirement benefits.

You are permitted, instead of taking the annuity from the life company with whom you hold the contract, to utilise the fund built up for your annuity in order to purchase an annuity from any other company, thus obtaining the best terms then available ('open market option'). If your PPP is provided by an organisation which is not a life assurance company, your pension (and life assurance) must be provided by a life company.

15.7.3 Contracting-out via a PPP

Scheme certificates

If a PPP has an 'appropriate scheme certificate' from the Occupational Pensions Board it will be able to receive protected rights contributions (and may be funded by them entirely) and so enable the individual employee to contract out of SERPS. A PPP which receives only protected rights contributions (a 'PPP(PRO)') can be effected by an employee who is a member of a contracted-in occupational scheme but wishes to contract out on an individual basis.

Contributions

Protected rights contributions are made up of the National Insurance rebate, the incentive (where applicable) and tax relief on the employee's share of the rebate (which grosses it up at the basic rate). The rebate is equal to the difference between the contracted-in and contracted-out National Insurance rates on the individual employee's band earnings (the earnings between the upper and lower earnings limits). Both employer and employee continue to pay full National Insurance but the rebate is paid by the DSS to the individual's plan after the end of the relevant tax year.

The incentive is currently 1 per cent of band earnings and is payable for those over 30 from 6 April 1993.

The protected rights pension must commence between State pension age and the age of 75. It must increase at 3 per cent per annum or the rate of the RPI, whichever is lower, and must not discriminate between males and females, married or single people in terms of the annuity rates offered. No lump sum benefit can be taken from the protected rights fund.

A protected rights pension must continue for the benefit of a widow/widower or dependant on the individual's death, at a rate not less than one-half of the individual's pension. On death before retirement age the protected rights fund can be paid to the deceased's estate or nominees but no life assurance sum assured can be included in the protected rights benefits.

15.7.4   Retirement annuity contracts (s 226 contracts)

No new s 226 contracts could be entered into after 30 June 1988 but contracts in existence by that date can continue much as before. Contributions can continue to be paid to such contracts and regular contributions can be increased in the future.

In many ways s 226 contracts were similar to the new PPPs but there are some key differences, eg no employer's contributions; contributions paid gross and the tax reclaimed; no facility for an employee to contract out through a s 226 contract and no general entitlement to take benefits before the age of 60. One important way in which a s 226 contract could be more favourable than a PPP was in providing a cash commutation equal to three times the annual annuity payable after the cash had been taken. This figure is often more than the 25 per cent of the fund available as a lump sum under a PPP. (Contracts entered into on or after 21 March 1987 are subject to a maximum cash lump sum of £150,000 per contract.) The earnings cap does not apply to s 226 contracts and the contribution limits are also different from those which apply to PPPs.

It should be noted that, although many s 226 contracts contain an open market option to allow the annuity to be purchased from a life company other than the one with whom the pension plan has been effected, exercising such an option after 30 June 1988 will have the effect of transferring the policy proceeds to a new PPP (unless the policyholder has a second s 226 contract already in existence with that other life company). Thus, in the absence of another s 226 contract, the benefits will be paid out of a PPP with the resulting less favourable calculation of the maximum cash lump sum compared to the s 226 contract.

15.7.5   Occupational schemes

These are schemes provided by an employer for the benefit of some or all of his employees but they are not available to directors of investment companies. To be effective, the scheme should be approved by the Pension Scheme Office (PSO) which is a branch of the Inland Revenue.

'Approval' will prevent contributions paid by the employer being taxed in the employees' hands as a benefit in kind. 'Exempt approval' will give the additional benefits of the gross roll-up in the fund and tax relief for the employee in respect of regular contributions he makes to the scheme. Exempt approval will also mean that the employer's contributions will be deductible business expenses without relying on the normal rules for deductibility applying to Schedule D income. In most cases approval is given under the PSO's discretionary powers which are extremely wide-ranging.

It is not possible for an employer to make membership of an occupational scheme (other than one providing death in service benefits only) compulsory. Employees are able to opt out of their employer's scheme and so become eligible to effect their own PPP, independent of the employer. In general, leaving an occupational scheme is unlikely to be wise except where its benefits are extremely poor and expert advice should be sought if this is contemplated.

Contributions

The employer must make some contribution to the scheme although the employee may indirectly provide the necessary funds by agreeing to a reduction in salary — 'a salary sacrifice'. Contributions by the employer to an exempt approved scheme are deductible business expenses, although relief in respect of non-regular contributions may be deferred by being spread over a maximum of five years. The employee may make personal contributions of up to 15 per cent of his remuneration. Personal contributions attract tax relief at the highest rate paid by the individual.

Unlike PPPs there are no specific limits on the amount of contributions which may be made to an occupational scheme, instead (subject to the various 'income capping' rules referred to below) the controls operate on the level of benefits which is allowed. If a scheme becomes 'over-funded' (ie where the scheme has more capital than is necessary to meet its prospective liabilities), payment of further contributions may be restricted or capital may have to be returned to the employer. If a refund is made to the employer it is taxable at a special rate of 40 per cent.

Benefits and limits

The benefits that can be provided by an approved occupational scheme are regulated by a series of Inland Revenue limits. These limits have been restricted over the years including important changes announced in the 1987 and 1989 Budgets. Each generation of limits has in general been preserved or 'grandfathered' for those who were members of existing schemes at the time of the Budget when the changes were announced. Other changes, the majority of them relatively minor, have also been made at other times. Details of the earlier limits can be found in previous editions of this work and in the *Allied Dunbar Pensions Handbook*. The limits which apply to members joining new schemes are summarised below.

The Inland Revenue limits are based on a percentage of the individual's 'final remuneration'. This must be calculated in one of the two ways permitted by the PSO, namely:

(1) the remuneration in any of the five years preceding retirement, leaving service or death (as applicable) together with the average of any bonuses, commissions, etc averaged over at least three consecutive years ending with the year in question; or
(2) the highest average of the total earnings over any period of three consecutive years during the last ten years of service.

Certain items are excluded from the calculation, such as share option and share incentive gains and golden handshakes, and some controlling directors have to use the second definition of final remuneration. There is also a maximum amount of earnings that can be taken into account and this is £78,600 for the 1995/96 tax year (previously £76,800 for the 1994/95 tax year). This figure should increase in future years in line with the RPI (although indexation did not apply for the 1993/94 tax year).

Within this framework, an individual can accrue a pension at the rate of one-thirtieth of final remuneration for each year of service with his employer up to a maximum of two-thirds final remuneration. In order to achieve this it is necessary to achieve 20 years of service.

The benefits can be taken on retirement between age 50 and 75. The benefits must be in the form of a pension but part of the pension can be commuted for a tax-free lump sum. The maximum lump sum is three-eightieths of final remuneration for each year of service or 2.25 times the pension available before commutation, if greater. The maximum lump sum, again available after 20 years of service, is one and a half times final salary.

It is also possible to incorporate widows' and dependants' benefits, including a lump sum of up to four times salary, together with a refund of personal contributions, which can be paid free of tax.

Company directors

In general, the same rules apply to 'controlling' directors as to any individual in an occupational pension scheme. However, because a director of a family company is in a rather different position from an ordinary employee, the Revenue have imposed some limitations on directors with at least 20 per cent control, eg the measurement of final salary is more stringent than for non-controlling directors. Directors with 20 per cent control and members of families controlling more than 50 per cent of the company are not eligible to join a company's approved pension scheme if it is an investment company.

15.7.6   Loans and self-investment

A very important development in recent years has been the use of pensions in connection with loans made to the pension planholder or occupational scheme member. This helps to reduce one of the disadvantages of pension schemes, ie capital invested in the fund is 'locked-in' until retirement.

Typically, a lender who makes an interest-only loan to the individual might expect him to repay the capital out of any lump sum to which he is entitled from his pension. Such lump sums will not be assigned to the lender as security for the loan but, for example where the loan is for house purchase, the mortgage over the property, assigned life assurance protection and the existence of the pension cash entitlement will usually satisfy the lender's requirements.

It is important that the pension contracts remain independent of the loan arrangements and that effecting the pension does not guarantee the availability of the loan. The pension must not be taken out in order to obtain the loan as the pensions legislation requires the pension scheme to be solely for the purpose of obtaining retirement benefits.

Another approach to 'unlocking' some of the pension fund is for the fund to be invested, in part, in shares of the employer company, in making the loans to the company or in purchasing premises from which the company trades.

Regulations following the passing of the Social Security Act 1990 have imposed tighter restrictions on the availability and amount of loans that can be made to the employer company but most small self-administered schemes and individual insured arrangements have escaped the restrictions entirely.

Inland Revenue rules have also restricted this type of 'self-investment'. Loans are limited, for the first two years of a scheme's existence, to 25 per cent of the value of the fund excluding transfer values, followed by a limit of 50 per cent of the fund. Previously the limit was 50 per cent of the fund throughout. The other approaches, which are also subject to restrictions, are usually only available to self-administered schemes in which the trustees have wide powers of investment compared to 'insured schemes' where the investment is usually confined to a policy issued by the insurance company concerned.

15.7.7   Contracting-out via an occupational scheme

As already mentioned, money-purchase schemes can now be used to contract out of SERPS without the previous requirement of a guarantee attaching to the benefits which are, in effect, replacing SERPS.

A contracted-out money purchase (COMP) scheme will receive protected rights contributions by way of National Insurance rebate and incentive payment, where appropriate, as is the case with a PPP. However, a COMP will receive the National Insurance payments monthly direct from the employer and not as a lump sum, a year in arrears, as does a PPP. With a COMP, the Inland Revenue's limits on maximum benefits apply to the aggregate of the protected rights and non-protected rights benefits; a contracted-in occupational scheme member may obtain the maximum benefits from the occupational scheme, in addition to the protected rights benefits, from a PPP(PRO) effected to contract out of SERPS. The age related incentive payable from April 1993 does not apply to a COMP.

In response to the European Court decision in *Barber v GRE*, with effect from 17 May 1990 the Social Security Act 1990 allows schemes to reduce the minimum age at which a COMP's protected rights can be taken by males. This was previously 65 but can now be as low as 60 (the age at which females can take such benefits).

15.7.8   Unapproved occupational schemes

These may be established by employers to provide benefits greater than those otherwise allowable. In this way, for example, benefits in excess of two-thirds of final salary can be provided and top-up pensions can be given to employees with short service or those who are subject to 'income capping'.

There are none of the special tax benefits normally received by approved pension schemes and employer contributions will only obtain relief under the normal business expenditure rules but lump sums can be paid free of tax from funded schemes. However, such schemes do retain certain tax benefits including, in some cases, the ability to roll up income at the basic rate of tax rather than at the special rate of tax applicable to some trusts. In appropriate cases this can result in a saving of tax where the employee is a higher rate taxpayer, as is likely to be the case. In addition, until 30 November 1994 it was also possible to set up offshore schemes with enhanced taxation benefits. Although the employee is subject to tax on payments into the scheme (whether set up offshore or not), it was also possible to arrange for a degree of tax-free growth and freedom from tax on lump sum benefits. This is no longer possible as the Finance Act 1994 will introduce a new tax charge on schemes set up to avoid tax in this way. The new rules apply to all schemes set up after the 1994 November Budget and existing schemes which are varied after that date.

15.7.9   Free-standing AVC schemes

Since October 1987, all occupational scheme members are entitled to top-up their pensions by making contributions to a separate pension scheme of their own. Such a 'Free-Standing' Additional Voluntary Contribution (FSAVC) scheme may not be commuted for a cash lump sum and must be aggregated with the occupational scheme to determine the maximum permitted benefits. The overriding limit on personal contributions, 15 per cent of salary (capped where appropriate), remains.

Although regulated by the occupational pension scheme tax legislation, FSAVC schemes also have similarities to PPPs in that they are individual arrangements independent of the individual's employer. The maximum limits on benefits and contributions are, however, those applicable to occupational schemes (see above). An employee's contributions to such schemes must be paid net of tax relief at the basic rate.

As long as contributions to the FSAVC do not exceed £2,400 per annum, the employer need have no involvement in an employee joining an FSAVC scheme. Even where the contributions exceed £2,400, the employer's involvement at the outset is restricted to providing sufficient information to allow the maximum contribution which can be paid to be calculated by the FSAVC provider. In some cases the funds built up in the FSAVC together with the benefits from the employer's scheme may exceed the Inland Revenue limits. Where a scheme is overfunded in this way any over-provision is returned to the scheme member subject to a tax charge. This charge also applies to AVC schemes established in-house by employers.

15.8 Suitability

Personal pension plans and occupational pension schemes provide highly tax-efficient benefits. In consequence they are suitable for and extremely attractive as investments for those with earned income who wish to provide for personal cash and income during retirement and protection for their wives and families during their working lives. Because the premiums are deductible for tax purposes from earned income, the effective cost is relatively low, while the tax-free growth inside the pension fund enables substantial accumulation of funds for pension benefits. The emerging benefits, in the form of tax-free cash commutation and pensions, receive beneficial tax treatment. However, the fact that pension benefits can only be taken after certain ages tends to make such schemes suitable only for those prepared to take a long-term view.

15.9 Preview of the year ahead

The industry will face a stern test over the coming months. Resolving the uncertainty surrounding the SIB review of pension transfers and opt-outs is the most immediate priority. The judicial review proceedings are scheduled to be heard quickly and an early resolution to the complex legal issues will be needed if confidence in the industry is to be restored.

Once the review process has started the focus will turn to the scale of the administrative task facing pension providers and occupational schemes. Resolving problem cases will take many months and the review process, as a whole, will last for several years. What is already clear is that the vast majority of personal pension planholders who have their pensions with large reputable organisations will be entirely unaffected by the SIB review. It is essential that this message is communicated clearly and effectively to the media and the public at large.

Many pension providers have redesigned their pension contracts to offer more flexibility and better value for money. This trend is likely to continue. In some cases this is a response to the new rules on disclosure at the point of sale of remuneration and services which came into effect at the beginning of 1995. However, some providers have also recognised the changing nature of the pensions market. Over recent years the concept of a 'job for life' has become an increasingly rare phenomenon. The importance of a pension plan which can adapt to changing needs without incurring further sets of initial charges has never been greater.

In making a choice of pension provider, factors such as the ability of the pension plan to change over time, the quality of the advice given and the financial security of the pension provider will all have to be considered, as well as the overall level of charges. As new pension providers enter the market, the decision as to which pension plan offers the best value for money can no longer be based solely on which plan offers the largest projected pension fund.

Finally, the current political uncertainty is likely to continue over the coming year. Aside from the effect of this uncertainty on the investment markets, there is no overall political consensus on pension matters. The valuable tax benefits of approved pension schemes and the role of personal pensions are all areas which are capable of being the subject of political debate. This should not be allowed to obscure the fundamental issues: State pensions are likely to prove inadequate for many and delaying the start of pension planning is likely to prove costly.

15.10   Conclusion

The tax-deductibility of premiums, tax-free growth and prospects of a tax-free lump sum make pensions an extremely attractive investment.

There are, of course, some restrictions (lack of access to the fund until a minimum age, ability to take only a proportion as a lump sum, limits on the investment permitted, etc) but these do not detract from the investment benefit of pensions where the pension is effected for the right reasons, ie as long-term planning for retirement.

Sources of further information

See end of Chapter 14.

16 Commodities

William Adams, Base metal research analyst, Rudolf Wolff & Co Ltd

16.1 Introduction to commodities

The commodity markets had their origins in the industrial expansion of the 19th century. Industrialisation led to a rapid growth in demand for basic commodities which caused increased volatility in prices as supply was increasingly dependent on the arrival of shipments from abroad. This price volatility meant more efficient means were needed to price and allocate commodites. The early commodity markets therefore enabled traders to buy and sell contracts for physical commodities, on the basis of today's prices for delivery in the future.

Today's commodity exchanges still provide this service, although they have generally evolved to provide more of a pricing mechanism, where traders buy and sell the right to a commodity (a future), rather than in trading the physical commodity. That said, the commodity exchanges are still backed by physical commodities and if a future contract becomes prompt, then it is the physical commodity that has to be delivered or taken-up.

The primary reason for the markets is still to provide a means whereby trade users can fix the price they sell or buy their raw material commodities at in the future. For fabricators using commodities, this means that the price of their finished goods can be determined before being produced, by locking-in (hedging) the cost of the commodities needed to produce the finished goods. Likewise a producer can plan in advance whether it is profitable to continue producing the commodity in the period ahead. If the future price is above the full cost of production, the producer can sell futures against forward production and guarantee a profit for the period ahead.

Today's commodity markets are very sophisticated and form an integral part of the world financial markets where banks, producers, consumers, merchants and investors are all participants.

This chapter will largely deal with the concepts of the commodity markets with insight into those commodities that can be bought and sold through, or are regulated by, the London Clearing House, the London Metal Exchange, the London Commodity Exchange, and the London International Financial Futures Exchange.

16.2   Types of commodities

16.2.1   Softs and metals

The raw material commodities can be sub-divided into two categories: soft commodities and metals.

The term soft commodities loosely describes all non-metallic commodities: cocoa, coffee, sugar, rubber, grain, potatoes, wool and edible oil, nuts, etc. The London Commodity Exchange is Europe's primary soft commodity exchange, operating markets in coffee, cocoa, sugar, the BIFFEX Freight Index and UK domestic agriculture markets.

The London Metal Exchange (LME) is the centre for trade in the main non-ferrous base metal futures such as aluminium, copper, zinc, lead, nickel, tin and aluminium alloy. The London Bullion Market Association (LBMA) looks after the interests of London's bullion markets. The bullion markets are physical markets and not futures markets.

The London Clearing House (LCH) deals with the clearing and settlement of the futures markets. Membership of LCH guarantees the fulfilment of the contract to both buyer and seller, thus avoiding the need for both buyer and seller to be concerned with each other's financial health. In effect, the LCH becomes the counterparty to each trade that its members carry out with other members.

16.2.2   Physical and futures

The commodity markets can be broken down into 'physical' and 'futures'. The physical markets deal with trading of the actual commodity and would normally result in a physical exchange of the commodity. A futures contract deals with commodities that are traded for delivery at a pre-defined future date and, in the majority of cases, the commodity is not expected to be delivered. As a futures contract is a tradeable contract, it will generally be liquidated before the contract becomes prompt. This means that the contract will be cancelled by a corresponding and opposite contract, which will mean the net position of the trader will be square and that any difference in buying and selling prices will be settled in cash.

By buying and selling in the futures markets against a physical position, the hedger is able to safeguard himself against the risk that the value of his unsold goods will depreciate through a fall in price or, alternatively, against the risk that pre-booked forward sales will show a loss if the commodity price rises.

Example

A merchant who has taken delivery of 25 tonnes of copper, but has not yet found a buyer for the metal, can sell one futures contract, the basis being the price at which he bought the physical metal. When he finds a buyer for the physical metal, he then buys back his futures contract on the basis of the price at which he sells his physical metal.

This means that while he holds the 25 tonnes of copper in stock, he is not vulnerable to a fall in the copper price, as any fall in the copper price will be offset by a profit on his futures contract.

This mechanism for hedging risk works when the futures markets are liquid, ie when there are sufficient buyers and sellers to make a two way market.

Market liquidity is increased by the existence of speculators. The speculator buys or sells a commodity on the expectation of making a profit. By taking the opposite view in the market to the hedger, the speculator takes on the unwanted risk that the hedger wants to avoid.

Investment in physical markets is complicated by having to pay the full cash cost of the commodity, the warehouse and insurance costs, etc. Metals have the advantage over soft commodities in that they are generally less bulky and are not perishable.

Investing in futures avoids many of the disadvantages of physical commodity investing. The speculator can avoid taking physical delivery of the commodity as long as the future contract is closed before the contract becomes prompt. By dealing in futures, the spectulator is able to trade softs as easily as metals, without the worry of the commodity perishing, or the more expensive storage costs.

16.2.3 Financial futures

The third category of futures is financial futures which regard money as another commodity. Financial futures grew rapidly in the 1980s and have enabled traders to use their money more flexibly, by trading and hedging interest rates, bonds and stock market indices in the same way they would trade other raw material commodities.

These financial futures contracts are structured, regulated and cleared just like the raw material commodities and provide opportunities for investment managers, financial treasurers and traders seeking profit opportunities.

The interest rate market contracts are the most important of the financial futures. These range from short-dated three-month papers to long-maturity government bonds and are denominated in most of the world's major trading currencies. The major contracts are traded in three time zones, providing around-the-clock access.

Stock index contracts are also well established and becoming increasingly popular, as are the option derivatives on the stocks. In addition to speculation, these products enable investors and fund managers to hedge their portfolio rapidly or to gain immediate access to the market.

16.3   Characteristics of commodities

Commodity markets are sophisticated, internationally traded and price movements are often volatile. It is these characteristics which provide many attractive trading opportunities.

16.3.1   International markets

The word commodity is defined in an economic sense as 'an exchangeable unit of economic wealth'. In most cases these units of economic wealth are internationally recognised and, therefore, have a real value which is recognised and traded internationally. This widespread need for the commodities also means the markets are liquid and have high turnover as each commodity often passes through many traders'/industrialists' hands before being consumed. The liquidity, high volume and interest in these commodities means that in most cases it is possible to trade large volumes fairly quickly without disrupting the balance in the market.

16.3.2   Frequent opportunities

The prices of commodities continuously fluctuate as buying and selling pressure shifts. The driving forces for prices in the long term are the supply and demand fundamentals. In the short term, the markets may move in the opposite direction to that suggested by the fundamental factors, but this divergence provides further opportunities for trading. In the futures markets, because the prompt date is a date in the future, the contract can be sold short. This means that the trader can sell the contract before buying it back at a later date. Therefore, even if you expect prices to fall, you can still trade and profit from a falling market. This second dimension to the futures market is not available to most private investors in equities. However, the futures markets can at times be very volatile and the investor directly involved in a commodity will need to follow the market closely and is best advised to seek the guidance of an established broker and investment adviser.

16.3.3 Real assets

Raw material commodities are real assets with intrinsic values. This means that they could always be sold for cash and in the long term they are a good potential hedge against inflation or currency depreciation.

16.4 Methods of participation in the commodity markets

There are many opportunities for investors to participate in the commodity markets and a host of investment vehicles that can be used to do so. This section will deal with the more direct approaches of investing in commodities and commodity futures.

16.4.1 Physical (cash) metals

Possibly the least speculative means of getting involved in metals is to buy physical metal. Once bought, the investor will have to pay insurance and warehousing costs, but because payment has been made in full and there is no gearing involved on the initial capital investment, the investor will not have to pay additional margin payments.

The time to buy cash metals is when prices have fallen considerably below the cost of metal production, which in theory should eventually lead to production cutbacks at plants that are no longer economically viable. This will bring about a change in the supply and demand balance of the metal.

It should be made clear that an oversupply situation in the metal markets can last for a number of years, so this type of investment should be seen as a long-term investment. In addition, it should be realised that world production costs will also fluctuate; in times of falling metal prices, producers will attempt to cut production costs in an effort to remain economically profitable.

The long-term cyclical nature of commodity prices is inherent in the markets, as high prices encourage additional production and less consumption, which will turn a market which has a balanced supply and demand into a market where there is a supply surplus. This will lead to lower prices. Conversely, in a period of low prices, consumption will increase and production will decrease, which will eventually lead to a drawdown in stocks and higher prices as demand for metal outstrips supply. These cycles mean that the further prices diverge from the world production costs, the more likely it is that there will be a change in the direction of the price trend. These factors influence the market over the long term and may take a few years to change the direction of a commodities price.

16.4.2   Cash and carry

The cash and carry is a risk-free way of trading in commodities, for a known return on funds employed. In addition, a cash and carry will sometimes provide opportunities for a capital gain.

This method of trading takes advantage of markets where forward prices are at a premium to cash (spot) prices. This premium is known as a 'contango'. In normal (contango) market conditions, the futures price is above the cash price (the exception to this occurs when there is a physical shortage of the commodity for nearby delivery, when this happens forward prices trade at a discount to the cash price; the discount is known as a backwardation). Normally the contango reflects the cost of storage, insurance, and the opportunity cost of tying up money while holding the physical commodity. In other words, the contango reflects the interest payments lost by not having the money in the bank, plus the cost of insurance, plus the cost of storage.

A cash and carry is traded by buying a commodity for immediate delivery and simultaneously selling an equal amount of the commodity for a future delivery date. In a contango market, this will mean that you are buying at a lower price and selling at a higher price. The difference will be the gross profit. Occasionally while the investor is holding a cash and carry, a shortage in the commodity will occur and the market's contango will narrow or even turn into a backwardation. In this case the holder of the cash and carry can sell his cash commodity and simultaneously buy back his future position, thereby making a capital gain.

16.4.3   Futures

The basic commodity traded on the exchanges is the outright futures contract. This provides the investor with a high risk vehicle to trading commodities and requires the services of a futures broker. The buying or selling of a futures contract by an investor/speculator involves them taking a view on whether prices are set to rise or fall during the period of the futures contract. At any time during the life of the futures contract, the contract can be closed-out by making a corresponding and opposite trade.

For example, if you buy one March 94 cocoa then to close out your position you need to sell one March 94 cocoa before the March 94 cocoa contract becomes due. If on 4 January you sell one LME three months copper, with a prompt date of 4 April, then when you sell the contract you will need to sell one lot of LME copper, on the basis of the three months price, and then adjust the contract to the prompt date of your original long position, in this case 4 April.

Because dealing in futures is for forward delivery, only a proportion of the value of the contract is initially required as payment. This initial payment, known as initial margin, is normally around 10 per cent of the value of the full contract. Therefore an investment in £100,000 worth of copper will only require an initial outlay of £10,000. This means that the funds you initially commit are geared at 10 per cent.

Your risk, however, is on the full £100,000 value of the commodity, therefore a 10 per cent move in the price of the commodity against you would mean a 100 per cent loss on your initial funds. Should the value of the commodity move against you, then you would be required immediately to provide funds equal to the open position loss of your futures contract. This difference is called variation margin and is paid in addition to the initial margin. Both initial and variation margin are used by the broker as collateral against any difference in the current market value of your contract and the starting value of the contract when you initiated the trade.

It is this gearing and the need for variation margin payments which gives the commodity markets their high-risk reputation. Of course, it is the ability to make 100 per cent on your funds with only a 10 per cent movement in price which makes the market attractive to speculators.

16.4.4 Options

A less risky way to invest in the commodities is to buy options. An option is a traded contract which gives the buyer the right to buy a futures commodity at a specific price (strike price) at a predetermined date in the future; the buyer is not, however, obliged to buy the futures contract. The risk is limited to the initial payment that the buyer has to pay for the option, this is known as the premium. The advantage of trading options is that for a predetermined cost there is the potential for a significant gain.

Traded options are based on underlying futures contracts. If the option becomes profitable, the holder of an option can, at any time prior to the declaration of the option, lock-in a profit by one of the following means:

(1)   trading a futures contract against the option position;
(2)   selling the option and making a profit out of the difference between the premium he paid to buy the option and the premium he collected when he sold the option;
(3)   waiting until option declaration and notifying his broker that he intended to declare the option, in which case the option position will be converted into a futures position at the strike price of the option. The investor then has to sell the futures contract to take the profit.

If the futures price moves in the opposite direction to the option, then the holder of the option allows the option to expire and his loss is limited to the initial premium he paid.

There are numerous types of options and by combining various types, the investor can produce option strategies which will provide different opportunities. The basic options are call and put options. A call option gives the buyer the right to buy a futures contract and a put option gives the buyer the right to sell a futures contract.

A grantor (uncovered seller) of an option takes on unlimited risk, as by selling the option he gives the buyer of the option the right, but not the obligation, to take up a futures contract at a predetermined price on a pre-determined date in the future. Option grantors are traditionally the trade (consumers and producers) who use options as a means of raising cash. Investment fund managers and risk seekers also grant options, but option granting is a high risk activity, whereas option buying will provide an investor with a high leveraged position with a limited liability.

16.4.5   Managed funds

Investing in commodities through managed funds provides the ideal vehicle for investors, who do not have the time, inclination or expertise to follow and trade the markets, to get exposure to the risk/rewards that the futures markets offer.

Types of fund on offer vary the level of risk/reward, some offer a guarantee that at least the initial sum will be returned after a pre-set period, but this guarantee means that the fund will be relatively low geared and, therefore, the level of potential rewards will be less than for a high geared fund where the initial investment is at risk.

Basically, there are two types of funds that invest in commodity futures, options and derivatives. The traditional type of fund is the Unauthorised Collective Investment Scheme, which pools investors' money so that the investment benefits from a diversified portfolio investing in futures and options. These funds are generally registered offshore and are open-ended funds which work on a unit allocation basis. The second category of funds are the Futures and Options Funds (FOFs) and the Geared Futures and Options Funds (GFOFs). These funds have recently been authorised by UK regulators and work in a similar fashion to authorised unit trusts, which traditionally were not allowed to invest in futures. At the moment these new funds have not been widely developed.

Funds generally operate on the basis that the fund manages the money it raises by investing the money with a number of Commodity Trading Advisers (CTAs). This enables the fund managers to select the best performing CTAs and, as market conditions change, the allocation of money with each CTA can be optimised. The fund manager monitors the returns from the CTAs and handles the administration and risk management of the fund.

Normally, the only cost to the investor will be standard brokerage charges plus a small management fee of between 1 and 3 per cent and an incentive fee which is assessed on the performance of the fund. This fee generally averages around 15 to 20 per cent of the increase in value of the fund in an agreed accounting period.

Commodity funds generally have full discretion over the money invested with them, although some funds will specialise in certain market segments and will have pre-set risk management principles. The performance of all funds relies heavily on the judgement of the fund manager and how accurately he anticipates the markets.

In selecting a fund manager, the investor needs to see how the manager has performed in the past. Although this by no means guarantees future performance, it does give some insight into how skilled the manager and the operation is.

The traditional funds are registered overseas to provide tax incentives for investors. Generally, the minimum investment into this traditional type of fund is around £10,000. The advantage of managed funds is that they provide individual investors and institutions with access to a market which is growing rapidly in volume and which provides numerous opportunities for investors to diversify their investment portfolio.

16.5   Commodities' recent market performance

16.5.1   Financial markets

After going from strength to strength in 1993, the rise in US interest rates in February 1994 put an end to the bull market for both bonds and equities. During the rest of 1994 the bond and equity markets fell and various rebounds have so far failed.

16.5.2   Soft commodities

A combination of improved consumption growth, especially in the developing countries and supply and quality disruptions sent soft commodities higher in mid-1994. The most notable example was coffee's threefold rise from 70 cents to over 200 cents. The rise was sparked by fears that the Brazilian crop had been damaged following two frosts and a drought.

The bull markets attracted fund buying, but the higher levels prompted aggressive profit-taking. Cocoa and coffee rose in mid-1994, but have since fallen back, while sugar has rallied strongly since mid-year.

16.5.3   Base metals

Base metals have undergone sharp price rises since October 1993 when the bear market hit a bottom. Table 1 below shows the extent of the 3 months' price and LME stock movements in 1994. During the OECD recession in the early 1990s, metal consumption was underpinned by strong South East Asian demand. Once North America and parts of Europe started to emerge from recession, demand for base metals increased as consumption rose and merchants and consumers started to restock.

Table 16.1   Summary of 1994's performance, price and stocks

	LME STOCKS					*1994 3Mths Prices*		
	END '93	*HIGH '94*	*END '94*	*+/−*	*Start*	*LOW*	*HIGH*	*% Chq*
Cu	599,500	617,800	301,850	−51%	1,727	1,727	3,032	+75%
Al	2,486,375	2,661,525	1,674,650	−37%	1,121	1,121	2,015	+80%
Zn	906,700	1,239,350	1,185,200	−4%	1,012	918	1,214	+20%
Pb	303,650	372,650	343,425	−8%	475	437	703	+48%
Ni	124,104	151,254	148,392	−2%	5,240	5,240	9,550	+82%
Sn	20,050	32,405	28,105	−13%	4,810	4,740	6,440	+34%
AA	49,260	49,260	30,480	−38%	992	992	1,920	+94%

In addition, 1994 saw the emergence of significant investor interest in the commodity markets. Funds and investment banks started to offer clients a host of commodity based investment vehicles, including investment trusts, base metal backed warrants and managed futures funds. This fuelled the bull market in base metals and helped carry prices to levels that had not been envisaged the previous year.

The sharp rise seems to have caught many merchants and consumers off guard. As the global economy now heads towards more synchronised growth in the main consuming regions of North America, Europe, Japan and South East Asia, further spectacular gains are likely.

There is, however, need for caution as the fundamentals of some of the metals suggest that the move up in metal prices has been premature and indeed the fundamentals themselves are set to change as new and idle production capacity is brought on stream.

16.6 Outlook for the year ahead

16.6.1 Financials

The determination by many leading governments to clamp down on inflation should provide some encouragement for the financial markets. The prospects for continued and more widespread economic growth is expected to underpin equities and with the bond markets now looking undervalued some recovery should be seen.

16.6.2 Softs

Sugar

Concerns of strong Chinese and Russian demand for sugar has underpinned the bull market and funds have fuelled the rally, but against a background of poor harvests in China and Eastern Europe, firmer prices look likely in the short term, although technical corrections look overdue.

Coffee

Prices rose from 70 to over 250 cents, before falling back to 140 as the market doubted the justification for such high prices. Market seems to be building a base around 150. Look for prices to rise further as there is still uncertainty over the size of the Brazilian crop and demand remains strong. The market should also be underpinned by the possibility of a supply retention scheme that a number of producers are considering.

Cocoa

Concerns over the effect of a late harvest in the Ivory Coast, following a dry pre-harvest period, sparked the rally in 1994. The market's concerns over quality also drove prices above $1500 per tonne as heavy rains may have damaged the crop. The involvement of funds added to the upward momentum.

With another deficit forecast and with further fund activity expected, we feel cocoa prices have further to run on the upside.

16.6.3   Base metals

As we move towards synchronised economic growth in the three traditional consuming regions of Europe, North America and Japan, we are also faced, probably for the first time ever, with the prospects of synchronised economic growth in a fourth region as well. The fourth being the rapidly growing South East Asian economies. This should lead to four major consuming regions all expanding at the same time.

The growth in consumption in North America has exceeded expectations and is lasting much longer than projected. This raises the question whether the markets have underestimated the impact of more widespread growth. If it has been underestimated, then the commodity prices are set to reach record highs. The uncertainty lies in whether the global economy can sustain such widespread growth without running into liquidity problems, high interest rates or a financial crisis.

For the moment we favour a continuation of the bull market in base metals, but expect the markets to become increasingly volatile and nervous as prices trade further above the average operating production costs.

Copper

The fundamentals in the copper market are very strong; stocks, as measured in the number of weeks' consumption that they represent, have fallen from ten weeks in 1993 to around five weeks at the end of 1994. Below five weeks' stocks are considered to be below that needed to ensure a smooth supply to industry. When stocks are below five weeks, prices can be sustained at much higher levels in the short term.

Before we get too bullish, two points need to be taken into account. Firstly, new mine production is scheduled to come on stream between now and 1996, this will reduce the current supply deficit. Secondly, with prices already up 90 per cent and with investment funds thought to be already long of copper, there will come a time when the funds decide to take profits. This could result in a sharp correction in metals prices.

Aluminium

Aluminium demand is soaring as can be seen by the rapid decline in stock levels. While this trend continues we expect prices to head even higher. Our concern is that although there is only one major new production project scheduled to start in 1995, the Alusaf smelter in South Africa, there are over 2m tonnes of idle production capacity that is likely to be restarted as the bull market gains momentum. The timing of these restarts will be very influential on aluminium prices. In addition, with a large fund presence there is the danger of large scale profit-taking at some time.

Overall, we expect higher aluminium prices to be followed by a sharp correction, a period of consolidation at lower numbers and then a more gradual rise while the global economy continues to expand.

Zinc

1994 saw zinc demand grow by 2.2 per cent; this is expected to increase during 1995/96 as global economic growth gathers momentum. Zinc is, however, suffering from an acute oversupply, as evidenced by the high stock levels. This should prevent zinc from following the spectacular performance of aluminium and copper. However, the markets do not always react in the way the fundamentals suggest they should. Much of the surplus zinc is held in LME warehouses, therefore, it is not known who owns it, or indeed whether the metal is for sale at the prevailing price. If the metal is not freely for sale, then higher prices could well be seen despite the high stock levels. This has been the case in the nickel market.

With very strong demand for zinc in North America, premiums for the physical metal are likely to force prices higher. Overall we expect zinc prices to trend higher over the course of 1995/96, although a sell-off in other base metals is likely to affect zinc as well.

Lead

The lead market is very tight. Supply is being restrained by a shortage in mine output, which in turn is suffering as a result of the depressed zinc market—lead is largely mined as a co-product of zinc. As demand increases we expect the drawdown of lead stocks to underpin a steady rise in lead prices.

Nickel

Nickel has shocked the metals market. Since the 1993 trough, prices have risen 150 per cent. This is despite a high level of nickel stocks. With the LME accounting for 50 per cent of total commercial stocks, it appears that the majority of metal held in warehouse has not been widely for sale at these price levels.

Nickel's biggest use is for stainless steel production, which has experienced tremendous growth in the past 18 months, up over 11 per cent in the Western World. The prospects for continued strong demand for stainless steel look good, it is finding strong demand in the emerging markets. Its use in pollution control equipment, which is benefiting from the ever stricter environmental legislation being applied to new and existing plant should see demand outpace industrial production growth rates.

However, another cause for concern is that around 15 per cent of the West's nickel supply comes from Russia. The deteriorating economic climate in Russia is expected to lead to a fall in Russian nickel production. With so much uncertainty surrounding Russia, the market will remain very vulnerable to supply disruptions.

New nickel production is scheduled to come on stream in 1995. This will help alleviate the supply shortage, but the main concern is the high stock level which could terminate the bull trend if it were released on to the market too quickly. Overall, we expect stronger nickel prices in the first half of 1995, but, as new production materialises, prices are likely to come under pressure.

Tin

Tin has recovered from its lows; however, the market is still suffering from oversupply. Economic growth should underpin demand, but there are concerns that Chinese exports may remain at a high level for some time to come and may increase if tin prices rise significantly.

Overall we expect the market to rise on the back of stronger demand and with prices only up 29 per cent in 1994, there still seems good potential for gains in 1995.

16.7   How to participate

Commodity markets involve a high risk and it is essential for the investor to fully understand the whole workings of the market. That said once the concepts and risks have been grasped then commodities provide a wide range of investment opportunities.

The key to successful investing in commodites lies in a full understanding of the opportunities available, to have access to up-to-date information, and most importantly to know how to interpret this information. This information can be found through experienced brokers and professional advisors.

Commodity markets involve a high risk and it is essential for the investor to fully understand the whole workings of the market. That said, once the concepts and risks have been grasped, commodities provide a wide range of investment opportunities.

The key to successful investing in commodities lies in a full understanding of the opportunities available, having access to up-to-date information, and, most importantly, knowing how to interpret this information. The information can be found through experienced brokers and professional advisers.

Sources of further information

Further information should be initially sought from the market exchanges and the London Clearing House, details given below:

Useful addresses

London Metal Exchange Ltd
56 Leadenhall Street
London
EC3A 2BJ

Tel: (0171) 264 5555

London Commodity Exchange
1 Commodity Quay
St Katharine's Dock
London E1 9AX

Tel: (0171) 481 2080

London International
   Financial Futures Exchange
Cannon Bridge
London
EC4R 3XX

Tel: (0171) 623 0444

London Bullion Market
   Association
6 Frederick's Place
London
EC2R 8BT

Tel: (0171) 796 3067

London Clearing House
Roman Wall House
1–2 Crutched Friars
London
EC3N 2AN

Tel: (0171) 265 2000

17 Gold and other valuables

John Myers, Lessia Djakowska and Susan Farrell of Solon Consultants

17.1 Introduction

17.1.1 A long-term hedge in precious metals

Three hundred years ago, a troy ounce of gold would pay for a fine man's wardrobe; an Indian diamond of quality would have funded the purchase of a house in the City. Today, the same ounce of gold would give just about enough money for an off-the-peg suit, and a Hatton Garden diamond might be eagerly snatched to pay off mortgage arrears on a flat in the Docklands. Fashions change, generations pass, but over the years these valuables have generally held their appeal for investors. That helps to explain why some financial counsellors encourage their clients to put a small part of their savings into gold, or maybe platinum or silver — but rarely into diamonds, and scarcely ever into ivory, which traders can no longer handle legally in many places.

The traditional worth of precious metals and other valuables is as a long-term hedge against political tumult or economic chaos. When inflation soars, when currencies look weak, when stock markets go black, precious metals have gained in attraction; in the past, the greater the uncertainty, the higher the price rise. Gold is of course the archetypal precious metal. Attractive to look at, and rare, it is an age-old standard of wealth with a habit of asserting itself when more ephemeral standards fail. Investors hold it not out of greed but out of fear. Nevertheless, the Gulf War and the Russian *putsch* had only a marginal effect on the price of gold; and various international incidents in the last decade produced only a ripple in gold prices.

Because gold is intrinsically valuable, internationally acceptable and negotiable, it retains its historical image as the ultimate form of money, a store of wealth transcending wars and political turmoil. Events have tarnished that image. Hedging, with the help of futures, options, gold mining shares, physical holdings and indices, has damped down oscillations. A weakening of exchange controls has made it easier for wealthy people who fear war and local hyperinflation to shift into dollars, marks,

Swiss francs or yen instead of gold. Recent political crises in the world have therefore had little impact on the bullion market of late.

The market in gold is complex. Demand is driven by dream and doubt more than industrial utility. But as the American poet Delmore Schwartz said, 'in dreams begin responsibilities', and gold supply is governed as much by the actions of the 'official sector', (central banks that are responsible for its role as a quasi-monetary standard and which control almost one third of total supply) as by the efforts of producers. Gold maintains a reputation, albeit sullied, as a long-term insurance premium paid against the collapse of economies, markets and currencies. Gold 'bugs' are still convinced that the metal will retain, or even increase, its value during times of great uncertainty.

J M Keynes may have dismissed the metal as 'a barbarous relic', but there are many who believe that 'something which has been a store of value for 5,000 years will not go out of fashion'. In their view, a holding of gold should counterbalance a severe downturn in portfolios of stocks and shares during a monetary or political crisis. Bullion (in the form of bars, wafers or coins) is largely immune to the effects of weather, moisture, oxidation or sea water, and to the corrosive effects of most acids and alkalis. Furthermore, as the prices of gold and platinum are usually expressed in US dollars, such metals can be a hedge against sharp falls in the value of other currencies, although they remain susceptible when dollar markets falter. In the shorter term, the volatility of the metals markets provides some opportunities for speculative trading.

The case remains strong enough for some level-headed financial planners to recommend that wealthy investors keep as much as 5–10 per cent of their assets in the precious metals market. Some bolder investors with cash to spare hold as much as 10–15 per cent in bullion, gold mining company shares, or mutual funds that invest in those companies. In principle, buying gold should help to even out the volatility of an investment portfolio. Nonetheless, prices of precious metals could oscillate in spectacular ways in a short time; and they are not investments for the nervous or the needy. In times of relatively low inflation — the early 1990s was an example — shares, bonds and unit trusts substantially outperform gold or the other noble metals.

Silver and platinum have also become respectable vehicles for investment. Respectable, but risky: silver is used primarily as an industrial material, so there is at least a chance that its price will fall during a recession. Platinum is highly volatile, and its popularity largely depends on its present use in automotive catalytic converters which, with technical development, now require decreasing amounts of the metal. Nonetheless worldwide demand for platinum has grown, boosted at the margin by sales of inexpensive jewellery in Japan. Jewellery is also a main outlet for gold, and sales can suffer when economies falter or bullion price rises deter buyers. The unpredictability of precious metals prices makes them unsuitable investments for individuals with limited sums to invest, or for investors who require a flow of income from their savings.

17.1.2 Gold coins

Gold coins are another form of bullion investment. They are minted by the governments of many countries. Examples are the American Golden Eagle, the Russian chervonetz, the Mexican peso, the Austrian corona and philharmonic (it has a fiddle on the obverse), the Luxembourg lion, the Australian nugget, the South African krugerrand and others enjoying culturally redolent names. Mauritius has its dodo; France, its Napoleon; China, its panda; Canada, its maple leaf; Japan, its Hirohito and its Akihito (of which more anon). The Royal Mint's Britannia has an aesthetic appeal to justify a premium over the coin's bullion value. Struck in 22 carat gold, with Britannia standing amid the waves with her trident on one side, and a shield and olive branch on the other, it was once awarded the *Coin of the Year* title. Although the Britannia competes with the American Eagle, there is one significant difference: the US Mint produces tens of thousands of Eagles, while Great Britain has limited production to only 500 each of the 1, ½ and ¼ ounce sizes. The set sells for $1,650 and the individual ⅒ ounce coins for $105. The retail price may seem high, given that bullion sells at less than $400 an ounce at today's prices.

A £2 silver coin was launched in April 1995 by the Royal Mint to commemorate the fiftieth anniversary of the United Nations. However, discerning collectors and traders are beginning openly to challenge the Mint and its play on the investment and collectable value of commemorative coins. Experts claim that they would not usually be part of a serious collection, and that they represent a poor return on investment. The value of modern commemorative coins is estimated to be between 40 to 60 per cent of their original purchase price.

Glendining's, the specialist coins and medals auctioneers, believe that the supply of commemorative coins considerably outstrips demand. Whereas their production was once a rare event, there have been many new issues since the 1980s.

A silver version of the Royal Mint's UN coin can be bought for £26.50, while base metal and gold versions are due to be issued in late 1995. The Royal Mint is also to produce a silver 36-coin collection, provisionally priced at £1,200, with each coin representing a Member State of the UN. The coins are to be issued on a monthly subscription basis, with a limited production of 100,000.

Sales of American Eagle bullion coins, though, plummeted in 1994, compared with 1993 sales and were on an extremely narrow trading range. Prices are determined on the basis of current gold and silver prices, plus a small premium, reflecting trends in gold prices throughout 1994. However, as they are all legal tender coins, they will attract the interest of collectors — with the possibility that demand may exceed supply.

Another example is the Australian 'kangaroo', launched in March 1991 as a series of gold bullion coins in the shape of 2 ounce, 10 ounce and 1 kilogram 'nuggets' which are 99.99 per cent pure gold. The largest coin has a face value of $A10,000 (more than £4,000), but sales prices of the coins are linked to the market value of bullion. The 1 kilogram nugget is the heaviest legal tender coin this century.

The krugerrand, still at the leading edge in the gold coin market, was largely responsible for the modern success of gold coins. In 1978 South Africa sold the highest amount ever recorded by any country in a single year. With the lifting of trade sanctions on the country, the South Africans are planning to re-launch the krugerrand internationally. However, a general deterrent for the UK private investor wishing to invest in gold coins, wafers, or bars is the liability for VAT which purchase incurs. Although the tax may be avoided if the gold is delivered offshore, the collapse in UK demand for this form of investment since the tax was imposed in 1982 means that few large dealers are now willing to take on new customers. However, the demand in Germany for gold coins and bars increased dramatically when the 14 per cent VAT rate was removed earlier in 1993.

As with all purchases of precious metals, the buyer is advised to deal only with reputable sources. A recent scheme launched in Florida claiming to turn US$60 into US$9,200 in gold coins is claimed by trading watchdogs to be nothing more than a classic pyramid scheme.

17.1.3   Coins manufactured in other precious metals

The silver 'Kookaburra' (released April 1990) and the platinum Koala stirred up new interest and visibility for Australia's ambitious bullion coin programme. The Koala is one of only a few platinum bullion coins currently on the market. One of the earliest was the platinum Noble from the Isle of Man, minted originally in 1983. The Australian Gold Corporation selected platinum instead of silver because of the metal's rarity. Only about four million ounces of platinum are produced worldwide annually, compared to 40 million ounces of gold. The Koala image was used partly to attract sales from Japanese buyers, who account for about 50 per cent of world demand for platinum. A day after the platinum coins were launched in Japan, 4,093 ounces of the platinum Koalas were sold at prices between \$510–\$520 an ounce, according to the Gold Corporation.

In parallel, Russia is offering a set of four historical commemorative coins that feature two made of silver, one of platinum and one of palladium. The full set has been selling for about £500. The Russians, in urgent need of currency, have been aggressively selling palladium coins to collectors and metals speculators. The Russian government has offered a bullion palladium coin, made of 99 per cent palladium and priced to sell at a premium of 20 per cent above the metal's daily spot market price. The coins, which bear a face value of 25 roubles, carry the image of a ballerina — the first of what the Russians hope will be a long-lasting series of 'palladium ballerina' coins. Only 30,000 have been minted so far; and 3,000 are of proof quality.

Knowledgeable dealers believe that the palladium coin serves as an important precedent, and that palladium could be the investment metal of the 1990s. Only three countries — Russia, South Africa and the United States — have enough palladium to mine the mineral commercially; it is primarily employed in electronic components. Other countries to issue coins manufactured from palladium are Bermuda, France, the Isle of Man and Tonga. All these coins were special-issue commemoratives. The Russian coins are just one case of the increasing competitiveness with which foreign mints are seeking customers. Mexico, for instance, is offering the Mexico Rainbow Proof Coin Collection — a set of silver, gold and platinum coins. When they were launched, the first year's coins, bearing 1989 dates, were priced at £440.

Since 1991, silver coins have become more popular with mints. A noteworthy example is the American 'Eagle'; more than 5.3 million silver dollar 'Eagles' were sold between December 1990 and March 1991 — a record volume for a silver bullion coin. One factor was the anticipated rise in silver prices; another was patriotism during the Gulf war. Investors also favour silver coins and bars to hedge positions in silver futures and shares of companies that mine silver.

17.1.4 Other valuables

Apart from precious metals, investors can also consider valuables such as gemstones — emeralds, sapphires, semi-precious stones and diamonds. In investment terms only diamonds are significant, and the market is still dominated by the Central Selling Organisation. This is the London-based marketing organisation of De Beers.

At the regular sales, the CSO's experts sort heaps of rough diamonds that represent about four-fifths of the world's annual production. De Beers chooses its 160 or so buying customers from thousands of applicants. Ten times a year, at the sales (called 'sights'), the favoured few are offered a selection of diamonds chosen by the organisation and placed in a simple container. The set can be bought as a whole, or not at all. The gems are then passed on to diamond cutters in the world's major centres: Antwerp, Tel Aviv, New York and Bombay.

Only about one in six of the diamonds mined ends up in rings or other jewellery, but these account for most of the diamond output's value. The remainder are put to industrial use. The market's performance therefore largely depends on the success of its promoters in stimulating demand. To this end, De Beers spends large sums on advertising and sales promotion — for example, in an effort to persuade more men to buy and wear diamonds as jewellery. One result had been to stimulate demand through retail jewellers, but the markups make it more difficult for the investor to achieve gains. The addition of VAT accentuates this problem.

Thus, over the decades, De Beers has succeeded in mass-marketing what was once an aristocratic luxury without greatly diminishing its value. Diamonds remain 'the gem of gems' even though millions own them. De Beers' aim is long-term stability and prosperity for the industry. In its view, price fluctuations would undermine confidence in the value of diamonds. So far, the strategy has succeeded, although it is potentially vulnerable to persistent recession. There may also be nervousness among governments which wonder about alternative approaches to marketing diamonds other than going through the Central Selling Organisation. Markets for many other commodities have suffered successive seizures, but rough diamond prices have remained steady over the last two years, against a long-term tendency to rise since the organisation began publicising price changes in 1964.

17.1.5   Selected forms of investment in valuables

There are alternatives to investment in physical gold and other precious metals. Some institutions have 'certificate programmes', through which a private investor can specify how much to invest (usually a minimum of £500 or £1,000), and the institution then puts all the orders together and makes an appropriate purchase in bullion bars or ingots at the going market rate. The institution then divides the purchase between all the investors, issuing certificates for each allocation. Delivery and storage subsequently can be arranged. Investors should make doubly sure that the company that they are dealing with is trustworthy, that the purchase is made and stored in their individual names, and that proof of ownership is provided.

Other forms of investment have recently had a conspicuous effect on the gold market, helping to change its structure. The growth of speculation in the futures and options market has been an area of some controversy. The gold price has declined gradually in real terms over the last four years, and some commentators see a vicious circle in the effects of hedging by producers. Mine owners sell gold forward before new mines are opened up by raising gold loans that have to be repaid at a fixed price at a later date, thereby limiting price rises. The more that prices are capped at $400 or less (the World Gold Council estimate) the greater the incentive for producers to hedge to protect their profitability. Other analysts disagree, pointing to a reduction in hedging by mining companies when the market hit a seven year low. Whether or not hedging by producers has a counter-productive effect on it, the options and futures market provides flexible instruments for speculators to exploit any short-term volatility in the gold price.

Mining equities and funds offer the investor an alternative route. Shares in technologically proficient mining companies with large reserves and low production costs may on occasion be more attractive than investing directly in their physical output.

17.2 Highlights of the previous year

17.2.1 Modest signs of revival

Gold began to regain some of its lustre when mutual funds' computers triggered buy orders in the last half of 1993. While gold remains a risky investment producing negative returns, some gurus still believe that, long-term, prices will rise and rewards will outweigh uncertainties and drawbacks.

So far in the 1990s, the metal has performed like a commodity; the price has tended to reflect demand from fabricators of jewellery and electronics. In parallel, new buyers have entered the market on a large scale, and, for a time, China surpassed the US as the world's largest buyer, importing 350 tonnes or 10 per cent of world demand in 1992, when China lifted exchange rate controls on semi-official currency swap markets. As China's dollar depreciated by 30 per cent within days, Hong Kong's gold outlets reported an immediate upsurge of 20 per cent to Chinese customers.

Gold sales by central banks and other official sector organisations dropped dramatically in 1994 and there was a similarly sharp fall in producer hedging. These substantial reductions in gold supply would have had a much more noticeable impact on the gold price in 1994 except for a reversal in the attitude of private investors, whose buying in 1993 was a major factor in pushing up the gold price, while 1994 saw a sustained and substantial level of disinvestment.

Demand was very high in the first half of 1993 because the price was perceived to be exceptionally low. There has since been a rise of about 20 per cent, and latest figures indicate demand stabilising. Countries monitored by the World Gold Council, a promotional organisation financed by some gold mining groups, account for an estimated 75 per cent of world demand. In these areas, 1994 third-quarter gold demand rose by 6.2 per cent, that is about the 1993 level at 593 tonnes. But for the first nine months demand was down 6.4 per cent at 1,690.9 tonnes.

The prospect of the gold market being caught in a 'death cross', which according to chartists' technical theory could signal a price fall, might have prompted selling by funds. The death cross began to loom over the market before Christmas; it occurs if the 200-day moving average is crossed by the 50-day moving average while both are falling. A similar situation in the silver market happened in November 1994, when there was a sudden 15 per cent fall in price. However, most analysts concur that gold is likely to remain above the key technical support level of US$375 an ounce.

To a degree, prospects continued to be influenced by the knowledge that the world's central banks and quasi-governmental agencies like the IMF hold massive stocks of gold. If released in bulk onto the bullion market, the effect would be to depress prices. Gold suffers when interest rates are high, and in recent years central banks have increasingly switched to interest-bearing financial instruments. Thus in the 1980s official reserves of gold worldwide almost halved. The Gulf war and its aftermath led to Middle Eastern banks selling gold in favour of dollars and sterling.

Generally, the impetus to switch from gold is restrained by central banks' desire not to upset the market, but methods other than outright sales may be used to 'mobilise' gold reserves. They can be physically disposed of through the minting of bullion coins. More indirect means are call options on reserves, and low-interest gold loans to producers. Gold loans have had a substantial effect on the market in recent years, as was mentioned in the last section. Gold interest rates rose sharply in the second half of 1994, while demand for borrowing increased. Strong demand brought the total offtake of 1,598 tonnes to only 1 per cent below the 1993 level. Quarter four 1994 demand was up 19 per cent over 1993. Consistently strong demand from East Asia raised the gold offtake by 21 per cent. Recovery in the second half of 1994 in China and India offset a slow start to the year; while demand in Turkey and Saudi Arabia was significantly down in 1994 due to economic difficulties in both countries.

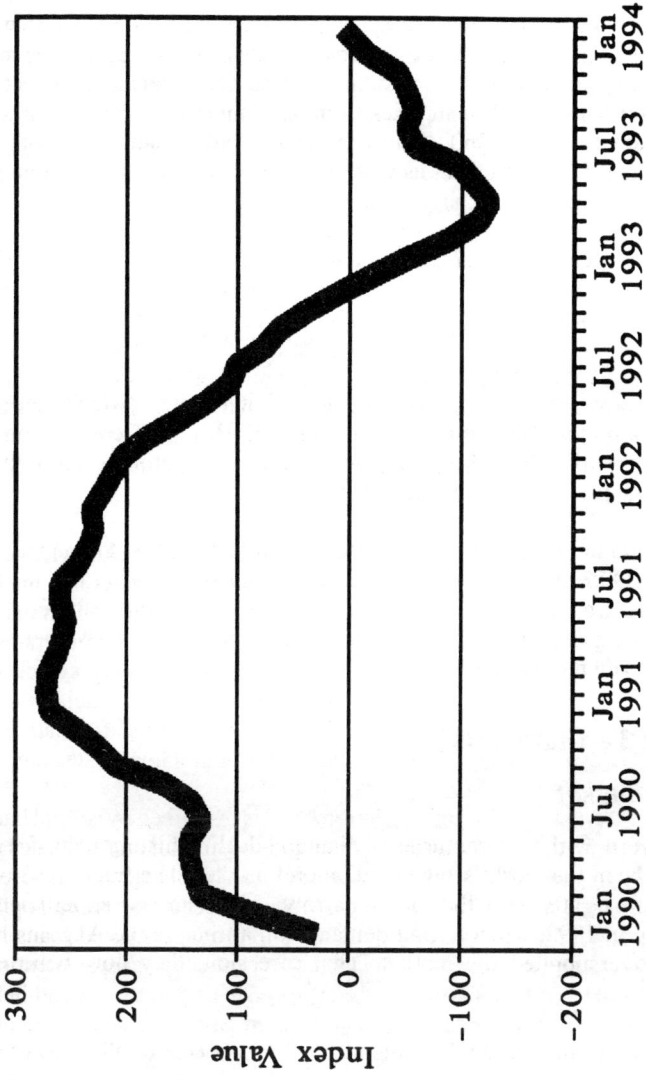

Figure 17.1 London gold price 1990–1993 ('cumulative sum' chart showing trend)

Source: *FT/Gold Field Mineral Services*

Estimated consumption of gold demand in 1994 in the 22 key markets monitored by the World Gold Council totalled 2,443 tonnes, showing only a 1 per cent change from 1993. India and the US continued to be the largest country markets, followed by Japan and China.

When the Soviet Union fell apart in 1991, it was revealed that it had exported more than half of its reserves in 1990, and that they stood at less than a quarter of previous Western estimates. This and more modest production led to a fall in supplies from 425 tonnes to 226 tonnes in 1991 and an estimated 160 tonnes in 1993. Production in Russia and Uzbekistan suffered from lack of capital and poor technology, output in South Africa was also slightly down, by about 3.5 tonnes. South African mine production is also now more capital intensive, and the low price has made some mine closures inevitable.

17.2.2   Demand for jewellery fabrication

1994 saw a record jewellery demand of 664 tonnes, which helped to maintain the 1994 overall demand at the 1993 level. Demand from the US was strong throughout the year, and there were strong signs of recovery in Japan for both jewellery and bullion.

Demand in Europe recovered in the second half of 1994 to bring the full year (290.3 tonnes) to virtually the same level as in 1993 (291.4 tonnes). Reports from the jewellery trade suggest that the recovery is based on the rebuilding of depleted inventory levels, and on renewed consumer confidence and purchasing.

17.2.3   Diamonds

The market

Antwerp, with four centuries of diamond dealing history behind it, has long been the world's biggest diamond market. The traders, who are packed tightly into the city's narrow seedy streets, experienced a slump in 1992, when falling demand and a truce in the Angolan civil war oversupplied the market. That recession, they now believe, is safely past.

About four in five rough diamonds, and 40 per cent of all polished diamonds come from Antwerp. On the world market, total dealings reached a record $17.1bn in 1993. America's rich went on a Thanksgiving and Christmas shopping spree; Hong Kong demand leapt 42 per cent; and Indian sales rocketed.

As the US economy began to emerge from the doldrums in 1993, Antwerp's total exports surged by 11 per cent. The recovery is continuing, although more slowly. There is confidence, expressed by Antwerp's industry association, the Diamond High Council, that the US will continue to grow and that the Japanese market will also recover. However, a question still hangs over Europe's resurgence. One major threat to Antwerp's monopoly is emerging cut-throat competition from other diamond centres, mainly in the Far East.

Diamond production

Russia mines top quality diamonds, and the country has some newly discovered diamond fields. These supply opportunities coincide with an acute shortage of cash that in turn exacerbates the political uncertainties and the weakness of the rouble. Russia's response is likely to have a radical impact on both the domestic and world markets by the turn of the century. At present, the Yakutia-Sakha Republic accounts for 99 per cent of the former Soviet Union's total diamond production. It is expected that these fields will be depleted by around 2010. However, the newly discovered fields in Asiatic Russia, around St Petersburg and in the Karelian Republic are expected to bring huge riches: De Beers conservatively estimates more than 250 million carats for one field alone.

The yield of gem diamonds from the new fields is much higher than the output from the Yakut fields, which is in turn superior to South African gem stones. The diamond content of the Yakut ore ranges from 0.6 to 4 carats per ton of ore, with 2–3 carats per ton considered to be most likely. Industry sources predict that an annual production of between 3 and 6 million carats is likely over the next 30–40 years. Although the actual prospecting and development of the fields is likely to be both expensive and time-consuming, American, British and Australian investors have already placed and won tenders to develop five diamond-bearing areas.

Russia and South Africa also face competition from other countries. For example, Australia is now the world's largest producer of diamonds. Most of the stones are industrial grade only, but some are of gem quality. Australia's Argyle diamond mine also produces some of the rarest stones in the world, some of which have sold for more than US $1m a carat.

De Beers and Russia

There have been more inklings of trouble for the international diamond traders from Russia. Large amounts of Russian diamonds by-passed De

Beers to be sold directly on the world market, circumventing the traditional diamond cartel, and threatening prices. This forced De Beers to buy more than $500m worth of these diamonds in 1994, to prevent a collapse of prices.

The dismemberment of the former Soviet Union had additional consequences for the diamond cartel. Yakutia, the largest region in the Russian Federation, took advantage of the political confusion to declare itself a sovereign state. To appease Yakutia, Moscow gave it control over 20 per cent of the diamonds it produced, and De Beers was forced to negotiate a separate agreement with the regional government.

Russian diamond producers have started selling gem diamonds to financial institutions and private individuals in an attempt to create a diamond market in Russia. The Moscow branch of the Central Bank of Russia and the Diamonds of Russia–Sakha company have established a National Diamond Trust. Its earnings will largely be reinvested in the Russian diamond industry. Annual sales are initially estimated at US$1.2m, but that figure is expected to rise as demand already exceeds supply.

The selling mechanism is based on the so-called investment diamond. The National Diamond Fund is attracting investments using diamonds as security. The stones are to be held by the investor until the agreement expires, when he can sell to the fund at their original price, plus a 22 per cent interest; or to any jeweller, including buyers outside Russia.

Another area for negotiation and dispute are the joint-ventures Russia has entered into to send diamonds abroad for polishing. De Beers considers these consignments as exports while Russia does not — as the diamonds remain Russian property.

Russia is now pushing to alter its buyer–seller relationship with De Beers: it is reportedly demanding seats on De Beers' board and an increase in the amount it sells outside De Beers. Russia produces 20 per cent of the world's diamonds and, under a deal which is due for renewal in 1995, is committed to sell 95 per cent to the Central Selling Organisation (CSO). De Beers may be forced into renegotiation if Russia's quota is increased. It could mean a fall in the quotas of other member countries — which include South Africa, Botswana and Australia.

Russia's aggressive stance is one difficulty among several for the diamond cartel. Under the terms of the 80-year-old arrangement, De Beers buys up the world's production of diamonds, and then fixes supplies on the market. When countries deal independently, as Angola and Zaire did during the early 1990s, the CSO's prices are directly affected. The Angolan approach alone caused profits to fall by a quarter in 1992.

As a girl's best friend

The traditional image of diamonds as a good investment is not as attractive as many perhaps imagine. While other commodities fluctuate in price — influenced by the weather and economics — the price of rough diamonds has tended to stabilize or rise. Given that kind of price performance, and the financial position of De Beers Consolidated Mines, which has largely controlled the flow of rough diamonds on to the world market, it would be natural to assume that investing in diamonds would be a secure investment. However, De Beers deals only in rough diamonds, and sells only to about 150 diamond dealers, a select client list. Membership is by invitation. Outside this narrow market, prices for cut and polished diamonds rise and fall, sometimes dramatically.

Diamonds can be used as a very compact way of holding wealth, with their long-term trend slightly above inflation. Large loose stones, free of jewellery settings, can be more easily examined for flaws, colour, 'fire' and brilliance, and it is easier to compare stones. The diamond, or diamonds, should be certified and sealed by an internationally recognised organisation, such as the Gemological Institute of America or the Diamond High Council of Antwerp.

17.3　Recent developments

17.3.1　Gold internationally

In this century, gold has recorded five major price rises in world markets. Its history, of course, is as a coinage metal and a measurement of national wealth. In 1934, as part of America's 'new deal', the bullion price was upgraded and fixed in US dollar terms at $35 per ounce. This lasted for 40 years until President Nixon severed gold's links with the dollar. On the open market, bullion reached $200 per ounce, principally as a consequence of petrodollar inflation and weak central banking strategies.

In the inflationary 1970s, with the rush to convert paper money into gold, the price of an ounce of gold rose to $825 in early 1980 — the last big surge in the gold price. It then dropped to $300 an ounce in mid-1982, only to rally again, reaching $500 per ounce in June 1983. Since 1987, gold has fallen back. In 1991 the dollar price averaged $362.26, down 6 per cent on 1990, and declined further to a six-year low of $336 in April 1992. This was despite the Gulf War, continued turmoil in South Africa, and the collapse of the Soviet Union. By March 1993, gold had tumbled yet again, and was fixed at a consecutive seven-year low of $326, with further falls to $325 being predicted by the most pessimistic. After gold's strong price performance in 1993, which led to the 1994 bull market in commodities, 1994 was a year of consolidation with prices remaining within a steady US$370–395 trading range. This left the average price for the year in US dollar terms around 7 per cent above its 1993 average, the first increase since 1990. However, the weakness of the dollar against other major currencies brought about significant declines in the price of gold, particularly against the Deutsch-Mark and the Yen.

Gold's stability was achieved against the background of a number of conflicting economic developments. The floor for the prices was provided by the combination of a weaker dollar and stronger than expected growth in the world economy. This helped encourage a buoyant level of demand in most markets.

The overriding factor in 1994 was the upward trend of interest rates led by the US, which began tightening monetary controls. With other monetary authorities following the US lead, the resulting widening of the margins encouraged gold producers to increase their forward sales.

The fourth quarter of 1994 started with gold testing the upper limits of the US$370–395 trading range. The higher prices prompted increased hedging by producers, and the market gradually eased lower to settle around US$385.

Gold interest rate movements were caused by a combination of factors that squeezed gold liquidity in 1994. These included an increase in forward sales; a seasonal upturn in the demand for gold lending to fund increased jewellery manufacture in Europe and the Americas for Christmas, India for the wedding season and the Far East for the Lunar New Year; large short positions created by hedge and commodity funds; and the uncertainty that surrounds the rolling over of swaps and deposits into the new year.

Central bank gold holdings, as indicated by IMF 'All Countries' figures of 909.4 million ounces at 1994 year end, were down 3.5 million ounces from 1993. The Canadian selling programme accounted for much of the decline. Canadian sales totalled 2.1 million ounces in 1994, a little over half the 3.9 million ounces sold in 1993. Canada continues to be the only country pursuing a continuing gold disposal programme. Its gold reserves stand at 3.9 million ounces, compared with around 20 million ounces in the mid-1980s.

With reductions in Canadian, Austrian and South African holdings, totalling 4.5 million ounces, small accumulations elsewhere more than offset fractional disposals by some other countries.

In Russia, gold is being used, to an extent, as a form of money. The Russians are minting gold roubles to steady their own currency and the current unfavourable economic climate. Gold output has risen in the Krasnoyarsk and Khabarovsk territories, the Irkutsk and Amur regions and the Evanki republic. The Chairman of the Russian Federations' State Committee for Precious Stones and Metals announced that Russia produced an estimated 160 tonnes of gold in 1993.

In some other countries, demand for gold is rising rapidly, particularly in China where consumption grew 132 per cent in the third quarter of 1994 as wages increased and people sought a hedge against inflation rates, which rose to a post-1949 high. Demand was high throughout 1994, due to the lifting of exchange rate controls, the rapid depreciation of China's currency, and a traditional cultural affinity for gold. Interest is also growing in other South East Asian countries, where gold is bought partly as a guard against economic, financial and geopolitical uncertainties. It is estimated that South East Asia now accounts for about one-third of the world's annual gold consumption. Thus, there have been steady sales of gold in Thailand, Taiwan, Singapore, Malaysia and South Korea.

Higher production and sales of hoarded gold have kept up with demand, holding down bullion prices. A further blow to the gold price was dealt by the Indian government's decision, in March 1992, to lift their ban on imports and allow nationals to import up to 5kg of gold at one time — abandoning futile efforts to stop gold smuggling. Approximately 200 tonnes of gold had been imported illegally into India annually, but since the announcement the premium on smuggled gold has fallen 14 per cent in rupee terms.

The Soviet disintegration has also had some repercussions on the market. Exports from Russia have reduced from the high levels of 1990, as has anxiety over the prospects of further sales, given the sharp cut in estimated Russian reserves. Some commentators hope that the Eastern Bloc's demise will provide a fillip to the market as the emergent nations of the region seek to back their currencies with bullion. These commentators also point to the traditional popularity of gold as a store of value in Eastern Europe, and anticipate a rise in private hoardings there. Some evidence for renewed interest in gold's monetary role was provided by the Baltic states' successful demand for the return of pre-war reserves held by the Bank of England. On the other hand, central bank sales from at least one erstwhile Eastern Bloc country are thought to have contributed to the weakness of the gold price in 1992.

A development which could affect UK purchasers of gold is the move towards VAT harmonisation throughout the EU. However, harmonisation is still in the discussion phase. Currently, transactions between wholesale bullion dealers are zero-rated for VAT in the UK, but the Treasury is under increasing EU pressure to apply a standard minimum rate, despite manifesto commitments to maintain all current zero-rating, which enables UK traders to react quickly to market changes. The imposition of VAT on wholesale trading could inhibit trading in the London Bullion Market.

17.3.2   Falling mine production

One factor likely to reduce gold supplies in the near future is a decline in mine production. Western mine production is considered to have reached a peak, and although it is not expected to fall immediately it is unlikely to be able to respond to growing demand. The main factors are rising production costs, reduced capital expenditure, and falling exploration — as well as the limiting effect on each of the low gold price. In the US, Canada, and Australia, surface ores have gradually become depleted. This means that extraction must increasingly focus on deep-lying deposits, and on sulphide ores, both of which involve more costly production. In the developed world it is also less likely that much in the way of valuable ore reserves remain to be discovered, and in the developing countries terrain is often more hostile and investment in production riskier.

In South Africa, still the world's largest producer, capital expenditure has fallen sharply since 1986. The industry has rationalised extensively, increasing productivity but focusing output on the highest grade ores and shortening the life of the mines. Continued low investment will reduce South African output. Some predictions suggest that production will fall by 30 per cent over the next five years.

Conversely, new advances in technology promise to boost the South African gold mining industry. Executives in the industry hope the technological advances will transform the production process and its economies.

In recent years, two large gold mines have closed, other mines have reorganised and South African gold output has steadied at about 600 tonnes a year. But to make profits the mines need technological advances that reduce costs, or consistently higher gold prices of at least US$450 an ounce, compared with around the US$385 of 1994 and the predicted US$360–410 for 1995 otherwise production is likely to go into slow and steady decline.

Russia and the former Soviet Republics also have production problems. The mining areas are often remote and hostile, and equipment poorly developed and limited in supply. Mine output is predicted to be 200 tonnes in 1993, 33 per cent down on 1989 levels. The way is now clear for development of Sukhoi Log in Siberia, the world's biggest known gold deposit, according to Star Mining Corporation, the small Australian company that has 34.9 per cent of the venture. The agreement had taken six years to nego-tiate, and if all goes well, the construction of a conventional hard rock, open pit mine will begin at the end of 1996. Production would rise from 300,000 troy ounces in 1998 to more than 2 million troy ounces by 2003. Cash costs would be among the lowest in the industry, no more than $180 an ounce, despite the difficulties of mining in Siberia.

The Lena gold fields, which contain Sukhoi Log — with its reserves of 50 million ounces and resources of 100 million, and several other substantial gold deposits—are in the Bodaibo region of Russia's Irkutsk province. While Sukhoi Log is being developed, the joint venture company, Lenzoloto (LenaGold) will have cashflow from alluvial mining, which has produced at least 30 million troy ounces of gold since 1850, making LenaGold one of the biggest gold producers in the history of the world industry. LenaGold expects to see a small profit during 1995, and to produce about 220,000 ounces from existing operations rising to 300,000 by 1998.

Kazakhstan, formerly part of the Soviet Union, expects a substantial increase in gold output in the next three to four years. During 1993 the Republic produced about 14 tonnes of gold and wants to increase this to between 42 and 56 tonnes rapidly to build reserves to back the country's new currency — with the aid of foreign investment. One of Kazakhstan's gold mines, the Bakyrchik, located in an arid region of the north-eastern steppes, is one of the world's biggest gold deposits with about 8 million troy ounces, but the ore is very complex and difficult to process. Bakyrchik Gold, a London quoted company, is in a joint venture with Altynalmas, the organisation responsible for Kazakhstan's precious metals and precious stones production.

17.3.3   Technological change

The two new techniques which could transform the industry are *diamond wire cutting*, pioneered by Gencor and Anglo American; and the *impact ripper*, an industry research project recently taken over by the mining house Gold Fields.

The diamond cutting technique applies the established method of quar-rying granite and other hard stones to underground mining. A synthetic-covered steel cable less than a centimetre thick studded with industrial diamonds saws through the rock face, cutting away the ore in large chunks. The impact ripper is an hydraulically powered chisel, mounted on rails, which attacks the rockface with an accuracy that blasting lacks.

The potential benefits of the two techniques are thought to be substantial, because both could transform the cost structure of the industry and underground productivity. Diamond wire cutters can work 24 hours a day, require less labour and minimise the amount of waste rock mined. They would eliminate the need for explosives used for the 900,000 blasts the gold mines make every day; they would lead to the redesign of underground mines, save on tunnelling timber, and on transport costs. They would also improve underground safety, and make better use of mechanised methods.

Much gold output comes from mines sunk to below sea-level, or more than 3,000 metres underground. The MacArthur Forrest cyanide process saved the South African gold mining industry when it was introduced in 1890. But existing mercury-based techniques, adequate for recovering gold from surface ore, were not effective in treating metallurgically difficult underground material. Gold recovery rates fell to less than 50 per cent, but the new process achieved recoveries of 85–95 per cent.

Despite refinements, the metallurgical and mechanical methods have not changed for decades. The cyanidisation process has been modified to push recovery grades to more than 99 per cent, allowing the retreatment of millions of tonnes of low-grade waste material, but leaving little room for improvement. The labour-intensive underground routine of drilling holes in the rockface, filling them with explosives, blasting once a day and cleaning up the broken rock before hauling it to the surface, is the same as it was 100 years ago.

South Africa's remaining gold reserves are vast and well-defined but deep — at depths of up to 5,000 metres below surface. The capital cost of sinking a new mine shaft to that depth is more than R2.5bn (£5bn).

However, those who adopted the new methods have experienced problems. For the moment, Gencor has given up on diamond wire cutting, and is monitoring Anglo American's progress with new technology.

Bacterial leaching

Some Western industrial groups, eager to win potentially lucrative stakes in the former Soviet Union's gold mining industry, have found that bacterial leaching technology can provide them with a keen edge over traditional mining methods. The technology, relatively new to the western gold industry, uses bacteria to break down refractory or difficult ores to release the gold locked inside. Another attraction of the technology is that it is environmentally friendly. For example, bacteria can deal with ores containing toxic material such as arsenic and leave no harmful waste.

Gold mining policy in the former Soviet Union was to leave its extensive refractory sulphide gold deposits untouched, mining only those ores from which gold was easily extracted — to boost investment and economic activity. The strategy has been to employ low cost means of production to provide wealth.

Two Western companies have recently signed gold deals with CIS partners which specifically called for the introduction of bacterial leaching in line with the economic strategy. Lonrho, the UK-based conglomerate has reportedly won the right to develop a gold mine in Uzbekistan, primarily because it had access to the Biox bacterial leaching process developed by Gencor of South Africa. Biox is presently used at the Fairview mine in South Africa, at Saõ Bento in Brazil, and the Harbour Lights and Wiluna mines in Western Australia, as well as Ashanti — Lonhro's associate in Ghana.

Although Gencor is so far the front-runner in gold bacterial leaching, rivals are beginning to emerge. The Moonstone Group, a small exploration company in the Channel Islands signed a joint venture to explore for gold and diamonds in a vast area of Kazakhstan in December 1994. It claimed the deal was made possible by the BacTech system, developed in the chemistry department at Kings College, London, with Australian backing.

17.3.4 Other precious metals

Platinum, and its relatives palladium and rhodium, have industrial uses in manufacturing, as well as jewellery fabrication, which make them prone to the effects of world recession. Around 34 per cent of platinum is used in the manufacture of catalytic converters for the automobile industry, but this demand is highly susceptible to the development of better technologies. In early 1992 the market faltered when a US company announced a breakthrough which eliminated the need for platinum. Prices recovered when it became clear that the new device was an add-on to existing converters.

Palladium's prime role is also as a catalyst, in electronics as well as the automobile industry. Demand for this metal shares platinum's susceptibility to the effects of substitution but, overall, cuts in percentage usage of palladium have been masked by continued expansion in the electronics industry. Rhodium plays a crucial role in the automobile industry, which consumes around 90 per cent of it. This role looks set to continue, as is demand for this more exotic member of the platinum family.

The wild card in the market for platinum and its siblings has been the uncertainty of supplies from its main producers. Civil disturbances in South Africa continue adversely to affect this sensitive market. In 1991

South Africa produced 75 per cent of the total world output of platinum, and the former Soviet Union 20 per cent. Although demand reached record levels in 1991, so did supplies. Russia increased exports by a third, causing a fall in prices to a six-year low. The closure of the South African Boschfontein shaft by Rustenburg Platinum, the world's largest producer, in March 1993, added to the continued downward trend in prices. Russia disposed of its precious metal stocks to reap the benefits of record worldwide platinum and palladium sales in 1994, according to Johnson Matthey. They suggest that platinum demand rose by 7 per cent to a new peak of 4.32 million troy ounces in 1994 driven up by the requirements of producers of anti-pollution car exhaust catalysts and jewellery makers. Palladium sales were expected to rise in 1995 due to an increase in demand from Japan's electrical industry and from the mobile phone, personal computer and pager industries.

The price for platinum reached its highest level for four and a half years in April 1995. This was after an American firm announced it had developed a new system for using the metal to clean up vehicle fumes. The price was fixed at $US459 per ounce, its highest level since September 1990. Palladium prices reached a parallel peak for the same reason making a six year high of $US175 in March 1995.

Russia, the world's biggest producer of palladium, and the second-biggest producer of platinum, has stepped up exports to provide much of the extra metal and increasing fears that the high prices seen during 1994 could trigger selling of its stockpiles in 1995. The size of the stocks and how long they might last is questionable — and only very few Russians have access to this information. Recovery prospects reflect a revival of confidence in the metal, accompanied by hopes for a world economic recovery.

17.4   Counterfeits and forgeries

17.4.1   Counterfeit coins

One of the problems of purchasing coins made from gold bullion or other precious metals is the risk of forgeries. In the 1970s, when inflation was soaring upwards, interest in UK sovereigns was so high that the Mint found itself unable to produce enough. As a result, there was an increase in the premium (the difference between the face value and the metal value). The coins began to sell at almost one and a half times their face value. The opportunity attracted middle eastern forgers, although, in practice, the vendors and buyers could easily detect the counterfeit coins.

The controversy over the long-running Hirohito coin scandal echoed into 1993, and still has residual effects on market sentiment in Japan. Originally issued in 1986 to commemorate the 60th anniversary of the late Emperor's accession to the throne, the Japanese police alleged in 1990 that 107,000 of them were suspected of being middle eastern fakes. Coin dealers affected by confiscations denied there was any conspiracy or crime. The affair took a new turn when a UK dealer began civil action against the Japanese government for the return of seized coins. The dealer alleges that the Tokyo police, contrary to their statements, had effectively abandoned their investigations in 1990.

As a result, confidence in the Hirohito coin collapsed and 2.8 million coins worth ¥280bn were cashed in for their face value and returned to the Bank of Japan.

The scandal of the Hirohito coins caused a delay in the issue of the Akihito coins (called Heisei after the new emperor's era). The number of coins released was reduced from 3.8 million coins to 2 million. In an attempt to discourage forgers, the coins contain 30 rather than 20 grams of gold. This amount represented about ¥50,000 worth of gold in a coin that the Japanese sold for ¥100,000. However, despite the Hirohito scandal and the delayed issue, the Japanese bought most of the 2 million coins.

17.4.2   Gold mine frauds

Precious metals investing also has been beset by fraud. The chief problem lately is with promoters selling interests in gold mines that are nearly worthless or non-existent. As a case in point, telephone salesmen may call offering gold not yet mined. They say they will sell it for £100 under the going price.

Such frauds are an international problem. One US commentator believes that there are 'probably 30 to 40 gold mining scams going on now in the United States'. He cautions investors to be distrustful of salesmen who offer interests in gold mines. They promise gold for perhaps half the market price; the explanation is usually that the mine owner has a special process or patented techniques for extracting the metal.

New fingerprinting techniques developed by scientists, led by John Watling and Hugh Herbert at the Western Australian Department of Minerals and Energy Centre will make salting of gold mines — a technique used since the mining industry began — a problem of the past. 'Salting' is the addition of precious metals from one mine to another, to give the illusion of great discoveries of gold, as happened in Kalgoorlie, the centre of the new Western Australian gold rush. A new mine suddenly was found to contain ores with a gold content ten times higher than normal.

Evidence presented by John Watling at a conference in 1994 proved that the gold came from two sources, and that one was added artificially.

This process, recently perfected, will give every mine a unique fingerprint. The fingerprinting technique will affect not only salters of mines and gold thieves but also fraudsters and drug barons. Watling hopes that much of the world's gold will be fingerprinted so its origins can be identified with certainty, and gold will no longer be an untraceable international currency. Watling is now working on a consignment of diamonds from De Beers to see if the same technique can be applied.

17.5   Opportunities and costs

17.5.1   Suitability

Who should buy gold, in what form should it be purchased and how much should one invest in the metal? 'It depends on the investor' says one dealer. 'Many large portfolios should have at least a small percentage in gold. A person who has little money to invest and is conservative should concentrate on gilts. If you are more aggressive, you could have a larger holding in gold.' These recommendations seem optimistic, given gold's resistance in recent years to the anxiety factor. For many investors who still wish to hold gold, coins make sense, because they are easier to sell than bullion. Alternatively, investors can buy precious metals in bars or wafers, which may, for an extra price, have decorative stampings. A 100-ounce gold bar is about the size of a brick. Wafers are sold in various weights, down to a few ounces, although premiums tend to be higher on smaller unit weights. Gold coins, bars or wafers could be stored in a safe-deposit box or home safe.

Some banks offer gold purchase programmes, and may be willing to finance these purchases. If an investor buys on credit, the bank will want to keep the gold in its vault, and charge for storage.

The safest way of buying gold, either in the shape of coins or bars, is at a high street bank, which will reduce the risk of theft, increase security and avoid VAT if the gold is held in offshore branches. For example, Lloyds branches in Jersey will deal in Kruggerands and Maple Leaf coins on behalf of mainland customers. Reportedly, they charge £1.50 per coin for the service, with a minimum charge of £10. Insurance during transit is 50p per coin. Storage is 25p per coin per quarter (minimum charge £5 per quarter). Insurance for storage is 0.175 per cent per annum of the gold's value, with the minimum premium set at £35.

With valuables like gemstones, which vary in quality, investors face problems. To follow the recommended practice in the alternative investment markets, investors are advised to purchase the best. The difficulty is that the best is becoming scarce and very expensive in many classes of alternative investments. Diamonds are no exception. One of the consequences is interest in other gemstones, such as sapphires, which are almost as durable as diamonds, and for which a grading system has been developed jointly by a Sri Lanka government agency and the Gemological Institute of America Gemological Laboratories. The established grading certificate is an important supporting document when buying or selling diamonds or sapphires. Other gemstones, for example, emeralds, are less attractive because they are still being mined in large quantities.

17.5.2   Recovering gold from wrecks

Recovering gold bullion and coins, and other precious metals and valuables from undersea troves has also attracted attention in recent years. The costs can often be considerable, and there are risks to the health of the divers. Nonetheless, treasure has been retrieved from wrecks in substantial quantities. As a result, the backers of these ventures have recovered gold, thousands of coins, and scores of bars of a type virtually unseen in more than a century.

17.5.3   Costs of ownership

Some investors are put off by, among other things, the transaction costs, the imposition of VAT, storage expenses and lack of dividends associated with precious metals investments. Investors should remember that, unlike bank deposits and securities, gold does not pay interest or dividends. Its value depends on changes in the general market for bullion. Storage and insurance costs can erode profits from investments in gold bars or coins.

17.5.4   Advisers

Even for investors who have good reasons for investing in precious metals, financial advisers offer words of caution. Anyone who buys gold or another precious metal, or gemstones, should use a bank, a specialist trading house or a reputable dealer. In any event, it is important for the investor to make sure he or she can obtain possession of the asset when it is needed. In times of great financial crisis, it is as well to remember that banks may be closed.

In Britain, gold coins can still be bought direct from certain members of the London gold market or, more commonly today, through dealers, precious metal brokers, investment consultants, some banks and jewellers. Gold sovereigns and half sovereigns are still being sold in quantity, and the products of other countries' mints can also be purchased. It should be noted that there are advantages in buying coins in popular demand. The premiums charged (ie the difference between the price of the coin and the value of the bullion it contains) tend to be higher for coins that sell in low quantities.

Gold options can now be bought in the UK through Sharelink, Europe's largest execution-only stockbroker, and are traded in Amsterdam and New York. The minimum dealing price is £30 plus £2.50 per contract, commission of 1.5 per cent and each option covers 10 troy ounces of gold.

17.6   Taxation

17.6.1   Tax planning

The income, capital gains, capital transfer and inheritance tax considerations reviewed in Chapter 18, on arts and antiques, are generally relevant to valuables. The same advice applies to careful tax planning.

17.6.2   VAT

Until 1982 purchase of bullion coins did not attract VAT if the coins were still legal in their country of issue. Following the Exchange Control (Gold Coins) Exemption Order 1979 and the Value Added Tax (Finance) Order 1982, there are now two main ways for UK private investors to buy gold bullion coins. One is to pay the VAT, which would make it more difficult to realise a gain from the transaction. The other is to buy the coins overseas and store them there at a cost.

Other approaches may be promoted in advertisements or through direct mail circulars — they should be carefully evaluated and treated with the utmost caution. It should be noted that, in the UK, where bullion coins are subsequently sold back by VAT registered traders (who buy and sell gold coins by way of business), the dealer who makes the purchase should now pay the VAT on the transaction directly to HM Customs & Excise.

A special scheme for accounting and paying for VAT on supplies of gold was introduced on 1 April 1993. The scheme will apply to certain supplies of gold which are liable to VAT at the standard rate. Under the new scheme a standard-rated supply of gold will be treated as a taxable supply by the buyer as well as by the seller for the purpose of registration. Under the terms of this scheme, the buyer must account for the output tax chargeable on the supply of gold by the seller. The buyer retains the right to claim input tax credit in the same VAT accounting period in which the supply takes place. A VAT leaflet 701/21/93, 'Gold and gold coins', available from HM Customs and Excise, provides full guidance.

The forfeiture provisions of the Customs & Excise Management Act apply, even if the smuggled gold is found in the possession of an innocent purchaser. It is, therefore, in the best interest of buyers to satisfy themselves that the gold has been properly imported before agreeing to complete a purchase. The questions to ask are: Where has the gold come from? Has it been imported? Has VAT been paid on it? Why is it being sold? How is it delivered? Is a quick settlement demanded? Is the seller new to the gold market? Does he regularly supply large quantities? What references can he offer? Such basic checks are clearly advisable in view of the growing number of frauds.

VAT regulations also apply to silver and platinum. As in the gold and silver markets, zero-rating for VAT applies only to transactions between wholesale traders. In the past, zero-rating was not necessary as transfers of metal among traders in London were relatively unimportant. The rapid rise in demand for platinum, together with remaining uncertainties about the political future of South Africa (the dominant supplier), has increased the need for rapid, inter-trader movements of metal. As previously noted, though, the future of zero-rating is in some doubt pending negotiations on EC VAT regulations.

17.7 Preview of the year ahead

17.7.1 Limiting factors

As the world economy struggles out of recession, fabrication demand is likely to increase and outstrip supply. Lower interest rates should make gold relatively more attractive to investors; and some of the massive cash sums that circulate around world markets may well find a home in gold. Buyers of bullion are concerned about structural weaknesses in OECD and ex-Soviet bloc economies, and the risks of inflation in countries that need to reflate either to sustain living standards or for electoral purposes. On the supply side, central bank and producers' sales are expected to be low.

One effect of rising gold prices will be to focus attention on gold mining shares. The valuation of these shares can be a complex art. Often gold stocks trade at several multiples of their net present value, calculated by discounted cash flow methods. The premium paid will not necessarily bring a return, although the investment does offer an element of insurance against economic, political or natural disaster. For investors, the key question is whether gold will rise above $400 or even $450 per ounce in 1995 or 1996.

The see-saw of prices between $350 and $400 per ounce in 1994 is attributed by commentators to massive speculative buying and selling by commodity funds. However, as prices rose, fabricators reduced their purchases, and demand fell in the Far East. Gold traders had a disappointing year in 1994 as prices remained largely in the narrow range of $375 to $395. Once the ultimate hedge against rising inflation prices, gold has lost much of its glitter. One cause is a release of gold firm hoards held by Asian investors and central banks. As the price rises to $400, they sell, leading to a reversal of the trend. For such reasons, analysts believe gold stands little chance of topping $425.

Some investors feel that the law of averages will mean that gold and other metals will have a good run at some point in 1995 — as global recovery gathers momentum. The law of averages does not work like that, but on 18 January gold rallied to a peak of $383 an ounce, up $11.20 above the 8½ month low reached at the beginning of the month. Low interest rates and the newly elected government in the world's biggest bullion producer, South Africa, have created hopes among international investors that Western gold bugs, Chinese speculators and Asian governments, will become buyers. Some specialist brokers favour purchases of gold-mining shares, since their prices rise faster than gold. With Nelson Mandela's government in place, top quality South African mining stocks may be worth serious consideration.

A few, like gold guru Julian Baring, are happy to look for a price of $500 per ounce at some point in the next five years. These optimists (or pessimists, depending on one's perspective) also expect platinum to break through the $400 barrier, and perhaps rise towards the $450 mark, while silver will stay in a range of $5–6 an ounce. Gold's 'sidesmen,' silver and platinum, have more industrial uses than gold so both should record price increases during 1995.

Bullish traders point to a healthy balance of demand, often exceeding production; and uncertainties bedevilling supplies from Russia, the world's second-biggest producer. They predict a correlation between gold and other metals, as the economic cycle swings worldwide from high interest rates and recession to low interest rates and recovery.

Although gold has started to regain its lustre, it remains a tarnished investment which has returned only 3 per cent in the last five years. Buyers take on faith the advice of experts, who believe that, over the long term, the rewards will outweigh the risks.

One factor to set against that optimism is the activity of the official sector. Central banks, particularly in EU countries, have little incentive to maintain their reserves at current levels. A widely reported recent prediction suggests that the prospect of European Monetary Union may eventually lead central banks to become net sellers of around 700 tonnes a year by the turn of the century. However, this possibility must be weighed against central bank conservatism, and the likelihood of delays in implementing plans for monetary union. Bullish prediction that former Eastern Bloc countries will seek to back their currencies with gold must also be seen against their desperate short-term need for hard currency, and the consequent incentive to sell existing gold reserves.

17.7.2 Growing jewellery demand

Demand for jewellery fabrication worldwide has surprised some with its ability to withstand the effects of recession, and growth has been a feature of jewellery's uses of gold for the past 25 years. In a recent paper, Stewart Murray, Chief Executive of Gold Field Mineral Services, outlined reasons for considering jewellery as 'gold's salvation'. Jewellery fabrication grew at about 1 per cent lower than growth in per capita wealth in the period 1968–1990, despite the fact that over the same period the real gold price almost doubled, and that jewellery demand is sensitive to price changes. Growth in demand is not restricted to the industrialised countries. Although jewellery holdings per person have grown faster in the OECD countries, reflecting their wealth, the developing countries — including China — are adding to demand.

If holdings of gold jewellery continue to grow at present rates the additional gold required will be considerable. Much of the potential for growth comes from increased prosperity in the developing countries, particularly in Asia. With the lifting of import restrictions on gold by the government, the Indian market saw significant increases in both jewellery fabrication and hoarding, and this trend looks set to continue. The Middle East also remains a strong market, in particular Saudi Arabia. Demand in Kuwait has also picked up as the country re-establishes itself after the destruction of the war.

A continuing growth of gold demand does, however, rest on several assumptions; that an increasing world population will become more prosperous, and, less problematically, that gold jewellery will retain its appeal. It is also a prediction for the rest of the decade, rather than the forthcoming year, and does not take into account current recessionary impacts on jewellery retail.

17.8 Conclusion

Platinum and its relatives palladium and rhodium will remain a fascinating, if risky, investment opportunity. The platinum metals will remain key resources for the automobile industry, with rhodium being the more resilient to the development of substitutes. Even with substitutes reducing the platinum content of catalytic converters, continuing environmental concern for greenhouse gas emissions is likely to increase the number fitted to new cars. In the short term, however, industrial demand will suffer from the weakness of car sales and pessimism in the Japanese market, the largest for platinum jewellery fabrication.

For gold, despite good prospects in the market fundamentals, there are few willing to forecast large price rises. Unless one takes into account financier and noted gold 'bug' Sir James Goldsmith's prediction, of a 'meltdown' in the global financial system, mutual funds holding mining equities and some bullion, or direct investment in major mining equities are likely to outperform the physical commodity itself in the immediate future.

Sources of further information

See end of Chapter 19.

18 Art and antiques

John Myers, Lessia Djakowska and Susan Farrell of Solon Consultants

18.1 Introduction

18.1.1 A form of alternative investment

The promoters of 'alternative investments' confidently advocate tangible assets as sound purchases for 'financially secure and intelligent buyers'. The assets they have in mind include works of artistic or historical significance — that is, items which are 'museum-worthy by any standards' or 'culturally significant', and which appeal to collectors. Small investors with capital to spare are generally recommended by advocates of alternative investments to allocate roughly 10 per cent of their investment capital (excluding the equity value of their main residence) to the acquisition of 'traded artifacts', ie possessions such as works of art and antiques, which will, it is hoped, protect investors against inflation and currency fluctuations in the future.

On occasion, larger institutional investors and corporate bodies are also advised to accumulate Old Masters and rare antiques to complement their investments in securities and real estate. The apologists argue that these investors can afford to ride out slumps lasting up to a quarter of a century, if beneficiaries can wait and the eventual return is sufficient. At present, one of the advantages of such investments for certain institutions, such as pension funds, can be freedom from tax on their gains. On the other hand, art and antiques cost money to insure, preserve and store. Capital appreciation has to be substantial to make up for the loss of income and the costs.

Nonetheless, art objects are increasingly seen as investments, the values of which rise and fall as new assessments are made of their aesthetic, historic or functional worth. Other factors stimulating the past evolution of this sector have been television programmes and media coverage, the marketability of art, and the sporadic success of the auction houses in improving the liquidity of art as an investment. Buyers are also influenced in their choices by critics, art historians, exhibitions, specialist magazines, and even by the track record of each field.

In general, the alternative investment is recommended by its promoters as an asset for the buyer to retain over a prolonged period to allow the value to mature. Speculative trading in works of art and antiques is frowned upon as too risky. There is, it is said, too much uncertainty in the rewards to justify gambling on the chance of making a perfectly-timed purchase and sale; it is difficult for even the expert to identify the under-valued piece which is certain to come into fashionable demand at some time in the future.

18.1.2   The dividends

The advocates of the alternative investment argue for including fine art and antiques in private or funds' portfolios as long-term investments on grounds which are, essentially, those of the economist: while the number of buyers in the markets is tending to go up, the supply is static or declin-ing. On the one hand, the volume of 'discoveries' or 'retrievals of lost works' is restricted. On the other, valued items do disappear through fires, thefts and other calamities; and, perhaps more significantly, there has been, until just recently, a steady drain from the market of works acquired for permanent retention by museums and institutional collectors.

Traditionally, 'coffin power' — ie the collections left for sale after death — has always provided a regular flow of material, but more recently a new source of works has appeared, which could be described as 'receiver power', as seen at the Philips sale of the contents of Asil Nadir's offices for £4.5m. In theory, the problems of Lloyd's Names should also ensure a steady flow of art on to the market. Christie's is offering a scheme through Coutts & Co for Names to use works of art as security for obtain-ing bank guarantees for 'funds at Lloyd's' purposes.

The features of the alternative investment market which should therefore attract buyers who are looking for assets of permanent value are a growing demand, a diminishing supply and a general upward movement in prices.

The cosmopolitan origins of buyers who attend major sales might seem to indicate that this argument has gained wide acceptance. There is an international demand for authentic items of quality. Apparently these buyers have been persuaded that works of art and rare antiques are safe assets to acquire with spare capital, or revenue which might otherwise be subject to tax — even though they bring their owners no income and involve some risks. Yet, many would deny an investment motivation. To them, such motives degrade the purity of artistic endeavour; they are aes-thetes who are seeking a cultural dividend, the delights of living with rare, historically important, satisfying works which give pleasure to their owners. Similarly, large institutions are buying works of art to improve their employees' working environments. Investment is then a secondary motive.

18.2 Highlights of the previous year

18.2.1 Structure of the market

In the 1980s and early 1990s, spectacular prices have been paid for works of art. Many people outside the art world — and some inside — consider £20m, or more, an absurd sum to pay for a painting. They fail to take account of the edifice of values that provide a logical basis and grounds for such prices. The Art Sales Index shows that in the past 20 years, the average price for all works by Cézanne, Degas, Manet, Monet and Renoir has risen from £37,000 to £271,000, despite the slump in the market for Impressionist works in the late 1980s and early 1990s.

Markets for art and antiques have developed considerably in recent years, especially over the last two decades. Their growth has been prompted by both negative and positive considerations. In the early years of this period, investors chose to buy these tangible assets because of failures of stock markets and interest-bearing securities to protect their capital against inflation. It is worth noting that immediately after the October 1987 Stock Market crash, record sales occurred in the auction houses, reflected in record prices. Sotheby's, for example, sold van Gogh's *Irises* for £30m. The highest price ever recorded at auction for a work of art was for van Gogh's *Portrait of Dr Gachet* which went for £50m in May 1990, the peak of the boom in art prices.

With the greater spread of higher disposable incomes and an increase in leisure time, a demand has emerged for assets which have a worth and an interest beyond their monetary cost. Social changes have also made an impact: for example, dealers and auctioneers report that young, wealthy buyers have been entering the market for works of fine art — paintings, prints, ceramics, engravings and sculptures. Antiques markets and fairs have also experienced a comparable rise in demand. Nowadays, important showings and sales are attracting bidders who are constantly setting new record prices for old furniture, oriental carpets, rare books and manuscripts, antique jewellery, furniture, arms and militaria, and other pieces of artistic and historic value. The conventional division between the fine and the decorative arts reappeared after the recent collapse of the market in Impressionist and 20th century paintings.

18.2.2   Signs of revival

The *Daily Telegraph* Art 100 Index, a proprietary figure that encompasses auction prices for 100 top artists and sectors from Old Masters to contemporary shows that, although overall art prices are still declining, the rate is slowing. It reached 4,541 in January 1994. It sank to 3,964 in July and to 3,856 at the end of November. The figure (in which 1975 prices equal 1,000) peaked in 1990 at more than 9,000.

The art market follows the economic cycle and, in the UK, the house market. After four depressed years, there are signs of revival, notably in New York. But the important London auctions did well too in December 1994, with the Marquess of Cholmondeley raising £21.3m (against a £15m estimate) for surplus furnishings from Houghton Hall, Norfolk.

However, Impressionist and 20th century art — the sector that led the price roller-coaster upwards until 1990 — remains convalescent, although Christie's was happy with its big November 1994 auction. This brought in £15.1m and was 85 per cent sold by value, mainly because vendors seem prepared to accept lower prices: a large painting by Miro went for £1.32m (against the £3.6m it made in 1990) and a Picasso head sold for £2.1m (£2.7m in 1989). A market is re-establishing itself, albeit at a lower level.

This sustained interest is reflected in other traditional areas, which have held up against the recession. For example, books, oriental carpets and furniture have continued to sell well.

Good provenance, quality and freshness to the market were, as usual, crucial factors in the sale of Impressionist and Modern pictures in London. A portrait of art dealer *Joseph Brummer* by Henri Rousseau sold for £3m — an auction record for the artist.

Similarly, the last complete copy in private hands of William Blake's *Jerusalem* was sold from a private collection for £928,000 at a sale of important Old Master, Modern and Contemporary Prints. A rare series of lithographs by Toulouse-Lautrec, entitled *Elles,* attracted a bid of £441,500 at the same sale.

The areas which have withstood the slump over recent times have been those which appeal to the connoisseur rather than the speculative trader. An increase in private buyers has been most noticeable at auctions both in London and New York, as falling prices attract the knowledgeable collector of the decorative arts and antiques. In the antique jewellery market, for example, dealers reported continuing keen demand for top quality diamonds, rubies, emeralds and sapphires. A survey of auction trends by Phillips, the London auctioneers, suggested that buyers should look out for Victorian wildlife jewellery, Burmese rubies and sapphires, and Columbian emeralds.

18.2.3 Concern for national heritage

The establishment of the Single Market has caused concern over the possible repatriation of art works to their countries of origin. However, this concern is not a recent phenomenon and governments have tried in various ways to prevent objects of long-standing cultural value and national heritage works from leaving the country permanently.

Holbein's *Portrait of a lady with a pet squirrel and a starling* was withdrawn from sale amid much public outcry at the prospect of the picture leaving the UK. It was eventually purchased by the National Gallery for £10m under private treaty. *The Old Horse Guards, London* by Canaletto, was bought by the composer Andrew Lloyd Webber for £10.2m, after similar fears that it would be sold abroad. In 1994, an export ban was placed on the £7.6 million *Three Graces* sculpture by Canova, which led to its staying in this country and out of the hands of the Getty Museum in California. Currently, British Institutions are trying to raise more than £500,000 to prevent *The Painter's Room* by Lucian Freud leaving the country.

The controversy over these sales illustrated the growing influence of the heritage lobby on what is an increasing international market for art and antiques. Recent stagnation apart, the price increases of 1989–93 tempted those responsible to offer prized works owned by cash-stretched private estates and public bodies; their decisions prompted a reaction. With museum purchasing funds still frozen, the government has come under increasing pressure to halt the export of major works coming onto the market.

Under the present system, the Waverley Rules, a specialist committee advising the government, can impose a moratorium on the granting of an export licence for up to six months, to allow museums and public galleries the chance to purchase. The success of this system depends, however, on these bodies having adequate funds to meet the high prices of works deemed of national interest. In 1991 the trade secretary resorted to placing long-term export bans on several items, limiting their potential market value. In December, the government's Review Committee recommended the drawing up of a list of art treasures whose export should be banned. This was condemned by some because of the impact it would have on the value of the works to their owners, who would not be compensated. The lack of any decision on the matter was also seen as instrumental in a rush to market by owners of many fine paintings, including the Holbein and the Caneletto.

Many works deemed national treasures are valued out of the reach of all but the wealthiest investor, but government heritage policy is likely to affect the art and antiques market as a whole, and EU policy proposals, reviewed in the next section, even more so.

18.2.4   Leveraged purchases and guarantees

There are perhaps a few hundred people today who might pay more than £10m for a work of art. For them, the main attractions are the market's performance and the opportunities to 'collateralise' art — a development that, until recently, seemed to have a bright future. After several years of rapid escalation, demand for works sold at auction declined amid controversy over Sotheby's leveraged sale of *Irises* to the Australian entrepreneur, Alan Bond. The arrangement led to accusations that auction prices were being artificially inflated. The painting was later sold to the J Paul Getty Museum for an undisclosed sum, after Bond failed to pay off his £16m loan from Sotheby's. The rate of interest on such loans can be as much as 4 per cent above prime.

The loan system tends to inflate prices, whether the borrower secures the painting or not: like a roulette player with chips on house credit, he will bid it up. Pre-financing by the auction house artificially creates a floor, while a dealer who states a price sets a ceiling. If the borrower then defaults, the lender recovers the painting, writes off the unpaid part of the loan against tax, and can resell the work at its new inflated price.

The auction practice that attracted the most criticism in 1989 and 1990 goes to the heart of the nature of auctions themselves and the ethics of the trade. Auction houses have been giving guarantees to the seller of a work of art and loans to the buyer. If a collector has a work of art that an auctioneer wants to sell, the latter can issue a 'guarantee' that the collector will obtain, say, £3m from the sale. If the work does not make £3m, the collector still receives the payment, but the work remains with the auction house for later sale. Guarantees are a strong inducement to sellers, but clearly risky for the auction house.

Most top private dealers dislike the system of guarantees and loans. They argue that it creates a conflict of interest. One dealer is on record with the comment: 'If the auction house has a financial involvement with both seller and buyer, its status as an agent is compromised. Lending to the buyer is like margin trading on the stock market. It creates inflation. It causes instability.' The advocates defend the policy as 'right, proper and indeed inevitable'. They claim that guarantees are given 'very sparingly'.

18.2.5 Consumer protection

In the US, there has been a battle between the auctioneers and consumer affairs bodies. For more than a year, a team of officials pored over leading auctioneers' records, identifying such exotic-sounding practices as 'bidding off the chandelier' (announcing fictitious bids to drive up the price) and 'buying in' (leaving a work unsold because it does not reach the seller's reserve price). Stiffer controls are being applied in the US, including those governing loans. The New York State legislature is also taking a close interest in the art market. It shares with the city's Consumer Affairs Department concerns about chandelier bidding, the undisclosed reserve and auction houses' lending practices. The current consumer affairs code says that 'if an auctioneer makes loans or advances money to consignors and/or prospective purchasers, this fact must be conspicuously disclosed in the auctioneer's catalogue'. These developments are likely to have repercussions in Britain and other parts of Europe, as auctioneers tend to apply the same rules worldwide.

According to a US official, the team found 'gross irregularities' in art auction houses. Chandelier bidding amounted to 'an industry practice, both above and below the reserve'. (A chandelier bid above the reserve violates present rules.) The spokesman was also concerned about the practices of not announcing buy-ins and of keeping reserves secret. The auction houses contended that, if bidders knew the reserve, it would chill the market. Art dealers, lobbying the agency, maintained that the reserve should be disclosed and that bidding should start at it.

Dealing in art, from a gallery or an auction house, is not a profession. There are representative bodies that attempt to set standards and to control their members' practices. Nevertheless, art dealing has the characteristics of a trade. The case is being argued for regulation, for setting up an independent regulator — an art-industry equivalent to the Securities and Exchange Commission. The auction houses and dealers have doubts about the ideas; some outsiders think they may have some merit.

18.3   Current developments

18.3.1   Continued internationalisation

Buyers around the world have been persuaded by plausible arguments that alternative investments can act as a form of insurance against a fall in currency values. As a result, many of the markets for art and antiques have become more international: since the 1970s, North American, Continental European and Middle and Far Eastern investors have begun to frequent salerooms in greater numbers.

More recently, new rich art buyers have appeared in Russia. Prime among these in Moscow and St Petersburg are six banks which have made immense profits in 1992 and 1993 from trading currencies during the upheavals of the rouble. They are, most notably, Inkombank, Stolichny, Alpha-Bank, Voznozdenie, Menatep and Moscovia. Five years ago none of them owned significant pictures, but now they are buying Old Masters and Contemporary Art. All have spent hundreds of thousands, if not millions, of US dollars.

Self-promotion is part of the answer as to why the banks are buying. More important is the anxiety to store the value of money in what appears, for now, to be a more stable international currency, art; what may matter most is that special tax protections are promised for banks and companies which invest in 'outstanding art collections' (this is a heritage measure to keep great art in Russia).

In recent years, London's traditional dominance as the centre for art and antiques sales has been challenged, in particular by New York, Geneva, Frankfurt and Paris, which nowadays are attracting important specialised sales. London still accounts for two-thirds of art sales in the EU, but it remains to be seen what effect possible EU regulations on VAT will have on London's position in the art world.

In some alternative investment markets — furniture is one example — the strength of American demand has meant that market prices have been set mainly in New York. Generally, the mobility of alternative investments, combined with the wider geographical spread of dealers and auctions, should mean that prices tend to be maintained in real terms and are somewhat less vulnerable to the effects of inflation and volatile exchange rates.

18.3.2   Market practices and government policy

Internationalisation tests market barriers created by differing auction practices, as well as government imposed controls and levies. The growth in art as an investment area has also encouraged auction houses to examine their own practices and develop the range of services they offer, but some of these have been controversial. Conflicts of interest and sharp practice have focused the attention of regulators, as has the growth of outright fraud and theft.

The auction houses have sought to demystify the auction process, to reassure the new breed of art investor. They have employed capable people to explain the significance of the terminology and the practices, and the business of reserves. One area which continues to be controversial is the practice of auction houses offering loans and guarantees. They are a strong inducement to sellers, but clearly risky for the auction house, as Christie's found when they recently failed to sell three major Modernist works reputed to have been guaranteed for £28m.

Unethical behaviour has come under the scrutiny of authorities in several centres of the art trade. For example, 'puffing the bid' involves fictitious bidders inflating the price by displaying false interest. In the UK, *The Times* newspaper found instances of questionable practices in an investigation of classic car auctions, leading to calls from legal and trading experts for a review of auction law.

The trade in art and antiques has traditionally thrived on links with the 'informal economy'. In Spain and Italy in particular, a thriving black economy pours money into art. For some buyers, art and antiques represent a store of value, a haven for assets and a form of currency, and their interest supports the market internationally, in fields which appeal to Latin tastes. However, many in the market, as well as in government, have become increasingly concerned about the growing internationalisation of art theft and fraud. For example, the Japanese police have strengthened supervision of art dealers. They suspected that art works were being used in tax evasion and as 'stage properties' in large-scale economic crimes. Similarly, in May 1992, a Swiss government report expressed concern at the country's role as a transit centre for objects of doubtful origin, and for 'money laundering operations'. New import controls are seen as likely, but perhaps not for a year or two.

18.3.3 Art and the Single Market

The establishment of the Single Market may affect the movement of works of art both out of the EU and between the member states. Changes affecting the UK market could occur in three main areas: export controls, VAT harmonisation and artists' royalties.

Since January 1993, imports and exports have been subject only to spot checks at member states' frontiers, making illegal trade much harder to detect. Some countries, notably Spain, Greece and Italy, fear the loss of many important works. The UK government, on the other hand, is concerned that trade restrictions will harm its predominance in Europe, while auction houses anticipate endless bureaucratic wrangles.

The recently introduced EC Directive on the return of 'cultural objects' has been a focus of controversy amongst some member states. This Directive entails the forming of central authorities or 'art tribunals' in each country with the power to demand the return of an item illegally exported — with compensation if the buyer exercised due care in the purchase. The right of return expires after 75 years for public collections and 30 years for private collections. However, because the legislation is not retroactive, the British Museum will not have to relinquish the Elgin Marbles.

An EC export licence is now required to export a cultural object out of the EU, if the value of that object is above a certain threshold. These thresholds are defined by age and value, much as they are under the current UK export rules, described in the next section. In some cases the thresholds are comparable with those set for a UK licence, in others the threshold is set at a higher level, as the chart below shows. For comprehensive details contact the Department of National Heritage, tel: (0171) 211 6164.

Category by type and age	*Threshold* *£*
Elements forming an integral part of artistic, historical or religious monuments which have been dismembered and which are:	
—more than 50 years old, but less than 100 years old	no licence required
—more than 100 years old	zero
Manuscripts more than 50 years old, including maps and musical scores	zero
Architectural, scientific and engineering drawings produced by hand, more than 50 years old	11,900
Arms and armour, more than 50 years old	39,600
Drawings by hand on any medium and in any material, more than 50 years old	11,900
Portraits or likenesses, which are more than 50 years old, of British historic persons	119,000

Paintings in oil, tempera or other media, which are more than 50 years old (excluding portraits), of British historic persons	119,000
Books which are:	
—more than 50 years old, but less than 100 years old	no EC licence required
—more than 100 years old	39,600
Collections and specimens from zoological, botanical, mineralogical or anatomical collections	39,600

Agreement was reached on the harmonisation of VAT payable on sale of works of art imported into the European Union in December 1993. The agreement is the outcome of several years of discussion on taxation relating to works of art imported into and sold within the EU. The UK, which has the largest art and antiques market within the EU, has sought to maintain the system of taxation which will retain its position as an international centre.

The margin in system for taxing works of art which is currently applied in the UK (ie VAT on the auctioneers' commission and premium, but not on the whole price) now applies throughout the EU.

For items imported from non-EU countries into the UK, there will be a rate of VAT of 2.5 per cent from 1 January 1995.

This special rate will apply until 30 June 1999 when Britain will have to come into line with the rest of the EU (not less than 5 per cent). However, it has been agreed with the EU that a review on the impact of the import tax will take place in 1998 prior to the ending of the British derogation in 1999.

The net effect of the 2.5 per cent on imports will make an imported work of art less than 1 per cent more expensive than it is at the moment when bought by an EU purchaser. For a non-EU purchaser, however, it will be cheaper than it is at present since any VAT payable will be refunded on re-export.

The third area of policy review concerns artists' royalties, known as *droits de suite*. The payment of these also varies across Europe — from none in the UK, Ireland, and the Netherlands, to between 3 per cent and 5 per cent of the selling price in other member states. These sums are payable by the seller, direct to the artist or his/her estate, provided the sale is over a threshold figure and the work is still in copyright (ie produced by a living artist or one who has died within 50 years). There is pressure to extend this system across the EU, with the Germans being particularly keen. Supporters argue that the levy assists artists; opponents, including the UK government, argue that it is a disincentive to trade. However, the issue likely to be decisive in settling the matter is whether or not it distorts trade in the EU. The Commission is investigating this issue.

18.4   Purchasing art and antiques

18.4.1   Quality and provenance

The consensus of expert opinion is that the buyer should be concerned with the features which establish a work as one of quality. The condition of a painting, for example, is an important factor, as is its provenance, ie its origins and history. An investor who acquires a work (which he plans to hold for some years before disposing of it, possibly in an overseas market) will want to make sure in advance that its ownership, authenticity and quality are established beyond reasonable dispute, and that it is marketable.

When negotiating to buy an asset, the investor will therefore need to go further in his investigations than would be necessary merely to check that the vendor has a good title to the piece. The research carried out into the history and previous ownership of the work should also indicate clearly the probability that it is a genuine item. A bill of sale which includes a full and authentic dossier of the purchase will be helpful both for the purposes of an inventory of assets and an eventual disposal. Preferably, the dossier will be endorsed by valuers of repute, who will be in a position at some time in the future to verify the statements made.

These precautions are advisable for several reasons. Basically, they provide the buyer with evidence that the vendor has a good title to the piece. Equally, the research is important because there are frauds and forgeries in the alternative investment market, as well as reproductions and 'restorations' which can be difficult to distinguish from the genuine article. Occasionally, the forgery may turn out to have a high value in its own right, but on the whole the investor will need to take due care that the authenticity of the work has been verified. It is also important to bear in mind that certificates may be counterfeited.

18.4.2   Fakes and forgeries

Dealers and auction houses take steps to reduce the risk of forgery and mistaken identity. Some offer the buyer a five-year guarantee against forgery. Because the largest houses trade in volume and compete intensively for material, they can sometimes be an unwitting conduit for fakes, particularly in ill-documented but now increasingly expensive areas of art. In sectors of the market where fakes are relatively common, some will inevitably turn up at auction; and where the rewards can be measured in millions of dollars, fakes will breed.

One growth area for forgery has been the work of the Russian *avant-garde* — Rodchenko, Popova, Larionov, Lissitsky and Malevich. Works by these artists are coming on the market in some quantity. Prices are moving up and authentication is difficult. There has also been a growing interest in Russian and Eastern European relics. Many of those now appearing on the market are fakes. The export of genuine icons, once encouraged by the Soviet government, is now actively discouraged, and bans are enforced in several East European countries.

The handiwork of some well-known forgers has itself become sought after. A case in point is the late British painter Tom Keating, whose works have fetched up to £27,500 at auction. One buyer, however, paid £1,500 for an 'original' Keating only to find that it, and its certificate, were themselves fakes.

18.4.3 Choosing an adviser

When making a purchase, it is usually helpful to have details in a dossier about the artist to whom the piece is ascribed. In the art market, for instance, it is common to use the names of artists to denote works 'in the style of' a particular painter, or paintings by unidentified members of a school associated with a famous artist. Therefore, not all paintings listed in an auction catalogue under the name 'Manet' will be by that painter; and it is important for buyers to appreciate the esoteric distinctions employed by the specialists in auction houses to indicate the provenance of a work. Ideally, those chosen to advise should have a wide knowledge of the field. Thus, a specialist offering guidance on the purchase of works of art should also be able to direct its installation, placement and maintenance.

Ideally, he or she should have a background in art history, curatorial experience, an intimate knowledge of the art market, and up-to-date familiarity with trends in prices and values. In addition, care should be taken to check that the adviser has a good understanding of handling, shipping, conservation, restoration, insurance and security. Curators of art galleries and museums will sometimes indicate formally which dealers specialise in particular areas.

18.4.4   Exporting art

There are further precautions which the intending buyer of art or antiques should keep in mind. Suppose, for instance, that the plan is to send an item out of this country; authorisation may be needed. Some categories of antiques, collectors' items and other artifacts do not need a specific licence. They are covered by the Open General Export Licence (Antiques), which does not need to be applied for. Exporters need only inform customs officials by quoting its title in export documentation. A Specific Export Licence must be applied for (from the Department of Trade and Industry) by those wishing to send historic manuscripts, documents and archives of any value out of the country. Any object covered by the regulations which exceeds the thresholds of age and value will need a UK export licence.

Licence applications have to be accompanied by a black-and-white photographic copy of the item; and the decision whether or not to permit export will be influenced by independent advice. Where the item is regarded as part of the national heritage the issue of a licence may be delayed or refused on the advice of experts in the field. The procedures may include reference to the Department of National Heritage's Arts and Libraries' Reviewing Committee on the Export of Works of Art. It bases its decisions on the answers to three main questions:

(1)   Is the object so closely connected with the country's history and national life that its departure would be a misfortune?
(2)   Is it of outstanding significance for the study of some particular branch of art, learning or history?
(3)   Is it of outstanding aesthetic importance?

In the past many licence applications have been made; few have been rejected. For example, in one recent year, 6,550 applications were made for export licences with a total value of £963m: only 24 failed to receive approval, subject to an offer to purchase at a specified price being made by a public collection in the UK within a reasonable time.

It is prudent to bear the requirement in mind when deciding to acquire a work of art or an antique of exceptional interest. When these items come onto the open market some foreign buyers may be deterred by the inconvenience and delays of up to seven months in the review procedure, and by the inherent risk that their offer will merely represent the buying-in price for a domestic museum. The absence of such foreign buyers could mean lower bids and less attractive gains when the time comes to dispose of the item.

For further advice and more detailed information, the prospective exporter should contact the Department of National Heritage.

18.4.5 National heritage bodies

The National Gallery

The National Museums of Scotland

The Ulster Museum

The National Trust for Places of Historic Interest or Natural Beauty

The Historic Buildings and Monuments Commission for England

The Trustees of the National Heritage Memorial Fund

The Historic Churches Preservation Trust

Any local authority (including National Park authorities)

Any university or university college in the UK

Any museum or art gallery in the UK which exists wholly or mainly for the purpose of preserving for the public benefit a collection of scientific, historic or artistic interest and which is maintained by a local authority or university in the UK

The British Museum

The National Museum of Wales

The National Art Collections Fund

The National Trust for Scotland for Places of Historic Interest or Natural Beauty

The Friends of the National Libraries

The Nature Conservancy Council

Any government department (including the National Debt Commissioners)

Any library the main function of which is to serve the needs of teaching and research at a university in the UK

Any other similar national institution which exists wholly or mainly for that purpose and which is approved for the purpose by the Commissioners of the Inland Revenue

18.5   Characteristics

18.5.1   Prospects of capital appreciation

Can alternative investments be justified by private investors or by trustees and fund managers with powers to buy fine art or antiques? Essentially the question is whether the capital appreciation over a period of say, ten years, 25 years or even longer, will warrant the temporary diversion of funds and the expenditure incurred in holding the asset.

Frequent reports in the press of record-breaking prices paid for pieces at auction may seem to support the case for alternative investment. In 1989, some ten-year and 20-year investments paid handsome dividends. The increasing number of investments which have provided significant capital appreciation short-term, also represents an interesting trend, that helps to endorse the advocates' case for buying arts and antiques.

Their counsel to both private and institutional investors is to buy the best examples that can be afforded and to take expert advice from a reputable dealer or appraiser. They suggest that an artist's early work will, in general, be less valuable than later, more mature, examples. Reasonably enough, they also point out that prices can fall, as happened with Georgian silver after a boom in the 1960s, with 19th century fine art in the mid-1970s, and with many categories of art and antiques in the early 1980s. However, even expert advice is fallible, particularly where attribution is concerned. A case in point is the work of Rembrandt, which has suffered the attentions of a Dutch government committee. Many, in fact the majority of works once attributed to him have now been reattributed to his pupils. Works have lost up to 90 per cent of their value, and the controversy has spawned a 'Save Rembrandt Society'.

18.5.2   Art as investment

A further characteristic of the alternative investment market is its appeal to investors who are nervous about the future. Some of the assets described are low in weight, small in size, and high in value: they are portable, easily concealed and readily negotiable in markets around the world. Those who fear political, economic, social or tax repression in their own countries tend to regard alternative investments as a means of safeguarding their wealth.

There are occasions when works of art and antiques do seem to meet demanding investment criteria. As a case in point, the Antique Collectors Club has reported that the value of furniture bought through dealers or at auctions has been rising. According to their figures, prices paid for these antiques between the end of the 1960s and the late 1980s rose by more than twice the Financial Times 500 Share Index, (after adding 4 per cent per annum for dividends). Even taking dealing cost into account, the rise in values has been appreciable. For example, a writing cabinet designed in 1904 in art-nouveau style by Glasgow architect Charles Rennie Mackintosh, sold for £793,500 at Christie's in February 1994. It set a record for Mackintosh and for any item of 20th century furniture.

On the other hand, there is anecdotal evidence to make enthusiastic bidders at auctions cautious. According to one press report, a battle tableau by Ernest Meissonier, a much-favoured painter of a century ago, sold in London in 1892 for £20,700; again in 1913 for £6,300; and again in 1964 for £4,340. Lazare reports that John Singer Sargent's oil sketch *San Virgilio* sold for £7,350 in 1925 and just £105 in 1952. A scholarly study of London art auction transactions between 1652 and 1961 found that the average work appreciated just half a per cent a year — a poor return in anyone's passbook. More recently, a painting by Henry Fuesli, an 18th century Swiss/British artist, bought by Rudolf Nureyev in 1988 for $1.16m, was sold in January 1995 for $761,500 (£488,141). There are also hundreds of Impressionist and 20th century paintings, the routine works of artists as celebrated as Renoir, Picasso and Chagall, hidden away in the vaults of Japanese banks. These were acquired late in the 1980s and are now valued at little more than half their purchase price.

To set against these warning illustrations, there are some promising examples of the gains to be made. Paintings by the Scottish Colourists — S J Peploe, J D Fergusson, Frances Cadell and Leslie Hunter — have shown an average annual appreciation rate of 19 per cent from 1975. Similarly, Renoir's *Tête du Femme* was sold for £1.35m in 1987 and exchanged hands again in 1988 for £1.98m (an appreciation of 35 per cent in one year).

18.5.3   Costs of ownership

Typically, rates of return are only attractive if the owner is prepared to put a value on the pleasure of holding such works of art in his home or at his place of work. The investment may also be justified if the money used for the acquisitions would have been taxed at a high rate. Conversely, some items could have been a poor investment for the buyer, after taking into account outlays to meet insurance premiums, dealers' or auctioneers' commissions, any liability to capital taxation, the interest foregone, and security and maintenance costs.

The lack of income flows, means that the buyer of alternative investments is dependent on capital appreciation; yet he has to deduct the following costs from any gains he may achieve:

(1)   costs of acquisition and disposal, including premiums and dealers' commissions;
(2)   holding costs (insurance, storage, etc);
(3)   valuation fees incurred;
(4)   revenue and possible tax benefits foregone by tying up capital in the asset;
(5)   the value of time spent learning about the market and, increasingly, the advice of market experts or consultants;
(6)   capital gains tax payable on realisation of the asset, or inheritance tax payable on its transfer.

Substantial gains are necessary to justify such an investment in financial terms; or, alternatively, the investor has to be convinced that the assets he acquires can be relied upon to sustain their worth in times when traditional investments fail.

18.5.4   The Chester Beatty collection

In 1991, 13 paintings from the collection of the late Sir Alfred Chester Beatty were offered at auction. They included works by Toulouse-Lautrec, Degas, Renoir and Chagall. The trustees had previously considered donating Van Gogh's *Sunflowers* to the nation: instead they sold at auction for £24.75m. Had they donated it, the family would have received £5.5m under the government's acceptance *in lieu* scheme. That returns a quarter of the tax deducted as an incentive to donate works of art to the nation.

The sale at auction was subject to combined inheritance and capital gains taxation. The capital gains tax of £3.07m was calculated as 30 per cent of the difference between the valuation and the sale price at auction. The inheritance tax was levied at a variable rate (between 65 and 80 per cent) because the painting had been exempted at the time of an earlier death in the family. Otherwise the rate would have been 60 per cent. At the 80 per cent rate, the balance left for the family would be £3–£3.5m, probably not enough to settle the full tax on the estate.

18.5.5   Buying at auction

Sales to meet tax bills provide auction houses with a flow of works to offer. Many people who like the idea of buying at a sale worry that they will find it hard to conform to usual practice, that a sudden twitch will leave them with an unexpected heirloom and an unwelcome bill. The pace can be fast, the enthusiasm contagious, and bidding strategy complex. The amount paid is also likely to include extras, such as a 10 per cent buyer's premium and VAT on the auction house's services.

In reality the buying process often begins a month or more before the sale date. Catalogues appear and can be bought on subscription, by order or at the auctioneer's offices. The descriptions of items have various nuances; for instance, only information printed in bold type may be guaranteed. There will be an estimated price range, but no disclosure of the secret minimum bid acceptable to the vendor, the 'reserve'. Critics ask, 'Is this secrecy necessary?' Should the buyer be told whether he is bidding against an actual rival or the consignor's reserve? Auctioneers argue that the confidential reserve is a defence against the collusion of 'auction rings'. It is only worth organising a ring when the participants know that the reserve is low enough to ensure a good profit.

Before the sale, lots are commonly exhibited. They are sold 'as seen' so it is important to study the condition of an item in advance. Before bidding at many major auctions, it is necessary to register — to give name, address and bank reference. A 'client card' for previous registrants can speed the process. At the auction, the registrant may take a pre-reserved seat and a bidding number. It is, in practice, virtually impossible to bid by accident. Just when to start bidding is a matter of strategy. Some buyers come in early and raise quickly to deter competitors; others wait to avoid inciting other bidders with their keenness. Care is advisable when the bidding pace seems unusually fast, or the auctioneer does not indicate the source of the bid. Often he or she will say 'on the left' or 'the bid is with me' or some similar words that convey the origin and authenticity of the bid. Payment may be cash, approved cheque or, in some instances, by credit card.

18.5.6 Independent sources of information

Research pays off before buying at auction or through a dealer. An independent source of information on the prices of paintings sold at auction is the Art Sales Index. This lists the results of auctions for about 60,000 items each year which were sold for £500 or more. Using this source, an analysis has been made of transactions for a representative selection of 20th century modern masters. The analysis shows a compound rate of appreciation in excess of 14 per cent per annum between 1971 and 1991. Such rates of growth make it easier to argue the case for the allocation of funds to alternative investments.

The growth of interest which has already taken place has prompted the development of improved sources of information on available media, prices and the advantages and limitations of particular types of investment. There are already computerised databases providing information to help determine sound investments. 'Artquest' provided by the Art Sales Index, holds details on paintings, drawings and sculptures which have been sold at public auction around the world. Another recently developed database is the 'Thesaurus Fine Art Information'. This allows dealers, collectors, and museums who subscribe to it to search through details of forthcoming auction sales, for any category of antique or collectable of interest. The gradual evolution of a more or less formal infrastructure of information sources in the alternative sector of the investment market will add to the understanding of the opportunities and prospects.

These sources and others tend to show that the average annual appreciation over the past 40 years has tended to outstrip the rate of inflation, although there has been considerable volatility from artist to artist and from sale to sale.

18.6　Taxation

18.6.1　Tax planning

It is equally prudent for the investor to plan so that he or she can properly avoid situations in which unnecessary tax liabilities could be incurred. For instance, if the investor eventually wishes to contend that isolated purchases are for the purpose of building up assets as long-term investments, then it may be prudent — indeed mandatory — to record the acquisition of chargeable assets in his tax returns. This step would help to support a claim that capital gains rather than income tax should be the basis for calculating any future liabilities when, despite the parity of the rates of tax, there are advantages in doing so for the individual taxpayer.

The private investor also may be faced with claims by the Inland Revenue that purchases and sales of alternative investments are adventures in the nature of a trade. This would lead to an income tax liability if the investor is held to be carrying on the trade on his own account, or to a corporation tax liability if he has set up a company for the purpose.

18.6.2　Capital gains

Alternative investments are subject to the general law on capital gains tax, although there are special exemptions. In broad terms the amount of the chargeable gain is the difference between the cost of the asset and the sale proceeds, less an adjustment for the inflationary element of the gain accruing since March 1982. For any asset held on 31 March 1982, there is the opportunity to base the cost of acquisition at its market value on that date. There is however no charge on unrealised gains on assets held by an individual at his death.

Special considerations apply in the case of works of art and other alternative investments. Thus, a gain accruing on the disposal of an asset which does not exceed £6,000 (from 6 April 1995) is generally exempt from capital gains tax with marginal relief (see Capital Gains Tax Act 1979, s128). In this connection the exemption on articles which provide a gain of not more than £6,000 (for instance, individual pieces of antique silver) would become particularly relevant.

There are also exemptions in relation to individual objects of artistic, historic or scientific interest (and collections of such objects) which are accepted by the tax authorities as forming 'an integral and major part of the cultural life of this country'. These are often referred to as 'national heritage property'. Under the '*douceur*' arrangements (referred to below), gifts of such alternative investments to national heritage bodies (and gifts of these alternative investments to charities) are not charged to capital gains tax. In the case of sales, the notional capital gains tax liability will be one of the factors relevant in calculating the sale price that can be negotiated. There is a similar exemption applying to gifts of qualifying heritage property made for the public benefit.

Where national heritage property (accepted as such by The Commissioners of the Inland Revenue) is transferred by way of gift from one individual to another, or where such property is transferred into or out of settlement, the transfer will be treated for capital gains tax purposes as giving rise neither to a gain nor to a loss, provided that appropriate undertakings are given with regard to location, preservation and access. This means that any gain is carried forward to be charged at such time as the donee disposes of the property in a manner which does not qualify for conditional exemption.

18.6.3   Inheritance tax and estate duty

Inheritance tax replaced capital transfer tax with effect from 18 March 1986. It was introduced in the 1986 Finance Act and applies to gratuitous transfers by individuals. The major difference between capital transfer tax and inheritance tax is the treatment of lifetime transfers. Outright transfers between individuals are exempt if the transferor lives on for seven years. Gifts made within seven years of death are charged at death rates, but the charge is tapered where the gift occurs more than three years before death.

The charge on death is retained within inheritance tax, as are most of the exemptions and relief available under capital transfer tax, including transfers between spouses domiciled in the UK. Trust-related transfers remain subject to the full range of charges, at the time the transfers are made. The cumulation period for all chargeable transfers has been reduced to seven years and the threshold below which tax is not charge-able is £154,000 (from 6 April 1995). A flat rate of 40 per cent will now replace the former four-rate system.

Estate duty applies to property inherited before 13 March 1975. This may still be relevant to the sale of objects which have been previously exempted from estate duty. Estate duty will not be charged if exempted objects are sold by private treaty to a national heritage body or have again been transferred on a death and have been conditionally exempt on that occasion. Special rules apply when property which has previously been exempted is sold after 6 April 1976. The way in which this property is taxed, depends on what had happened since the original exemption was granted — either capital transfer tax or inheritance tax or estate duty only may be payable. This is a complex issue and is dealt with fully in Appendix III (p 46) of *Capital Taxation and the National Heritage. See* bibliography at the end of Chapter 19.

18.6.4   Tax liabilities in practice

The Treasury has become more flexible about the art it will accept in the form of heritage sales to museums as a means of saving tax. On the other hand, museum purchasing grants have been severely curtailed, which limits the opportunity for private treaty sales.

Suppose a beneficiary has inherited a painting that auction houses believe will fetch £100,000 under the hammer, after allowing for commission and expenses. When the painting was bequeathed it was worth, on valua-tion, £80,000. Capital gains tax would be payable on the difference between the valuation and the sale price (on £20,000). Inheritance tax would be payable on the sale price net of capital gains tax, leaving the vendor with just over £50,000.

If a museum will buy the painting the vendor receives a *douceur* (usually a quarter of the amounts payable in capital gains and inheritance taxes). In this instance a museum would gain the painting at a bargain price, and the beneficiary would receive more than £65,000. The problem is that museum purchasing grants have been frozen for six years, and the National Heritage Fund and the National Art Collections Fund have limited resources. There is also a sum of about £12m a year set aside by the Treasury for selling works of art to the State *in lieu* of tax. The object has to be a 'pre-eminent addition to a national, local authority, or uni-versity collection' and can only be set against inheritance tax, not against capital gains tax. Decisions are made on the advice of the Museums and Galleries Commission. It is a field in which the leading auction houses and dealers have built up expert knowledge.

18.6.5 VAT

HM Treasury has produced The Value Added Tax (Works of Art etc) Order 1983 (SI No 809) which exempts from VAT disposals of works of art and other objects (including manuscripts, prints and scientific objects), which are of national, scientific, historic or artistic interest, or which have an historical association with a particular building. To qualify for exemption, these heritage objects have to be disposed of by private individuals in the course of business either as private treaty sales or gifts to one of the approved list of public galleries and similar institutions or in settlement of tax debts under the '*douceur*' arrangements. This change is also now incorporated in the Value Added Tax Act 1983, Sched 6.

On 1 January 1986 a new harmonised system of customs duty and temporary importation reliefs came into effect under the Value Added Tax (Temporarily Imported Goods) Relief Order 1986 (SI No 1989). The relevant HM Customs & Excise Notices are 361 and 712. The latter is a new information 'package' about the VAT second-hand scheme for works of art, antiques and collectors' pieces (mainly for dealers in fine art and antiques who are VAT-registered). VAT leaflet 701/12/89 gives guidance on 'Sales of antiques, works of art etc from stately homes'. The new regulations apply to works of art brought in primarily for exhibition but later sold. VAT leaflet 701/36/86 also contains guidance on the insurance of second-hand goods such as works of art.

From the beginning of 1995 changes occurred arising from the first stage of implementing the European Union's Seventh VAT Directive. Further changes will follow the Royal Assent to the Finance Bill. The measures affect dealers in works of art and antiques. From 1 January 1995, VAT on all these goods may be accounted for on the margin between their buying and selling prices. Details of the new arrangements are explained in HM Customs and Excise VAT Information Sheet 1/95 which supersedes Information Sheet 3/93, dated 1 June 1993. The new arrangements require traders registered for VAT who make supplies of second-hand goods to traders registered for VAT in other Member States to submit EC sales lists showing the full net value of any supplies made. Full details appear in HM Customs and Excise Notice 725: VAT; the Single Market.

The Finance Bill 1995 introduces a 2.5 per cent effective reduced rate of VAT on imports of those works of art and antiques which are currently fully relieved from VAT at importation. Details can be found in HM Customs and Excise Notice 712. The relief previously afforded by Regulation 47 of the VAT (General) Regulations will cease to be available and such importations become subject to VAT at the standard rate.

Supplies of goods through auctioneers and agents who act in their own names will be treated for VAT purposes as supplies both to them and by them. A special accounting scheme will allow auctioneers who sell works of art and antiques to calculate their VAT on a margin basis. A new VAT Notice 718 gives more detailed guidance on these changes.

The works of art eligible for the margin scheme include:

- Pictures, collages and similar decorative plaques, paintings and drawings, executed entirely by the hand of the artist, with some exceptions.

- Original engravings, prints and lithographs produced in limited numbers from plates executed entirely by hand by the artist.

- Original sculptures and statuary in any material, executed entirely by the artist (subject to certain provisos).

- Tapestries and wall textiles made by hand from original designs in limited numbers (not more than eight copies).

- Industrial pieces of ceramics executed entirely by the artist and signed by him.

- Enamels on copper, executed entirely by hand, limited to eight numbered copies, bearing the signature of the artist or studio, with certain exceptions.

- Photographs taken by the artist, printed by him, or under his supervision, signed and numbered, and limited to 30 copies.

Antiques are defined as objects, other than works of art or collectors' items, which are more than 100 years old. *See also* Chapter 19, section **19.5.2.**

18.6.6 Stamp duty

Stamp duty will normally be payable only when the transfer is of an interest in an alternative investment, and not when it is the work itself which is being transferred, since chattels are transferable by delivery and no document is required to effect a transfer of the interest.

18.7 Mechanics

18.7.1 Suitability

Research on individuals' investment preferences indicates that works of fine art and antiques only begin to figure to a significant extent in the portfolios of the wealthy. Initially, investors concentrate on property, building society investments, insurances, unit trusts or investment bonds, and possibly equity investments or gilts or National Savings certificates.

Thus the more esoteric investments tend to be bought when extra capital is available. Neither individuals nor pension funds have so far engaged in the purchase of alternative investments as a routine policy, although the British Rail Pension Fund was, at one time, an exception; the Fund invested approximately £40m in about 2,000 works of art, but its trustees and managers subsequently decided not to make any more purchases in this market.

In November 1988 the BR Pension Fund disposed of 31 museum-worthy pieces of silver for £2m having paid £400,000 for them ten years previously. In 1989, the Fund sold paintings and sculptures, including works by Manet, Renoir, Monet, Picasso, van Gogh and Cézanne. Altogether the items put on sale realised £38.5m, leaving the pensioners with more than £30m after paying all expenses and commissions. In 1990, the Fund sold its collection of 19th century continental European and Victorian paintings for £6m compared with its mid-1970s pruchase price of £1.2m. One of a batch of 16 Old Masters, owned by the Fund, which were sold at Sotheby's in December 1994, went for £3.4m, compared with a purchase price of around £150,000. The Fund has seen a 14.3 per cent annual cash rate return and a 6.6 per cent real rate of return.

In general, pension fund investment managers see a problem in the marketability of such assets. It is not easy to convert alternative investments into cash at short notice without sustaining losses. In addition, pension fund trustees and investment advisers are cautious about committing themselves to a line of action which might be criticised in the future.

Trustees and investment advisers say that it is difficult to obtain accurate valuations on a regular basis and, even when valuers can supply a dependable service, there are few reliable and independent indices on which to compare their portfolio's performance, as with equities. There is also a lurking suspicion that funds should not be invested in areas which are regarded as unsuitable for investors who may need income or capital at short notice, and which cannot be readily converted into cash.

On the other hand, the infrastructure for making alternative investments is gradually being established, and in the course of the next few years there may be improvements in the information sources and the indices available to investors and trustees. A well-publicised example is the service provided by London-based art investment managers Poensgen Sokolow. They produce the quarterly *Art Market Analysis*, and offer portfolios of important works with starting prices of around $10m. The improvement of the information facilities and the build up of reputable sources of impartial market intelligence might eventually help to make such alternative investments attractive — both for individuals and for investment managers with responsibilities for closed funds such as small self-administered pension schemes.

18.7.2   Sources of information

For the moment, the sources of information and intelligence are diverse and scattered. There are, in each of the areas of alternative investment, several specialist journals. In addition, there are various societies or clubs, which give the collector access to specialist knowledge. Auctioneers produce useful catalogues which highlight pieces coming onto the market; and those interested can find out about the prices paid at these sales.

The specialist journals and some of the directories produced by associations of dealers and auctioneers identify the areas in which particular firms are knowledgeable. The dealers will usually charge high commissions to cover their costs of holding expensive assets for periods, which can sometimes be prolonged, before a buyer emerges. Auction sales are, on the whole, a source of more competitively priced items, although many of the leading London firms now charge a commission to both vendors and buyers.

It is, however, becoming more difficult for the private collector to keep pace with developments in his or her chosen fields of alternative investment. Although London remains an important centre of trading activity in art and antiques, many important sales are nowadays being held outside the UK, which has become a net exporter of such pieces. In earlier times, collectors could rely on a steady flow of fine works.

18.7.3   Advisers

In recent years the established London firms have been experiencing parallel competition in specialised fields from provincial dealers and auctioneers. Consequently, keeping abreast of news and intelligence on alternative investments today, requires a complex web of contacts and information sources. In this context, it is important to locate one or two of the specialists among the dealers and in the auction houses who can be relied upon to assist the dedicated and wealthy enthusiast.

To a degree, investors seeking advice on specific pieces can depend upon appropriate museums or art galleries, where curators are normally willing to give an opinion on the quality and authenticity of a work. Curators are also likely to be familiar with the market, or dealers who specialise in a sector, although they are usually reluctant to be seen to recommend a particular firm. Curators will not normally give opinions on market values.

Leading auctioneers are more willing to express a view on the price a piece might command if offered for sale, and specialist dealers will also have an opinion on the value of an item in their field of expertise. Such valuations are important if the investor plans to make a sale; they will help him or her to arrive at a sensible reserve figure.

Dealers and auctioneers are generally keen to offer help, in particular to itemise and appraise assets. At the outset, their valuers will advise on insurance cover and the security of precious items, pending sale. They will then prepare a full inventory of the chattels, identify those which are of value and make arrangements for the disposal of the residue. Any gifts or bequests will also be valued for inheritance tax purposes; and recommendations will be made on the handling of any works which have national or historic interest. The experienced auctioneer or dealer will also advise on how best to sell items for disposal. Given that the market for art and antiques has become international, it is important to choose with care a time and a place when specialist collectors are likely to be at a sale.

The valuer will charge a fee, and the auctioneer or dealer will be thinking of a commission on sales. Before confirming instructions for an inventory and appraisal, it is advisable to discuss the eventual consignment contract for an estate which may include important pieces. Some firms in the art and antiques market will refund part of their valuation fee if any of the items they appraise are sold through their auction or dealing rooms within a year or so of the appraisal. There may also be opportunities to negotiate lower commission rates on sales. Within the trade, auctioneers and dealers are often prepared to cut their selling commission from 10 per cent to 6 per cent, and there is certainly scope for reductions in standard rates when the estate is large and valuable.

A further point to bear in mind when negotiating commission rates is the possibility that an item at auction may not reach the reserve price suggested by the valuer. In some instances, the auctioneer may be willing to make no charge to the vendor, or levy a reduced commission, if a lot fails to sell at the reserve which the firm has recommended. Auctioneering and dealing in art and antiques are highly competitive businesses and many firms are willing to consider special terms when an estate contains a number of worthwhile items.

For buyers who use the services of dealers there are often the attractions of 'buy-back' offers. These usually have many caveats attached to them.

The dealer may undertake to buy back at a price geared to his valuation at the time of the repurchase; or he may only be willing to commit himself to buy back at the original price paid by the investor. Almost no dealer is willing to purchase at the original price plus inflation since the date of the transaction; and, if any do make such an offer, the buyer might well consider it prudent to make such checks as he can that the firm is likely to be still in business at a future date when a resale might be contemplated.

The professionals who advise on alternative investment can also help when it comes to reviewing a portfolio. To offer sound advice, they should be in close touch with the market trends, so that they can recommend optimum times for the disposal of pieces which have reached a current peak in value. Equally, they should be well placed to identify pieces coming onto the market which would make a collection more representative and therefore more valuable in terms of the chosen theme.

18.7.4   Commercial galleries

New collectors may not necessarily understand the more recondite points of aesthetics when collecting art, but they are often keenly aware of the financial implications. They are also conscious of the social benefits of being a part of the collecting 'realm', and the prestige of owning museum-calibre works. In this context, one American dealer offers a useful checklist for those entering the art market for the first time:

'Use the expertise of dealer-owned galleries which represent the artists they exhibit. Ask for biographical materials on the artists. Seek advice from individuals in the art industry.

'Let the dealer know which artists you are interested in, so you can be notified of exhibits or new works. This way you'll get first-hand, fresh information and will likely be placed on a special list for private preview showings.

'Galleries don't always display everything they have either. Ask gallery owners to show you their "backrooms" and remember to ask questions. Galleries often present themselves as quiet enclaves, but staff ought to be knowledgeable and helpful.

'Dealers seldom give what is called a "collector discount" to occasional buyers. In major centres, it's not uncommon for dealers to discount up to 10 per cent. That's because most works are marked up substantially to take price negotiations into account.

'Whenever possible, view a one-person exhibition to see several pieces of an artist's work. This will help you see the depth of an artist's vision and quality of work.

'If you see a piece that strikes you, go for it. If you need a companion's approval or review by a trusted adviser, most dealers will hold it for you for 24 hours. This will give you right of first refusal — and time to think.'

Commercial galleries normally put on three kinds of exhibition: one-person shows, theme shows, and exhibitions from stock. Galleries tend to show from stock at the quieter times of year. From the standpoint of the exhibitor, the one-person or theme show is the best way to achieve the preferred effect: they allow the gallery to suggest the cultural significance of an artist's work. A few galleries can put on first-class exhibitions from stock because their backroom holdings are strong. They are able to mount exhibitions of acknowledged masters, or works that can reasonably be described as 'museum-quality'.

Some of the galleries and dealers are promoting art and antiques as alternative investments, because they believe there are worthwhile opportunities to plan and manage portfolios. They contend that the investor can specialise in one or two categories of investment but still spread the risks by diversifying the selection within these categories. In addition, they suggest that it is possible to use market intelligence and research to time purchases and sales to maximum advantage and to build up interest among potential bidders.

18.8   Maintenance

18.8.1   Safeguarding the investment

A prime consideration in the mind of the investor who buys works of fine art or antiques ought to be security. Theft, accidental damage, fires, floods and other catastrophes remove many works from the market each year, usually forever. Computer systems are now being introduced to log details of missing works such as the Art Loss Register and the New York-based International Foundation for Art Research. Their aim is to deter thieves by making details of stolen works quickly available to auction houses, dealers and collectors.

The immediate conclusion is that a purchase should be held safely. For economic reasons, a bank vault may be considered when items are not continuously on display. Even when the items are bulky, the cost of hiring vault space will be far lower than the valuation and subsequent insurance premiums for pieces held in less secure places. In other cases, the collector's pieces should be insured against all risks, and the items in a collection should be revalued at five-yearly intervals, or more frequently, to ensure that the insurance cover is adequate.

18.8.2   Insurance

Brokers and insurers who carry out these valuations with the aid of expert dealers or auctioneers will at the same time advise on cost-effective outlays on security measures — cost-effective in the sense that they bring more than compensating savings in premiums. The valuers will, in particular cases, photograph pieces in a collection to provide a record in case of damage or theft.

A point to note is that the London head offices of insurers charge travelling and subsistence expenses, so it is usually sensible to contact the nearest regional office. However, if the item is a particularly specialised work of art, it may be advisable to consult fine art brokers. They may advise that it is unnecessary to insure well-known items against theft, giving substantial savings in premiums, on the grounds that any subsequent disposal by the thief in the art market would lead to his capture. For example, in 1994, the gang that removed, in 50 seconds, one of Norway's greatest icons, Edvard Munch's painting *The Scream*, from Oslo's National Gallery, were captured when they tried to sell it to members of Scotland Yard's Art and Antiques Squad, who masqueraded as unscrupulous dealers.

By and large, burglars usually avoid stealing such items, unless they already have a buyer or can realise the value of precious metal or gemstones from which an antique is made. Most thefts of antiques are opportunistic and involve works of art valued at less than £1,000. Some are planned, either through handlers, or because the thieves mistakenly believe they can convert antiques into cash.

Steps are now being taken to create one global law on stolen goods, which will enable the owners to repatriate their property while the unwilling buyers can seek compensation from the auction houses or dealers that handled the sale. The new law is in draft form, and more than 50 nations will gather in Rome in June 1995 to pursue an agreement.

A collector may also wish to put his art or antiques on show. This can present problems. As values shoot up, it can be difficult to insure valuable exhibits. When the Metropolitan Museum of Art's show 'van Gogh at Arles' was being planned in the early 1980s, it was assigned a global value for insurance of about £1bn. Today it would be £5bn, and the show could never be considered. In the wake of the May 1990 sales, every van Gogh owner wants to believe his painting is worth £50m and will not let it off the wall if insured for less. Even then, the problem is compounded by enthusiastic dealers or auctioneers: when consulted on insurance values, they may be tempted to set the maximum imaginable price on a painting to maintain the image of its market value and tempt the owner to sell.

18.8.3 Security

One of the security measures which is often overlooked is to preserve confidentiality when buying an alternative investment. News of purchases attracts those inclined to steal — a problem also faced by owners who have to allow access to the public to gain the tax exemptions referred to earlier.

In addition to tighter security, it is important with some works of art and antiques to consider the 'ambient' conditions in which a piece is to be displayed. Adverse lighting can, for instance, cause a valuable watercolour to fade, and many items of antique furniture need a suitably humidified atmosphere to survive without deterioration.

Normally, specialists in the field will advise on the best methods of preserving the qualities of a piece. They are also a useful source of information on firms which carry out restoration and repair work to appropriate standards, and on removal firms which have a good record of handling delicate and valuable pieces with due care.

18.9 Preview of the year ahead

18.9.1 Renewed confidence

Prices have been held back by a shortage of good objects: unless under pressure from the three Ds — death, debts or divorce — potential sellers have been hanging on for higher prices. This year they could feel more confident about entrusting their antiques to the marketplace. The reigning themes for 1995 are 'high quality' and 'fresh to market'. It is expected that people will be looking for arts and antiques that have not been available for 20, 30, 40 or 50 years, that is items that justify the description 'rare'.

One sign that bodes well for the market is that art dealers, who for a long time have been sitting on too much inventory to add any, are far more willing to buy works at auction and privately than they were just a year ago.

Renewed confidence was seen in sales of Modern and Impressionist paintings, in both London and New York, where works from celebrated collections and fresh to the market attracted bidders from Europe, South East Asia and the Americas, particularly from the private sector.

Before the recent hints of recovery, the art market had collapsed under the weight of speculative bidding, especially in the field of contemporary art, which is still suffering the adverse effect of hype and inflation in the 1980s. At that time works of new artists were bought and sold like stocks, and some blue-chip pieces fetched astronomical prices.

Art experts now report a revival based on more realistic prices and the re-entry of connoisseurs, who had been deterred by speculative buying. The market has been further strengthened by new Asian investors buying works of quality and value. At Sotheby's Impressionist sale, Cézanne's *Still life with apples* — which had been hawked around the world's sales rooms for two years at £17–20m — was expected to reach £6.5m; it sold for almost £18m in May 1993. Eight other lots sold for more than £5m, and the sale generated over £50m — the highest total in three years at Sotheby's.

At Christie's New York Impressionist sale at the same time, six of the sale's top works were bought for prices high above their estimates, including Monet's *La Jette du Havre* for £6.4m.

In June 1993 Sotheby's had its best Impressionist sale in four years, when it sold 84 works for £20.2m. Christie's found buyers for 82 per cent of the Modern pictures offered including Renoir's *Jeune Fille* for £5.6m, and Modigliani's *Tête de Jeune Fille* for £2.8m. It was the highest ratio of works sold to works offered for the auction house in London since April 1990. Four years ago, the market was so weak that more than half of Christie's and Sotheby's contemporary offerings went unsold at auction.

As in other sectors of activity, the signs of recovery, though seemingly consistent, should be viewed with some caution — it is always tempting to claim total recovery at the slightest flicker of life.

The markets for contemporary works and Old Masters have not suffered as badly as the Impressionist market, and good prices are being paid for top quality pictures with impeccable provenance. In hard times, the art market freezes, as only the most hard-pressed owners offer their precious possessions. The fall in supply helps to sustain prices — one reason why art can be a reasonably sound defensive investment. Even in the great slump of the 1930s, only those sectors which had been ultra-fashionable in the 1920s suffered at all badly.

In January 1994, a work that turned out to be *A boy drinking* by the 17th century Bolognese artist Annibale Cerracci, was resold for £1,478,190 in New York, giving the most spectacular price in a highly successful run of Old Master painting sales. The painting had first appeared at an auction in Somerset in 1984, when it fetched a mere £209. At the Somerset sale the painting was thought to be a copy, but bought by an intermediary and put into Bonham's sale in London in 1985, when it sold for £5,500 to a dealer who proved the painting's authenticity to his advantage.

18.9.2 Far Eastern interest

The importance of the Japanese as a market force was demonstrable as much by their absence in the last few seasons as by their predominance in the previous two. Their departure from the Impressionist market, where they accounted for a third of the activity in the 1990 boom, as well as the record-breaking purchases, is widely credited with the slump since then.

Dealers and collectors from the nations of South East Asia have made their presence felt in the auction houses in the last few seasons. There has been a corresponding interest in artwork from the region — a reflection of their booming economies. Korean, Taiwanese and Hong Kong buyers have been particularly active. Their main interest, for the present at least, is in reclaiming their cultural legacy that has been in the possession of Western collectors. A Chinese splash landscape by Zhang Daquien, estimated at £15,000–£20,000, was bought by a private Asian collector at Sotheby's in June 1994 for £170,000. A pair of Chinese jade lanterns, estimated at £28,000–£40,000 was sold for £200,000 to a Taiwanese buyer. At Art Asia last year, Chinese painter Liu Yuyi's kitschy *Song of Legendary Goddess Nuwa* fetched $1.2m, said to be the highest price ever paid for a contemporary Chinese painting. In New York, a 15th century Korean dish broke the record for any porcelain after selling for $3.082m (£2m) at Christie's in April 1994. It also broke the record for any Korean art.

The strong interest shown in works of the South East Asian nations, coupled with the anxieties of wealthy Hong Kong collectors ahead of 1997 and the possibility of renewed Japanese interest, are likely to ensure the region's continued emergence as a key player in the market.

18.10 Conclusion

Recently it has been the private buyer, with a sound knowledge of the determinants of quality and provenance in a specialised niche, who has sustained the market in art and antiques. Collectors can take both pleasure and gain from a work of art — two forms of appreciation. It also seems possible that ownership of art will seep out of America towards Europe and the Far East. Art management specialists who take on responsibility for high value portfolios are likely to increase in number.

In the UK and Europe, governments will continue to re-regulate the market, inhibiting it in some cases, but ensuring wider access in others, not least through better protection for the consumer.

The last few years have illustrated that if art is a market it is a highly knowledge-intensive one. To make informed judgments, the prospective investor needs expertise or access to it: the connoisseur's intuition, and familiarity with the patois of the auction house and dealer, are as vital as knowing what is on sale, where, and when. As the French art expert Jacques Attali recently pointed out, 'nobody is in a position to establish laws for a market as unstable and as irrational as this. Each work of art is singular; each motivation is unique; each transaction has its own requirements'. In the coming years, he says, buyers will become more and more discriminating. The supply of recognised works of art will diminish, but new types will appear on the market. The art market will become 'a kind of avant-garde of museums, a selection process of what may subsequently become part of our collective memory'. It is in keeping with his remarks to add the footnote now *de rigeur* on investment sales literature: 'investments can go down as well as up'.

Sources of further information

See end of Chapter 19.

19 Collectables

John Myers, Lessia Djakowska and Susan Farrell of Solon Consultants

19.1 Introduction

19.1.1 Collectables as alternative investments

The fashionable urge to collect seems to extend to an ever-widening range of items with memorable, nostalgic or merely eccentric qualities — classic postage stamps, old cars, numismatic coins, Oriental carpets, banknotes, scrips, medals, vintage wines and spirits, musical instruments, playing cards, *objets de vertu*, bric à brac, scientific instruments, cars, printed ephemera to name but a few. The enthusiasm for collecting such items stimulated the formation of various bodies, including the Ephemera Society, which was set up in 1975; its membership, of more than 1,800 worldwide, benefits from a lively range of activities and publications.

Despite this evidence of enthusiasm, many investors remain wary of collectables. Caution is, of course, sensible when considering esoteric investment media, but several factors have recently made them more appealing. Many players on the stock markets have become acutely aware that equities are highly volatile. Every hint, or rumour of a crash, sends shareholders on a hunt to spread their risks.

Collectables seem comparatively safe refuges for spare capital: they are unlikely to lose a quarter of their value in a single day's trading. In times when inflation threatens, collectables can offer a hedge against escalating prices and, for many people, they warrant a small proportion of an investment portfolio.

An understanding of the field can best be illustrated by the examples in this chapter drawn from a wide range of collectable media.

Collectables do, however, have one factor in common with arts, antiques and valuables: they attract wealthy buyers from all corners of the world. They use their cash or borrowing power to diversify their assets, in the manner of new Renaissance merchant princes. Quality of life is their target.

Such nonchalant aficionados of the good life collect primarily for lifestyle motives, rather than mere speculation on the chance of high gains, although there is also an investment motivation. The buyer of an alternative investment compares an opportunity to buy a collectable with the risks involved with stocks and shares. After a substantial fall in the equity markets, he or she may see an art deco ornament or a rare musical instrument as more likely to hold its value.

A case in point was a Venini glass vase which, in the 1960s, sold through a run-of-the-mill department store at no more than £20. At a Geneva sale only two years ago, a bidder paid 176,000 Swiss francs (£70,000) for it. The glass had original qualities. Successive valuations of the few remaining examples of the piece to be offered for sale had proved inaccurate. At first, the bidder who paid £500 for one such Venini in 1978 could not find a buyer to take it off his hands at a profit. He was wise to wait: at an auction in 1984, the same vase fetched £25,000 — over 12 times the auctioneer's estimate — equivalent to an annual compound rate of return of 92 per cent. In 1987, another Venini vase attracted a successful bid of £52,000. The pre-sale estimate was less than half that amount. The latest £70,000 figure was also double the auction house's estimate.

Another Geneva sale of 20th century collectables produced a similar result. French and Japanese dealers bid strongly for a delicately carved glass table lamp. The lamp, originally produced commercially by Daum and Louis Majorelle less than a hundred years ago, was bought by a Japanese dealer for 1.58 million Swiss francs (£675,000). The seller had bought it about 20 years ago for less than £5,000, a compound annual rate of appreciation equal to approximately 30 per cent.

19.1.2   Numismatic coins

Rare coins have recently been treated almost on a par with the holding of shares and bonds, and some stockbrokers, particularly in the US, have recommended them to their clients as a substitute for stock market investments. The market for coins has been greatly enhanced by a wider acceptance of a grading system. Agreed methods of categorising coins according to their quality help to structure the market for collectors and investors.

Knowledgeable players would like coins to become respectable as the basis for investment funds they are setting up. A typical institutional scheme requires an initial tranche of capital — say £50m — to fund dealing in collectable coins. The essence of the plan is to acquire enough coins which will appreciate over a short enough period to generate worthwhile returns for the investor. A key question is how to calculate 'worthwhile'. Some coins will gain in value, others will lose. Whatever happens, the fund has to meet its overheads, which will include regular valuation of its portfolio. One analyst estimates that sets of coins will need to appreciate, on average, by more than 40 per cent to give investors a 20 per cent return. In the case of one such fund, the promoter's filings with the US Securities and Exchange Commission claim that similar types of investment company have previously achieved returns of this figure or more.

The promise of success is echoed in fresh price records at coin auctions. Not long ago, a Wall Street investment fund paid £600,000 for an 1804 United States silver dollar — a record at the time for a coin sold at an auction. The coin was one of only 15 known examples. The earlier record price paid for a coin was for an American doubloon, dating from 1793, sold in 1979 for £250,000.

19.2   Highlights of the previous year

19.2.1   Auctions of collectables

Collectables generally continued to escape the worst effects of the recession in the arts and antiques market, and there were signs of recovery in trade buying and highly successful sales, at which collectors paid spectacular prices. But there were exceptions. Watches, a favourite several years ago, have had variable results, and pop memorabilia attracted less attention, with the exception of a recording by former Beatle John Lennon singing with his first band, the Quarrymen, which sold for £78,500. On the other hand, rare books and coins, toys, glassware, ceramics, jewellery, basketball cards, and Hollywood posters have continued to sustain interest, and rarity almost always excites bidders. Annie Oakley's rifle was sold in 1993 for £84,000, a teddy bear made a record £110,000 in 1994, and a Dinky toy of a Bentall's van fetched a record £12,700 also in 1994. Opulence, intricacy, ethnicity, and authenticity, and the bizarre continued to attract buyers.

Perfume bottles, biscuit tins, slot machines, costumes, dolls and typewriters are cherished as never before. In the US, memorabilia related to slavery and American historical manuscripts are fast becoming favourites. In May 1993, a handwritten manuscript by Abraham Lincoln, part of a speech denouncing slavery, sold for nearly $1m. A month earlier, a photograph of Frederick Douglas, a former slave who became an outspoken abolitionist in the 1880s, went for $20,900.

The manuscript of Robert Schumann's second symphony was sold for £1,486,500 in December 1994 — the highest price paid for a manuscript of any single musical work. As all other surviving manuscripts of symphonies by Schumann, Beethoven, Schubert, Mendelssohn, Brahms and Bruckner are in public libraries, it is the only one likely to appear at auction.

Eighteenth century costumes are particularly sought after by both private buyers and museums. A ballgown may fetch £10,000. So might a Swedish Malling-Hansen typewriter of the 1870s. Matthew Bolton corkscrews change hands for up to £2,000 and a rare Baccarat perfume bottle in the shape of a butterfly was recently auctioned for £18,000.

A hoard of Old Master prints found inside a trunk that was home to a family of mice sold at Sotheby's in December 1994, for £587,952, more than twice their estimate. The sale included two Durer prints. One, *The Rhinoceros*, is one of his most famous images: of the first such animal seen in Europe. They went for £111,500. A second Durer print, *Samson Rending the Lion*, achieved an auction record for the artist, when it was sold for £199,500.

Noire et blanche, a photographic print by Man Ray depicting Kiki of Montparnasse fondling an African mask, sold for $354,500 (£239,527), double its estimate and a record for the artist, at Christie's in New York in April 1994. It was the second-highest price paid at auction for a photograph. Alfred Stieglitz's image of the hands of his wife, the artist Georgia O'Keefe, made $398,500 at Christie's in 1993.

Unusual early film posters have become highly collectable, and private deal prices in the US have reached £68,000 — a threefold increase in three years, despite the recession. Dealers predict that unique posters will fetch $250,000 when released onto the open market. Horror and animation art are among the biggest attractions, with a 1933 King Kong poster fetching £71,980 in New York at a recent sale. While the lucky individual who discovers a poster for Steamboat Willie, Mickey Mouse's first talkie (1929) will be able to retire for life.

To the British, posters have hitherto meant Kitchener pointing, Toulouse Lautrec, Mucha and British Railways. The record for a British poster is £68,200, paid at Christie's in February 1993 for an 1895 Charles Rennie Mackintosh of an Art Nouveau female figure. Not quite a King Kong, but the figure was attractive enough.

19.2.2   Where eagles dare

Recently Christie's sale of Dan Dare strip cartoons and front covers of the *Eagle* attracted many private dealers. Items sold well attaining prices of between £300 and £600. For example, 'Reign of the Robots' from 1958 sold for £580. Illustrations of Dan Dare by his creator, Frank Hampson, attracted particular interest, especially from the US.

Vintage comics are regularly included by auction houses such as Christie's and Sotheby's in New York. Interest has grown since 1991, when at Sotheby's comic book auction, a first edition Batman comic brought $55,000 — an auction record in this field.

19.2.3 Scope for creative imagination and knowledge

Another group of entrepreneurs specialise in kitsch, mementoes, and bric-à-brac. The souvenirs of today can be the alternative investments of tomorrow, or so the retailers argue. The souvenirs of the age become the memorabilia of generations to come — as garish as seaside postcards, and as uncouth as water-filled, shake-up, domed paper weights that snow on the Houses of Parliament.

Paperweights have continued to climb in value during a period in which the value of other items has stagnated. A record $258,000 was paid at auction for a rare Clichy magnum basket weight. The market is strong, with the motivation being the artistry, craftsmanship and colours, much the same as collecting paintings.

Packaging has become another popular collectable item, and recent sales have featured biscuit tins produced between the 1870s and the 1930s, the great period of the British tin. Shaped tins tend to be the most prized, with the best examples fetching hundreds of pounds at auction. One, in the shape of an ocean liner, recently went for £880.

19.3 Current developments

19.3.1 Vintage stock certificates

Collectables with obvious appeal for the alternative investor are vintage stock and bond certificates. Enthusiasts and scripophilists will pay up to £70,000 for a particularly rare item — the sum paid in 1991 for a Bank of England promise-to-pay bill, issued to back loans to the pre-communist Russian Imperial government. The value of the certificates lies in their historic and aesthetic appeal, or the signatures which appear on them, rather than their face value. Thus an 1856 share certificate of the American Express Company, signed by Mr Wells and Mr Fargo and with a nominal value of $500, recently sold for £500. Certificates from the early industrial revolution are currently in high demand, particularly from shipping and railways enterprises.

Some collectors hold on to certain pre-communist bonds in the half-expected hope that they will eventually be redeemable. The market in these took an unexpected turn in 1991 when the (then) Soviet government paid out 54 per cent of the face value of busted bonds. The compensation settlement had a time limit however. Dealers have been overwhelmed with certificates from those who missed out, causing a slump in the market for Russian bonds. The trade in vintage bonds from other pre-revolutionary regimes should be an interesting area for speculation.

19.3.2   Rare books

Books have been collected since the times of monasteries and chain libraries. From the Renaissance to the French Revolution, books were mainly collected and used for what was in them rather than their appearance. By the time Jane Austen's novels were gaining shelf space, the nouveau riche began to see books as artifacts which granted status to their owners. Among some buyers, the appearance began to transcend the content.

The market is segmented. One sector is the 'first edition market' — a very specialised field. With some works, a book's value may depend as much on the presence and quality of its dust jacket, as the rest of its make-up. Scott Fitzgerald's *The Great Gatsby*, for example, had a typographical error on the jacket of some copies of its first edition. With this, a copy might fetch £3,000, without, a mere £30–£250. Inscriptions in books by the author or a famous owner, or a relative, or an influential friend of the author, can also enhance values. A copy of the late Graham Greene's rare first novel, inscribed with a message to his wife, was sold at Sotheby's for £13,200 in 1991, double the previous record for this volume, set the previous year. In other cases, inscriptions have increased values by even more.

In collectable books, as in other areas of the market in art and antiquities, it has been works of fine quality which have withstood the downturn in the last two years. The market in Impressionist and Modern paintings has suffered a particularly severe decline in the last few years. Standard reference works or *catalogues raisonnés*, on the other hand, have experienced little change in demand. These volumes have more than aesthetic appeal, they are in constant demand from art dealers and can fetch four figure sums at auction. The attractions of very rare works have also weathered the recession. Phillips had their most successful book sale in March 1992, raising more than £500,000, with the main attraction being manuscript material by David Garrick, the 18th century theatre luminary. Another generally successful area has been antiquarian textbooks. Christie's sale of the Loughlin collection, of mainly 16th to 18th century works on mathematics and other sciences, did very well for the vendors. The highest price, £280,000, was for an exquisitely bound copy of du Bellay's 1549 *Instructions sur le faict de la Guerre*.

The advice to collectors of rare books could easily be restated in many other fields of alternative investment: 'Buy the best of what you like. Rely on your own instinct, but work closely with knowledgeable dealers. Develop a collector's eye by looking at a large number of books. Browse in specialist shops. Search out auctions, fairs and even car boot sales.'

One of the latest trends in collectables are the 'hypermoderns' — books which have been published within the last two decades, or even the last two months. For example, John Grisham's *A time to kill* — his first mystery will fetch $750 today: of the 5,000 printed, 3,000 were destroyed, and in the meantime, John Grisham became, well, John Grisham. In American hypermodern-speak, the author 'Garped' — a term used to describe a breakthrough book derived from *The world according to Garp* — the book that put John Irving on the map with critics, readers and collectors.

19.3.3 Numismatic coins

As indicated in **19.1.2**, rare coins have one of the longest-established markets among collectables. This market has suffered a downturn over the past ten years, particularly in the US, as more exotic or eccentric ephemera have attracted the enthusiastic collector. However, the trade has proved fairly resilient, perhaps because of its continuing wide appeal, and generally very reasonable prices under current market conditions. Rarity still exacts a high premium nonetheless.

A 1982 gold coin commemorating the release of the Falkland Islands from the invading Argentinians sold for £2,200. It was in mint condition and was one of only 25 struck.

At a recent Christie's firearms sale, an 1890 halfpenny was sold for the astonishing price of £1,380. This ordinary halfpenny is stamped with the word 'Oakley' on its obverse and is deformed by a bullet shot. Apparently, Annie Oakley, the great American sharpshooter, used to shoot coins thrown up in the air. These were then stamped with 'Oakley' and given to the audience.

A temporary collapse in world demand for Greek and Roman coins is feared following the sale of a vast collection belonging to mint mogul Bruce McNall.

Over the last two years the rare coin market has also attracted a share of the controversy caused by selling practices in other alternative investment markets. Some dealers in the US have sought to encourage investment in coins by establishing certifiable grades of quality. Associated with this is the practice of 'slabbing'. Coins graded by one of two grading houses, the Numismatic Guarantee Corporation or the Professional Coin Grading Service, are sealed in plastic 'slabs'. However, the market in slabbed coins has slumped, and the Federal Trade Commission has repeatedly indicted the PCGS for making false claims about the objectivity and consistency of its grading.

Certification of quality, if done consistently, could show pointers to how the market in collectables might develop. Through the American Numismatic Exchange some coin dealers have sought to create their own version of the modern stock market. The Exchange enables dealers to trade over a computer network. Investors can buy and sell as they wish through the network, without having to wait for auctions and sales. Critics argue that coins are not equities, they are 'limited edition art objects', so values tend to be set on a subjective basis. Nor, they argue, are coins liquid assets. Investors should allow for delays in finding a buyer who will pay the 'right price' for a rare coin.

Advocates of the coin bourse claim that it has helped to stabilise a volatile market. If it develops as it might, the Exchange could trade in coin futures and coin options. Equally, it could extend its remit into other alternative investments. Syndicates and funds could be set up to trade in certificates backed by physical assets, hedged on the Exchange. An information infrastructure could follow, as the traders and investors seek better intelligence on the fundamentals and technical performance of particular assets. Far fetched? Possibly, but informal coffee house trading years ago in the City led to the spectacular and speculative commodity, insurance and shipping markets of today. At the time, it seemed an equally unlikely proposition.

19.4   Purchasing collectables

19.4.1   Strategies

Collectors need to plan their strategies. Do they intend to become expert collectors, who gain thrill and pleasure out of the artifacts in which they invest? Or will they instead rely upon dealers to feed their hobbies or their alternative investment portfolios? If the latter, the player should realise that they will miss out on the social ambience of the market — the real enthusiasts will be in the know, as the dealers are.

19.4.2 Collectables in general

In recent years, activity in the market for collectables has increased, just as it has in the markets for art and antiques and for valuables such as gold and jewellery. Two factors help to account for the popularity of these alternative investments: changes in exchange rates, and uncertainties about the future. A further significant factor is the entry of players from countries not hitherto on the scene.

As in markets for other alternative investments, the entrants come from Asia, particularly from China and Hong Kong. The players from these countries are taking advantage of the 'globalisation' of alternative investment markets. Improved communications, both telematic and physical, have helped to create an alternative investment village peopled by cosmopolitans.

The rapid, sometimes sensational, growth; the record prices featured in reports of sales; the apparent robustness of demand — all tend to obscure one critical fact about all investment markets, actual and alternative. They are cyclical. As new groups of collectors emerge, they push up prices. As their demand is absorbed into the markets' infrastructures, growth rates tend to tail off, and both buyers and sellers become more selective.

Some markets are naturally cosmopolitan, some are limited by national or cultural appeal, some are restricted in their development by language. An example, which crosses the boundaries of all three, is the market for rare books and manuscripts. It offers many opportunities for many people. Incunabula appeal to those who value antiquity in their collectables. A thematic set of works by a famous author may appeal to a collector who is able to read and enjoy them. A historic set of works about a great event in a nation's development may attract those with a personal interest in the subject. There are opportunities for collectors who want to pay no more than £100 for a book or a manuscript, and opportunities for enthusiasts who may be willing to bid a four, five or six figure sum.

Collectable cars

Classic cars have a more limited appeal, but remain cosmopolitan. A Porsche 959, a Ferrari F40 super car, or the Bugatti Royale may attract bidders from almost any part of the developed world. Their chances of gain can be considerable. Within a single year, 1988–1989, the price of some Aston Martin DB6s rose tenfold, from £10,000 to £100,000. Prices have fallen since their boom in that year, however, and in the past year have steadied to a 'realistic' level, to around £50,000 maximum in the case of the Aston Martin.

The frantic activity in the market arose, to some extent, from interest by wealthy, middle-aged enthusiasts, nostalgic for the cars of their youth. Foreign buyers also stoked the price furnace. Their more powerful foreign currencies made goods bought abroad a bargain. Luxury-car lovers helped too: faced with a £35,000 price tag for a new import, many opted for the 1950s' 'chromosaurus', at no more than £18,000.

These buyers have not disappeared, although ageing Rolls-Royces and Bentleys currently glut the market. Enthusiasm for the highly charged sports car is undiminished, and the old Ferraris, Jaguars, Maseratis and MGs continue to command high, but not hyped, prices. One area which has proved more popular recently is what one dealer described as 'good, honest, clean cars'. Old family cars with character; the Volkswagen Beetle, the Morris Minor, the Mini-Cooper, are attracting a new generation of enthusiasts willing to pay around £5,000 for a model in good condition.

Intending purchasers are recommended to buy through a private transaction after placing a classified advertisement in a car magazine, or from an enthusiast who belongs to a specialist automobile club. Some experts believe that, when buying cars, auctions can be particularly hazardous. They argue that there may be little opportunity to inspect the car, and they suggest that an iron will is needed to avoid being swept away by the bidding excitement.

Another simple recommendation is not to buy a car unseen. It is advice that applies equally to many other alternative investments. Skilled salesmen may give 'cast-iron assurances that there will never be another chance to buy a car like this again, and urge the investor to send money without delay.' As a cynical commentator put it — 'Two weeks later, you will find a pile of rust on your doorstep. The chance of a lifetime comes along about once a week'.

Buyers of classic cars are also encouraged to drive them. Unless it is a museum-quality machine, an ageing vehicle could benefit by being fired up to full running temperature on a regular basis. If it costs too much to insure the car for the road, the buyer is advised to change the oil periodically, to jack up the car to protect the suspension, and take other steps, such as dehumidifying the garage, to prevent deterioration.

Collectable wines and spirits

Some French wines, for example, fine vintages of Latour, have recorded an average annual appreciation of around 20 per cent in the past 15 years. At the recent sale of the late Robert Maxwell's collection, a dozen bottles of Latour 1982 sold for £800. Bidders paid around 20 per cent above the market average, perhaps attracted by the new found notoriety of the cellar's previous owner.

Some specialists believe that wines can be restored. In one cited instance, a buyer paid £425 for a double magnum of 1865 Château Lafite in 1967. Fourteen years later the buyer took the bottles back to the chateau to have the bottles topped up and new corks inserted. Sold at auction after a few months, it reached £12,000 per double magnum — that is, 25 per cent a year compound. The same connoisseur believed its value in mid-1990 would be about £48,500.

A sale of whisky fetched £98,000, including 14 bottles from the *SS Politician*, the ship which inspired the film classic *'Whisky Galore'*. The bottles sold for £11,000.

19.5 Taxation

19.5.1 Tax planning

If purchases can be justified as requirements of a business — for instance, acquisitions of furniture or wall decorations for an office — investors paying high rates of tax may obtain benefits. They may be able to offset the costs of acquisitions as legitimate business expenses, but with a corresponding liability on disposal. If, on the other hand, the chattels which form the alternative investment portfolio are not regarded as income-producing, the owners will not normally be able to secure income tax relief in relation to insurance premiums or maintenance expenses.

19.5.2 VAT

A uniform system of VAT calculation for trade in second-hand goods took effect in the EU on 1 January 1995, when the 7th VAT Directive came into force. Commercial transactions now carry VAT levied on the profit margin, while transactions between individuals will not be liable to VAT. Second-hand cars are now defined as those more than six months old or with more than 6000 km mileage (twice the previous lower limits). The UK is allowed a transitional period up to 30 June 1999 at the latest, during which VAT will be charged at the reduced rate of 2.5 per cent. The changes to VAT explained in chapter 18, section **18.6.5**, also apply to collectors' items and second-hand goods. Collectors' items are defined as:

- Postage or revenue stamps, postmarks, first day covers, pre-stamped stationery and the like, franked, or if unfranked not being of legal tender and not being intended for use as legal tender.

- Collections and collectors' pieces of zoological, botanical, minerological, anatomical, historical, archaeological, palaeological, ethnographic or numismatic interest.

19.5.3   Sets of collectables

The investor may want to avoid acquiring 'a set of similar or complementary things' rather than a number of separate items which do not constitute a single set. The definition may affect future tax liabilities if the value of the set would exceed capital tax thresholds whereas the individual items would be exempt. Thus the Inland Revenue is of the opinion that a collection of postage stamps *per se* constitutes a single set, although, in their view, the stamps of one definitive or commemorative issue would not necessarily do so.

One of the issues in the field is whether the acquisition of a set or sets of collectables is a mere hobby or a pukka investment. Implicit in the question is whether expenses will be deductible. On balance, if the collector is in it strictly for investment and capital gains, and keeps accurate records, including purchase dates, prices, provenance, current values, then it may be possible to make a case for deducting certain expenses — insurance, relevant publications, even travel to sales and auctions. In the majority of cases, however, the collector will be trying to create legal and tax history — in itself an expensive hobby.

When a collection is sold at auction, or after exhibition at a dealer's shop, the authorities may also be interested in the gains secured. In a case where someone has purchased collectables 'under the table', without a clean provenance, the Revenue may argue that the cost basis is zero. The gain would, therefore, be 100 per cent. The advantages of documented evidence are clear. Where the authorities take the view that efforts were being made to evade payment of tax, the legal penalties can be stiff, even if the action was innocent.

19.6   Suitability and mechanics

19.6.1   Risks

An abundance of snares awaits the buyer. Markets may be thin. Collectables can be difficult to sell quickly, and meanwhile they pay no interest. Instead they can soak up considerable amounts in insurance, storage, and maintenance. Repair and restoration can also be expensive. It might cost £60,000 to renovate a Ferrari; and only the reckless would drive it along the road. The car has a hand-formed aluminium body. If a passer-by leans against the fender it can easily dent.

Despite such costs and risks, enthusiasts still pay massive sums for rare vehicles. Recently, a 1936 Mercedes-Benz 500K Roadster, one of the most stunning automobiles ever built, was sold at auction for £1.6m. It was not in first-class condition. According to one report, rats had eaten through the upholstery. A butcher had left it sitting in his shed, unused, for more than 30 years. Originality means a great deal with great cars.

19.6.2 Precautions

Independent advisers who specialise in collectables recommend that an investor should carefully check a dealer's reputation, before deciding to employ his services. They suggest that enquiries should be pursued to find out how long the dealer has been in business, and to what professional organisations he belongs.

In practice, it is also prudent to make sure that the collector fully understands what is being offered and promised. By way of illustration with coins, questions might be asked about the grade of the coin, and the backing for any guarantees. Does the dealer guarantee to buy back an investment? If so, at what price, and on what terms? Are there, for instance, any deductions affecting buy-back warranties? Is a service charge levied?

With collectables of any value, it may be worth seeking a second opinion on quality and provenance, before confirming a decision to buy. Familiarity with sales and the publications in the field will also reveal whether an asking price is in line with the market, or well above it.

19.7 Preview of the year ahead

The ideal alternative investment is, by definition, extraordinary. The swan-shaped vehicle with its pedestrian-spraying 'beak', and its £187,000 hammer price, is a possibly extreme example. Some collectors favour such conventionally sought after items as the intricately crafted manuscript. Others find passionate interest in obscure examples of the mundane; the telephone card for instance.

Recovery of property values in London have brought fresh confidence to the top end of the classic car market. In company with top-quality houses, top-quality cars are now selling well. So this year may be a good time to put a classic car in your garage, if you have the space. Not since the collectable car boom of 1988, when vintage cars became an investment craze, have prices been so low.

Apart from cars, collectors are currently displaying an interest in photographic equipment — an early Leica, with its mystique of Henri Cartier-Bresson, Andre Kertesz and 1920s Paris, may be worth thousands in mint condition. Even the humble box camera, the 'ordinary' Kodak which sold for £3 in the 1890s can fetch £1,200 today. In 1993, Christie's sold a Hegelin watch camera, one of only two examples known, for £18,700, and an 1880s Lancaster ladies watch camera for £39,000. A camera made of gold for the Sultan Abdel Aziz of Morocco in 1901 sold for £39,600.

Other collectables that Antiques Roadshow valuers favour include dolls, toys and the memorabilia of the early cinema. Dolls could fetch from £10 to £150,000; a 1939 German triplate Mickey Mouse £12,000. And film posters may reach between £35 and £70,000. There is a diversity of choice to suit the taste and pocket of the most eclectic of collectors.

19.8   Conclusion

In this field of alternative investments, the vital step is to decide whether to be an investor or a collector, or both. Those who take the trouble to understand a particular market well, and be a player, can gain the knowledge to be a specialist collector. In practice, only a limited number of people have the enthusiasm, dedication and resources to pursue the opportunities on a systematic basis. As indicated, any of these markets for collectables is also a social network. The participants derive much pleasure from being involved in this network. Keeping in touch with fellow devotees is rewarding in the interchanges and in the exchanges.

The investor will quickly learn that he or she spends much time learning about the subtle connotations of hallmarks on metalware, manufacturers' symbols on ceramics, makers' names on antique clocks, the marks of well-known furniture craftsmen and many thousands of other characteristics which influence the attribution of collectors' pieces. Those for whom time is scarce will quickly recognise that they need the services of a specialist. The real collectors develop a burning fervour and could scarcely stop, even if they wanted to, or were forced to by circumstances. In essence, to be a mere investor is to miss out on the social rewards, and to enjoy only vicarious or second-hand advantages. But then collectables are second-hand!

Sources of further information

Bibliography

Sponsoring the Art: New Business Strategies for the 1990s, The Economist Intelligence Unit (0171 830 1000)

Antique Dealer & Collectors Guide (monthly), IPC Magazines Ltd

Art Sales Index 1993–4 (26th edition), Art Sales Index Limited (01932 856426)

Art Market Bulletin, Art Sales Index Limited (01932 856426)

The Guide to the Antique Shops of Britain 1995, compiled by Carole Adams, Antique Collectors Club (01394 385501)

Guide Emer 1993 (bi-annual European guide) available from Mr G Gillingham, 62 Menelik Road, London NW2 3RH (0171 435 5644)

Antiquités Info (monthly European guide) (0171 435 5644)

Capital Taxation and the National Heritage, The Board of the Inland Revenue, London 1986, (amended 1988)

The Ephemerist (quarterly), Ephemera Society (0171 935 7305)

The Death Tax, Towry Law, (01753 868244)

Works of Art: A Basic Guide to Capital Taxation and the National Heritage, Office of Arts and Libraries, 1982

Works of Art in Situ: Guidelines on In Situ Offers in Lieu of Capital Taxation, Department of National Heritage, 1984 (0171 270 3000)

Gold to 1992, The Economist Intelligence Unit (0171 830 1000)

Diamonds: A Cartel and its future to 1996, The Economist Intelligence Unit (0171 830 1000)

Manuscripts and Archives, Office of Arts & Libraries, 1991

Works of Art Private Treaty Sales: Guidelines from the Office of Arts and Libraries, Department of National Heritage, 1986 (0171 270 3000)

Gold 1995, Goldfields Mineral Services, Greencoat House, Francis Street, London SW1P 1DH

Picture Guide to the UK Art Market 1995, Duncan Hislop, Art Sales Index Limited (01932 856426)

Official Antiques Review 1995, Tony Curtis (ed), Lyle Publications

Antiques Price Guide 1995, Martin and Judy Miller (eds), Millers Publications

Art Newspaper, PO Box 1, Tonbridge, Kent TN9 1HW (01732 770823)

Gold Demand Trends (quarterly), World Gold Council (0171 930 5171)

Platinum 1995, Johnson Matthey plc, New Garden House, 78 Hatton Garden, London EC1N 8JP

Useful addresses

Arts Council of England
14 Great Peter Street
London
SW1P 3NQ

Tel: (0171) 333 0100

British Antique Dealers
   Association
20 Rutland Gate
London
SW7 1BD

Tel: (0171) 589 4128

Ephemera Society
4 Marylebone High Street
London
W1M 3DE

Tel: (0171) 935 7305

Incorporated Society of Valuers
   and Auctioneers
3 Cadogan Gate
London
SW1X 0AS

Tel: (0171) 235 2282

International Association of
   Professional Numismatists
11 Adelphi Terrace
London
WC2N 6BJ

London and Provincial Antique
   Dealers Association
535 Kings Road
London
SW10 0SZ

Tel: (0171) 823 3511

Oriental Ceramic Society
30b Torrington Square
London
WC1E 7JL

Tel: (0171) 636 7985

Royal Academy of Arts
Burlington House
Piccadilly
London
W1V 0DS

Tel: (0171) 439 7438

Royal Fine Art Commission
7 St James Square
London
SW1Y 4JU

Tel: (0171) 839 6537

Society of Antiquaries of London
Burlington House
Piccadilly
London
W1V 0HS

Tel: (0171) 734 0193

Wine and Spirit Association of
   Great Britain (Inc)
Five Kings House
1 Queens St Place
London
EC4R 1XX

Tel: (0171) 248 5377

20 Tax beneficial investments and savings

Mike Wilkes of Pannell Kerr Forster, Chartered Accountants

20.1 Introduction

The most important aspect of savings planning is to identify appropriate investments which offer good value and tax benefits and privileges are only one aspect of this.

An investment which is appropriate for one person may not necessarily meet the needs of another person in different circumstances. Some of the questions to be asked are:

(1) How long can the savings be tied up?
(2) Are the savings for a particular purpose (school fees, daughter's wedding, retirement, etc)?
(3) When will the money be needed?
(4) Is income required?
(5) Will fluctuations in stock market and/or property prices be such a worry that the investments become unattractive?

Another aspect is that you may want to strike a balance. The criteria for investing the short-term part of the portfolio should be different from the method of investing in more volatile investments on a longer-term basis. Striking the right balance is one of the hardest aspects. If savings are fairly modest they may have to be invested on a conservative basis — and the return will reflect this. At the other extreme, a high net worth individual who has covered all his short-term requirements may deploy a proportion of his capital in more risky investments which offer the prospect of a very high return.

Once these decisions have been made, the next step is to identify investments which meet the specifications and offer good value. An investment may offer good value if the managers' charges are reasonable and the tax treatment is favourable.

This chapter starts by looking at tax privileged investments from the standpoint of the most cautious investor who may want access to capital at short notice and who is, therefore, not well disposed towards investments which may fall in value from time to time. Then a look is taken at tax privileged investments which involve a degree of risk arising from fluctuations in The Stock Exchange, etc. Finally consideration is given to bank deposits and 'near cash' investments most of which involve little or no risk but do not have a privileged treatment. Many of these investments are provided by the government through the department of national savings or local authorities.

20.2   Tax privileged investments

20.2.1   TESSAs

One of the government's more successful innovations are TESSAs (tax exempt special savings accounts). These are available to any individual who is resident in the UK and aged 18 or over.

The investment will normally run for five years. It offers a secure return since the money has to be deposited with an authorised bank or building society and the risk of capital loss is therefore remote. The investor can withdraw his capital within the five year period but the tax benefits will be forfeited if such withdrawals exceed certain limits. Subject to this, the benefit of having a TESSA is that the investor receives tax-free interest.

The maximum amount which may be withdrawn during the first five years without jeopardising the tax benefits is the interest credited to the account less the basic rate tax which would have been deducted if the account had not enjoyed its special tax exempt status.

Example

Sid deposits £3,000 in a TESSA. In year one the bank credits interest of £195. The interest has not borne any tax. Sid can withdraw £195 less 25 per cent notional tax, ie £146.25 without affecting the exempt status of the account. The remaining £3,048.75 will continue to attract tax-free interest. However, if Sid withdraws £146.26 the bank will have to account to the Inland Revenue for the tax of £48.75 and the account will thereafter be treated as an ordinary deposit account. Once five years have elapsed, Sid can withdraw the entire amount with no tax consequences.

There are limits on the maximum amount which may be invested in a TESSA. An individual may invest up to £3,000 in the first year and up to £1,800 each year thereafter, subject to the total not exceeding £9,000. Alternatively, an individual can invest up to £150 per month.

In order to encourage reinvestment, the Finance Act 1995 contains provisions which increase the limit of the first year deposit, for a second TESSA account, opened after a previous TESSA account has matured. Providing that the new TESSA account is opened within six months of the maturity of the previous account, the whole of the capital held in the matured account, excluding any interest element, up to a maximum of £9,000 can be invested in the new account in the first year. If however the maximum is invested, no further investment will be permitted. Individuals who invest less than £9,000 in the first year of their second TESSA account will be able to continue saving over the next four years, within the usual limits for each year, subject to the overall limit of £9,000.

An individual cannot have two TESSAs at any one time. However, the above limits apply separately in relation to husband and wife. The terms under which banks and building societies accept deposits for TESSAs will vary. The government regards it as a matter of choice as to whether the deposit carries a rate of interest which is fixed for five years or a variable rate. TESSAs are 'portable' so an investor will be able to transfer his savings from one financial institution to another without losing his tax benefits. However, the investor should check the level of any transfer penalty.

Uses of TESSAs

Older investor who needs income

The prime user of a TESSA is an older person who needs to take a regular income and who would rather avoid fluctuations in the value of his or her savings.

School fees provision

TESSAs are also suitable investments for individuals who wish to accumulate capital to cover school fees and similar costs — especially school fees payable in the medium term.

Quite sizeable sums can be accumulated. Thus if an individual makes the maximum deposits allowed, and interest is earned at a gross rate of 6.6 per cent, he will accumulate a total of £11,319 at the end of five years (this assumes that interest is credited on an annual basis). Thus a married couple could accumulate just over £22,600 between them over five years. If we assume that they have put this aside to cover school fees payable when their son reaches 13, and the fees are currently £2,000 per term and likely to rise with inflation at 4 per cent per annum, they will still have covered the first three to four years' fees and this will allow other savings plans (such as PEPs — see below) to fund later years.

Why waste the tax exemption?

TESSAs may also be attractive to wealthy individuals who happen to have £10,000 on deposit and who may or may not keep it there for five years but would like to obtain the tax exemption if it is held for the full period (see also **2.3.15**).

20.2.2   National savings certificates

These are another investment which provides a totally tax-free return. However, the yield reflects this and so TESSAs offer better value for most people.

National savings certificates are a five year investment but they can be encashed early although this involves surrendering a small amount of interest.

The 42nd issue of national savings certificates is now available and if held to redemption (ie five years) give an overall net yield of 5.85 per cent.

Once certificates have matured, they attract tax-free interest at the national extension rate (currently 3.51 per cent) until they are redeemed.

Practical aspects

The certificates may be a suitable form of savings for children but children's bonus bonds are likely to be a far more attractive proposition for small savings. They are not, however, suitable for non-taxpayers or for short-term savings; but for the investor paying tax at the higher rate, the certificates may be attractive.

Application forms are available from most branches of the Post Office and banks. Between £100 and £10,000 can be invested in the 41st issue, plus up to £20,000 reinvestment of earlier issues which have matured.

Holdings should be reviewed from time to time, particularly since new issues may carry more attractive rates of capital appreciation than those already held. A review of holdings should certainly be made at the end of the specified period.

Any number of certificates can be cashed at one time, on at least eight working days' notice, and repayment forms are available at most branches of the Post Office and banks.

20.2.3 Children's bonus bonds

As the name suggests, these bonds are specifically designed for children and are intended as longer-term savings, as the bondholder can retain the bonds up to the age of 21. The current issue (Issue G) has a guaranteed tax-free return of 7.85 per cent if held for five years. Anyone over 16 can purchase bonds for anyone under 16, and children under 16 who wish to purchase bonds for themselves will have to ask a parent or guardian to sign the application form. The maximum total holding in all issues of children's bonus bonds is £1,000 per child (excluding interest and bonuses) regardless of the number of donors, and can be purchased in £25 units. Shortly before each five year period ends the next guaranteed interest rate and bonus will be advised. No action is necessary unless it is decided to cash in the bond. Once the bondholder is over 16, the next offer of interest rates and bonus will be for whatever length of time remains until he or she reaches 21. The bonds can be encashed at any time, with one month's notice, but there will be a loss of interest unless this is at a five-year bonus date, or at age 21.

As with savings certificates, this investment is particularly suitable for parents, as the interest is not aggregated with their own income for tax purposes, even if the growth in value produces interest in excess of £100 per year.

20.2.4 National savings index-linked certificates

As with national savings certificates, these certificates are guaranteed by the government. They cannot be sold to third parties.

There is no lower age limit for holding these certificates, although encashment is not allowed until a child reaches the age of seven, except in special circumstances.

If a certificate is encashed within the first year, the purchase price only is repaid. If the certificates are held for more than a year, the redemption value is equal to the original purchase price, increased in proportion to the rise in the RPI between the month of purchase and the month of redemption. In the event of a fall in the RPI, the certificates can be encashed for the original purchase price. After the death of a holder, indexation can continue for a maximum of 12 months.

The latest issue (8th) guarantees a return above the rate of inflation for a five-year term by offering extra tax-free interest of 3 per cent as well as indexation. The amount of extra interest credited to the holding rises in each year of the life of the certificate and is itself inflation-proofed.

As with national savings certificates, capital appreciation is exempt from income tax and capital gains tax.

Certificates are suitable for individuals who do not need immediate income but are seeking protection in real terms for the amount invested. Higher rate taxpayers in this category will find the certificates particularly attractive. The investment limit here is £10,000 with a minimum of £100, in addition to holdings of all other issues of savings certificates.

Application forms are obtainable from most branches of the Post Office.

Comparison with TESSAs

There are circumstances where index-linked certificates could provide a better return than TESSAs. Interest rates are affected by a number of factors other than the rate of inflation and if you are pessimistic about the likely rate of inflation over the next five years index-linked certificates offer a low risk alternative.

20.2.5   Premium bonds

Premium bonds are guaranteed by the government. They cannot be sold to third parties.

Any person aged 16 or over can buy the bonds, and a parent or legal guardian may buy bonds on behalf of a child under 16. A bond cannot be held in the name of more than one person or in the name of a corporate body, society, club or other association of persons. Prizes won by bonds registered in the name of a child under the age of 16 are paid on behalf of the child to the parent or legal guardian.

The minimum purchase for a bondholder aged 16 or over is £100. Above this amount you can buy bonds in multiples of £10, up to a maximum of £20,000 per person.

No interest is paid, but a bond which has been held for one clear calendar month following the month in which it was purchased is eligible for inclusion in the regular draw for prizes from £50 to £1 million. Bonds can be encashed at any time, and all prizes are totally free of UK income tax and capital gains tax. Although the top prize may not compare favourably with potential National Lottery winnings, unlike the lottery the original stake will never be lost.

20.2.6 Personal equity plans

PEPs were introduced by the Chancellor of the Exchequer in the 1986 Finance Act to encourage wider share ownership by individuals in UK companies by offering investment tax incentives. Successive Finance Acts have introduced changes which make PEPs even more attractive.

Anyone who is over 18 years old and resident in the UK for tax purposes can take out a PEP. Crown employees working overseas are deemed to be resident for this purpose. Should a plan holder subsequently become non-resident, the plan can be maintained and its tax benefits preserved.

The tax benefits take the form of total exemption from capital gains tax and income tax on the appreciation and investment income earned from equities, unit trusts and investment trusts held within the plan. A plan can be terminated at any time and the funds withdrawn without loss of the tax benefits.

There are two distinct types of plan, general plans which have been available since the introduction of PEPs, and single company plans which were first introduced on 1 January 1992. Single company plans allow investment only in the shares of one designated company, and are subject to an additional condition that substantially the whole of the cash subscribed to the plan, or from the realisation of plan shares, must be reinvested in plan shares within 42 days.

There is no restriction on the investment switches that can be made within the fund and no liability to income tax or capital gains tax arises. A PEP can be transferred from one manager to another.

The maximum investment into a general plan is currently £6,000 per tax year and up to an additional £3,000 may be invested in a single company plan. Both husband and wife can invest this sum. The investment must generally be in the form of cash although shares acquired through a public offer may be transferred into a plan within 30 days. In addition, many managers offer share exchange schemes or will reduce their normal charges for selling shares so that cash can be raised for investment in a PEP.

The cash held within the PEP can be held on deposit. The interest earned is paid gross and will be exempt from tax provided that it is eventually invested in plan shares or units.

The full £6,000 may be invested in qualifying unit trusts or investment trusts who in turn invest at least 50 per cent of their funds in UK equities and shares quoted on EU stock exchanges. This range of investments will be extended to include specified corporate bonds and convertibles of UK non-financial companies, and preference shares in UK and EU companies, providing they are quoted companies. This was announced by the Chancellor in his 1994 budget speech, and will become effective on, or as soon as possible after 5 April 1995. The precise date is uncertain because consultation on the necessary changes to the regulations will have to be made. As an alternative, up to £1,500 may be invested in a non-qualifying unit trust or investment trust, although from 6 April 1993 at least one half of the assets must consist of qualifying quoted securities.

Although no relief is available on the investment into the fund, the plan is virtually a gross fund in the same way as a pension fund. There is an important advantage over most pension funds in that all proceeds are tax free when drawn whereas at least part of what emerges from a pension scheme will be taxable. It is therefore a useful addition for individuals to enhance retirement benefits. The fund can be used in the same way as a pension, ie tax-free cash can be taken or the fund could be used to purchase an annuity.

PEPs are not 'no risk' investments but in the past a combination/selection of unit/investment trusts and direct investment in bluechip or 'alpha' stocks have generally produced a reasonable return where the investment was kept for between three and five years (see also Chapter 3).

20.2.7   Insurance policies

Insurance policies are another type of tax privileged investment. Investors in qualifying policies are not subject to any tax on the maturity of the policy. We look at such investments in greater detail in Chapter 14.

20.2.8   Friendly society investments

Friendly societies issue qualifying insurance policies and there is no tax charge for investors when such policies mature. In this respect the position is no different from policies issued by insurance companies. The difference lies in the way that friendly societies are treated for tax purposes. Friendly societies are treated favourably as they are not normally subject to tax on life assurance business and this has generally enabled them to produce attractive returns.

Friendly society policies are, however, essentially a long-term investment since the surrender value can be very low where plans are cancelled or surrendered before the ten-year term has expired, as penalties tend to be heavy and frequently the charges on friendly society plans are high.

The maximum premiums are very low. The maximum annual limit is £200, but will be increased to £270 from the day that the Finance Act 1995 receives Royal Assent. Some societies do permit a lump sum investment to be made to cover the full ten-year plan. Policyholders must be between the ages of 18 and 70.

At least 50 per cent of the underlying fund of a friendly society must be invested in narrower range securities as defined in the Trustee Investment Act 1971. This could put restraints on the investment performance although on the other hand it offers a reduced level of risk. All investment income and capital gains within the fund are free of all UK tax, which enhances the rate of return.

Finally, the Policyholder's Protection Act 1975 does not extend to friendly society plans and there is no compensation scheme in the event of a friendly society having financial difficulties.

20.2.9 Pension policies

Personal pension policies and additional voluntary contributions to approved pension schemes are amongst the most favourably treated of all investments. Full tax relief is available for the individual's contributions and the fund enjoys total exemption from tax. This is discussed in Chapter 15.

20.2.10 Enterprise zone property trusts

These trusts are effectively collective schemes whereby an individual acquires an interest in a portfolio of properties located in one of the designated enterprise zones. The minimum investment is usually £5,000 but unlike the Enterprise Investment Scheme investments (see **13.5**) there is no maximum, and it is therefore possible for investors to shelter very large or exceptional income during a tax year. Investors are issued 'units' or 'shares' but in law they hold an interest in the properties as members of a syndicate.

The investment is allowable as a deduction from the investors' taxable income to the extent that the managers invest the cash raised by them to construct buildings or purchase newly constructed and unused buildings within an enterprise zone. There is usually a small part of the investment which attracts no tax relief representing the cost of purchasing the land on which the building has been constructed. Generally this is between 4 per cent and 8 per cent of the total investment.

Example

Mark invests £50,000 in an enterprise property trust on 3 March 1995. He has income of £75,000 which is subject to the 40 per cent top rate.

The managers of the trust invest all the money raised in qualifying property before 6 April 1995. The land element is 4 per cent. Mark, therefore, gets a tax deduction of £50,000 × 96 per cent, ie £48,000. This deduction saves Mark tax of £19,200 so the net cost of the investment is £30,800.

Current yields on such investments are between 6 per cent and 7½ per cent of the gross investment. The income is paid gross and is treated as rental income for the investor. The final investment return on such an investment is difficult to predict. Investors should expect to retain their units for a term of 25 years. A disposal within this term could give rise to a clawback of some or all of the income tax relief given in year one (although no such clawback need arise in the case of a gift).

The yield becomes more attractive when one compares it with the net cost of the investment, after tax relief. Thus if the trust yielded 6 per cent on the gross cost, the yield on Mark's net cost becomes 9.7 per cent.

These investments are tax privileged because of the relief due to the investor when he makes the investment. However, they are not risk free as the investment produces income only if the properties are fully let. In practice this risk can be minimised.

The trust managers can generally secure rental guarantees of at least two years where they buy properties from developers. Sometimes the developer offers a further guarantee which in the short term provides effectively a guaranteed income. In many cases the managers buy enterprise properties which have been 'pre-let' and this means the investor is securing a guaranteed income, usually with upward only rent reviews for a 25-year period. If good rent reviews are achieved the capital value of the investment can be expected to appreciate.

Investors may also take a qualifying loan to acquire the units. The interest being set first against the rental income from the properties and any surplus is then available to be set off against any other Schedule A rental income for the same year. The balance of any unused interest relief is available to carry forward against rental income of future years.

In addition to the long-term nature of these investments, it is often difficult to dispose of the units as there is no established market through which units can be bought and sold. The managers do, however, offer to assist investors on a matched bargain basis.

Planning in later years

One planning possibility involving the use of these investments relies upon the fact that the clawback (or 'balancing charge') need not arise on a gift. Thus, Mark might transfer the shares in the enterprise property trust to his wife if she is not subject to the 40 per cent rate. If she had no other income at all she would have no tax liability on the rents she received of £3,000 per annum.

20.3   Conclusion

Some of the tax benefit investments offer the prospect of outperforming inflation. The return on a TESSA might very well be 6.5 per cent or more per annum. PEP's invested in a range of equities should produce a comparable return over the medium to longer term. Index-linked national savings certificates are guaranteed to do so.

The return on some of the other privileged investments looks less attractive. Where savings certificates have matured the current rate of interest added (3.51 per cent) barely keeps pace with the current rate of inflation.

The various types of deposit schemes offer a poor long-term return to anyone who cannot enjoy the income gross. They are, therefore, sensible investments for a married woman with little or no other income, but less attractive for a person who is subject to tax at 25 per cent or 40 per cent. That is not to say that these investments are not appropriate from time to time, as a way of investing money short term or in order to secure a known commitment or liability.

21 Investor protection

Peter Howe, LLB, Barrister, Company Secretary, Allied Dunbar Assurance plc

21.1 Introduction

The Financial Services Act 1986 was enacted following widespread concern at the collapse of a number of investment firms in the early 1980s. The legislation is based on the recommendations of Professor Gower who, on behalf of the government, carried out an investigation which revealed a lack of consistency (and in some cases the absence of any controls at all) in the regulatory systems controlling different types of firm.

Professor Gower's approach was to recommend regulation only in so far as necessary for the protection of investors and that the regulatory structure should remain flexible so as not to impair market efficiency. The aim was to introduce a consistent regulatory structure which would produce a 'level playing field' (ie rules which do not put some firms at a competitive disadvantage compared with others). His view was that regulation should not try to do the impossible by protecting investors from their own folly but rather to prevent reasonable people from being deceived.

Finally, Professor Gower recommended self-regulation by the industry as preferable to the regulatory system in the US where the Securities Exchange Commission is a government agency. Although the UK system is backed up by statute, the day-to-day regulation of investment businesses is undertaken by self-regulatory organisations made up of practitioners drawn from the various types of investment business which operate in the market.

The Financial Services Bill was enacted in 1986 and brought into force by a number of Commencement Orders. The key provisions were implemented in 1988. A two-tier system of regulation was introduced with the creation of a Securities and Investments Board (SIB), responsible for several self-regulatory organisations (SROs) which are referred to in the paragraphs below. They each produced their own rules and determined their compliance and monitoring approach.

21.2   Highlights of the previous year

21.2.1   The Personal Investment Authority (PIA)

Although there were doubts whether it would ever get off the ground the PIA finally received recognition by the SIB and became operational on Monday 18 July 1994.

Seen as key to the SIB's aim of setting and delivering higher standards of investor protection the PIA is now the primary SRO for the retail sector. It effectively merges the regulatory activities of FIMBRA and LAUTRO as well as covering some of the non-stockbroking private investor responsibilities of IMRO and the SFA (See **21.3.1**).

At the time of writing over 3,000 firms, mainly ex FIMBRA and LAUTRO Members, have been admitted to membership of the PIA with an estimated 2,000 applications still to be decided. On the assumption that most of these applicants are accepted into membership the total membership of PIA should be 5,000 out of a potential total of 5,500.

Using appropriate risk-assessment techniques and compliance visits the PIA must now meet the challenging task of ensuring compliance with its rules.

Now that the PIA is operational, FIMBRA and LAUTRO have had their recognition orders revoked by the SIB but with transitional provisions lasting, unless modified, until 1 October 1995.

Those firms which obtained their authorisation from FIMBRA or LAUTRO but which have so far not been accepted into membership by PIA may continue to operate provided that they applied to PIA (or another regulator) by 1 October 1994. Any firms which failed to do this ceased to be authorised on that date.

21.2.2   Disclosure

New product and commission disclosure rules for life companies were published in April 1994 following directions from the Treasury and SIB.

From 1 January 1995 Key Features setting out the essential elements of the product including charges and expenses must be given to an investor before an application form is completed. The document must disclose the commission or other remuneration payable to the intermediary (whether independent or tied) and must give further important information about the product.

Until 1 July 1995 the key information can be given on a 'specimen' basis but after this date it must be presented in a way that is specific to the circumstances of the purchasing investor.

The rules require life offices to use their own charges instead of industry standard charges when preparing illustrations of future benefits and the clear disclosure to investors of the consequences of surrendering a policy before the end of its term or maturity. They also permit product providers to make charges which differ according to which distributor outlet is used to obtain the business.

The rules on disclosure do not apply at present to unit trusts and other non-life assurance packaged products. A consultation document on a disclosure regime for these products is awaited with a view to probable implementation in Autumn 1995.

21.2.3 Training and competence

Since the publication of the McDonald Report ('Training and Competence in the Financial Services Industry') in May 1990 the SROs have each produced training and competence schemes which meet the standards set by SIB's Training and Competence Panel.

The aim of the new SRO for the private investor, the PIA, is to introduce unified training and competence arrangements across its membership so that common standards will apply whether the adviser is independent or tied (see **21.4.2**).

The PIA issued a consultative paper in December 1994 proposing that:

*   most new entrant advisers must pass the full Financial Planning Certificate (offered by the Chartered Insurance Institute) or the Investment Advice Certificate (offered by the Securities Institute) depending on the type of investment business undertaken;
*   experienced advisers must demonstrate their competence but will be able to do so in a number of ways including a mixture of examination, assessment and the demonstration of appropriate experience;
*   all advisers must undertake appropriate Continuing Professional Development.

The aim is to begin implementation from 1 July 1995 with all elements of the scheme fully implemented by 1 July 1997. In order to assist firms, particularly small firms, the PIA is considering setting up a Training and Competence Advisory Service.

21.2.4   Complaints and compensation

The PIA Ombudsman Scheme has been established with the appointment of an Ombudsman, Mr Stephen Edell, independent of the PIA itself. The scheme covers most investments (see **21.3**) and the maximum award is £50,000 including up to £750 for 'distress and inconvenience'. PIA member firms are in general bound by the Ombudsman's decisions but an investor is entitled to reject it and go to court.

The PIA's complaints handling requirements came into operation on 18 July 1994. Complaints first received by a firm after its admission to membership of the PIA are subject to these requirements. Those received before membership is confirmed continue to be governed by the firm's current regulator's requirements, whether FIMBRA, LAUTRO, IMRO, SFA or SIB (see **21.5**).

Owing to significant pressures on the funding arrangements of the compensation scheme (see **21.4.4**), a SIB Consultative Paper was issued in February 1994 with proposals to amend the scheme. The principal change is the ending of the requirement of cross contribution whereby funding of compensation by members of an SRO above a set threshold is met by a levy on firms in other SROs. The emergence of three large, broadly based SROs (see **21.3.1**) means that compensation liabilities can be limited to those arising from members of each SRO separately.

In June 1994 the Court of Appeal overturned a decision of a lower court and held that the directors of the Investor Compensation Scheme should in general award what a court of law would award. The case effectively prevented the directors from exercising discretion not to compensate investors in home income plans (the mortgage of homes in order to invest the sum borrowed) for cash withdrawals spent on, for example, holidays. The case is going on further appeal to the House of Lords.

21.2.5   Pension Transfers and opt-outs

The SIB set up a Regulators' Steering Group in December 1993 to examine and make recommendations on this issue. The problem is that, since 1988, many investors may have, against their best interests, opted out of existing pension schemes or made transfers of their benefits from such schemes into individual personal pension plans.

In 1994 two important papers were published:

(a)   Pension Transfers and Opt-Outs—Further Safeguards for Future Business.

(b)   Pension Transfers and Opt-Outs, Review of Past Business, Statement of Policy and Specification ('the SIB Statement').

The first paper set out new standards effective from 1 July 1994 for the protection of investors including the use of a 'transfer value analysis' whereby investors must receive, and have explained to them, a comparison of the advantages and disadvantages of staying with an occupational scheme or moving to an individual pension arrangement. Firms are required to demonstrate that they have special double-checking arrangements to ensure compliance with the rules and must notify the regulator of their intention to carry out this type of business.

The SIB Statement, addressed to PIA and other SROs set out standards for a programme of review by firms of their pension transfer and opt-out business between 1988 and 1994. The PIA will have the leading role in implementing the 'guidance' laid down by the SIB.

A principal objective is for the reviews to be implemented and, where appropriate, remedies effected without the need for litigation. In a consultative paper issued by the PIA in December 1994 a number of proposals are put forward for amending the PIA's powers and those of the PIA Ombudsman to make it less likely that either firms or investors will pursue cases through the courts in order to achieve a more favourable outcome than that offered through the PIA complaints procedure (see **21.5.1**).

Although a number of firms have already commenced implementation of the review the SIB has laid down a detailed timetable for completion of various case categories with a view to completing most of the exercise by December 1997.

21.2.6 Occupational pension schemes

Following the Goode Report in 1993 a Pensions Bill has been introduced which, if enacted, will provide for the appointment of a pensions regulator and a compensation scheme. It gives scheme members the right to appoint trustees of their choice and there will be tighter controls on investment choice of trustees. A new minimum solvency requirement will be imposed which will encourage trustees to hold more pension fund assets in the form of gilts instead of equities.

21.2.7 EU Directives

The Third Life Insurance Directive came into force on 1 July 1994, introducing the single European Licence for life assurance companies with their head office in a member state to offer their products within the European Economic Area on the basis of the authorisation granted to them in their 'home' state. The Directive does not harmonise the different systems of supervision in each member state, which may apply stricter rules to companies which they supervise where they consider this necessary. The member states in which companies operate with a licence from their home state have no power to intervene unilaterally in the financial supervision of the company but retain powers to prevent persons entering into contracts and prohibit advertising provided that such measures are for the 'general good' of investors.

A Consultation Document was issued by H M Treasury on the implementation of the Investment Services Directive (enabling share dealers to operate throughout the European Economic Area with a single licence issued by their home country regulatory authority) and the Capital Adequacy Directive (setting minimum Community-wide levels of capital needed by investment firms. These directives must come into force by 1 January 1996 and regulations are expected to be laid before Parliament in early 1995.

21.3   Basic framework

The key provision in the Financial Services Act 1986 (FSA) makes it a criminal offence to carry on investment business in the UK unless the person concerned is authorised or exempt. Investment business is defined as carrying on certain activities, eg buying and selling, advising, arranging or managing 'things' which are investments under the FSA. The definition of investments includes most 'paper' securities such as stocks and shares, collective investment schemes, most life and pension policies, gilt-edged securities and futures and options. The definition excludes real property, bank and building society accounts or alternative investments such as antiques and works of art. Although most National Savings products satisfy the definition of investments they are specifically excluded.

The FSA has only minor application to the regulation of occupational pension schemes which are largely governed by trust law. Financial services regulation is only concerned with the investment management aspects. In particular the Act requires trustees to be authorised (see **21.3.1**) unless they have delegated day-to-day investment decisions to professional investment managers.

21.3.1   Authorisation

Firms carrying on investment business may obtain their authorisation from the SIB or more likely from one of the SROs which the SIB has recognised:

(1) The Securities and Futures Authority (SFA) which resulted from a merger, in April 1991, of The Securities Association (TSA) and the Association of Futures Brokers and Dealers (AFBD). TSA regulated the activities of those who deal in, advise on or manage securities whilst AFBD regulated those who advise on or deal in futures and options, including those handled by the commodity exchanges and the London International Financial Futures Exchange;

(2) The Investment Management Regulatory Organisation (IMRO) which regulates the managers of investments including the managers and trustees of collective investment schemes, eg unit trusts;

(3) The Life Assurance and Unit Trust Regulatory Organisation (LAUTRO) which regulates the marketing activities of life companies, friendly societies and collective investment scheme managers;

(4) The Financial Intermediaries Managers and Brokers Regulatory Association (FIMBRA) which regulates the many intermediaries who advise and arrange deals in life and pension products, collective investment schemes and other investments.

(5) The Personal Investment Authority (PIA), which became operational in July 1994, effectively merges the regulatory activities of FIMBRA and LAUTRO as well as covering some of the non-stockbroking private investor responsibilities of IMRO and the SFA. LAUTRO and FIMBRA will cease to be recognised by the SIB as SROs once the process of transfer of membership to the PIA is completed.

Another way in which authorisation to carry on investment business can be obtained is through membership of a recognised professional body (RPB). Most solicitors and accountants obtain their authorisation from their respective professional bodies (eg The Law Society or one of the accountancy bodies) where their investment business is only a small proportion of their overall professional activities. The Insurance Brokers' Registration Council regulates insurance brokers whose main business is general insurance but who may undertake investment business so long as this does not exceed 49 per cent of their total business.

Finally, there are firms such as insurance companies and friendly societies which obtain their authorisation under separate legislation from the Department of Trade and Industry or the equivalent authorities in the EU member state in which the company's head office is situated, and the Registrar of Friendly Societies respectively. These firms do not need to seek additional authorisation under the FSA although their marketing activities are subject to regulation by LAUTRO/PIA or, in a very few cases, the SIB.

21.3.2   Exemptions

Some firms are exempted from the requirement to obtain authorisation under the FSA. These include the Bank of England, recognised exchanges and clearing houses and members of Lloyd's.

An important category of exempt person is the appointed representative. This is an individual or firm which acts as the agent of an authorised person and for whose activities (within the limits of the authorised person's business activities) the authorised person takes legal responsibility. Although it is open to any firm which is authorised to appoint such representatives, the practice is most common in the case of insurance companies and firms that market life policies and collective investment schemes.

21.3.3   The SIB Central Register

The SIB is required under the FSA to maintain a public register of firms authorised to carry on investment business. This Central Register permits investors as well as firms to check on the authorisation status of firms including appointed representatives who trade under their own names and not that of the authorised firm which has appointed them. It will now be possible to check whether such an appointed representative is the agent of a particular company.

The Central Register can be contacted by telephoning 0171–929 3652 or by using Prestel or Telecom Gold services.

21.3.4   Authorisation criteria

In deciding whether to authorise a firm the SIB, SROs or RPBs consider such matters as whether those involved in the business are fit and proper persons having the financial resources and competence to operate the business in a way which is unlikely to result in unreasonable risk to investors. In addition, the SIB has published ten Principles (see below) which it expects all firms to observe. The breach of any principle might call into question whether the firm was fit and proper to carry on investment business.

The Principles

(1) **Integrity**
A firm should observe high standards of integrity and fair dealing.

(2) **Skill, care and diligence**
A firm should act with due skill, care and diligence.

(3) **Market practice**
A firm should observe high standards of market conduct. It should also, to the extent endorsed for the purpose of this principle, comply with any code or standard as in force from time to time and as it applies to the firm either according to its terms or by rulings made under it.

(4) **Information about customers**
A firm should seek from customers it advises, or for whom it exercises discretion, any information about their circumstances and investment objectives which might reasonably be expected to be relevant in enabling it to fulfil its responsibilities to them.

(5) **Information for customers**
A firm should take reasonable steps to give a customer it advises, in a comprehensible and timely way, any information needed to enable him to make a balanced and informed decision. A firm should similarly be ready to provide a customer with a full and fair account of the fulfilment of its responsibilities to him.

(6) **Conflicts of interest**
A firm should either avoid any conflict of interest arising or, where conflicts arise, should ensure fair treatment to all its customers by disclosure, internal rules of confidentiality, declining to act, or otherwise. A firm should not unfairly place its interests above those of its customers and, where a properly informed customer would reasonably expect that the firm would place his interests above its own, the firm should live up to that expectation.

(7) **Customer assets**
Where a firm has control of or is otherwise responsible for assets belonging to a customer which it is required to safeguard, it should arrange proper protection for them, by way of segregation and identification of those assets or otherwise, in accordance with the responsibility it has accepted.

(8) **Financial resources**
A firm should ensure that it maintains adequate financial resources to meet its investment business commitments and to withstand the risks to which its business is subject.

(9) **Internal organisation**
A firm should organise and control its internal affairs in a

responsible manner, keeping proper records, and where the firm employs staff or is responsible for the conduct of investment business by others, should have adequate arrangements to ensure that they are suitable, adequately trained and properly supervised and that it has well-defined compliance procedures.

(10) **Relations with regulators**
A firm should deal with its regulator in an open and cooperative manner and keep the regulator promptly informed of anything concerning the firm which might reasonably be expected to be disclosed to it.

Source: *The Securities and Investments Board*

21.4   Rules and regulations

The FSA contains only the bare framework of the total investor protection legislation. The detailed rules and regulations with which authorised firms are expected to comply are contained in rule books maintained and enforced by the SIB and the relevant SRO or RPB. The original rule books of individual SROs and RPBs were required to give investor protection which was equivalent to that given by the rules of the SIB itself. In an effort to avoid unnecessary duplication whilst preserving the ability of SROs and RPBs to make practitioner-based rules relevant to the particular business in which their members operate, some amendments have been made to the FSA. These amendments have allowed the SIB to make certain core rules which are directly applicable to all investment firms (except members of RPBs) whichever SRO they belong to. The designated core rules (of which there are 40) were intended to provide a degree of uniformity and common standards which the individual SROs could supplement by additional rules geared to the activities of the firms which they regulate. Instead of having to convince the SIB that their rule books are equivalent, the new proposals will require the SIB to agree that the rule books, together with the SRO's monitoring and compliance arrangements, provide adequate protection to investors. Since these amendments were made the SIB has had second thoughts about the need to designate core rules although most of them have been incorporated into the SRO's own rule books.

21.4.1   Business conduct

The detailed rules and regulations cover a number of areas relating to the conduct of investment business by authorised persons. These include:

(1) the way in which authorised firms and their appointed representatives seek new business;
(2) the ongoing relationships between authorised firms and their customers where such relationships exist;
(3) the way in which authorised firms must deal with complaints by investors.

21.4.2 Seeking business

There are detailed advertising rules which prohibit misleading advertisements and statements and claims which cannot be substantiated. For example, LAUTRO has required its member firms to submit their marketing material for with-profit bonds and guaranteed bonds which offer potential growth in line with a stock market index but with a guaranteed return of capital if performance is poor. If any advertising material is found to be potentially misleading, LAUTRO will expect its member firms to check that investors have not been disadvantaged and to compensate any that have.

There are rules which require authorised firms to know their customer before making a recommendation or arranging an investment transaction and to make sure that any investment that is recommended or transacted is suitable having regard to the investor's personal and financial requirements. Poor completion of 'fact finds' (the questionnaires which intermediaries normally use to get to know their customers) have been the subject of criticism by some SROs and the Insurance Ombudsman and is receiving significant attention in the proposals for training and competence.

In the case of packaged product investments such as life assurance, pension plans and collective investment schemes, the polarisation rule requires intermediaries to disclose in a Buyer's Guide (to be replaced by a 'Terms of Business' letter) and on business stationery whether they are independent from any particular product company, in which case the obligation is to recommend a suitable product from those available on the market or company representatives, who must recommend a suitable product from the product range of the particular company they represent.

Independent intermediaries and company representatives are permitted to make unsolicited calls (personal visits or oral communications other than at the investor's invitation) which cannot be made in relation to non-polarised investments. Investments which can be the subject of unsolicited calls normally give the investor cooling-off rights enabling the investor to cancel an investment transaction within a reasonable period (normally 14 days) from entering into the contract. Detailed product disclosure rules are designed to provide sufficient information about the product to enable the investor to decide whether to continue with the contract.

21.4.3   Customer agreements

The rules prescribe the terms of customer agreements between authorised firms and their customers including how such agreements are made, how instructions are to be communicated and how such agreements are terminated.

There are also rules requiring authorised firms to place client money in designated trust accounts to ensure that investors' money is kept separate from other money belonging to the firm. The rules provide for the payment of interest except in specified circumstances.

21.4.4   Complaints and compensation

There are rules requiring authorised firms to operate detailed monitoring and compliance procedures to ensure that the rules are obeyed and to have suitable procedures for dealing with complaints from investors. A breach of these rules may also result in a breach of SIB Principle 9 (see **21.3.4**).

Authorised firms are required to contribute a levy to a compensation scheme established by the SIB and administered by the Investors Compensation Scheme Limited under which, in the event of an authorised firm going into liquidation, investors may recover up to a maximum of £48,000 if the firm is unable to meet its liabilities.

21.5   Complaints and remedies

21.5.1   Basic procedures

If an investor has a complaint about an authorised firm, the investor should raise the matter initially with the firm's compliance officer who is usually an employee of the firm with responsibility for ensuring that the firm complies with the rules. If the firm does not handle the complaint to the investor's satisfaction, the investor may refer the matter to the relevant complaints body. The appropriate complaints body will depend upon the arrangements which that firm's SRO or RPB has made. For example, nearly all life assurance companies and many unit trust companies are members of the PIA and it is the PIA Ombudsman that would deal with the investor's complaint. Disputes between members of IMRO and their customers are dealt with by the Investment Ombudsman. It is the authorised firm's responsibility to inform the investor as to the appropriate complaints body. The complaints body has a range of sanctions which can be imposed including awarding appropriate compensation for any losses suffered by the investor.

Referring a complaint to one of the relevant complaints bodies does not normally prevent the investor from pursuing any other legal remedies. In addition to bringing civil actions for breach of contract or negligence, the private investor is given a right, under the FSA, to sue an authorised firm for any breach of the investor protection rules which causes the investor loss.

Individual SROs as well as the SIB have a range of intervention powers which can be used in the interests of investor protection. These include the SIB's power, which it has now exercised in relation to five individuals to prohibit the employment of persons considered to be unfit, to apply for an injunction or restitution order where a breach is threatened or where investors have suffered loss, to restrict the business of investment firms, to restrict any dealings with a firm's assets or even to vest those assets in a trustee. SROs have the power to discipline their members for misconduct and may impose fines.

21.6   Overseas aspects

Overseas firms are subject to the FSA if they carry on investment business in the UK. Unless an overseas company is authorised to carry on investment business in the UK, it is difficult for it to market its products and services to UK investors. It is possible for the overseas firm to promote its products and services in the UK through an authorised person.

If the investment is a recognised collective investment scheme or an insurance policy issued by a recognised insurer, which it may be if the scheme or insurer is authorised in another EU member state or in a territory designated by the Secretary of State for Trade and Industry (eg the Isle of Man, the Channel Islands), the authorised firm may market it freely within the UK. Although such a scheme may not be subject to the UK compensation scheme it is possible that it will be subject to a compensation scheme set up in the home country or territory concerned.

If the collective investment scheme or insurance policy is not a recognised scheme, there are severe restrictions on the extent to which it can be promoted in the UK. For example, an authorised person is able to promote such a scheme to established customers under the terms of a sub-sisting customer agreement but cannot market to investors generally.

21.7   Preview of the year ahead

The regulatory system is now seven years old and in this time the pace of regulatory change has not slackened. Fundamental questions have been raised which go to the very heart of the system as conceived by Professor Gower. It is to be hoped that the year ahead will be one of consolidation in which existing proposals and developments are fully implemented. These include the initiatives on disclosure and training and competence.

All eyes will be on the newly established PIA and its objective of setting and delivering higher standards of investor protection. In particular it will be judged on its success or otherwise in weeding out, through its appli-cation process, those who are not fit and proper to carry on investment business and in its implementation of the review of pension transfers and opt-out business.

The new pensions regulator should be appointed and a compensation scheme for occupational pension schemes introduced.

The PIA is likely to produce rules requiring product companies and inter-mediaries to provide statistics on their persistency — the extent to which products sold remain on the books for a reasonable period. A company's or intermediary's persistency rate is seen by the regulators and consumer representatives as an important indication of competence and compli-ance. The issue of whether such statistics should be published generally or confined to the use of regulators for monitoring purposes is likely to be hotly debated since 'poor' persistency can result from factors other than mis-selling by intermediaries.

21.8   Conclusion and future developments

The FSA provides the framework for the most comprehensive investor protection system ever seen in the UK or elsewhere in Europe. In the past seven years considerable progress has been made by the SIB and the SROs in putting the flesh on the bare bones provided by the FSA.

Changing circumstances brought about by an innovative and competitive financial services industry as well as developments in Europe will require further adaptations of a system which needs to be responsive to such changes.

21.8.1 Future developments

Looking ahead, the scope for change and future development of the regulatory system is significant. The principle of self-regulation continues to be questioned and might not survive the election of a Labour government or a new major scandal affecting the industry. Developments in Europe may also provide a focus for such questioning.

The implementation of the Third Life Insurance Directive will pave the way towards a workable investment protection system across member states. This process will be accelerated from 1 January 1996 when the Capital Adequacy Directive (setting minimum Community-wide levels of capital needed by investment firms) and the Investment Services Directive (enabling share dealers to operate throughout the European Economic Area with a single licence issued by their home country regulatory authority) enter into force.

Increasing resources will need to be expended on monitoring compliance, meeting the costs of the compensation scheme and financing the initial and ongoing costs of the training and competence proposals. These expenses, together with the cost of initiatives like the revised product disclosure regime and the setting up costs of the PIA for the retail sector, will add to the competitive pressures on investment firms. This is likely to produce an increasing number of mergers or take-overs and a search for more cost-effective methods of securing the distribution of financial products and services. Predictions have been made that the number of life companies will reduce substantially over the next few years and that the number of independent intermediaries will halve from 20,000 to 10,000 by 1997. New methods of distribution such as the sale of more products by telephone will occur. In this environment new challenges will be created for the regulators as well as for those regulated. It is possible that the regulators will focus their attention on minimising the risk of fraud and other market failures instead of concentrating on the improvement of the detailed standards of industry practice.

The FSA introduced a dynamic system capable of responding to change. There is little doubt that the system will be severely tested during the next few years.

Sources of further information

Useful addresses

PIA (Personal Investment
   Authority Limited)
Hertsmere House
Hertsmere Road
London
E14 4AB

Tel: (0171) 538 8860

LAUTRO (Life Assurance and
   Unit Trust Regulatory
   Organisation)
Centre Point
103 New Oxford Street
London
WC1A 1QH

Tel: (0171) 379 0444

IMRO (Investment Management
   Regulatory Organisation Ltd)
Broadwalk House
6 Appold Street
London EC2A 2AA

Tel: (0171) 628 6022

SIB (Securities and Investments
   Board)
Gavrelle House
2–14 Bunhill Row
London
EC1Y 8RA

Tel: (0171) 638 1240

FIMBRA (Financial
   Intermediaries, Managers
   and Brokers Regulatory
   Association)
Hertsmere House
Hertsmere Road
London
E14 4AB

Tel: (0171) 538 8860

Investors Compensation
   Scheme Limited
Gavrelle House
2–14 Bunhill Row
London
EC1Y 8RA

Tel: (0171) 638 1240

SFA (Securities and Futures
   Authority Limited)
Cottons Centre
Cottons Lane
London
SE1 2QB

Tel: (0171) 378 9000

The Law Society (of England
   and Wales)
The Law Society's Hall
113 Chancery Lane
London
WC2A 1PL

Tel: (0171) 242 1222

The Institute of Chartered
  Accountants (in England
  and Wales)
PO Box 433
Chartered Accountant's Hall
Moorgate Place
London
EC2P 2BJ

Tel: (0171) 920 8100

Insurance Brokers' Registration
  Council
15 St Helen's Place
London
EC3A 6DS

Tel: (0171) 588 4387

The Insurance Ombudsman
  Bureau
City Gate One
135 Park Street
London
SE1 9EA

Tel: (0171) 928 7600

The Office of the Investment
  Ombudsman
6 Frederick's Place
London
EC2R 8BT

Tel: (0171) 796 3065

Personal Investment Authority
  Ombudsman
6th Floor
1 London Wall
London
EC2Y 5EA

Tel: (0171) 600 3838

Index

ALLIED
DUNBAR

Allied Dunbar Library Series

- Allied Dunbar Business Tax   Anthony Foreman
  and Law Handbook   Duncan Taylor

- Allied Dunbar Expatriate Tax   David Phillips &
  and Investment Handbook   Nigel Eastaway

- Allied Dunbar Pensions Handbook   Anthony Reardon

- Allied Dunbar Retirement   David Vessey
  Planning Handbook

- Allied Dunbar Tax Handbook   Anthony Foreman

All of these titles are available from leading bookshops.

For more information please contact:
Allied Dunbar Library Series,
21-27 Lamb's Conduit Street, London WC1N 3NJ
or telephone: 0171 242 2548